D0146697

Money in the People's Republic of China

By the same author:
A Short History of Socialist Money

Money in the People's Republic of China

A Comparative Perspective

Gavin Peebles

ALLEN & UNWIN
Sydney London Boston

4-30

First published in 1991
Allen & Unwin Pty Ltd
8 Napier Street, North Sydney, NSW 2059

UK distribution
University College London Press
Gower Street, London WC1E 6BT

US distribution
Paul and Company Publishing Consortium Inc.
141 Old Bedford Road, Concord MA 01742

National Library of Australia
Cataloguing-in-Publication entry:

Peebles, Gavin, 1947– .
Money in the People's Republic of China.

Includes index.
ISBN 1 86373 033 8.

1. Monetary policy – China. 2. China – Economic conditions – 1976– . 3. China – Economic policy – 1976–
I. Title.

332.4951

Set in 9.5/11pt Times by Graphicraft Typesetters Ltd, Hong Kong
Printed by Chong Moh Offset Printing, Singapore

Contents

Figures

Tables

Acknowledgements

It is often said that research in the social sciences is largely autobiographical. To a great extent this is true. One's education will determine the tools and methods one is able and likely to use. One's employment history will determine the projects one chooses or has chosen for one and the amount of spare income available for language lessons, travel, books etc. One's geographical relocations will determine the people, ideas, experiences and influences one encounters, which are bound to influence any research. So it is with this book, and I would like to acknowledge the influences on its form and content in a largely autobiographical manner. Most of the acknowledgements are to institutions for their agreeing either to educate me or to employ me, and sometimes both, or for inviting me to talk to them.

The belief that an empirical study of money in the People's Republic of China might be possible came to me on the morning of 4 July 1981 when, in Hong Kong, I read a newspaper report that the People's Bank of China had released monetary data for the first time and would continue to do so. I sat down, wrote out a research outline and sketched out some theoretical concepts. That outline has guided me ever since. Its approach, structure and content were determined by my experiences until then. I had studied economics at Quarry Bank High School for Boys in Liverpool (England), the University College of Wales, Aberystwyth, and the University of Liverpool. At these institutions I was taught, among other things, the then orthodox British interpretation of Keynesian macroeconomics. I also studied the emerging Post Keynesian interpretation, especially its American variant, and realised the importance of the history of economic thought as an academic subject. I worked as a tenured university lecturer, and while teaching macroeconomics (which in the West is exclusively about market economies) I found it useful to ask how things would be in a planned economy. I returned to being a student and financed myself through the intensive postgraduate course in Russian language at the University of Strathclyde and then did research on the Soviet economy at the University of Glasgow. I returned to teaching and in 1980 became lecturer in economics at the University of Hong Kong, where I was able to continue my studies of the Chinese language at the University's Language Centre. I taught my own courses on comparative economic systems, macroeconomics and the history of economic thought and contributed to courses on development economics and the Hong Kong economy. The reading and thinking necessary to do this have influenced how this book has turned out. I believe strongly in going back to basics and taking nothing for granted, even to the extent of labouring what will be obvious to some readers. I also believe in putting events and ideas into a comparative context.

While in Hong Kong I published some articles on China, the Soviet Union and Eastern Europe and a book about Hong Kong's economy. I am grateful to the people who have commented on these works or reviewed them or cited them in their own work. This was a mainly encouraging experience. In Hong Kong I received a research grant from the Hang Seng Bank Golden Jubilee Education Fund in 1987, for which I express my thanks. This allowed me to obtain material and to employ Miss Grace Chow for a few months as a research assistant. I am grateful to her for her very competent assistance.

This book was written during the period July 1989 to October 1990, my first sixteen months as senior research fellow of the Contemporary China Centre in the Research School of Pacific Studies at the Australian National University in Canberra. I am grateful to the university for so employing me and for still believing in letting its research fellows get on with their own research largely unencumbered by any other duties. In April 1990 the Contemporary China Centre supported a research visit to Hong Kong. Although this mainly concerned a different project of mine I was able to spend some time on the topic of this book, meeting former colleagues and talking to Professor Audrey Donnithorne. I would like to thank Dr C.H. Chai for drawing Davis and Charemza (1989) to my attention and Veronica Pearson for her hospitality.

In Canberra I would like to thank my colleagues for agreeing to the occasional consultation about a language problem that was beyond my abilities and experience and Dianne Stacey for help in accustomising myself to Microsoft's Word program, with which I wrote this book. I would also like to thank You Ji for drawing Chen Wenlin (1989) to my attention, Christopher Buckley for showing me Tsang (1990) and Dr On-kit Tam for providing me with data I needed from his specially obtained advance copy of *Zhongguo Tongji Nianjian 1989* before my own copy arrived.

Some of the information and ideas in this book have been presented at various seminars, and I would like to thank the participants for their questions and comments. In particular, they were on two occasions at the economics workshop of the Department of Economics of the University of Hong Kong in the mid 1980s, at the National Centre for Development Studies of the Australian National University in 1989, at a seminar arranged by the Department of Economics of the Victoria University of Wellington in New Zealand in February 1990, and at a seminar organised by the Centre for Chinese Political Economy at Macquarie University, Sydney, in May 1990. I also presented a related paper at the Eighth Biennial Conference of the Asian Studies Association of Australia held at Griffith University, Brisbane, in early July 1990, and I thank the Contemporary China Centre for supporting my attendance. In addition, I would like to thank the audience and the discussant, Dr Shoichi Ito of Osaka University, who attended a presentation of some of the following material and commented on it at the First Convention of the East Asia Economic

Association in Kyoto in October 1988, and I thank the association for inviting me.

Finally, I would like to thank Anna Beth McCormack and Bernadette Foley for their work of editing and re-designing my typescript.

Gavin Peebles
Canberra
1 November 1990

Notes

Transliteration: I have used *Hanyu pinyin* to transliterate all Chinese proper and place names and quotations from the Chinese with the following exceptions. If I think that a Chinese word has entered the English language with a spelling different from that of *pinyin* I have used the English word (for example, Kuomintang, Peking, Canton). Words in *pinyin* are in italics except when they are titles of articles in the bibliography.
Chinese characters: I have used modern, simplified characters in the few places were characters are used for clarification.
Coverage of the data: All data for China in this book relate to 'Mainland China' as it used to be called (including Hainan island, now Hainan province, and Tibet) but excluding Taiwan, Hong Kong and Macau.
Billions: One billion means 1000 million, a milliard in European languages and *shi yi* (十亿) in Chinese. Most Chinese data of this order of magnitude are given in the original sources in units of 100 million, *yi*, and so the data in the original tables must not be taken for billions; they just require to be divided by ten. For example, 50 *yi* (5000 million) equals 5 *shi yi* (5 billion).
Units: 1 ton equals 1.016 tonnes.
Fiscal year: The Chinese fiscal year is the same as the calendar year.
Regressions: Regressions were performed in various places and at various times using Microfit (and the same program when it was known as Datafit) and Stata programs. As someone who first ran regressions after having to write most of the required program in Algol on punchcards and wait overnight for the results I appreciate how useful, quick and productive such programs are and I would like to thank their authors for creating them. Regression results are given to the fourth decimal place as this is how they appear and this now seems to be the convention but this practise implies a far higher degree of accuracy than is justified. Results to two decimal places are really all that is needed.
Labelling variables: In the text the prefix 'pd' before a variable means its simple percentage increase. Δ means the absolute increase or first difference in a variable, so, for example, ΔSPP represents the absolute annual increase of Social Purchasing Power, usually in billion *yuan*, and pdSPP indicates the percentage increase in Social Purchasing Power for a particular year. $\Delta \ln P$ means the first difference of the natural logarithm of P, which is approximately equal to the percentage increase expressed in decimal form. Lower case letters for variables indicate average annual rates of change calculated, unless otherwise indicated, by log-linear regressions of the original variable on time. So, for example, *crc* indicates the

average annual growth rate of currency in circulation during a specified period.

Guiding thoughts: In conclusion, some thoughts on method and its subject matter that have guided this work:

'. . . the avoidance of naïveté and ambition is most unscientific.' (P.J.D. Wiles)

'Perhaps economic problems are so intractable that storytelling is the best we can do.' (Mark Blaug)

'It is a capital mistake to theorize before one has data.' (Sir Arthur Conan Doyle)

生人不能一日无用即不可一日无财

(Living man cannot go one day without using things, therefore he cannot go without using money.)

钱可通神

(Money talks.)

China's money

The Chinese currency is known as the *Renminbi* (人民币) which means people's currency. Its basic unit is the *yuan* 元, which is represented by the symbol ¥. This represents the first letter of the *Hanyu pinyin* transliteration of the character with two lines added to represent the first two strokes made when writing the character itself. Sometimes the two lines are omitted. Each *yuan* is divided into 10 *jiao* (角), which in spoken modern Mandarin Chinese are called *mao* (毛), and each *jiao* into 10 *fen* (分). There are thus 100 *fen* in a *yuan*. Each *fen* is divided into 10 *li* (厘), but such small units (one-thousandth of a *yuan*) are hardly ever mentioned.

Some translators, especially in American works, even call the *yuan* a dollar. In English one sometimes hears people say that something cost 2 *Renminbi*, but that is like saying that something cost 2 sterling. This confuses the name of the currency with its basic unit. In spoken Chinese the word '*yuan*' is generally not used, and the word '*kuai*' 块, meaning lump, is used in conjunction with a number and the word '*qian*' 钱, which means money. Hence *liang kuai qian* (两块钱) (literally, 2 lumps money) means 2 *yuan*, and *liang kuai si mao si* (两块四毛四) means 2 *yuan* and 44 *fen*. In the Cantonese dialect the word '*man*' (文) is used for a *yuan*; so *leung man* (两文) means 2 *yuan*.

Since 1980 Foreign Exchange Certificates (*waihui quan*), printed in 1979 and bearing that year, have been issued for tourists and business visitors to spend in selected locations, some of which will accept only them and sometimes levy a surcharge on payments in the official currency. Their unit, the *yuan*, is the same as that of the *Renminbi*. For regulations concerning their use see Sherer (1981: 160). In 1987 a new set of paper banknotes was issued adding two high-denomination notes, ¥50 and ¥100.

The *Renminbi* is an inconvertible currency with its exchange rate now being determined by the State General Administration for Exchange Control. As with most inconvertible currencies, there are a number of exchange rates existing for different traders as there is no unified free market. The general trend of the official rate was one of continued depreciation for the period of this study, 1949–88 (although there was a strengthening of the *Renminbi* against the US dollar in the 1970s after the latter was floated), with major official devaluations in July 1986 and December 1989. The official rate from March 1955 (which was maintained through to late 1971) was 2.4618 *yuan* to the US dollar. After the December 1989 devaluation the official rate became 4.7221 *yuan* to the US dollar.

For an excellent history of Chinese currency to the early 1980s I recommend *A History of Chinese Currency (16th Century BC–20th Century AD)* Hong Kong: Xinhua Publishing House with NCN Ltd and MAO Management, 1983. See also *Jingji Da Cidian—Jinrong Juan* (1987: 23).

1 Subject and plan

This chapter will review the subject matter and scope of this book, the methodology and data used, the perspective and approach chosen, and the plan of the book.

1.1 Subject and method of this book

This book is an historical and empirical examination of money in the People's Republic of China over the period 1949–88. For reasons explained below, the statistical analysis concentrates on the period 1952–85. The approach is mainly macroeconomic in nature. I ask the simple questions: What is money, what is it used for, how much of it is there, and who has it? As money, like the common cold, is something a person can only get from other people, where does it come from in the Chinese economy, and how? And as it only benefits a person when it leaves their possession, where does it go to, and on what terms? What is the relationship between money and prices, as this relationship may be thought to determine its value, and what is the relationship between monetary growth and the government's budget? How did economic reform in the 1980s affect monetary flows? How do monetary relations in China differ from those in other countries? And so on. The approach is firmly analytical and does not contain detailed descriptions of institutions, their political position and reform, although references are made to this type of literature.

Most books about the Chinese economy are descriptive and contain very little actual analysis. This to some extent is understandable, especially for works published before about 1980 when there were very few data available, with the exception of some for the 1950s. It was important to understand what the new Chinese economic institutions were and how they differed from those of capitalist economies and even from those of the Soviet Union, from which country many were adopted in the 1950s. In these books the authors hardly ever asked why: Why was this institutional form adopted? Why did prices rise? Why did the money supply increase rapidly in that period but not in this? I have tried to tackle these latter questions using a simple consistent analytical framework developed from a simplified model based on the actual nature of Chinese institutions and the policies followed. Many articles about money and prices in China, even now, concentrate on very short periods for analysis—some just on the 1950s—and modern works concentrate on the new features of the economy, such as inflation, that emerged in the early 1980s. Some do this on a year-to-year basis for a short period. For such short periods very few patterns emerge, especially if the data are not examined in the light of the same consistent theory or belief about such basic things as the reasons for changes in the money supply, the direction of causation between money and prices, reasons for retail price increases and so on. I have tried to put the events of the entire period 1952–88 into a consistent framework of analysis.

Data to do this was obviously required, and in this I have been very fortunate. There was an almost complete statistical blackout in China for the period of roughly 1960 to 1980. Since then the open door policy has seen the republication of national statistical yearbooks on an annual basis, economic almanacs, specialised yearbooks and publications on such things as agriculture, agricultural procurements, retail sales and prices. These materials are extremely useful and important, but these sources are not very good at giving precise definitions of the terms used nor of their coverage and methods of compilation, unfortunately. Many economic journals recommenced publication and have progressively contained more and more serious analytical articles on many aspects of the Chinese economy, including money and inflation, and they often include interesting data. China has joined certain international financial institutions, and since October 1981 its recent monetary data have been published by the International Monetary Fund (IMF). Unlike the case of the Soviet Union we now have currency data for the entire period since 1952 and much more detailed price data. World Bank delegations visit China, conduct joint research projects and publish their views and policy advice. China has adopted Western methods of compiling gross domestic product (*GDP*) data and has published them in the *Statistical Yearbooks* for a few recent years,[1] although it continues to stress and publish estimates based on socialist material-accounting conventions.

The publication in the early 1980s of complete sets of hundreds of time series back to the early 1950s obviously raised the question of their reliability. How could such a poor country collect all the data and store it safely? How was this done throughout the Cultural Revolution period when statistical work and education were not highly regarded? There are hardly any breaks in the important series. What about the well-known inflationary biases in the reporting of output figures and the under-reporting of inputs that are common to all socialist countries? These problems have not really been adequately resolved by students of the Chinese economy, probably because they were so grateful to get hard numbers in Chinese sources other than page numbers and the occasional figure from *Peking Review* or at a meeting with an important politician or at an official reception. Li Chengrui (1984), then Director of the State Statistical Bureau, explains how statistics were able to be collected even during the Cultural Revolution period and states that they are 'basically reliable' and 'basically conform to the political and economic changes of the times' (p. 23). Kane (1988: 3–4), relying on other explanations by Li Chengrui advocating faith in Chinese statistics, concludes that output statistics, for example, probably do correctly 'represent the general level and trend of activity'. Egawa (1981) shows the main biases in Chinese economic statistics revealed by Chinese economists, and Molodtsova (1985) reviews the recent improvements in statistical work. These latter two analysts do not, unfortunately, discuss the accuracy of the actual earlier macroeconomic data that have been published. Relevant to any monetary study is Gregory Chow's (1986) judgement that the macroeconomic data *are* reliable. However, his conclusion is based on the fact that, when using such data in his models, he gets reasonable results; so he concludes that the data must be accurate. He does not check them against any alternative sources or against what could reasonably be expected.

The macroeconomic data have been used to present a rather gloomy picture of the economy before 1979, which is probably what the reforming Deng Xiaoping leadership intended them to show. They were put to such use by Li Chengrui (1984) to condemn the policies of the 'gang of four' and earlier policies. They show the economic collapse after the Great Leap Forward and huge population losses very clearly, stagnation in productivity growth despite high investment ratios and stagnation in food consumption in the 1970s. The new regime probably intended the world to see what it thought were the hopeless consequences of Maoist development for efficient economic growth. The economic statistics were used for political purposes. Whether this means that the data are completely fabricated I do not know, but I very much doubt it. They do seem consistent with what we might expect from our knowledge of the historical background. Output data do fall, for example, when there are major political campaigns and upheavals. Unlike in the case of the many developing countries that produce depressing and heavily adjusted data in order to obtain foreign aid (Griliches, 1985), China was probably not influenced by this possible motive.

Accepting the basic reliability of the data collection processes does not, however, solve the problem of the accuracy of the actual printed figures. On a number of occasions I have found data that are self-contradictory and tables where the subitems do not add up to the given totals. There is not much one can do about this except to point it out and take the more reasonable figures, if there is such a choice. Different versions of what should be the same data often contain different figures. Some important series were redefined in 1985, making it difficult to obtain a consistent series for the entire period 1952–88. I have explained how I have coped with this problem at the relevant points in this book. What is needed is a team of interested outsiders to comb the statistical yearbooks, identify the mistakes and ask for clarification. Basic 'economic archaeology' is still required despite the pages and pages of data now available. I have not got very far in this endeavour by myself.

Another aspect of the data used here is that they are national in coverage. They are unable to indicate the likely huge variation in regional experiences in a country so large and diverse as China. This problem is probably more serious in data for the latter part of the 1980s when such things as regional inflation rates became different, with the relatively prosperous southern provinces, such as Guangdong, experiencing higher rates than elsewhere. This problem must always be borne in mind.

As argued by Hsiao (1971), it is felt that Chinese currency and monetary data are likely to be among the most reliable of all the major macroeconomic series published. This is because currency issue emanates from one single central authority, the People's Bank of China, which is able to record every unit issued and has a large and well-trained staff to do so. Bachman (1989: 169–70) argues that the Ministry of Finance and the banking system have information that is 'more comprehensive and reliable than that flowing through the physical planning system'. There is much in these arguments, but they do not address the question of the reliability of data actually published for outsiders to see and study. I have taken monetary data at face value, but I would not be at all surprised to discover that some of the currency data published for the mid 1980s were somehow far less than the actual amounts in circulation.

The methods I have used to analyse these figures is mainly historical and descriptive, being based firmly on Chinese institutions and policies. I have, however, made some use of simple econometric techniques. I firmly believe that any explanation of the relationship between money and prices and any other variables should be shown to be supported by quantitative analysis over a long period. I also believe that the theories proposed should stand up to examination using the simplest of techniques with unadjusted annual data. Many macroeconomic econometric studies have forced their data into the preferred model by means of smoothing the original data, regressing on previous values of the independent variable, introducing arbitrary dummy variables, re-estimating some of the data series and so on, making it very difficult to put the explanation into simple straightforward English. For a market economy the process of averaging data is acceptable. Macroeconomic statistics are published for arbitrary periods of years, quarters, months and sometimes days. The natural rhythm of the business cycle may not show up in such arrangements, and data collected for periods of 527 or 1891 days, for example, may better show the workings of the economy. As these periods are not used in statistical sources, econometricians average the available data over periods longer than a year to approximate them. This is natural and correct. However, for the planned economies, for which very little empirical work has been done, we do not know which periodisation may be appropriate. Planners may have a very short time horizon in reacting to problems in the economy. Their reactions may show up more quickly than in the natural process of the capitalist business cycle. Hence, annual data may be sufficient to identify the relationships between variables. Anyway, this is an empirical matter, and it is settled by seeing whether using the crude original data without averaging and introducing arbitrary lags can account for the important macroeconomic relationships.

Apart from works specifically about China there are at least three econometric studies of relevance to this book: Howard (1979) on the Soviet Union; Friedman and Schwartz (1982) applying the Quantity Theory of Money to the United States and the United Kingdom; and Bordo and Jonung (1987) on the long run behaviour of income velocity of money. All three works have been subject to severe criticism over the nature of their econometrics.[2] This leaves the non-professional econometrician in the position of not knowing how much trust to put in the quantitative results. I have stuck to the simplest of graphical and statistical techniques, hoping that the reader will be able to see quite clearly the extent to which the evidence supports the views offered here. For the purposes of this book I remain a 'scatter diagram empiricist', and this is a book of economic history, not an econometric study. Regression analysis often hides exceptions to the pattern shown by the resulting equations. The methods I have used show when, and perhaps why, there are some slight historical exceptions to the general pattern proposed here.

Macroeconomics, and its empirical branch, macroeconometrics, are based on a mechanistic view of the working of the economy underlying much of economic theory, which adopted it from the eighteenth-century scientific view of mechanics. In such a view, similar quantitative causes are assumed to have similar quantitative results in the same circumstances. Of course, if these results did not appear in the data, other additional explanatory variables would be sought to explain the anomalous observations. It has been recognised that stable empirical relationships are not likely to be observed during wars, for example, and this is allowed for in research, sometimes by including a dummy or shift variable in the regressions. In the case of China, however, it does not follow that similar quantitative causes will consistently have the same quantitative impact, and this makes the automatic application of econometric testing inappropriate. This is due to two factors. First, many variables change in China, not because of mechanistic market forces but because planners decide to change them, and it is not at all certain that planners have responded to similar circumstances with the same quantitative reactions. This is in fact a basic hypothesis advanced to explain monetary events in planned socialist economies. Even if planners did so respond in some decades, it does not mean that we should expect to discover the same quantitative relationship between the extent of monetary growth and open inflation, say, in different decades when different political leaders will have had different ideas about the permissible extent of price increases. It is not reasonable to include a Cultural Revolution dummy variable just to produce better regression equations. Second, economic reforms will in themselves change the nature of the relationship between money and prices. As more prices are decontrolled the price level is more likely to be responsive to increases in demand. In addition to the quantitative examination of this relationship we should therefore consider the qualitative. If a proposition says that in certain circumstances prices will rise and in the absence of those circumstances they will not rise or will fall, this view can be examined simply by identifying those years which manifested those circumstances and seeing what happened to the direction of change of prices, not the size of the price change. This does not require any regression analysis, which may be inappropriate for the reasons given above.

When discussing the move away from broad historical studies in the field of monetary economics, Cagan (1989: 118) criticises 'the now common practice of gathering a handful of time series from a data bank and running them through a regression meat grinder'. Although he is generally referring to the non-theoretical technique of vector autoregression, which has been applied to the Chinese data, his criticism is applicable to other studies of China that ignore the institutional setting and mechanically apply Western models to the data. I believe that the description of the relationship between money and prices offered in chapter 6 is more realistic, based as it is on Chinese institutions and policies, and better supported by the data for a longer period than anything else I have seen.

I have written this book from a comparative perspective. This perspective has two aspects: the empirical and the theoretical. I fully agree with Wilczynski's (1978: 15) view that one cannot make direct quantitative comparisons between monetary stocks in capitalist and non-capitalist economies; their institutions and the role given to money differ enormously. This, however, does not rule out our making *dynamic* comparisons of the rates of growth of money, output and prices for a number of different economies. What is important here is, not that the economies have different institutional structures and roles for money, but that for each of the economies these institutions do not change the role of money within each economy too much. I have made such comparisons across countries and have also made them for different periods within China. I argue that Chinese economic institutions relating to monetary flows were generally unchanged for the entire period 1952–85. It is permissible to apply the same approach for the entire period. Some monetary studies of China do not even broach this problem and just assume an unchanged institutional background. By 1984 enterprise reform had substituted tax payments for profit remittances, and price reform had become a policy of freeing prices rather than just adjusting them; the government continued to buy all agricultural output offered to it only until 1985. In 1984 the specialised banks took over many of the day-to-day functions of the People's Bank of China, which became the central policy-making bank. After 1985 things changed, so I make a further comparison between the reformed economy and the traditional economy in chapter 7. An additional problem is caused by the fact that certain statistical series were redefined about the period 1985–86.

In addition to empirical comparisons I attempt to view the events in China in the light of basic monetary theory. I review three branches of modern monetary theory: that for market economies; that underlying the interpretation of monetary events in the Eastern European socialist countries and the Soviet Union; and that underlying monetary policies in developing, mostly market, economies. I argue that the dominant paradigm of Western monetary economics, the Quantity Theory of Money, is inapplicable to China and anyway does not offer to explain very much when it is so applied. Any alternative approach must be firmly based on the nature of Chinese economic institutions and policies. An alternative Western paradigm is discussed. This is still a very loose set of propositions and theories that does not yet have the history, simplicity or rigour of the Quantity Theory. It does, however, have two important virtues: it offers to explain more than the Quantity Theory can; and it has recently been much better supported by certain monetary events in the leading market economies. The Quantity Theory was unable to cope with these events.

The perspective of the monetary events in Eastern Europe and the Soviet Union and their interpretation are relevant to understanding

China's monetary experiences. Their monetary systems are essentially the same: a pure fiat currency is used whose value is supposedly guaranteed by the state's responsibility for, and ability to supply, consumer goods at stable prices; and the major channels of monetary creation are through the state sector of the economy. It is relevant to discuss and explain the extent to which China's monetary experiences differ from those of these countries as they operate essentially the same monetary system. Another aspect of Eastern European and Soviet monetary developments relevant to China is that some economists noted for their views on their monetary experiences, such as Kornai and Portes, have begun to study China's monetary developments and that their views have been noted and discussed by students of China.

Eastern European and Soviet developments are of interest for the reason that East Germany actually abandoned its own currency in July 1990 without foreign invasion or conquest—a remarkable event. The Soviet Union has adopted plans to transform the administrative-command system into a market economy, make the rouble convertible and increase many retail prices. This is the abandonment of the traditional planned-economy monetary system in these countries. Monetary events in these countries played a role in causing the financial crises that precipitated these events. China had many monetary problems during the 1980s but did not solve them by abandoning the system that had caused them; it retained the system, used severe deflationary policies and retreated somewhat from reform. A review of the extent to which Western economists understood and predicted Eastern European crisis, and in particular of the methodology used by those who were correct in their predictions, is thus relevant to monetary events in China. We can learn which methodologies have been supported by events and which have not.

The approach used in this book to explain monetary developments and the relationship between money and retail prices is based on earlier ideas in both Chinese studies and Western monetary theory. In Chinese studies a clear precursor is Perkins (1966), who uses what Peebles (1983) calls the 'purchasing power approach'. This approach examines the *flows* of expenditures going onto and coming from the consumer goods market in an attempt to explain both monetary and price changes. This empirical application of this approach is now possible because Chinese statistical sources publish complete ex post data of such flows. In fact a recent official account of the excess demand problems of the 1980s uses the same approach as used in chapter 6 and in Peebles (1986b) to identify and quantify excess demand.[3] I have used a very simple measure of excess demand on the consumer goods market, which I have called purchasing power imbalance (*PPI*).[4] It is a simple operational measure of excess demand. It is non-theoretical and rather crude. Its virtues are that it is simple, that it can be computed from Chinese data, that it is similar to a measure that Chinese sources have recently started to discuss, that it is reasonable to assume that monetary planners monitor its behaviour and, most importantly, that they consistently react to it in a number of ways. It is thus able to explain, in a general way, the timing of price increases, why there was rapid or slow monetary growth, why budget deficits emerged and so on. This *PPI* approach is in sharp contrast with that of most other studies that use the Quantity Theory, which takes the *stock* of money as an explanatory factor and indicator of demand pressure, not as an explanandum. It is necessary to explain exactly why this stock changes.

From Western monetary theory the obvious foundation of the approach used here lies in the rejection of the Quantity Theory and the use of Post Keynesian (deliberately without the hyphen) ideas, the most important of which are that monetary changes are the result of developments in the economy, that cost factors play a role in determining the aggregate price level and that the money wage is not 'just another price' that adjusts through a market process to monetary changes. These ideas have to be applied to a system that is different in many important respects from that of the market economies for which these competing theories were developed.

1.2 Plan of this book

The basic plan of this book is: events, theories and analysis. An analogy with detective fiction would be that the events constitute the 'case', the theories are the location and *modus operandi* of the main actors, and the analysis is the 'solution'. Chapter 2, concerning events, reviews the main macroeconomic experiences in China for the period 1949–85. Before 1952 this can be only descriptive as we have no official monetary data for this period. The period 1953–85 is divided into seven subperiods, and the major macroeconomic events and time series are discussed in their context. The purpose is to show the background to events and policies that would have had an affect on money and prices in the economy. The periodisation chosen is the same as that commonly found in Chinese statistical publications. The periods can be easily identified with planning periods, but this is rather a nominal feature of them rather than any real determination of their developments. It is important to note that these periods were chosen *before* any analysis was made. They have not been obtained ex post by means of trying different periods to derive various averages to see which periodisation produced the best statistical results.

Chapter 3, on theories, surveys the main terms and concepts used in modern monetary analysis. It also surveys the main features of monetary theory and evidence from the developed capitalist economies, the Eastern European socialist economies including the Soviet Union, and developing countries. There is, and always has been, less agreement on money in capitalist economies than meets the eye in traditional textbooks and teaching. This is also true about the role of money and the interpretation of monetary events in the planned socialist economies. It is important to know the basic paradigm of Western monetary theory as this has been applied to China by both Western and Chinese economists. It is important to realise that this paradigm is not universally accepted and that it cannot account for some important recent monetary developments. It is very helpful to know something about the concepts and problems concerning money in other socialist economies and about Western debates about them as these are clearly of relevance to China. It is also helpful to know what monetary experiences the developing countries have had and what policies are recommended for their specific circumstances.

Chapter 4, on the scene of the events and the *modus operandi* of its actors, surveys the nature of Chinese economic institutions to establish how they affect the nature of monetary flows. It shows the money supply process in detail using two methods of presentation for the modern period. It also looks at Chinese statements on aspects of economic policy and its objectives that are likely to influence money and prices.

Chapter 5 is the first analytical chapter. It reviews certain important works on money and prices in China in order to provide some clues about the correct method of analysis and to show which approaches do not lead very far. Works from both inside and outside China that I have found informative and helpful are surveyed in probably more detail than in most other works. I believe that this rather old-fashioned way of doing things is helpful in showing the origin of certain arguments about the nature and extent of inflation in China, for example. There is an already large and rapidly growing literature on money in China, especially in Chinese, and I, as a sole researcher, have only been able to include what I consider to be the most important and relevant analytical works.

Chapter 6 presents an analysis of money, prices and related variables for the period 1952–85 that accounts for the events described in chapter 2. I believe that the assumptions about institutions and policies necessary to make such an analysis hold good for this period; so I use the same approach for the entire period. An interview with Li Guixian, president of the People's Bank of China published towards the end of 1989, reveals similar concerns and attitudes to monetary policy as can be shown to have existed in earlier periods.[5] Commodity *huilong*, an important concept that will be defined, discussed and illustrated in sections 4.8, 4.9 and 4.10 and used in the theory of chapter 6, was specifically identified as having played a role in restraining monetary growth in 1987 (*Zhongguo Jingji Nianjian 1988*, p. IV-38). It is also the preferred way of dealing with monetary imbalances in the opinion of Hong Yuncheng, up until early 1990 the director of the General Office of the People's Bank of China (Li Ping, 1990: 27). Obviously, economic reform in the 1980s had not changed the basic nature of the money supply process, and planners' attitudes and the same institutional assumptions are valid for the entire period studied statistically in this book, that is, 1952–88.

Chapter 7 compares the results of chapter 6 with data from China for the period after 1985 to establish the extent to which things changed in the monetary field after 1985. It reviews the effects of economic reform on monetary variables and behaviour for the entire 1980s. It also makes some comparisons with some of the countries mentioned in chapter 3. Some conclusions are offered.

An alternative order for the reader who might prefer the progression of institutions, evidence, theories and analysis would be chapters 4, 2, 3 and then 5, 6 and 7.

Appendixes I to IV present the data used in the body of the book and their sources, and appendix V presents a short reading list arranged by topic. I have not used any confidential or unpublished data; data sources are detailed in the appendixes, and I recommend the original sources to anyone intent on serious work on the issues raised in this book. I have in places pointed out numerical errors and data mistakes in the works of others. As someone who has himself made such a mistake in published work, and acknowledged it, I appreciate how it can happen. My purpose has merely been to try to establish the correct figures to use and to put on record the results some analysts have published in different forms in different places.

2 Events and periods

This chapter reviews the macroeconomics of money, output and prices for the period 1952–85 and discusses the main events of the seven subperiods that will be subsequently used in the statistical analysis of these variables and their interrelationships.

2.1 General features of money, output, prices and money holdings, 1952–85

Figure 2.1 presents time series graphs of the main variables of interest. They are presented in the order suggested by the main paradigm of Western monetary theory. This paradigm will be critically discussed in the next chapter, and it will be argued that it is not suitable for the analysis of these events in China. An alternative view will be proposed there also. The dominant paradigm assumes that the nominal money supply is exogenous to the economy; that is, it changes because of events external to, and independent from, the actual current or past behaviour of the economy. There is also assumed to be a stable demand function for real money balances. A major determinant of this demand is real income. Changes in real income are often taken as a proxy for changes in the demand for real money balances. Any discrepancy between the rate of growth of the nominal money supply and real income is supposed to show up in price inflation, which will reduce the real value of the excess nominal money supply to equal the real quantity demanded. If there is a stable real-demand function for money, the ratio of money to income should show a growth pattern devoid of any noticeable instability but expressing constancy or smooth change.

The top section of Figure 2.1 shows two series of narrow measures of the nominal money supply, which are presented in Table I.1 (see Appendix). *CRC* represents currency in circulation and is held by households, enterprises, units, organisations. The other monetary series is *SDR* plus *CHR*, savings deposits held by households (residents, hence the use of the letter *R*) plus their cash holdings. The second section shows real national income[1] in index form (*RNI*) over the same period.

The third section shows two indexes of retail prices. *P* is the general retail price index (*quan shehui lingshou wujia zong zhishu*), and *MP* is the free market price index of consumer goods (*jishi maoyi jiage zhishu*). The data are in Table II.1. The general retail price index covers state-determined prices (list prices), negotiated prices and market prices. It is a

Figure 2.1 Money, output, prices and money holdings, 1952–85

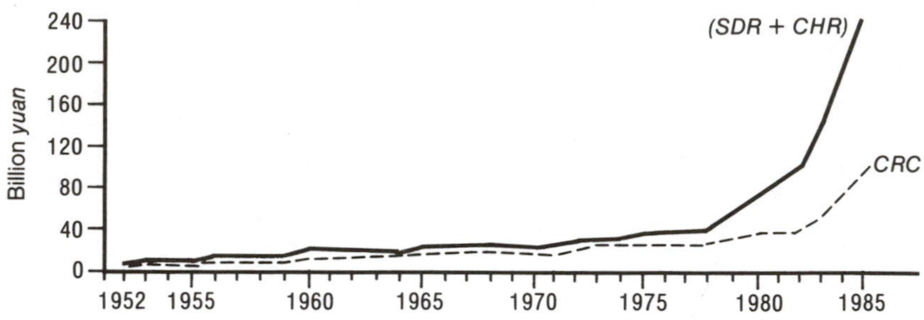

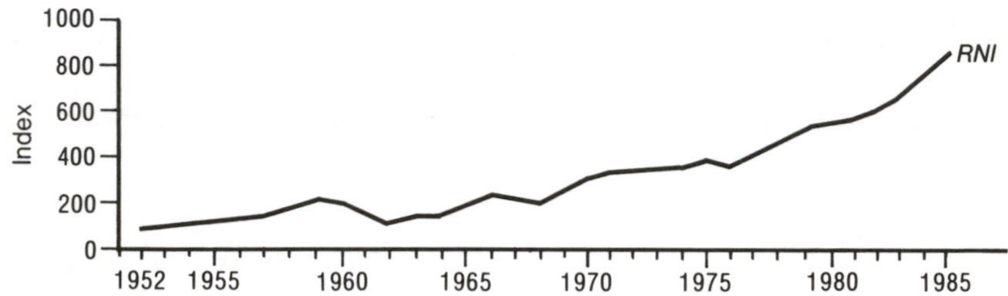

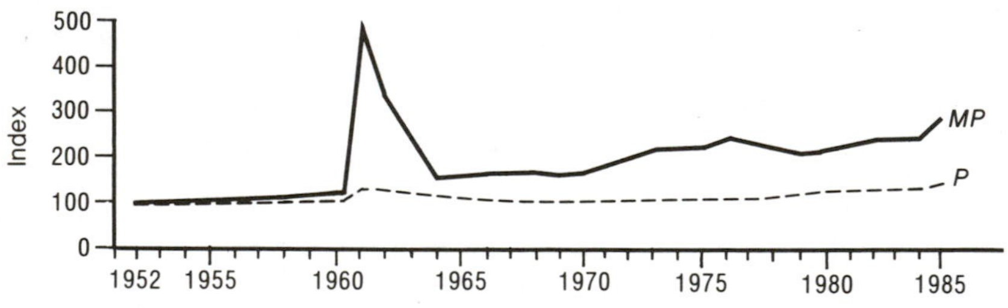

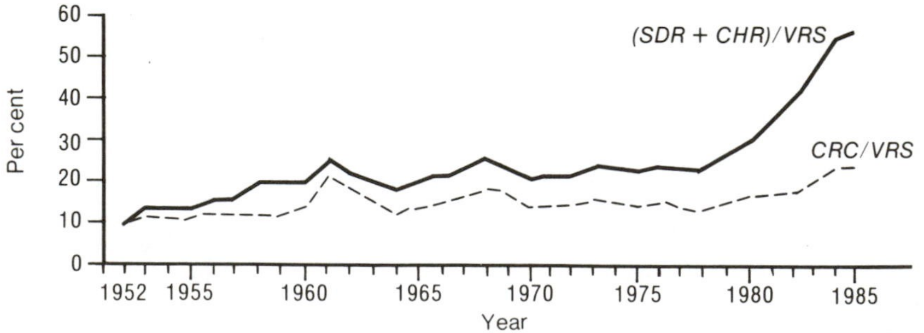

weighted average of these prices. The retail price index covers not only consumer goods but also the means of agricultural production sold to the rural sector through the retail trade network (*nongye shengchan ziliao lingshou e*). It is discussed in section 4.5. The free market price index covers a narrow range of goods sold by individual traders (*getihu*) and by peasants directly to non-agricultural purchasers on urban and rural markets (*nongmin dui feinongye jumin*). Most of the products are food or handicraft items, and only consumer goods are included in the price index used here. (For examples of items traded see *Zhongguo Maoyi Wujia Tongji Ziliao 1952–83*, pp. 335–8; and *Statistical Yearbook of China 1986*, p. 580.) This form of trade was discouraged for many years and has constituted a varying proportion of retail sales. For example, in 1953 this private trade constituted nearly 60 per cent of total retail sales. By 1956, the year usually judged to be the time when socialisation of production and distribution had been completed, it was 7.7 per cent, and by 1977, at the end of the ten years of chaos, it was down to only 1.7 per cent. By 1983 it had reached 11.2 per cent, and it continued to increase as part of the economic reforms of agricultural marketing during this period (*Zhongguo Maoyi Wujia Tongji Ziliao 1952–83*, p. 65). Hence, the index covers a very small part of retail trade for many years in this study.

The bottom section of Figure 2.1 shows the ratio of the two monetary concepts to the annual value of retail sales (*VRS*). The data are in Table I.5. It would not be sensible to express some of these monetary magnitudes as a proportion of total national income or gross domestic product (*GDP*), as would be done for a capitalist economy, simply because holders of currency cannot buy most of output and a large proportion of production is transferred without the use of currency. Chinese monetary planning has been concerned with the ratio of these monetary magnitudes to retail sales, not national income. The inverse of this ratio is a type of velocity of circulation of money, a concept that will be discussed in chapter 3 and analysed subsequently.

The general features of the series can be described briefly here. The following sections examine them in more detail and put them into the broader context of general economic development divided into seven subperiods. Over the period 1953–58 there were steady increases in money, real output and the two price indexes, with retail prices increasing at an average rate of 1.1 per cent a year. The money ratios increased quite smoothly. After 1958 currency in circulation continued to increase, but after 1959 real output fell dramatically during 1960–62. The general retail price index increased considerably, by 24 per cent from 1959 to 1962, and market prices exploded, increasing to four times their 1959 level by 1961. The money ratios also increased substantially. After recovery was achieved, real output and money grew relatively smoothly after 1963. There were declines in real output in 1967 and 1968 and then again in 1976. The money ratios rose in these years although there were no marked increases in prices. The market price index drifted up after 1970 until 1976, when it fell until 1979, whereupon it began to increase again quite steadily. The narrow money ratios were quite stable for the period 1963–78. For example, the currency-in-circulation ratio (*CRC*/*VRS*) fluctuated between a value of 12.6 per cent in 1964 and 18.2 per cent in 1968 (Table I.5). After about 1978 the nominal monetary magnitudes started to rise more rapidly, as did real output, but the money ratios rose, especially for the measure that includes household savings deposits. Periods of open inflation were clearly 1960–62 and the period after 1978. These periods of open inflation have been frequently identified by Chinese economists such as Luo (1982a; 1982b), Wang and Wang (1982: 223), Huang (1988a) and others. The clear period of relative stability of the general retail price index and the narrower money ratios was the 'ten years of chaos' from about 1966–76, sometimes also called the 'decade of disturbances' (Hsiao, 1987: 67) and the Cultural Revolution, although the latter term is reserved by many for the earlier period of 1966–68.

Three interesting generalisations can be drawn from this general evidence, which can be found in statistical form in appendixes I and II and the tables of the following sections.

First, in terms of short run variations there is an inverse relationship between nominal money and real output. In the years when real output fell the nominal money supply increased. The sole exception is 1962, when real output fell 6.5 per cent and currency in circulation fell 15.3 per cent. In 1960 and 1961 real output fell 1.4 and 29.7 per cent respectively. Currency in circulation rose 28 and 31 per cent in these years. In 1976 real output fell 2.7 per cent and currency in circulation rose 11.7 per cent. In the years of recovery after these falls in real output, that is, in 1963, 1964 and 1977, currency in circulation fell. This pattern is also true of a measure of the money supply including savings deposits. This inverse relationship between nominal money and real output is interesting and has to be explained by any theory of money in China. It is interesting because it goes against the experiences of market economies when there are large falls in real output. The period 1959–61 in China has been called the Great Depression by at least one authority on the economy (Howe, 1978: xxix). A comparison with the Western world's Great Depression might be instructive. In the United States real gross national product (*GNP*) fell 29.5 per cent over the period 1929–33 and *M1* and *M2* (two measures of the nominal money supply) fell 25.2 and 31.0 per cent respectively (Gordon, 1987: 582). In Canada also the money supply fell significantly during this period (Friedman and Schwartz, 1963: 352), but in the United Kingdom it fell only slightly (Capie and Webber, 1985: 60–76). A major controversy in monetary history and theory is, of course, the nature of this relationship. Did the fall in the money supply cause the fall in real output, or was the fall in the money supply the consequence of the fall in output? Different theories representing these different explanations will be discussed in the next chapter.[2]

A second feature of the evidence is that, over the long run, there is a positive relationship between open inflation and changes in the money supply. The periods of open inflation are associated with increases in the money supply. This feature of Chinese experience will be shown more clearly towards the end of the next chapter. It also holds for the seven subperiods and, to some extent, for annual changes.

Third, the money ratios held by households tended to rise when there were falls in real output and when there was open inflation. They rose in 1961, 1967 and 1968 and slightly in 1976, the years when real output fell. They rose consistently over the period after 1978 when open inflation became noticeable. An increase in money holdings in real terms (here they are expressed in terms of the proportion of annual retail sales value) at times of falling real output and rising inflation is somewhat odd. In market economies falling output tends to reduce money holdings, and inflation, it is always argued, reduces the amount of real money people wish to hold.

These three features of China's monetary experiences have to be explained by any theory of money and prices for China.

2.2 Detailed background to these events by subperiods

Subsequent statistical analysis of the period 1953–85 will use seven subperiods. The main features of each them will be discussed in this chapter. The events of the period 1949–52 will be discussed here also. This period does not feature in the statistical analysis because reliable data have not been published. It is, however, an important period as many of the basic institutional features of the economy, especially in terms of monetary policy and institutions, were established in this period.

The periods used and their names are as follows:

	1949–52	Rehabilitation or recovery
Period I	1953–57	First Five-year Plan
Period II	1958–62	Second Five-year Plan—including the Great Leap Forward (*Da Yue Jin*) and the Great Depression of 1959–61
Period III	1963–65	Period of recovery
Period IV	1966–70	Third Five-year Plan—beginning of the Cultural Revolution
Period V	1971–75	Fourth Five-year Plan
Period VI	1976–80	Fifth Five-year Plan
Period VII	1981–85	Sixth Five-year Plan

Periods IV and V together approximately cover the period sometimes known as the Great Proletarian Cultural Revolution (*Wuchan Jieji Wenhua Dageming*) of 1966–76. Some analysts would categorise both periods VI and VII (1976 and after) as the period of economic reform and modernisation, starting with the fall of the 'gang of four' in September 1976 and Hua Guofeng's supporting the policy of the 'four modernisations' and the 'foreign leap forward' (*yang yue jin*). Others put economic reform as beginning in late 1978. Period VII clearly covers the period of continuing economic reform in agriculture, industry, banking and commerce.

2.3 Rehabilitation or recovery, 1949–52

During this period three important events shaped much of the subsequent economy's structure and the attitudes of its planners and inhabitants: land reform; the establishment of new monetary institutions and the process of learning how to institute monetary reforms and policies; and the fight against inflation in the newly occupied cities.

The People's Republic of China was established in Peking on 1 October 1949. Well before this the Communist Party and its various armies had carried out some of its policies in its occupied areas and cities.[3] Land reform had been carried out in liberated areas of northern China from mid 1946 onwards. As the communist armies were occupied with fighting rather than administration, many features of this early wave of reform did not accord with party policy as was later expressed in the Outline Land Law of October 1947. The party wished to abolish feudal economic relations in the countryside, not any buds of capitalism. Peasants just wanted land, so they often ignored party directives that the land and assets of the rich peasants were not to be confiscated. It was the landlords' land, draft animals, farm tools and surplus grain that were to be redistributed as stipulated in the Land Reform Law of June 1950.[4] There was to be no confiscation of land or other assets used by landlords or rich peasants in industry and commerce. Confiscated land was reallocated to poor peasants and the landlords, self-employed people such as pedlars, handicraft workers and professionals, monks, nuns and so on, and those unemployed returning to their villages. Local governments could keep some of the land for establishing state farms. This last provision did not cover very much land, and the bulk of it (about 47 per cent of the nation's total cultivated area) was redistributed to 300 million peasants with the intention that it should be controlled freely by the recipients in a market environment. Peasants also received confiscated houses, tools and surplus grain of the landlords. Land could be rented or sold, and hiring labour was permitted. Lippit (1974) and Wong (1973a; 1973b) cover the main events and intention of the reform well, and Moise (1977: vol. 1) surveys these and other interpretations. A speech by Mao Zedong, at the Third Plenary Session of the Seventh Party Central Committee in June 1950, made clear his view that it was impossible to eliminate capitalism in China at that time.

An important monetary consequence of this land reform followed from the fact that recipients did not have to pay any compensation whatsoever to either the previous land or property owners or to the government. Previously, rents had been paid to landlords in grain. The peasants could now keep this, and they did not have to raise cash to pay compensation either. They could take the benefits of the land reform programme in terms of higher personal consumption. They had no great need to market their grain to raise money. This aspect of reform has been blamed by Chao (1970: 21–2, 41–2) for the phenomenon that the rural sector fell back to being a subsistence economy. No similar feature is said to have occurred in land reform in Japan and Taiwan where compensation was required. This reluctance to market grain is said by Chao to be the main reason for the government's introduction of compulsory purchases in November 1953. Peasants would not sell to the government voluntarily, so they had to be forced to do so. This change in 1953 produced a rural Chinese economy completely different from that probably envisaged in 1950 and introduced a system that had profound implications for the nature of monetary flows, marketing, income determination, price setting and inflation for the next 25 years.

The economy inherited by the communist government in 1949 was shattered. Fighting with the Kuomintang continued to at least late 1949, and Shanghai was bombed in February 1950. China fought in the Korean War from 1951. In 1949 agricultural output was at least 20 per cent lower than in 1937; industrial output was 50 per cent lower, as was the output of cotton and coal. Communications were broken; trade was minimal. At least 40 million people had been displaced as a result of flooding connected with the continuing civil war; there was unemployment; demobbed soldiers, including those of the Kuomintang, had to be resettled. There was rampant inflation in the cities, especially Shanghai, which experienced one of the twentieth century's most pronounced hyperinflations.[5] Shanghai had been occupied by the communists in May 1949; they found stocks of rice and coal to be very low, and private textile firms had only one month's supply of cotton in stock (Liu, 1980: 51; Liu and Wu, 1986: 17). China had been through twelve years of war and inflation. The government budget was in deficit, and the money supply was growing rapidly. The budget and wages were calculated in units of millet because of the inflation, and in 1949 revenues equalled only about half of expenditures. The new government had to have a balanced budget, a policy to stop inflation and a financial system for raising revenue and financing the government, the army and the increasing numbers of state-run enterprises.

The People's Bank of China had started operations on 1 December 1948 after it had been established by merging the Beihai, North China and Northwest China Peasants' Banks (*A History of Chinese Currency*, p. 189; Miyashita, 1966: 55–6; Ma, 1982a: 464). In the previously occupied areas various communist banks had issued their own currencies, and Soviet governments and worker–peasant banks and other organisations had been issuing their own currencies since at least 1927. (See *A History of Chinese Currency*, pp. 150–88 for examples of such issues, many bearing the portraits of Marx, Lenin, Stalin and Mao Zedong.) The Kuomintang government had also issued many different types of currency, which were rapidly depreciating. There was no national currency system.[6] The Kuomintang government carried out a currency reform as late as August 1948 when for 3 million *yuan* of existing legal tender notes a gold *yuan* note worth 1 *yuan* was issued. It instituted wage and price controls, which were enforced by means of public executions (Pan, 1984: 215–16; Barber, 1979: 49–50). When these controls were lifted in November prices rose about elevenfold in one month (Chou, 1963: 48). As successive cities were occupied by the communists, existing Kuomintang currencies were recalled and replaced by the appropriate locally issued Soviet notes. After the establishment of the People's Bank of China a national currency, the *Renminbi*, was issued, and one of the bank's main tasks became the recalling of all other currencies and the replacing of them with this unified currency. The six-year process by which existing currencies were recalled and replaced, first by other currencies and then by the *Renminbi*, was particularly complicated. Qian and Guo (1985: 238) present a chart, a virtual genealogy of the *Renminbi*, showing the various conversions. The communist government did, however, refuse to accept Kuomintang silver *yuan* notes issued in Canton in early 1949. Other currencies, gold and silver, and Hong Kong dollars were forbidden to circulate in China. Different rates of exchange for the new currency were established in different cities as they were occupied, and favourable rates for certain people were applied (Miyashita, 1966: 65–6; Qian and Guo, 1985: 237–9). It is said that all old currencies, both those of the Kuomintang and those of the communists, had been recalled by November 1951 (Peng, 1976: 26). This was the first time in decades that China had a single currency in circulation. Some of the proceeds of this currency recall, or 'confiscation' as some sources put it, were used for communist expenditures in areas where the old currency still circulated. Miyashita (1966: 58) quotes a contemporary report that argued that the communists would confiscate notes in newly occupied towns and send them to the big cities to buy up supplies on the market, thus driving up prices. By 1952 the *Renminbi* was the only currency legally circulating in China (with the exception of Tibet and Taiwan, as Chinese sources put it). By 1959, when Tibetan notes where recalled, China, with the exception of Taiwan, had achieved monetary unity (Liu, 1980: 65).

The control over the use of the new currency was established from 1950 onwards when the 'Decisions on Unifying the State Financial and Economic Work',[7] adopted in March 1950 (Chen, 1950b), were put into effect. Their basic aim was to increase central government revenues, encourage saving and reduce currency in circulation. An important means of doing the latter was the decision that all government organisations, army units and state-owned enterprises had to deposit all cash in excess of that required for immediate needs (about three days' expenditure in areas where there were branches of the People's Bank and not more than one month's elsewhere) in the state bank and not in private banks (Liu, 1980: 65; Miyashita, 1966: 70–1; Liu and Wu, 1986: 34). This served to lay the foundation of the system under which state units would not use cash for transfers between themselves as well as ensuring private banks would be deprived of funds. According to Miyashita (1966: 117), by the end of 1952 the People's Bank of China dealt with 90 per cent of deposits and loans. Together with joint state–private banks this proportion reached about 99 per cent.

Much economic activity in the cities was speculation, and there was an obvious distrust of private banks. Barter transactions and the use of commodities as money substitutes were common (Barber, 1979: 37–8). The major private and local Kuomintang banks were confiscated by the new government, but many banks were acquired through the more subtle means of establishing joint administration with communist-appointed directors (Cheng, 1954: 47–50). Already there were quite a few state-owned enterprises, commercial units and other productive assets, mainly confiscated from the 'top Kuomintang bureaucrats' (Liu and Wu, 1986: 21). The government was able to obtain important commodities for itself to use and sell. This played an important role in the fight against inflation. The anti-inflation policy is frequently described as a fight against capitalists, particularly against speculators. Its method is a model of the entire Chinese retailing and price control methods of the next 25 years. The government saw itself as able to control both sides of the market for important commodities. It controlled the issue of the new currency through the state bank, forbade its use within the state sector, and approved its use for wage payments and purchases from private traders. It also increased supplies of important commodities to the occupied cities starting in early 1950, a time when private businesses were closing down (Liu and Wu, 1986: 39). This supply effort was aimed at defeating inflation. Many private traders were locked into short term loans at high nominal rates of interest. Falling prices bankrupted them. Tsiang (1967: 328) argues that prices fell as businessmen dumped goods in order to raise cash to meet compulsory bond subscriptions. In 1950 wholesale prices fell by about 30 per cent over the period February–May 1950 (Liu and Wu, 1986: 37; Liu, 1980: 63).

Strenuous efforts were made to increase voluntary savings and to make government bonds more attractive. Private savings deposits had been index-linked against a basket of important commodities since mid 1949, and government bonds, issued from January 1950, were also index-linked. Their real value was thus preserved at a time of inflation. The term '*zheshi*', often translated as 'calculated in terms of commodities', describes this indexation. The system as applied to savings deposits was simplified in March 1950 (Cheng, 1954: 52–3). Wages and salaries were also indexed to the price of commodities. The chosen basket of commodities and the period from which prices would be taken varied from place to place (Miyashita, 1966: 75–7). Private savings deposits are said to have increased fivefold over the period February–June 1950. Cheng (1954: 53) and Tsiang (1967: 328) point out a disadvantage of the indexation system when prices began to fall. The People's Bank at first stuck to the view that the value of Victory Bonds (those issued from January 1950) should fall along with prices, but this policy was dropped, and the original value of all savings deposits was to be preserved if prices fell and protected if prices rose.

The Kuomintang government had followed a policy of low nominal interest rates, even during the rapid inflation, as it believed that interest rates were an important element in determining costs and hence prices. The communist policy of indexation was a very sophisticated financial innovation and one that seems to go against the communists' possible ideological view of unearned interest in a capitalist economy. Indexation of certain savings deposits was again introduced in September 1988. How the communists came to adopt such a sophisticated policy so early is a mystery. In his announcement of the issuing of indexed bonds Chen Yun (1949: 36) gives no clues as to the origin of the idea. Tsiang (1967: 325–6) states that he himself put forward such a proposal in April and May 1947 while a lecturer at the National University of Peking. He says that the idea attracted some attention among fellow academics but was not adopted by the Kuomintang government.

It is generally agreed that price stability had been achieved by about March 1950 (Yao, 1952: 221; Peng, 1976: 29; Tsakok, 1976: 8; Eckstein, 1977: 167; Liu, 1980: 63). Revenue collection, much of which was in terms of grain, was centralised, and throughout 1950 revenues rose, even exceeding planned amounts. It is claimed that by the end of the year balance had been approximately achieved (Liu and Wu, 1986: 36–7). Currently available official figures show a deficit for the whole of 1950 and a surplus for 1951. No official monetary data have been published for this period, but

Tseng and Han (1959: 43) state that currency in circulation fell 10 per cent from March to May 1950.

By the end of 1952 China had a banking system led by the People's Bank of China that controlled virtually all deposits and loans in the country and held the deposits of all state-run organisations, a stable currency and experience of defeating inflation.[8] This was done by state agencies' controlling the supply of certain commodities in an environment where currency issue was monopolised by the state bank. The politicians and planners could now try to build the economy they wanted.

2.4 Period I, 1953–57

The First Five-year Plan period (see Table 2.1) was seen as the first necessary step to secure the socialist transformation of the economy, which was expected to take fifteen years.[9] Some experience with planning had been obtained in northern China in 1949, and a tentative plan for the entire country had been drawn up for 1950. The State Planning Commission and the State Statistical Bureau were established in 1952. The economy consisted of a mixture of state-owned enterprises, co-operatives, individual peasants and handicraft producers, the state–capitalist economy and the private economy. At the end of 1952 the state sector produced 19 per cent of national income and the individual producers 72 per cent with the balance coming from the other sources (Liu and Wu, 1986: 110). It was an aim of this period to transform the structure of ownership to enable more widespread planning to take place in order to achieve socialist transformation, industrialisation and development. The Soviet Union was a close ally, contributing large amounts of aid and technical assistance on 156 planned industrial projects as well as training many students and technicians in Soviet bloc countries. Planning state industrial enterprises implies formulating a plan, ensuring that enterprises fulfil it and allocating the resulting output in accordance with the plan. State enterprises were given output quotas and plans for quality, variety, productivity and costs. It is hard to be certain about the extent of central planned allocation of industrial products in this period. Tang (1987: 229) gives a total of 227 nationally and ministerially allocated goods for 1953, rising to 532 in 1957, as do Liu and Wu (1986: 176). These covered all the major means of production and were centrally allocated. By 1956, 380 products were manufactured according to the plan, constituting about 60 per cent of total industrial output (Liu and Wu, 1986: 173–4). The period 1953–56 saw the state taking over many jointly run and private enterprises in industry, wholesaling and retailing. By 1956 industries that were said to be under socialist public ownership—that is, state-owned, collectively owned and joint state–private—accounted for 98.8 per cent of total industrial output. In retail trade private traders supplied only 7.6 per cent of total retail sales, the balance being supplied by state shops, co-operatives and state–capitalist businesses (Liu and Wu, 1986: 158–9). Former capitalist owners were effectively bought out of control over their enterprises, which became state operated under the plan. They received interest payments on their shares for seven years starting from 1956, which period was extended until 1966.

Table 2.1 Period I: main economic indicators
(percentage increase over the previous year except *ACC* and *B*)

Year	*RNI*	*IND*	*AGRIC*	*VRS*	*ACC*	*B*	*CRC*	*P*	*MP*
1953	14.0	33.6	1.6	25.7	23.1	0.28	43.3	3.4	3.9
1954	5.8	19.0	1.6	9.5	25.5	1.61	4.6	2.3	2.3
1955	6.4	6.3	8.0	2.9	22.9	0.27	−2.2	1.0	−0.2
1956	14.1	29.6	4.4	17.5	24.4	−1.83	42.2	0.0	−0.2
1957	4.5	11.6	3.1	2.9	24.9	0.60	−7.9	1.5	2.8

Definitions and sources: The variables and their sources are as follows:

RNI: real national income, percentage increase over the previous year (*Statistical Yearbook of China 1986*, p. 42).

IND: real industrial output, percentage increase over the previous year (*Statistical Yearbook of China 1986*, p. 42).

AGRIC: real agricultural output, percentage increase over the previous year (*Statistical Yearbook of China 1986*, p. 42).

VRS: value of retail sales (current prices), percentage increase over the previous year (*Statistical Yearbook of China 1986*, p. 448).

ACC: accumulation rate, percentage of national income invested (*Statistical Yearbook of China 1986*, p. 49).

B: government budget balance, billion *yuan* (*Statistical Yearbook of China 1986*, p. 509).

CRC: currency in circulation, percentage increase over the previous year, calculated from Table I.1, series CRC_2.

P: general retail price index, percentage increase over the previous year (*Statistical Yearbook of China 1986*, p. 535).

MP: market price index of consumer goods, percentage increase over the previous year, calculated from Table II.1.

The Ministry of Commerce was able to set prices for the state wholesale and retail trade sectors. Chen Yun (1950a: 70) revealed one of the tasks of state trading organisations when he announced that it 'is the responsibility of State wholesale companies to recall currency from circulation and to stabilize wholesale prices'. Such companies would buy products from the private sector and resell them with a markup. This difference would be the amount of currency the companies could withdraw from circulation. Any sale of state-supplied goods for currency would withdraw currency from circulation, and it is obvious that state retail trade would do this also. It is also obvious, but worth noting, that this would work only if the retail price exceeded the wholesale or procurement price. If this were not true, these state agencies would be increasing the amount of currency in circulation by buying at prices higher than those at which they resold. This monetary function of state trade was recognised from a very early period.

The Ministry of Foreign Trade, established in 1952, controlled a number of import and export corporations under the plan, and individual enterprises and units were not allowed to trade with foreign bodies. Domestic producers would have no idea what international prices were and could not be influenced by them, either in deciding what to produce or in determining their incomes. The State Planning Commission determined import requirements implied by the national plan, and the Ministry of Foreign Trade then drew up export plans so that imports could be realised. Wages were centrally set from 1956 onwards and were increased in that year. In 1956 wages were 14 per cent higher than in the previous year and the labour force expanded more than planned, resulting in the wage bill's increasing 37 per cent. Even though light industry output expanded 20 per cent, it was felt that this was a year of inflationary pressure and bad co-ordination between the demand and supply of consumer goods. There was no open inflation, however. Liu and Wu (1986: 181–5) summarise contemporary criticisms of this 'highly centralized economic system' under which state enterprises dominated most industries and were subject to rigid central control.

A major change in economic organisation occurred in November 1953. Government purchases of agricultural produce for its shops and industries had not been going well during that year, and in October only 38 per cent of that month's purchase plan was fulfilled. In November a system of planned purchase and planned supply of grain was adopted (Perkins, 1966: 48–51; Lardy, 1983a: 30). This entailed putting compulsory quotas on grain producers and organising the sale of grain[10] to urban residents and to those in certain deficit rural areas by the state. The system was applied to edible oils also and in September 1954 was extended to cotton, thus covering the major crops. Such a system transformed the entire nature of the economy and its monetary flows. The government now determined the prices for the bulk of agricultural output and thus played a major role in determining the money incomes of the rural sector, which constituted about 87 per cent of the population in 1953. The government controlled sales and stockpiled grain for bad years. As state industry expanded its scope, more and more of its products were sold to the rural sector at state-determined prices. The government was thus in a position to determine the terms of trade of the rural sector because it controlled the prices of its inputs (fertilisers, seeds, fuel, tools, consumer goods and so on) and of its output. Although there was not yet full collectivisation the government was in the same position as the Soviet Union government had been after collectivisation there in 1929. It could control rural incomes and extract a surplus for industrialisation. Rural incomes, and hence consumption, could be kept low, allowing resources to be devoted to investment. The food from the countryside, procured at fixed prices, supplied the urban workforce at fixed prices and in state-determined quantities. Urban rationing was instituted from August 1955. The state was able to control rural food trade, and many private traders disappeared. The accumulation rate (investment as a percentage of national income) was 24.2 per cent on average during this period. It showed some cyclical variation, and it has been pointed out that in the years after a good harvest (which occurred in 1952 and 1955) the accumulation rate rose (see Table 2.1).

The First Five-year Plan was for rapid industrialisation and socialist transformation. In 1952 about 42 per cent of gross industrial output value came from state-owned enterprises. It had reached 54 per cent by 1957 and 90 per cent by 1965 (*Statistical Yearbook of China 1986*, p. 224). By 1957 light industry's gross output in real terms (in 1952 prices)[11] had increased 83.3 per cent over the 1952 level, but heavy industry's output had increased nearly 211 per cent (*Statistical Yearbook of China 1986*, p. 225). Table 2.1 shows how industry grew more rapidly than agriculture during this period. It also shows that during this period, on an annual basis, there was no clear relationship between changes in currency in circulation and price changes. In 1955 currency fell 2.2 per cent and open inflation was 1 per cent. In 1956 currency increased 42.2 per cent and there was no open inflation. Changes in market prices were never very different from those of the general retail price index. This period saw rapid industrial growth, particularly of heavy industry, a high accumulation rate and a moderate rate of open inflation of 1.1 per cent per annum for the entire period.

In March 1955 a major currency revaluation was carried out under which all nominal units were reduced from 10 000 to 1 and new *Renminbi* notes were issued to replace the old. This reform removed the legacy of the earlier inflation; it will be discussed in section 4.12 on monetary policy.

2.5 Period II, 1958–62

The First Five-year Plan period saw rapid industrial growth, but agricultural output did not increase very rapidly and average living standards remained very low. The Second Five-year Plan period (see Table 2.2) envisioned even greater development of heavy industry. This approach to development was adapted from that of the Soviet Union and was laid down by the Eighth National Congress of the Chinese Communist Party in September 1956. After March 1958 a new line was adopted at the instigation of Mao Zedong. This policy stressed immediate and fast economic growth based on heavy industry. Already some plan documents had argued that China could equal Britain in the production of iron and steel and other industrial products within fifteen years or so (Liu and Wu, 1986: 228; Ashbrook, 1967: 26), but the new approach wanted even faster development of industry. The slogan 'Great Leap Forward' was first used in a *Renmin Ribao* (People's Daily) editorial on 13 November 1957, but the policy was really pushed again from early 1958 onwards. Completely unrealistic targets were set for industrial production, and attempts to achieve them by administrative, almost militaristic, means caused severe problems and the collapse of industrial and agricultural output. From the spring of 1958 control over many state enterprises had been decentralised to the local authorities in seven newly created administrative areas. Each area was ordered to industrialise its region, and a mass campaign of factory construction began. In August 1958 the Political Bureau of the party held a conference at Beidaihe at which completely unrealistic output plans were proposed for 1959. Cotton output was to double compared with 1957, and grain was to show a 60–90 per cent increase. Britain's industrial output was to be reached in the immediate future (Liu and Wu, 1986: 235). Steel production was to be a key element of the newly launched Great Leap Forward. In 1958 the accumulation rate was 33.9 per cent, and in 1959 it reached 43.8 per cent. In this fervour for production at any cost statistics of output were widely fabricated, and the currently available official statistics are highly suspect even today. For what they are worth, they suggest that from 1957 to 1959 light industry's gross output increased by 63 per cent and that of heavy industry by 165 per cent, making an overall 111 per cent increase in gross industrial output (*Statistical Yearbook of China 1986*, p. 225). Workers were ordered to move into industry;

Table 2.2 Period II: main economic indicators
(percentage increase over the previous year except *ACC* and *B*)

Year	*RNI*	*IND*	*AGRIC*	*VRS*	*ACC*	*B*	*CRC*	*P*	*MP*
1958	22.0	56.8	0.2	15.6	33.9	−2.18	28.4	0.2	7.9
1959	8.2	30.8	−16.4	16.4	43.8	−6.58	10.8	0.9	1.3
1960	−1.4	8.0	−16.9	9.2	39.6	−8.18	27.7	3.1	14.8
1961	−29.7	−41.7	1.4	−12.8	19.2	−1.09	31.1	16.2	260.0
1962	−6.5	−15.4	4.7	−0.6	10.4	0.83	−15.3	2.8	−35.0

Note: Variables are defined in the note to Table 2.1.

240 000 small-scale blast furnaces were built in the first eight months of 1958; people took to the hills to dig out coal using any means possible. More than 100 million people were mobilised for building water conservancy projects. Agriculture was neglected. In 1958 agricultural output rose only 0.2 per cent although a bumper harvest had been expected. At the end of that year state purchases of all agricultural produce were well short of needs, and supplies on rural markets were low. In 1959 agricultural output fell 16.4 per cent. Disaster loomed. Some adjustments were tried in 1959. The purchasing power of state organisations was frozen, the number of state workers was reduced, wages were frozen, and the State Council issued a directive to 'educate' the people to make savings deposits (Perkins, 1966: 169). Agricultural loans were frozen, and sales on credit were banned. Urban rations were reduced by about 10 per cent. There was no real adjustment in political thinking, and in early 1960 a new Leap Forward was launched.

A major organisational change during this period was the establishment of the rural people's communes during 1958. These were launched on the instructions of Mao Zedong as they were supposed to be a higher stage of socialist organisation than the existing producer co-operatives in agriculture. The latter were merged into 26 425 people's communes containing 121.94 million farm households by the end of September 1958. The communes took over the peasants' poultry, domestic animals and private plots of land as well as any sideline occupations they followed, thus abolishing any means for them to carry on private economic activity. By 1959 the proportion of retail sales that were peasant sales to non-rural residents was a mere 0.5 per cent. The communes were political as well as economic organisations, mobilising their members into projects dictated by the Great Leap Forward strategy. Most of them provided communal kitchens in which all members had to eat, as well as kindergartens, nurseries etc. Most of these facilities were provided free of charge (Luo, 1985: 80–1), thus reducing the need for purchases and the use of money. Wages were distributed partly in money but mostly in grain. Chow (1985: 111) provides an interesting economic explanation for the adoption of the communes,[12] and Howe (1978: 46–7) stresses the fact that such an organisation gave planners greater control over the acquisition of agricultural output. Communal kitchens were a means of limiting rural food consumption even further.

It has been argued by several that communisation prompted the rural population to increase their own consumption and reduce savings rates as they now felt that the state would provide everything. Kane (1988: 48–51) cites evidence of this changed attitude and the reduced saving that is supposed to have occurred towards the end of 1958 and in 1959. In fact, the macroeconomic data show a *fall* in the proportion of residents' nominal purchasing power remaining unspent in 1959 and 1960 but a marked *increase* in total social purchasing power remaining unspent in 1958 and 1959 (Tables III.1 and III.2).

Banks and commercial units were, of course, obliged to follow the Great Leap Forward strategy, thus aggravating the monetary situation. Commercial departments bought anything on offer irrespective of quality. Such goods accumulated in warehouses. The banks had to support these units if they ran short of money by granting them loans, which they just used to buy unsaleable goods. Liu and Wu (1986: 254, 269) comment that the gap between society's purchasing power and available commodities reached 5 billion *yuan* in 1959 and widened in subsequent years. Wang and Wang (1982: 223) remark that in 1960 the supply of consumer goods was only 87.9 per cent of purchasing power. Such a situation would, of course, make it difficult for peasants to realise their desired increased consumption remarked on above and would explain why the proportion of social purchasing power remaining unspent increased. The theory developed in chapter 6 will investigate the consequences of such imbalances.

An interesting monetary phenomenon occurred during this period. It seems to have occurred earlier in 1955 also. During the second half of 1955 a growing number of agricultural producers' co-operatives started to issue their own currency (Durand, 1965: 61). These were described as 'vegetable tickets', 'cash circulation notes' and 'co-operative currency'. Such names suggest limited usability, but Durand states that they were widely accepted in rural areas as a money substitute for all sorts of transactions and that their use was tolerated by the government because of the insufficient degree of monetisation of the rural areas. In his view this was a partial failure (*un échec partiel*) of the government's policy of ensuring an adequate supply of currency in the rural areas. In the period 1958–59 the same phenomenon recurred under the newly established commune system when communes started issuing their own notes (Donnithorne, 1967: 71–2). As Donnithorne points out, this practice must have been fairly widespread as it was explicitly condemned by the Minister of Finance, Li Xiannian, in the party's main journal *Hong Qi* (Red Flag). He affirmed that:

> ... the power of issuing money is centralised in the state bank and communes are absolutely forbidden to print and issue any disguised forms of money [*bianxiangde huobi*]. In order to reduce formalities they can, according to needs and within the commune, print and issue meal tickets [*fan piao*], hairdressers' and washroom tickets. However, these are merely vouchers [*shuyu pingzheng xingshi*] and must be strictly differentiated from currency. Their use must be limited and they must not circulate. (Li, 1959: 5)

Here we see a case of decentralisation to commune level, leading to communes' taking over one of the functions of the state bank, issuing currency, and influencing the distribution of income within the commune independently of members' ability to earn state-issued currency by performing tasks rewarded by the receipt of currency. Peasants would be motivated to obtain commune 'meal tickets', not official state 'meal tickets'. This is a reasonable way of defining the official currency at most times as it was generally only usable in state shops and a large proportion of purchases consisted of food. It obviously had to be stopped. As far as I know this phenomenon did not recur. However, another similar monetary phenomenon involving the use of a substitute for the official currency has been reported at various times. For example, Solinger (1984: 25–6, 35) gives examples of times when ration coupons circulated as money in the late 1970s and private sales were made for grain coupons. With rationing that requires the purchaser to produce both money and a ration coupon, neither in itself is sufficient to make the purchase but both are desirable.

The bare national statistics of Table 2.2 show what happened to output and prices. Agricultural output fell 16.4 and 16.9 per cent in 1959 and 1960 respectively. Real national income fell 1.4, 29.7 and 6.5 per cent in the three years 1960–62 respectively. The value of retail sales fell 12.8 and 0.6 per cent in 1961 and 1962 respectively at a time when retail prices rose significantly. The 16.2 per cent increase in the general retail price index in 1961 was the largest recorded. Part of it was due to the 260 per cent increase in free market prices. It is in this period that free market prices exploded and began to change by amounts very different from the annual changes in the general retail price index. In 1962 market prices fell 35 per cent but the general retail price index increased 3.8 per cent. This is an important observation. Changes in the general retail price index cannot be equated to changes in the free market price index. These latter prices have only a minor weighting in the general index and, except in a year like 1961, cannot be an important explanation of the size of the change in the general index. There is something else in the general retail price index that accounts for its movements.

The accumulation rate had peaked at 43.8 per cent in 1959 but was reduced to 19.2 per cent in 1961 and further to 10.4 per cent in 1962. Obviously, an effort was made to divert output to consumer goods. China became a net foodgrain importer in 1961, but this did not prevent the obvious inflation of this period. Exports of cereals rose 44 per cent in 1959 but fell 35, 50 and 24 per cent in the years 1960–62 respectively. Cereal imports in 1959 were a mere 2000 tons and in 1960 were only 66 300 tons. In 1961 they reached 5.81 million tons, exceeding that year's exports by 4.445 million tons (*Statistical Yearbook of China 1983*: 422, 438). This huge change in the cereals export balance was obviously a reaction to the domestic disaster (Jiang, You and Zhou, 1989: 160), but it was insufficient in itself to solve the problem.

The limited extent to which information about China was readily available during this period led many to underestimate the extent of this disaster, although there were many refugee reports being collected in Hong Kong that implied a major famine (Redl and Hughes, 1962) and writers such as Ashbrook (1967: 31–2) provided an early realistic appraisal. An overly sympathetic observer of the Chinese system such as

Joan Robinson (1979: 141–2) could apparently believe, for she certainly wrote as late as the end of the 1970s, that China came through the years 1959–61 'without either famine or inflation'. This was supposed to have been achieved through rationing and price control for necessities but using high prices for inessentials to 'mop up the excess purchasing power'. Even if this last policy was used, and I believe it was, it was obviously not enough in the face of such huge output losses. Deleyne (1973: 38–42) also believes that even during periods of economic expansion or of famine there were no serious inflationary pressures.

The extent of famine during this period cannot be stated accurately. However, we now know that the national population fell by about 13.5 million people from the end of 1959 to the end of 1961, with the national deathrate increasing from 11.89 per 1000 in 1958 to 25.43 in 1960. The rate had been 20.00 in 1949. The rural deathrate increased from 12.50 to 28.58 during the same period. Both the urban and rural birthrates fell continuously until 1961 but doubled in 1962 and remained high for a number of years (*Statistical Yearbook of China 1986*, p. 73). Lardy (1983a: 150–2) discusses various estimates of excess deaths during this period, and Riskin (1987: 136–7), doing the same, concludes that there was a 'demographic catastrophe' caused by both natural disasters and human error. Kane (1988) provides a comprehensive coverage of the famine. Although the statistics are likely to be very inaccurate as statistical work was obviously disrupted during this period, there can be no doubt that there was widespread starvation and death during this period. The Soviet Union withdrew all its technicians and aid from July 1960, abandoning uncompleted projects, which the Chinese could neither finish nor operate. China had lost the unique chance of major industrialisation in many fields using foreign technology adopted wholesale from the Soviet Union. For many years China chose to rely on its own resources and technology, although there was some limited importation of a few important industrial plants from several Western European countries (Ashbrook, 1967: 34–5). When China tried to buy plants from some Western countries the United States sometimes vetoed their sale.

Policies aimed at recovery obviously had to deal with the agricultural problem. From 1960 state agricultural purchasing prices were increased and taxes in kind were reduced, as was the size of state procurements. Free rural markets were allowed to operate on a wider scale from the winter of 1960 although the State Council decision to allow this was made on 23 September 1959, the time given by Eckstein (1976: 335–6) for the actual reopening of these markets. The delay was caused by left bias among cadres that opposed this policy (Zhao Dexin, 1988: 675; Bucknall, 1979: 70). Workers were transferred from administration and investment projects to agricultural work. About 26 million people were transferred from towns to the countryside in order to reduce the commercial demand for grain (Jiang, You and Zhou, 1989: 160). The state monopoly over grain, cotton and edible oil continued, but quotas on other products were reduced and producers could now sell them freely. State industry diverted inputs to the rural sector and increased investment in agricultural machinery. The extent to which normal trade relations with the agricultural sector had been disrupted is illustrated by the fact that the government had to pay in terms of grain to obtain required amounts of cotton, oil-bearing crops, cured tobacco, jute, sugar and other important cash crops. This was done from April 1961. There was a recentralisation of industrial management, and enterprises were allowed to retain a smaller proportion of their profits. The purchasing power of social organisations was 'slashed' (Liu and Wu, 1986: 278).

An important adjustment policy was based on retail pricing policy. It is important to document this policy here although it will be discussed later as a general policy in chapters 4 and 6. Many observers do not believe that it happened, although Joan Robinson refers to it and, as will be argued later, it provides a general explanation of most of the change in the general retail price level during this and other periods. It is clear that for purposes of monetary control many retail commodities were sold at high prices. This policy was used not for basic necessities, which were rationed, but for many other goods. It is worth quoting one source in some detail:

> During this period, the state rationed at cheap prices 18 kinds of basic daily necessities including grain and cotton cloth, which accounted for 50–60 percent of the total expenditure of the workers and staff. Higher prices were set according to a plan for some of the other consumer goods.
>
> In early 1961, sweets and pastries were sold on the market in the big and medium-sized cities at a high price; in February that year, the scope of supply of high-priced sweets was extended nationwide and the supply of such pastries was extended to all cities and towns—areas inhabited by 130 million people.
>
> In March 1961, restaurants which charged high prices were opened in over 100 cities in the country. Later on, it was also decided that a certain portion of the bicycles, clocks, wrist-watches, wines, tea and knitwear was to be sold at high prices.
>
> Statistics showed that in 1961 and 1962, a total of 7.45 billion *yuan* worth of high-priced goods was sold, which increased state revenue by 3.85 billion yuan. By so doing, not only were the workers and the staff ensured of their supply of basic necessities, but the needs of different people were met and a large amount of currency was recalled, including a portion of the money in the hands of the farmers who had sold their agricultural and sideline produce at high prices. (Liu and Wu, 1986: 278–9)

Wang and Wang (1982: 224) specifically state that high-priced goods were sold in state shops to withdraw money from the market. Xue Muqiao (1982a: 69) states that the state 'had to sell some high-priced commodities to withdraw some money from circulation' and that between 1961 and 1964 currency to the value of 4–5 billion *yuan* was withdrawn from the market. Cheng (1981: 34) translates the original of this passage as saying that the state 'had to raise the prices of a number of high-priced commodities in order to contract currency circulation'. At the end of 1960 the amount of currency in circulation was 9.59 billion *yuan*, so these are not trivial amounts. Zhang Yigeng (1985: 32–3) also points out the effects of this policy of selling high-priced goods and says the aim was to withdraw currency from circulation. He states that 3 billion *yuan*'s worth of commodities was able to withdraw nearly 10 billion *yuan* of currency, which seems a remarkably high figure given the amount of currency actually in circulation. Jiang, You and Zhou (1989: 165) also pinpoint the policy of selling high-priced goods as one element of fiscal adjustment and state that in 1961 this policy withdrew 3.3 billion *yuan* of currency from circulation. Zhao Dexin (1988: 665–6) attributes the high price policy to Chen Yun and dates its start as January 1961 with its being extended to industrial goods in March 1962. Over the period 1961–65 the policy is said to have withdrawn 6 billion *yuan* of currency from circulation. These sources establish the fact of, and reason for, increases in certain state-determined retail prices, even during such difficult times. The aim was to withdraw currency from circulation, which state-supplied goods can uniquely do. As Xue (1982a: 69) remarks: 'Price increases in farmers' markets boost peasant incomes. But they could not withdraw money from circulation for the state. Therefore the state had to sell high-priced commodities the prices of which were 2 to 3 times higher than plan prices.' Xue (1985: 5) also states that it was necessary to sell high-priced goods (principally foods) and that 5 billion *yuan*, or 40 per cent of currency in circulation, was withdrawn from circulation through this policy. So, at a time of famine, monetary policy dictated that the government had to open high price restaurants and sell sweets and pastries and other goods at increased prices, to reduce the money supply.

The policy of strict expenditure reductions (*jieliu*) ensured that 'currency that was withdrawn from circulation was not reissued' (Liu Hongru, 1980: 113). Jiang, You and Zhou (1989: 165) state that social purchasing power in 1963 was 17 per cent lower than in 1960[13] and that urban collectives' purchasing power over consumer goods was reduced 47.2 per cent. Social purchasing power would have fallen anyway without there being these restrictive policies as production fell, which would have reduced the wage bill and agricultural procurements automatically. As Table 2.2 shows, currency in circulation fell 15 per cent in 1962. There had been government budget deficits for the period 1958–61, but by 1962 a small surplus had been achieved.

In 1962 agricultural output rose, and it is generally conceded that by July and August 1962 conditions were improving as state agricultural purchases rose and free market prices fell (Liu, 1980: 112). Policies had involved increased central control, slashing purchasing power, redundancies for state employees, reduced rations in the cities and towns, high prices for certain goods together with the freeing of farmers to produce for the market. The new approach was not to last.

2.6 *Period III, 1963–65*

This period represents three years of readjustment, but it still contained ambitious attempts to industrialise the country (see Table 2.3). Policies decided on early in this period were to affect the economy for the next twelve years at least. There was great distrust of the so-called capitalist elements that had been allowed to re-emerge to deal with the agricultural crisis. Private plots had been restored, individual farming under contracts

Table 2.3 Period III: main economic indicators
(percentage increase over the previous year except *ACC* and *B*)

Year	*RNI*	*IND*	*AGRIC*	*VRS*	*ACC*	*B*	*CRC*	*P*	*MP*
1963	10.7	12.5	11.5	0.1	17.5	0.27	−15.6	−5.9	−24.5
1964	16.5	24.7	13.1	5.6	22.2	0.05	−11.0	−3.7	−30.4
1965	17.0	27.4	9.8	5.0	27.1	0.70	13.5	−2.7	3.2

Note: Variables are defined in the note to Table 2.1.

with the government had been used to boost production, and rural fairs had been reopened. The Communist Party was not prepared to leave well alone. From early 1963 the party launched an 'anti-five evils' movement against corruption and embezzlement, speculation, extravagant spending and waste, decentralism and bureaucracy. In rural areas it launched a 'four cleanups' socialist education campaign. Class struggle against feudalism and capitalism was on the agenda. In practical terms it involved such things as limiting the scope of village fair trade from March 1963 onwards, increasing the role of state-controlled agencies in trade, controlling market prices and acting against speculators and profiteers (Wang and Wang, 1982: 224–5). In December 1962 a ten-year plan for the period 1963–72 was proposed and drawn up. In December 1964 Zhou Enlai called for the establishment of an industrial economy within fifteen years and first mentioned the concept of the 'four modernisations' (of industry, agriculture, national defence and science and technology). Central control of allocations was tightened, and the General Administration in Charge of Materials was established in early 1963. At the same time the National Commission in Charge of Prices was established, and a readjustment of prices was carried out in 1963. This involved increasing agricultural purchasing prices, adjusting many industrial prices and reducing some retail prices. The government continued to subsidise the retail prices of important commodities. Prices were not adjusted to any significant degree until 1979. There was an increase in state wages for about 40 per cent of workers and staff in April 1963. After 1964 and until 1978 the average nominal wage in the state sector of the economy was virtually unchanged, falling in some periods and on average falling 0.5 per cent per annum (*Statistical Yearbook of China 1984*, p. 459). This price reform and wage increase ushered in a long period of stability of nominal variables.

Real national income started growing and did so at an average annual rate of 16.7 per cent for 1963–65. Industry and agriculture grew, with agriculture growing well in 1963–64 but still having a long way to go. Retail sales did not grow as fast as output. Currency in circulation fell in 1963 and 1964, and the general retail price index fell in all three years 1963–65. Market prices also fell, with the exception of 1965 when they rose. A survey of 85 country fairs showed that by 1964 free market prices were only 29 per cent higher than state list prices whereas they had been 220 per cent higher in 1961 (Xu and Chen, 1981: 123–4). By 1965 the accumulation rate had reached 27.1 per cent, higher than at any time during the First Five-year Plan period and the fourth-highest ever in the fourteen years since 1952. Even after three years of recovery per capita food consumption in 1965 was still less than in 1957. The party and the planners had turned their backs on the policy of using the market to boost supplies and reaffirmed their determination to industrialise with a high accumulation rate using strict central control over material allocations and prices.

2.7 *Period IV, 1966–70*

In the Third Five-year Plan period (see Table 2.4) there began the Cultural Revolution. Politics, mass mobilisation, class struggle, destruction, near civil war and murder dominated economics. Mao Zedong launched the movement from August 1966, calling on the people to rise up and throw out bourgeois capitalist roaders who were said to have infiltrated all levels of the Communist Party. School and college students became Red Guards and took up the call, travelling the country and destroying many aspects of the old society. Transport facilities, especially the railways, were disrupted, certain products were arbitrarily banned from sale, and production was disrupted as political meetings took precedence over work. Private houses were broken into, and foreign currencies, gold and silver hoards as well as Chinese currency were seized.[14] Banks were broken into and money stolen. The party's call to stop such activities in January 1967 ordered such money to be returned together with excess wages that had been paid out. Money given to Red Guards for their travels and refunded tax receipts were to be repaid also. Wages were to be frozen and so were the accounts of organisations and units. Private savings deposits were specifically exempted from this freeze.[15]

Amazingly, 1966 output figures show reasonable growth. The intensification of the movement into 1967–68 brought 7.2 and 6.5 per cent reductions in real output in these two years respectively and a fall in agricultural output and retail sales in 1968. As output fell in these two years, currency in circulation increased. It fell in 1970 when output grew rapidly. The budget in 1967 showed a deficit for the first time since 1961, and in 1968 expenditures were slashed by about one-third compared with 1966. The accumulation rate was reduced from 30.6 per cent in 1966 to 23.2 in 1969. Mao Zedong had to call upon the People's Liberation Army in 1969 to restore order in many provinces, and the army took control of twelve (Field, McGlynn and Abnett, 1978: 255; Liu and Wu, 1986: 357). Although there were signs of recovery in 1969, that year's plan was not met and the output of most industrial and agricultural products did not reach 1966's levels. Agricultural growth lagged far behind that of industry, and heavy industry continued to grow rapidly and to receive disproportionate amounts for investment. A policy of investing in the interior provinces was followed, mainly for purposes of national defence, at the expense of investment in manufacturing industries in the relatively developed coastal provinces. A special plan for 1970 was drawn up by the National Planning Conference early that year. A major change was the transfer of many centrally controlled enterprises to local authorities. These included huge undertakings such as the Anshan Steel Company and the Daqing oilfield. Some were put under dual central–local control, causing problems

Table 2.4 Period IV: main economic indicators
(percentage increase over the previous year except *ACC* and *B*)

Year	*RNI*	*IND*	*AGRIC*	*VRS*	*ACC*	*B*	*CRC*	*P*	*MP*
1966	17.0	25.3	7.4	9.3	30.6	1.71	19.5	−0.3	1.2
1967	−7.2	−15.7	1.7	5.1	21.3	−2.25	12.4	−0.7	1.7
1968	−6.5	−9.1	−1.9	−3.3	21.1	0.15	10.0	0.1	0.0
1969	19.3	35.7	0.4	8.7	23.2	0.09	2.2	−1.1	−0.1
1970	23.3	37.3	7.7	7.0	32.9	1.35	−9.8	−0.2	0.0

Note: Variables are defined in the note to Table 2.1.

of supply of materials to previous endusers and hence disrupting production. The newly empowered local authorities were incapable of managing the enterprises handed over to them. The following period, that of the Fourth Five-year Plan, inherited many problems caused by these policies.

2.8 Period V, 1971–75

At the start of the Fourth Five-year Plan period (see Table 2.5) ambitious targets for industry were set for 1971, putting a strain on agriculture, which failed to meet its plan for that year. The problems that were perceived came to be known as the 'three excesses' (Liu and Wu, 1986: 373–5): the high accumulation rate; a large above-plan increase in the number of staff and workers in the state sector and above-plan wage payments; and sales of grain requiring grain imports and unplanned sales from stocks. These problems became worse during 1972, and it was not until the next year that measures were taken. These policies are familiar from earlier periods. State investment was reduced, greater central control over wage payments was instituted, workers employed in excess of state plan totals were to be dismissed, and workers who had moved into towns and cities without permission were to return to the countryside. Investment in agriculture was to be increased, and workers were to be sent to the countryside. Central control over enterprises was intensified, particularly with regard to wage payments. The banks were to exercise tighter control over enterprises, and taxes were to be remitted promptly. In February 1973 Zhou Enlai warned that currency issue had reached its limit. Agriculture had been affected by the policy of promoting grain production irrespective of local conditions. This was the policy of 'taking grain as the key link' (*yi liang wei gang*). From 1968 there had been new prohibitions on private trade, and prices had been frozen from 1967. From 1975 marketing and supply co-operatives were to be merged with state commercial units, urban markets closed down, rural fairs limited and price control there continued. Peasant and private sales constituted no more than about 2 per cent of total retail sales until 1978 (*Zhongguo Maoyi Wujia Tongji Ziliao 1952–83*, p. 65). This period is often portrayed as one of struggle between, on the one side, the ailing Zhou Enlai, who tried for reasonable economic policies, and, on the other, Lin Biao, who wished to build up the military, and Jiang Qing of the 'gang of four', who opposed any policies that seemed to

Table 2.5 Period V: main economic indicators
(percentage increase over the previous year except *ACC* and *B*)

Year	*RNI*	*IND*	*AGRIC*	*VRS*	*ACC*	*B*	*CRC*	*P*	*MP*
1971	7.0	13.0	1.6	8.3	34.1	1.25	10.2	−0.7	8.8
1972	2.9	6.3	−0.5	10.1	31.6	0.02	11.0	−0.2	8.2
1973	8.3	8.6	9.1	8.2	32.9	0.04	9.9	0.6	5.3
1974	1.1	−0.9	4.3	5.1	32.3	−0.77	6.3	0.5	1.9
1975	8.3	14.4	3.0	9.2	33.9	−0.53	3.4	0.2	4.0

Note: Variables are defined in the note to Table 2.1.

have in them any vestiges of capitalist elements such as private trade and rural markets. Luo (1985: 89–97) describes and criticises the 'ultra-"Left" policies' of the 'gang of four' in agriculture. Political struggle and disruption became most acute during the period 1974–77 with three major political campaigns. As Field, McGlynn and Abnett (1978) nicely show, there is a clear positive correlation across provinces between the degree of political instability and the disruption to industrial output.

The accumulation rate remained high, and agricultural output fell in 1972 as there were five years of bad weather starting from 1970. The general retail price index remained virtually unchanged, but market prices continued to increase at an average annual rate of 4.6 per cent, the most significant increases since the early 1960s. The stability of the general retail price index prompted a flurry of articles and a pamphlet aimed at outside readers stressing the extent of price stability in China (Chi, 1975; Wang, 1975; Wei, 1975; Yang, 1975; Peng, 1976). A cynic might say that this is the only thing, and not a very important one at that, that could be used to make propaganda points about the nature of economic development during the previous ten years. 'Leftist' ideas flourished, and it was debated whether it was possible to abolish the use of money. Liaoning province came close to instituting a system whereby goods would be directly distributed to households without their having to turn up at the shops and use money (Goodstadt, 1976: 32). The consumer sector had been neglected, there were fewer and fewer shops, goods were of poor quality and variety, and there were serious shortages of non-staple foods in the cities. Rural life had not improved (Liu and Wu, 1986: 412–13). As Lardy (1983a: 159) cogently points out, China is probably unique in modern times for being able, in a twenty-year period, to double national income per capita while producing a constant or possibly slightly declining level of per capita food consumption. High accumulation rates, emphasis on industrialisation, distrust of market elements in the countryside and the neglect of the consumer had produced increased national income but not higher living standards. In 1976 changes in the leadership made a new approach possible.

2.9 *Period VI, 1976–80*

At the start of the Fifth Five-year Plan period (see Table 2.6) in 1976 both Zhou Enlai and Mao Zedong died and the 'gang of four' were arrested.

Table 2.6 Period VI: main economic indicators
(percentage increase over the previous year except *ACC* and *B*)

Year	*RNI*	*IND*	*AGRIC*	*VRS*	*ACC*	*B*	*CRC*	*P*	*MP*
1976	−2.7	−5.3	−0.1	5.4	30.9	−2.96	11.7	0.3	4.0
1977	7.8	14.5	−1.1	7.0	32.3	3.10	−4.2	2.1	−2.6
1978	12.3	17.1	4.8	8.8	36.5	1.01	8.5	0.7	−6.6
1979	7.0	7.6	7.2	15.5	34.6	−17.06	26.3	2.0	−4.5
1980	6.4	10.1	0.6	18.9	31.5	−12.75	29.3	6.0	2.0

Note: Variables are defined in the note to Table 2.1.

Hua Guofeng became Chairman of the Party Central Committee. His approach, enshrined in Zhou Enlai's term the 'four modernisations', still contained ambitious ideas about rapid industrialisation, which were described in an 'Outline Plan for the Development of the National Economy (1976–85)'. A major difference in approach was that, now that China had been recognised by more Western countries and diplomatic relations had been restored, foreign capital could be used for development. Entire second-hand industrial plants were bought from Western countries, and attempts were made to install them without much preparation. This approach lasted until the end of 1978. The accumulation rate increased to 36.5 per cent in 1978. There had been serious natural disasters in 1976 and 1977, and agricultural output fell slightly in both years. These were not the best circumstances for instituting another investment drive. A year that began with ambitious plans for industrialisation ended with a completely different policy based on agricultural development.

The entire policy line was changed at the Third Plenary Session of the Eleventh Party Central Committee in December 1978 when the policy adopted was to achieve a 'readjustment, restructuring, consolidation and improvement' of the economy. A genuine attempt was made to improve the performance of the agricultural sector. Experiments had been undertaken in Anhui and Sichuan provinces in 1978 to reduce the extent of interference in production decisions, to tie reward to performance and to encourage family sideline production. A whole new approach became national policy from 1979. In March or April that year the state purchasing prices of eighteen agricultural and sideline products were increased substantially and from the summer harvest those of grains by 20 per cent. Purchasing prices for pigs, eggs, cotton, sugarcane, beet and other products were all increased substantially, and on average purchasing prices increased either 24.8 per cent (Wan, 1984: 395; *Zhongguo Nongye Nianjian 1980*, p. 146) or 22.1 per cent (Luo, 1985: 103). State quotas were not to be increased over the 1971–75 levels, and higher bonus prices were paid for above-quota sales to the state of grain, cotton and edible oils. These price increases are said to have increased peasant incomes in 1979 alone by either 10.8 billion *yuan* (Wan, 1984: 395; Luo, 1985: 103) or by 7.8 billion *yuan* (*Zhongguo Nongye Nianjian 1980*, p. 146). The increased use of the bonus scheme had an important, possibly unexpected in magnitude, impact on the prices paid by the state and on rural incomes. Its impact on monetary flows will be examined in section 6.2. Urban and rural markets were reopened on a large scale, and trading surplus output on these markets became legal. The number of markets increased substantially, and by 1983 11.2 per cent of total retail sales were supplied by individuals and peasants (*Zhongguo Maoyi Wujia Tongji Ziliao, 1952–1983*, p. 65). Peasants were exhorted to *zhuan qian* (make money), a phrase echoing the injunction of Nikolai Bukharin to Russian peasants to *obogaschaites* (make yourself rich) during the Soviet Union's New Economic Policy (Nove, 1982: 123). Agricultural output increased by 4.8 and 7.2 per cent in 1978 and 1979 respectively while free market prices fell.

The general retail price index increased 2 per cent in 1979 when free market prices fell, providing another example of a year when the two indexes moved in opposite directions. The general index rose 6 per cent in 1980, its largest increase under communist rule since the 16.2 per cent of 1961. However, output and retail sales were now increasing substantially, not falling as they had in 1961. The value of retail sales increased by 15.5 and 18.9 per cent in 1979 and 1980 respectively. Along with this increased rate of open inflation there were large budget deficits in 1979 and 1980. These were not eliminated until 1985, and then only for that single year. In September 1979 the State Council decided that from 1 November the retail prices of eight important non-staples would be increased. It was also decided that a food subsidy of 5 *yuan* a month would be given to industrial and office workers in most areas and 8 *yuan* to people in livestock-breeding areas, who tended to eat more meat than the average person (Wang and Wang, 1982: 225). At this time 5 *yuan* represented about 8.5 per cent of the average monthly wage in the state sector. At the same time there were substantial wage increases in the state sector; the average wage increased 13.9 per cent in 1980 compared with 1979, and the total state sector wage bill increased 18.7 per cent.

2.10 Period VII, 1981–85

The agricultural reforms instigated in 1979 had effects that continued into the Sixth Five-year Plan period also (see Table 2.7). The question of price changes is an important one that can be clarified here. The sequence of events for 1979 can provide a hint as to the mechanism operating.

First, agricultural procurement prices were raised. This can be interpreted as both an increase in the cost to the state of obtaining inputs for state retail trade and industry and as an increase in the monetary purchasing power of the population. To the state, procurement prices and wages are costs; to their recipients they are incomes and hence purchasing power over state-supplied goods and goods on the free market. For many goods the retail price was less than the procurement price and necessary subsidies rose, contributing to the budget deficit.[16] Retail prices were increased, reducing somewhat the per unit subsidy, and compensatory wage and subsidy increases were granted, thus increasing nominal purchasing power even further. The purchase price and wage increases were the result of government policy, not spontaneous market forces.

We could explain the sequence briefly in four ways:

Table 2.7 Period VII: main economic indicators
(percentage increase over the previous year except *ACC* and *B*)

Year	*RNI*	*IND*	*AGRIC*	*VRS*	*ACC*	*B*	*CRC*	*P*	*MP*
1981	4.9	1.1	7.5	9.8	28.3	−2.55	14.5	2.4	5.8
1982	8.3	5.7	11.6	9.4	28.8	−2.93	10.8	1.9	3.3
1983	9.8	8.8	9.6	10.9	29.7	−4.35	20.7	1.5	4.2
1984	13.5	13.6	14.5	18.5	31.2	−4.45	49.5	2.8	−0.4
1985	12.5	17.5	6.4	27.5	33.7	2.16	24.7	8.8	17.2

Note: Variables are defined in the note to Table 2.1.

1 Costs went up, so the government increased prices to reduce losses.
2 Purchasing power went up, so the government increased prices to balance demand and supply.
3 The increased subsidies the government had to pay caused a bigger budget deficit, so prices were increased in order to reduce the deficit.
4 The excess of purchasing prices over retail prices together with the wage increases caused a net injection of currency into circulation, so the government increased retail prices to recall some of this extra currency and limit the rate of growth of the money supply.

It is tempting to abbreviate the last two to say: budget deficits caused prices to rise, and increased money supply caused prices to rise. Such explanations are not correct and do not offer an explanation of why the budget deficit or the money supply increased in the first place and how all these variables are interrelated. The longer explanation shows that both the budget deficits and the increase in the money supply are *consequences* of the change in policy, not exogenous external initiating causes of price increases. Most of the price increases, that is, those not on free markets, were the result of government policy. This important point has been noticed but not really followed up analytically. As Chen and Hou (1986: 817) ask in their study of the inflation of the early 1980s, 'But why did the government raise prices and hence contribute to inflation, especially in the past few years?' This extremely pertinent question will be pursued in chapter 6.

The introduction of free markets and allowing retail products to be sold at negotiated and market prices make explaining changes in the general retail price index more difficult, because these prices now have a greater weight in the index. In the 1970s virtually all goods were sold at state-determined list prices, so changes in this index were due to government policy of the kind described above. Now there are two influences on the general retail price index: state list prices and market prices. For analytical purposes there is a choice of which element to emphasise in explaining changes in the general index.

That government price changes still occurred and played a role in change in the general index can be shown by citing an article by Liu Zhuofu, head of the State Price Bureau. In the journal *Hong Qi* (Red Flag) in 1982 he outlined the reason for price rises in 1981, aiming to reassure the people that the situation was not dangerous. He identified three components of the general retail price increase, which was only 2.4 per cent compared with 6.0 per cent in 1980. The first component was the result of the State Council's approval of two sets of retail price increases: first, in the second quarter, of products whose procurement prices had been increased (bamboo, wood and leather-based products); and second, towards the end of the year, of cigarettes and wines. These price increases were accompanied by price reductions for such goods as manmade fibre cloth, nylon stockings, rubber shoes, watches, electric fans, televisions, tape recorders, tapes, electric watches and refrigerators. The second component was that enterprises took it on themselves to increase prices. A policy of linking bonuses to profit performance had been introduced, and these price increases were used to boost profits as the management and supervision (*jiandu*) of enterprises under the new system had not developed sufficiently (Liu, 1982: 34). Furthermore, enterprises were able to sell low-price good-quality products to friends and connections surreptitiously on the side (through the back door, *houmen*, as he puts it). This increased the burden on the broad mass of ordinary people, he says. The third component was that free market prices rose. One reason was because demand was greater than supply for certain commodities. The other was because certain small middlemen (*er dao fanzi*) engaged in forcing up prices.

This shows that any increase in the retail price index can be caused by government price increases, unofficial price increases and free-market price increases. In that year government list prices (*paijia*) were increased 1.3 per cent, market prices rose 5.8 per cent, and the general retail price index increased by 2.4 per cent.[17] It is an empirical question which type of price change exerts a dominant influence on the general index. This question will be discussed in the concluding section of this chapter.

Liu also discusses the reasons for the price changes. He says that manmade fibre prices were reduced in order to widen the market, reduce stocks, encourage production and improve the standard of people's clothing. There were two reasons for increasing cigarette and wine prices: to reduce subsidies because costs had risen due to increases in input prices, and to increase state financial revenue in order to help the current budget problem. Here we have an important insight into the planners' way of thinking. State enterprises and shops remit their revenues to the state budget. Increasing those remittances reduces currency in circulation (if they come from the retail sector) and contributes to budget revenue. Ma Kai (1984: 80) also states that high planned prices were set for alcohol and tobacco products to withdraw currency from circulation. In 1982 the index of list prices for the category 'cigarettes, wines and tea' was 16.5 per cent higher than in 1981, showing the effect of the government price increases undertaken towards the end of 1981 (*Zhongguo Maoyi Wujia Tongji Ziliao 1952–1983*, pp. 374–7).

There were important changes in agricultural organisation in this period. They can be summarised by the expression 'household responsibility system'. Various methods were tried throughout the country in a short period of experimentation,[18] but they all meant the end to the commune system. By the end of 1983 virtually all households practised this system, according

to Riskin (1987: 290), and Ash (1988: 539) dates the virtual disappearance of rural communes at the end of 1984. Now individual households were allowed to lease land for at least fifteen years and for 50 years for such activities as forestry and orchards, which require long term investments.[19] It was intended that land should not be sold or rented completely freely[20] nor used for non-agricultural purposes such as housebuilding,[21] but there are reports that land was used for housing when the government would not have approved and that land was rented quite freely. The households became responsible for supplying the state on a contract basis, and once such a contract was met they could sell any surplus product on free markets at market prices. This led to a diversification of production away from basic staples such as grain, which had been emphasised under the commune system, to cash crops, fish farming, chicken raising and so on. Propaganda trumpeted the triumphs of peasant households who bought a few chickens, for example, bred them successfully and became 10000 *yuan* households. The land area devoted to grain fell, much to the consternation of the party. Rural industries blossomed, and private traders, transport companies and housebuilders emerged to meet the needs of the expanding agricultural sector. Until 1985 the government was prepared to buy any products offered to it in excess of the contracted amount. In 1985 it abandoned this policy and adopted solely a contract system of procurement (Ash, 1988: 545–6). The state was prepared to buy only contracted amounts and reduced its procurement and marketing of agricultural products to nine main products (*Zhongguo Jingji Nianjian 1986*, pp. V-34, V–48–9). By 1985 nearly 22 per cent of total retail sales came from the private sector with individual traders supplying 15 per cent of the total and peasants selling 6.8 per cent of the total to non-agricultural residents (*Statistical Yearbook of China 1986*, pp. 445–6). In many cities the proportion of such products as beef and mutton, fish, eggs and poultry freely marketed on urban markets increased notably in the early 1980s (Taubmann and Widmer, 1987: 361), but that of grain and edible oils, the staples the state had always marketed, remained low. From 1982 the supply and marketing co-operatives, which carried out a large amount of rural trade, were taken out of state control and turned into truer co-operatives as shares in them were sold to the peasants.[22] The rural sector was transformed with rapidly rising farmers' incomes. As Travers (1984: 246–7; 1985: 126–7) points out, virtually all of the increase in per capita retail sales over the period 1978–81 went to the rural sector. As he notes, it was the command system that was able to divert goods to the rural sector in order, we would assume, to maintain incentives by ensuring that output was available for the increased incomes to be spent on. He argues (1985: 127) that the increase in urban saving during this period reflected involuntary saving and that planners diverted commodities 'not to areas of effective monetary demand but to areas of effective political demand'. Despite increasing marketisation of certain sectors of the economy it was planners who still allocated the bulk of retail supplies. Riskin (1987: 294–5) extends the analysis to 1984, cautiously concluding that the trend continued until 1984.[23] The privileged position of urban residents was finished.

In industry, reform was slower because of the difficulties involved. Like reform in all planned economies its purpose was to make enterprises more independent and able to meet the demand for their products. They were to become responsible for their losses and able to keep part of their profits. Rewards for both managers and workers were to be tied more closely to enterprise performance. The co-ordinating mechanism chosen for this purpose was both plan and market. The question of whether to close down or to bankrupt unprofitable state enterprises was not tackled on a national scale despite the reports of some enterprises being bankrupted. Dismissed workers were expected to be re-employed, and there was no move to create an urban labour market with mobile workers seeking the highest-paid jobs. Workers were still allocated jobs, and many were tied to their enterprises by the houses and welfare facilities they provided. State enterprises were still expected to produce part of their output according to their plan at fixed prices, but they were allowed to market excess output at negotiated prices. A two-track price system, sometimes called a dual price system, was thus created (Byrd, 1987b; Perkins, 1988: 620–1; Wu and Zhao, 1987). Marginal output decisions were taken on the basis of the market price, and the state quota could be regarded as a tax obligation on the enterprise. Peebles (1990: appendix B) shows that this is an optimistic interpretation of the nature of the dual track system. Much of industrial price reform revolved around the questions of how and how quickly a unified price could be established and whether this should be a purely market-determined price or whether the state should set the price.

From 1983 a system of substituting tax payment for remitting profits (*li gai shui*) was introduced although it had been introduced on an experimental basis during the period 1979–81 (Ma, 1982a: 103; Ho, 1987: 562). Instead of handing over the bulk of their profits to the state budget, enterprises were now to be taxed at predetermined rates. The government would still share in the post-tax profits, but enterprises could keep the balance for investment, bonuses and welfare facilities. A certain amount of workers' bonuses was allowed to be counted as a cost, but bonuses in excess of this amount had to be paid out of the enterprise-retained profit. A limit of 40 per cent was put on the amount that could be used for the staff and workers' welfare and bonus fund (Ho, 1987: 565). The government still tried to control the way enterprise income was used and to limit the growth of the wage fund. In 1983 profits of the enterprises using the tax system rose, and the state took 61.8 per cent of this increase. Profits retained by the enterprises rose to 17.9 per cent of total profits compared with 15.7 per cent in the previous year, with workers receiving 13.3 per cent of the increased profits in that year (Ho, 1987: 567). A new wave of tax reform was introduced in October 1984, and there was still to be control over the way enterprises used their retained profits.

An important aspect of the reform policy was the encouragement of private enterprises. Most of these were at first in the service sector, especially retailing, catering and repairs. They played an important role in increasing services in the cities. A policy of leasing small state-owned enterprises to individuals or collectives was also adopted. The intentions of urban reform were described in the important document *Decision of the Central Committee of the Communist Party of China on Reform of the*

Economic Structure, adopted at the Third Plenary Session of the Twelfth Central Committee meeting on 20 October 1984.[24] This document specifically recognised the important role of the private enterprise sector and pledged to protect its property, as had the new 1982 Constitution. In February 1985 Zhao Ziyang affirmed that such private businesses would not be nationalised (Kraus, 1987: 67–8).

During this period China increased its involvement in the international economy. By 1985 total foreign trade had increased to 3.7 times its 1980 level. China became a member of the World Bank (the International Bank for Reconstruction and Development), the International Monetary Fund (IMF) and the Asian Development Bank. Loans from these bodies were accepted, and capital was raised in Japan, Hong Kong and Germany (Wilson, 1986: 19). World Bank teams visited China and produced reports on aspects of the economy. Collaborative research was conducted, such as that in Tidrick and Chen (1987). Direct foreign investment in the form of joint ventures was encouraged. Many Hong Kong entrepreneurs in the textile and electronics industries relocated their factories to the Pearl river delta in Guangdong province, taking advantage of its cheaper labour as Hong Kong's economy continued to specialise in advanced services (Peebles, 1988: 69–70). Four Special Economic Zones were opened in Zhuhai, Shantou and Shenzhen in Guangdong province, and in Xiamen in Fujian, each of them near an independently administered region in the form of Macau, Hong Kong or Taiwan. Jao and Leung (1986) review their experiences, especially those of Shenzhen, which lies just north of Hong Kong.

Shenzhen and, to an extent, Guangdong province experienced a phenomenon that had not been seen on a large scale since the Kuomintang era: the open circulation of foreign currencies in China. In the Shenzhen zone three forms of currency circulated: the *Renminbi*, Foreign Exchange Certificates and Hong Kong dollars. By the first half of 1983 at least 17 per cent of retail sales were denominated in Hong Kong dollars and 25 per cent in Foreign Exchange Certificates (Jao, 1986: 173). The Chinese currency circulated at a discount against the other two. It is generally agreed by observers such as Jao, and the Chinese economists whom he quotes, that people preferred foreign currencies not because of fear of inflation but simply because they could buy a greater range of goods, both within China and outside it, for example, in Hong Kong. The inconvertibility of the *yuan* limited it to being able to buy solely what the state supplied in China and what was available on free markets. Foreign currencies were more powerful in this respect.

Fourteen coastal cities and Hainan island, which later became a province in its own right, were opened to foreign investment (Su, 1986). Joint ventures with foreign firms were encouraged, and these built many of China's new hotels in the country's attempt to attract world tourists and accommodate visiting businessmen.

The financial system was also affected by the reform programme, one important aim of which was to 'pay full attention to economic levers'.[25] Sometime early in the Cultural Revolution the People's Bank of China had been absorbed into the Ministry of Finance, losing its identity (Hsiao,

1984: 5; Tam, 1986: 428). This was restored in March 1978 when the People's Bank of China was separated from the Ministry of Finance (Tam, 1986: 430). In September 1983 it was announced that the People's Bank would become the country's central bank, and this became reality on 1 January 1984. The idea was that the bank would cease to carry out day-to-day banking business but would oversee the reformed banking system, using 'economic levers' for purposes of macroeconomic control to guide the economy rather than administer it. The newly created Industrial and Commercial Bank of China now became responsible for taking savings deposits, making short term loans to enterprises and settling interenterprise accounts. It took over many of the branch premises, staff and financial assets of the People's Bank and now is the country's retail bank with which people deal every day.[26] The Agricultural Bank of China, which had been resurrected in February 1979 (Ma, 1982a: 467; Hsiao, 1984: 12; Tam, 1986: 431), became responsible for rural banking and overseeing the operations of the rural credit co-operatives. The new central bank was established at a time of increasing output, a drive for increased investment and bank loans, and it had difficulty controlling the growth of the money supply, one of its main responsibilities. Planned money supply targets were exceeded by large amounts in both 1984 and 1985 (Lee, 1985: 17–18; Tam, 1986: 435). A large part of the 1984 increase in currency is described as 'irrational' (*bu helide*) by an official source (*Zhongguo Jingji Nianjian 1985*, pp. IV–37).

The reasons for this are now well understood and were connected with the way banking reform was carried out. More reliance was placed on bank loans instead of budget grants for providing enterprises with funds for investment. This was part of the policy of trying to make enterprises behave responsibly in their use of such money, as they would be expected to repay their loans and would be monitored by the banks, which wanted to get their money back. However, the old ideas of centrally determined quotas remained. Towards the end of 1984 it was announced that the maximum amount of loans each bank and its branches would be able to extend in 1985 would be based on the amount it lent in 1984. Hence, the various banks, in competition with each other, rushed to extend loans to enterprises in order to increase the following year's lending quota. Similarly, state enterprises were told that their maximum wage bill, including the newly introduced bonuses, for 1985 and after would be based on that of 1984. Obviously, they tried to increase their wage and bonus payments, and this occurred just at the time the banks were trying to increase their loans to enterprises (Lee, 1985). According to Komiya (1989: 88), the national wage bill in December 1984 was 75.4 per cent higher than in December 1983, and fourth-quarter wages were up 38 per cent (*Zhongguo Jingji Nianjian 1985*, pp. IV–37 documents the monthly increases in the wage bill towards the end of 1984 and also indicates that the system of setting 1985's quotas on the basis of 1984's lending was a main cause of the large increase in loans). The bulk of the increase in bank lending and wage increases occurred in the last quarter of 1984, which accounts for this high figure. On an annual basis the state wage bill in 1985 was 21.6 per cent higher than in 1984 (*Statistical Yearbook of China 1986*, p. 559). As a result of these reforms and badly judged attempts at setting quotas on future bank lending, 1984 became a year of rapid growth in nominal variables such as wages, bonuses, bank loans and currency in circulation.

The performance of the economy during this period is summarised in Table 2.7. The accumulation rate was reduced to below 30 per cent in the period 1981–83 but rose in 1984 and 1985, illustrating the real aspect of the credit and monetary expansion of these two years. Agricultural output continued to grow rapidly as did industrial output, especially in 1984 and 1985. The value of retail sales grew rapidly also, but some of this is just the effect of the increase in prices. The general retail price index in 1985 saw its largest increase since 1961, at 8.8 per cent. In the years immediately before this it did not increase substantially and was always less than the 6 per cent of 1980.[27] It will be useful to try to account for this increase as it was so large and as this may give us a clue to the extent to which reform had altered the reasons for changes in the retail price index. The *Communiqué on the Statistics of China's 1985 Economic and Social Development Plan*[28] tells us the following:

> The smooth take-off of the price reform in 1985 accelerated the development of the commodity economy. But market prices rose considerably. The general price indices for state purchases of farm and sideline products rose an average of 8.6 percent over the previous year. The general retail price index in 1985 increased 8.8 percent over 1984. Of these, the general retail price level, being influenced by the readjustment and decontrol of commodity retail prices for some farm and sideline products, rose 5.4 percent. The general retail price level, influenced by other factors, also went up by 3.4 percent. The general retail price index in the cities rose an average of 12.2 percent and 7 percent in the countryside. (Liu and Wu 1986: 467–8)

This is not much help as it gives two figures for the increase in the general retail price level and is obviously confused.

Currency in circulation increased by nearly 50 per cent in 1984 and 25 per cent in 1985. The government budget had shown a deficit of 17.06 billion *yuan* (about 5 per cent of national income) in 1979, and it remained in deficit right through to 1985 when a small surplus was achieved (Chinese definition).[29] Period VII is notable for its very much higher increases in currency in circulation, retail prices, and the sizes of the budget deficit and trade deficits. An important feature of this period occurred in 1985: the large increase in imports of consumer goods in this year. In US dollar terms the value of imports increased by 54 per cent. Imports of such things as televisions, tape recorders, radio-cassette recorders, motor vehicles, watches and electronic calculators were all running at at least twice the rate of 1984 in volume terms, with televisions being imported at 3.5 times their 1984 rate. Exports only increased by 4.7 per cent in US dollar terms, and a US$14.89 billion trade deficit was recorded (*Statistical Yearbook of China 1986*, pp. 181–91; Lin, 1989: 21).[30] Why was there such a large increase in imports? Komiya (1989: 74–5) sees it as a deliberate anti-inflationary policy of importing consumer goods for sale on the domestic market in order to withdraw currency from circulation. He calls it a policy of 'Merchandise *Huilung*'[31] through which the sale of imports withdrew currency from circulation (*huilong*, in *pinyin*). It is seen as a deliberate central-government policy reaction to the monetary situation. It soon became known that the government had allocated US$2 billion for the importation of consumer goods during 1984 and that this was said to have contributed to the large increase in retail sales in the first half of 1985 (Nambu, 1985: 6). Tsang (1990: 231) attributes to the trade deficit of 1985 a 'strong dampening' effect on 'the issuance of currency'. He states that the amount of currency in circulation in 1985 was 'actually smaller than in 1984'. His own table 3 (p. 230) shows an at least 20 billion *yuan* increase in currency in circulation in 1985, which was less than the increase in 1984. He has confused flows with the stock.

Here again, just as with the importation of cereals in 1961 and 1962, deteriorating domestic monetary conditions had an important impact on trade policy. Now the means were electronic goods, not food, but the principle was the same. The economy was still being managed by means of central directives in the case of both international trade in 1961 and 1985 and domestic trade in the early 1980s (Travers's argument that planners diverted retail supplies to the countryside). These were real resource reactions to domestic monetary conditions, but they still resulted from central policy changes.

2.11 Conclusions

The Chinese economy has always used money, but attitudes towards it changed enormously during the period under study. During the 'communist wind' of creating the communes, Zhang Chunqiao published an article in the *Renmin Ribao* (People's Daily) in October 1958 advocating the abolition of monetary wage payments and substituting payment in kind.[32] This was proposed again in 1975. During the 1970s, in much of the countryside money was very little used and little desired as there were hardly any goods available for purchase (Solinger, 1984: 23–8). Communes distributed a large part of their members' income in kind. Free markets were suppressed for much of the 1970s, reducing the role of money. If communes distributed food and services freely or in exchange for their own money substitutes, this further reduced the need for official money in the countryside. By the 1980s peasants were being exhorted to 'make money'. By the mid 1980s money was being used as a reward and a disciplinary device in schools. Students who gained 'titles of honour' were rewarded with up to 10 *yuan* a semester. Schoolchildren as young as nine and ten were fined for a whole list of disciplinary offences, a phenomenon called 'economic punishment' (*jingji zhicai*).[33] Whether ordinary people's attitudes towards money had ever changed much is unknown, but the rhetoric of the Communist Party, its general development policies and its reliance on monetary incentives certainly had.

An important question is whether the reforms of the 1980s, and in particular the urban and banking reforms that intensified after 1984, were sufficient to change the mechanisms of the economy, its monetary system, and the nature of the relationships between nominal and real variables. In other words, can the same institutional assumptions about the economy be made for the entire period 1953–85? This section and the description of monetary institutions in chapter 4 will argue that reforms did not sufficiently change the nature of the economy to make the same assumptions invalid. The major changes that differentiated the 1985 economy from any earlier period were the spread of small private and individual businessmen and traders and the concomitant increase in the proportion of retail sales emanating from outside the state sector. As has been noted already, this made market or free price increases a more important component of changes in the general retail price index. As Cheng Zhiping (1986), who was by then the head of the State Price Bureau, shows in his explanation of the price increases of 1985, these were mainly due to the decontrol of the system of pork purchases and pork prices and the decontrol of vegetable prices in many cities. He does not give detailed data, but this can be obtained elsewhere.[34] The general retail price index increased by 8.8 per cent, list prices by 7.8 per cent and market prices by 17.2 per cent. The extent of the general retail price increase was still similar to the increase in list prices. Most of the increases in list prices seem to have been due to the large increases in list prices of food items, with the category 'foods' increasing by 13 per cent, 'grain' by 11.5 per cent, 'fresh vegetables' by 36.1 per cent and 'non-staple foods' by 17.7 per cent. It could be argued that in 1985 list prices were being increased in response to the increases in market prices, but it is clear that list price increases still occurred and contributed to the increase in the general retail price index.

The major change in the industrial sector was the scheme whereby enterprises paid taxes, not full profit remittances. Now they could keep part of their profits for bonus and welfare payments, and this factor must explain much of the increases in the wage bill in the state sector by 17.1 and 21.6 per cent in 1984 and 1985 respectively, as must the policy announced in 1984 of determining enterprises' wage bills for 1985 and after on the basis of their 1984 levels.[35] The state sector remained an important channel through which money was put into circulation. Reform had not changed this important aspect of the economy. It is easy to agree with Chai (1987a: xvi) that the reforms had modified the economy but had 'not changed the basic characteristics of the Chinese economic system'. Most large enterprises were state owned and financed, much of retail trade was carried out by the state, labour was allocated to jobs determined by the state, and the banking system was government-owned and controlled. Kueh (1989; 1990) argues that much of the Maoist development strategy remained in Dengism. For analytical purposes it is acceptable to assume that the economic and monetary systems were fundamentally the same during the entire period 1953–85.

Certain empirical regularities in the relationship between money, output and prices were discovered earlier. In the short run there is an inverse relationship between real national income and currency in circulation. This was apparent in such years as 1960, 1961, 1967, 1968 and 1976 when real income fell but currency in circulation increased. In 1962, 1969 and 1977, when output increased, currency in circulation fell. In the long run, however, there is a positive relationship between output and currency. In both the short run and the long run there is a positive relationship between currency in circulation and the price indexes. Any theory of money and prices must explain these relationships.

It is easy to see many of the important changes in these major macroeconomic variables as being due to major external, politically motivated, shocks to the economy. They were not the result of the internal workings of a dynamic macroeconomic system producing familiar business cycles. The 1960 and 1961 shocks to real output were due to the attempt at the Great Leap Forward inspired by Mao Zedong. The 1967 and 1968 reductions in real output were the result of the chaos caused by the spreading Cultural Revolution launched, again, by Mao Zedong. The fall in 1976 was due to the demonstrations and disruption following the deaths of Mao Zedong and Zhou Enlai, the arrest of the 'gang of four' and the affects of natural disasters. The major changes in the accumulation ratio were also the result of important political changes and resulting policies. The large increase in the period 1958–60 was clearly the result of the Great Leap Forward and the increases of 1977–78 the result of Hua Guofeng's adoption of the 'four modernisations'. Similarly, some of the major nominal changes can be viewed as shocks imposed on the economy. The wage reforms and increases of 1956 and the early 1980s produced unexpected increases in the wage bill. The agricultural price reforms in 1979 caused large increases in rural money incomes. When there are such nominal changes there is no mechanism to ensure that real output will respond unless planners make the necessary reactions. The industrial and banking reforms of 1984 produced large increases in the wage bill also. The economy and its planners, including those in the banking system responsible for monetary policy, had to adapt to such large shocks to both the real and nominal variables.

In order to discover the nature of the relationship between the major variables presented in the tables in this book and some other aggregates not included there, correlation analysis was conducted on the simple annual percentage changes in some important variables.[36] In addition to the variables in the tables the following were added: the annual increase in the state wage bill, and the budget expressed as a percentage of national income. Such analysis tells us nothing about the direction of causation between any two variables, nor does it reveal the quantitative importance of that relationship. Two variables can be closely correlated, but our chosen explanatory variable may exert only a small quantitative effect on the dependent variable. Such results do indicate whether some of the relationships often postulated are supported by simple quantitative evidence on an annual basis, and they do suggest relationships to follow up in any further empirical study. For example, it is often suggested that decentralisation in the economy leads to high accumulation rates and that these caused large increases in the state wage bill, in government budget deficits and in currency in circulation. Such relationships are implicit in much of the narrative of Liu and Wu (1986) used above. Correlation analysis shows that there *is* a significant positive relationship between the accumulation rate and the rates of growth of industrial output, the state wage bill and currency in circulation. The accumulation rate is negatively correlated with agricultural output growth and the budget as a ratio of national income. The inverse relationship between the accumulation rate and the budget position implies that high accumulation rates are associated with either small budget surpluses or budget deficits. The eras of high accumulation rates discussed above were always associated with budget deficits; this relationship held for the entire period and on an annual basis. It is tempting to explain the negative correlation between accumulation and agricultural growth simply in the terms implied by Liu and Wu; when accumulation rates were high, resources were diverted to industry (which after all provides much of the necessary inputs to maintain a high accumulation rate) to the neglect of agriculture, even to the extent of ordering workers off the land and into industry, as was the case during the Great Leap Forward. Eckstein (1976: chapter 11) proposes a cyclical theory of the interaction between agricultural output and political and ideological change. In his view causation went from a good harvest to increased industrialisation and socialisation of the economy under Mao Zedong's insistence. The effect worked with a time lag and is not incompatible with the finding that years of high accumulation are associated with bad agricultural performance. The rate of growth of currency in circulation is significantly positively correlated with the growth of the wage bill, the value of retail sales, and increases in the general retail price index and the list price index but not in the market price index. It is significantly negatively correlated with the budget balance implying that budget deficits are accompanied by rapid currency growth. Budget deficits are also associated with rapid wage growth. Increases in the general retail price index are closely correlated with increases in the list price index ($r = 0.84$) and in the market price index ($r = 0.76$), but, as we have seen, there were periods when the general retail price index changed by amounts very different from changes in the market price index and, in some years, in the opposite direction.

This chapter has simply described the main economic trends and the changes in the major macroeconomic variables in China after 1949 with more detailed description of the events of the period 1953–85, divided into seven subperiods. Some features of the relationships between money, output, prices, wage growth and the budget position have been discovered. However, no theory of the nature of their interrelationship has been offered. This cannot be done until we have an idea of what is implied for such relationships by modern monetary theory and until we know in what institutional setting these events took place. Some of the assumptions of modern monetary theory may be completely inapplicable to the case of the Chinese economy, as will be argued in chapters 4 and 6. Accordingly, the next chapter will review three branches of modern monetary theory relevant to a study of China to discover propositions that may be capable of accounting for the nature of the relationships described above. Chapter 4 will describe the nature of Chinese institutions and policies to see which of the explanations of these relationships are possible and likely, and which are impossible in China.

3 Concepts and theories

China is a developing Asian economy using many institutions originally modelled on those of the Soviet Union. It also possesses institutions found in capitalist economies such as banks, money, market prices and interest rates. Because of this, existing analyses of money in China often approach the problem from one of three perspectives, drawing on the relevant monetary theories of capitalist, socialist or developing economies to explain events in China. It will be useful to summarise the basic concepts and theories found in each of these different aspects of modern monetary theory before reviewing existing analyses of China and applying some of their insights to the evidence.

3.1 Institutional assumptions underlying Western monetary theory

The basic assumptions of Western monetary theory are that there is private ownership of the means of production, that trade is voluntary and that prices are by and large set by market forces. In such a system money is everywhere completely active; that is, the possession of money is sufficient to obtain any commodity for which there is a willing supplier if the purchaser can meet the required price. Suppliers do not care who purchasers are or whether they have permission to buy. As long as the purchaser can pay the price and deliver the money the exchange will be made. In many markets, such as stock exchanges, the sellers do not even know who the buyers are. Changes in the pattern of demand are expressed in changes in money flows, which in turn bring about changes in prices that induce profit seekers to supply greater quantities of the needed commodity. At certain times and in certain countries restrictions have been placed on people's ability to use money alone to obtain commodities. In particular, rationing of retail goods and important producer goods has been imposed, usually during wars, and foreign exchange control has been used to restrict access to foreign exchange. However, in most advanced industrial countries these restrictions no longer exist and money is everywhere active.

Commercial banks are generally privately owned joint-stock companies responsible to their shareholders for making profits. Banks decide who should receive loans on the basis of commercial criteria, not on the basis of government orders. In some countries, particularly developing countries, many banks are government owned and are subject to government control. These governments raise money from the population by means of compulsory savings schemes, wage deductions, bond sales etc. and allocate these funds to specialised government banks, which allocate the funds to industries favoured by the government. Some of the rapidly developing Asian economies such as Japan, Taiwan and Singapore have allocated part of their investment funds this way. Generally, however, monetary theory assumes that banks are profit-seeking financial intermediaries that cannot be directly ordered to carry out government monetary policy against their private interests. Monetary policy must act on the banking system indirectly by changing such things as interest rates and possibly the availability of high-powered money. Monetary policy is carried out by the central bank, or a monetary authority, using economic levers, not direct orders. Banks are the only financial intermediary that can create money. Banks take deposits from their customers and provide a range of financial services for them such as safeguarding these money balances, paying interest, and transferring them whenever the owner of a deposit draws a cheque to settle a debt incurred in making a purchase. Banks can create deposits, which are part of the money supply, by granting loans to their customers or by buying earning assets from the non-bank public. Loans can be granted to the household sector for the purchase of consumer goods and houses, to firms, probably for investment purposes, and to the government. Influence over the ability of the commercial banks to meet their customers' demand for loans and hence their ability to expand the money supply is, in theory, the main way governments are supposed to control the money supply process to restrict monetary growth to within its target range. The rise of monetarism as a major influence on economic policy making in such countries as the United Kingdom has meant that monetary targets have become the guiding force for many aspects of government policy.

3.2 The functions and definition of money

Generally speaking, economists have identified three functions that must be carried out before something can be identified as money: it must be a unit of account, a means of exchange and a store of value.

The first function is supposed to have evolved in primitive times when some commodity was chosen as the unit of account and all exchange ratios that existed in a barter economy could be expressed in terms of their exchange rate against this common commodity, whether it be shells, feathers, cattle or whatever. This commodity did not actually need to be used in transactions as barter could still proceed, but it would be used to express all values. This is the basis of the standard economics textbook paradigm in which money then evolved to solve the double-coincidence-of-wants problem of barter by becoming the means of exchange. The anthropological evidence for this is virtually non-existent, and such writers as Heinson and Steiger (1989) propose an alternative explanation for the institutions of money and interest, said by them to be unknown in custom and command societies. They see money as the only means of settling debt in a private property economy. An implication is that non-private property, or command, economies do not require such an institution. They see modern China as developing private property relations (p. 192).

In modern societies the unit of account is no longer based on any actual commodity. Intrinsically valueless pieces of paper called currency or cheques are used. Currency is not backed by any commodity such as gold or silver. It is pure fiat money, issued by fiat (command) of the government, generally without there being any constitutional or legal restraint on the amount that can be issued. The government invests the currency with value by decreeing that it is legal tender for settling private debts and that it is acceptable as a means of discharging tax obligations to the government. As Hicks (1986: 7–8) argues as a general principle, in an economy with a well-established government and with no foreign trade the government could invest virtually anything with value on the basis of these two factors. These two government commands are usually sufficient to make its fiat currency desirable to its citizens and hence valuable.

Briefly, this is relevant to China in two ways. First, for many years up until 1978 international trade was relatively unimportant to China and was always conducted with an inconvertible currency. During this period it is likely that monetary management was relatively easier as all the government had to do was to ensure that its own citizens perceived its own currency as having value. Second, the above two traditional methods for ensuring a currency's value and use have not been relevant to China. For one reason, private contracts that required settlement in legal tender were not the basis of economic activity and trade in China for most of the period under study. For another reason, individuals pay hardly any direct taxes, so there is no need for them to obtain currency for this purpose. As we saw in section 2.3, during the land reform period the government did not insist that recipients pay monetary compensation, thus ignoring a method of making its currency desirable to the huge peasant population. The Chinese government attempts to invest its currency with value using a different method, which will be discussed in section 4.6.

Banks create another kind of money, bank deposits, by lending to their customers or buying assets from them. Owners of bank deposits are willing to hold them, and recipients of cheques entitling them to the payer's bank deposit are willing to accept cheques because they believe that the cheques can be converted into fiat money at a known rate (a 10 dollar cheque is worth 10 dollars in currency) if necessary. Of course, if all holders of bank deposits tried to obtain currency from the banks at the same time the banks would be unable to supply it. It has been pointed out many times that this is a shaky foundation for such an important institution such as money, but that is the way it is in most modern economies. Money consists of fiat, intrinsically worthless currency, and bank deposits, the total of which could not be converted into currency at the same time.

The unit of account and the nature of the currency can be changed by the government at will, as, for example, occurred in Israel when shekels replaced pounds or when a new 'heavier' unit replaces an old one although the name remains the same. In France in 1960, for example, 1 new franc replaced 10 old francs and all prices in the economy were changed in the same ratio. In certain inflationary Latin American countries a new currency is often issued, replacing thousands of units of the old, and very often a new name is devised for it. These examples show that even in private-property capitalist economies government edict is sufficient to change the unit of account and that such policies are not confined to socialist countries.

The means-of-exchange function is the most easily understood and is the basis of early monetary theories. Money is what we use to make purchases and settle debts. It commonly has the form of bank notes or currency or bank accounts transferable by cheque. In an advanced computer-using society, however, we could imagine electronic transfers at the point of sale such that people's accounts are simultaneously debited and credited on a central computer. There would still have to be a unit of account, but there would be no need for a physical object called money. However, we do use pieces of paper called money or pieces that represent money (cheques). As money is used to make transactions many monetary theorists have concentrated on this function when building up theories of the demand for money and what determines it.

Last, money is a store of value. Some forms of money are not very good stores of value. Bank notes can be lost or destroyed and, in most modern economies, pay no interest whereas bank deposits are safe from loss or theft (as long as the bank holding them is 'safe') and pay interest. The fact that holding some forms of money incurs an opportunity cost of foregone interest had been taken as the basis for certain theories of the demand for money. In some, money was assumed to be a non-interest-bearing asset. In modern economies, however, the picture is complicated by the fact that many bank deposits that we would be prepared to define as money, as they are a medium of exchange, do pay interest. This makes both theory formulation and economic policy much more difficult than formerly. In the relatively simpler monetary system in China there is a clearer demarcation between different forms of money, as the range of financial assets available to households is limited compared to that in advanced capitalist economies, where people can hold deposits of various types at commercial banks and at other non-bank financial intermediaries such as building societies or savings and loan associations.

There are two basic approaches to the definition of money: the a priori and the empirical.

The former starts from the three functions of money described above and argues that anything that performs these functions in a particular economy should be defined as money. This is not as easy as it seems. Clearly, currency meets this criterion as it is a means of exchange and a store of value. Current account or sight deposits at banks do also; they are a store of value and they can be transferred by cheque to settle debts. Time deposits pose a problem for this definition; they are clearly a store of value, but they cannot be transferred by cheque as they themselves have to be converted into current account deposits, sometimes after a delay and sometimes incurring a penalty. This impaired liquidity of time deposits at banks makes them less likely to be included in a definition of money from the a priori point of view.

In capitalist economies there is a whole range of monetary assets that are very close substitutes for money, the possession of which could influence the holder's expenditures and which certain economists have argued should be included in the definition of the money supply. Each country must decide how to define such things as foreign residents' holdings of the domestic currency and the government's own holdings of money. Different countries use different conventions.[1] As Gowland (1984: 2) argues, 'it is impossible to define "money" correctly. Money is a theoretical construct devised by economists.' For this reason the empirical definition has become prevalent recently. This is also because certain governments have adopted monetarist economic policies that stress the importance of limiting the rate of growth of the money supply. Obviously, governments first have to know which aspect of the money supply to control. The empirical approach tries to tell them. Monetary theory suggests which observable variables would be closely correlated with the money supply, and the empirical approach uses statistical techniques to determine which defined monetary aggregate actually is most closely connected with these variables, such as nominal income. Whichever monetary definition is most closely and predictably correlated with whatever variables the government wishes to control is announced to be money. Darby, Mascaro and Marlow (1989) are just one recent example of this approach. Unfortunately, this approach has had its problems and is sometimes ridiculed by outside observers because it seems that economists cannot even define what money is. It is not just outside observers who find this puzzling. In her presidential address to the American Economic Association in 1986 Alice M. Rivlin (1987: 5) remarked that 'no one seems to know what money is any more'. In the early 1980s the British government adopted a wide definition of the money supply for controlling. At first it targeted *M3* and subsequently sterling *M3* (£*M3*) because this was closely correlated with nominal income. In the early 1980s the relationship between this monetary aggregate and nominal income broke down and the government, for a time, stressed the importance of a narrow measure of the money supply, *M0*, which was now announced to be the important monetary variable (Chrystal, 1989: 46–7).[2] The empirical approach to defining the money supply is the main method that has been applied to China.

3.3 Changes in the money supply

The major cause of changes in the broad measure of the money supply is changes in bank lending. If net borrowing is positive, bank deposits will increase as banks make loans to their customers in excess of the repayment of loans to the banks. Households and firms (known as the private sector) borrow from banks, as does the government (the public sector). Their combined demand for loans, combined with the banks' ability to give loans, will determine the growth of the money supply.

Government fiscal policy can have an impact on the money supply. Government expenditures and purchases of assets from the private sector act to increase the money supply directly, and government taxes and sale of assets to the private sector reduce it. If the government has a budget deficit it can cover it in three ways: it can borrow from the domestic population, from abroad or from domestic banks. The first two methods have no impact on the money supply. If the government borrows from the domestic population, existing money is merely transferred from the private sector to the government in return for government debt. The government spends the money, thus keeping it in circulation. If the government borrows from abroad in foreign currencies, this can be used to obtain existing domestic currency for the government to spend. There is no direct impact on the money supply. The part of the government debt that is covered by these two forms of borrowing is said to be 'funded' in British monetary economics. When the government borrows from domestic banks to meet the 'unfunded' part of its deficit the money supply increases. Furthermore, whenever the private sector borrows from the banks the money supply increases. The easiest way this happens is when the banks grant overdraft facilities for their clients, thus creating an additional deposit for the borrower and an asset (the loan to the customer) for themselves. When the overdraft facility is used to pay a third party the money supply increases.

Economic relations with the foreign sector also can have an impact on the money supply. They involve both government and private actions. Very often governments intervene on the foreign exchange market to stabilise the value of their currency. If a government intervened to support its currency, it would buy the currency using its reserves of foreign exchange; government holdings of the domestic currency would rise, and the money supply would fall. If a government intervened to keep its currency from appreciating, it would sell the currency; the supply of the domestic currency would rise, and the government would accumulate extra foreign-currency reserves. Hence, observing changes in a government's holdings of foreign exchange indicates the extent to which this cause is contributing to monetary growth. Private sector actions with the foreign sector can influence the money supply, but their precise treatment depends on whether foreign residents' holdings of the domestic money supply are counted in the statistics. For theoretical purposes they perhaps should be as they can be used to buy domestically produced goods and can be transferred to domestic residents. Settling debts incurred in international trade by using cheques drawn on domestic banks obviously has an effect on the domestic money supply. Bank lending to foreigners can also have an effect as the non-domestic resident can transfer the deposit to a resident, thus increasing the money supply held by domestic residents.

Reasons for changes in the money supply, conceived as a broad definition including all time deposits with commercial banks but excluding deposits with other financial institutions, can be summarised as follows. This summary uses terms commonly found in the British explanation of the money supply process, but the general principles are the same for most open-market economies. In any given period

ΔMs = Public sector borrowing requirement
minus
Private sector lending to the government
plus
Bank lending to the public
plus
Δ Banks' net claims on foreigners
plus
Δ Government holdings of foreign currency reserves

The relative importance of each of these factors will vary from country to country depending on such things as the extent of its involvement in foreign trade, the type of foreign exchange regime it has adopted, the government's willingness to run budget deficits and its ability to borrow from the private sector, and the extent to which people are willing to use bank credit to finance purchases. Beliefs about which of the above reasons for changes in the money supply dominate can change and cause major changes in many aspects of government policy. For example, in the United Kingdom from the mid 1970s, and especially under the Conservative government of Prime Minister Thatcher, it was argued that the government's borrowing requirement was the dominant cause of changes in the money supply and so it should be strictly controlled. This could be done by reducing expenditures, increasing taxes or selling government assets to the private sector. Fiscal policy was thus formulated in the light of its monetary implications.

The extent to which fiscal policy actually does cause changes in the money supply is an important question for any economy and has often played a dominant role in determining the government's fiscal stance. For example, the Hong Kong government's well-known policy of fiscal conservatism has always been justified on the grounds that such a policy ensures that government activity has a neutral impact on money supply growth. It will then be the private sector's borrowing requirement that determines the rate of monetary growth. Peebles (1988: 154–5) quotes a former Hong Kong Financial Secretary to this effect. The empirical question of whether, in fact, the dominant influence on monetary supply growth is fiscal policy became particularly controversial in the United Kingdom once the policy of determining fiscal policy on the basis of its monetary implications became the cornerstone of policy in the 1980s. Such a view became the basic determinant of British government policy in the 1980s and was justified in the *Financial Statement and Budget Report 1980–81*, where it was stated that 'there is no doubt that public sector borrowing has made a major contribution to the excessive growth of the money supply in recent years'. Quoted from Kaldor (1985: 89). Kaldor (1985: 87–94) tests this view and finds no empirical support for it whatsoever for the period 1971–79. The best statistical explanation of changes in a broad measure of the money supply during this period was bank lending to the UK private sector, not government borrowing. Other periods when government deficits have had no appreciable impact on monetary growth spring to mind. In the United States during 1988 and 1989 there remained a significant federal budget deficit, yet the Federal Reserve Board was able to limit the growth of the money supply to zero in real terms, provoking accusations from monetarist economists that, unless reversed, this policy was bound to cause a recession. It is a gross oversimplification, which is very often completely wrong, to ascribe changes in the money supply mainly to the government's budget deficit. Bank lending to the private sector can often dominate this impact and produce monetary growth rates that are completely different from what would be expected from looking at the budget deficit alone. This caution should always be borne in mind when trying to explain monetary growth in any economy, and it will be analysed for China in chapters 4 and 6.

3.4 Controlling the money supply

This is an extremely difficult policy to accomplish in market economies, and textbooks oversimplify the methods by which, and the extent to which, it can be accomplished. Very often a textbook will illustrate the problem and the required technique by using the money multiplier concept.

This concept was developed by Friedman and his colleagues in order to classify reasons for changes in the money supply in any economy with a commercial banking network. Textbooks, however, have tended to interpret it as a valid theory of money supply creation whereas, like the quantity equation, it is a truism. Money, M, is defined as cash outside the banks, C, plus bank deposits, D. Banks seek to hold reserves, which consist of cash and the reserves that the monetary authorities insist that they hold, R. These two forms of reserves are generally called high-powered money, H, or the monetary base. So,

$$M = C + D$$

and $$H = C + R$$

so that $$M/H = (C + D)/(C + R)$$

which gives $$M = H(1 + C/D)/(C/D + R/D)$$

or $$M = H(1 + c)/(c + r)$$

where c is the public's desired cash-to-deposits ratio and r is the banking system's reserve-to-deposits ratio. The money supply is thus seen as a multiple of the amount of high-powered money in the economy, as c and r are fractions. Now, this expression is always true. It can only be a useful theory if c and r are relatively stable. Then, changes in high-powered money will cause a multiple change in the money supply. The expression can mainly be used for historical analysis to account for observed changes in the money supply. This multiplier model of the money supply process suggests that the way to control money supply is to control high-powered money.

Despite the fact that textbooks persist in implying that controlling high-powered money is the main technique monetary authorities use to control the money supply, this has not in fact been the case. The general approach has been to act on the costs and availability of loans from the banking system to discourage private sector borrowing (which, as we have seen above, can cause changes in the money supply) and to reduce the public-sector borrowing requirement. This latter element can be reduced by spending cuts or tax increases and asset sales to the private sector. Private sector borrowing can be discouraged by high interest rates, which will also probably encourage the public to buy government debt, thus reducing the impact of any budget deficit on money supply growth. Gowland (1984: 9–10) lists '17 methods of controlling money' and elsewhere (pp. 26–7) outlines 'seven basic methods of controlling the money supply'. An important point he stresses is that 'no government or Central Bank in the developed world seeks *directly* to control the total quantity of currency' (p. 27). There are two main reasons: because currency is a small proportion of the money supply in an advanced economy; and because controlling the creation of deposits when people borrow from the banks will control the growth of currency anyway. However, currency control can be much more important in a planned economy where currency plays a much more important role in certain sectors of the economy, and this is the case in China.

As Gowland (1984: 52) stresses, the textbook approach of money control by controlling the money base has never been used in the United Kingdom. There, monetary control has been based on interest rate effects on the price of credit, attempts to control the government's borrowing requirement, asset sales to the public and, for many years in the United Kingdom as well as in France, direct controls over bank lending to the private sector. Such controls are really ceilings on the acceptable rate of growth of bank deposits in any period. They have often been coupled with quotas for lending to particular sectors of the economy, such as export industries in the United Kingdom. Such direct methods of control over the privately-owned, profit-seeking banks were an important part of British monetary policy for the period 1952–71 and have been extensively used in France. Gowland (1984: 34) states that such controls were used in the United States for the first time in 1979 but were quickly dropped. This illustrates that even in market economies the monetary authorities have been prepared to rely on direct quantity controls on the behaviour of the private sector in an attempt to limit monetary growth. Prachnowny (1985: 194–208) argues that the main method of monetary control in Canada for the period 1975–82 was the use of interest controls. He also argues that the Federal Reserve Board in the United States used the same technique before, in October 1979, switching to control of the banks' holdings of non-borrowed reserves, not the monetary base. These are forms of indirect control over the money supply, even though both authorities were committed to controlling the money supply.

Despite the array of tools available and the years of experience, there has been constant experimentation to try to establish effective means of controlling the money supply in market economies. Their actual experiences in meeting the targets set for monetary growth has not been particularly good. Recent policies have been anti-inflationary, hence aimed at reducing the rate of growth of the money supply, rather than increasing it in an attempt to reduce interest rates and unemployment, as might have been the case in the 1950s and 1960s. If inflation is seen simply as 'too much money chasing too few goods', which is all the Quantity Theory of Money implies, then the monetary authorities have been able to act on only the money side of the problem. In a market economy the government has no direct control over the availability of goods, although 'supply side economics' of the 1980s did promise that tax cuts would boost output growth and hence reduce inflationary pressures. The monetary authorities' inability to hit their own monetary targets in many years during the 1980s is chronicled by Gowland (1984: 204–6) for the United Kingdom and Gordon (1987: 426–8) for the United States. Macesich and Tsai (1982: 201–6) summarise the evidence for a number of industrialised economies and conclude that 'central banks only rarely succeed in hitting monetary targets' (p. 201).

3.5 Theories of the effects of changes in the money supply

Like much of microeconomics, the basic paradigm of monetary theory revolves around the concepts of demand and supply. In monetary theory, however, these concepts relate to aggregates and they relate to stocks of real money balances in existence at a particular time, not to flows of goods or services over time. Theorists construct theories of the demand for real money balances, which show the determinants of the quantity of real money balances that people wish to hold in any given circumstances. The functions of money as both a means of exchange and a store of value figure in deriving this demand function. It is generally argued that the demand for real money balances is a positive function of real incomes and an inverse function of the rate of interest. It is a positive function of income because of the transactions demand for money; at higher incomes people make more purchases and higher real value purchases, and this requires greater money holdings. Demand is thought to be an inverse function of interest rates on the basis of various theories, including Keynes's speculative motive or Baumol's (1952) inventory model, a proposition also derived by Tobin but predated by Allais's analysis (Baumol and Tobin, 1989). Extensive evidence supports these parameters in the demand function. Laidler (1985: 121–34) surveys the evidence, concluding that it is 'overwhelming' (p. 134) that there is an inverse relationship between money holdings and the rate of interest, a view echoed by Thomas (1985: 306–8).

The dominant assumption of mainstream theory is that changes in the nominal money supply are exogenous to the economic system; that is, they occur independently of what is happening in the economy. An additional important assumption is that demand and supply are always in equilibrium. The paradigm then is that exogenous changes in the money supply must bring about changes in the factors determining money demand, so that demand changes to equal the changed supply and people voluntarily hold the increased money supply. There are four possible consequences of an increase in the nominal money supply according to this approach: real income could increase with other factors constant; interest rates could fall with other factors constant; the price level could rise to reduce the real value of the increased nominal money supply to what it was, with the other factors constant; or a combination of all three reactions could occur. Furthermore, the short run response could be different from the eventual long-run outcome. The disputes in monetary theory revolve around which of these four possible reactions is most likely. This means bringing in arguments about which variables can change. For example, Keynes argued that money demand was interest-elastic, so an increase in supply would lower interest rates, thus stimulating investment, which, through the multiplier process, would increase real incomes. His analysis was for an economy with widespread unemployment. He thought that an increase in the price level was unlikely, so the effect of the increased money supply, in the short run at least, would be lower interest rates and higher real income. In contrast, quantity theorists argue that the income elasticity of demand is very low and that real income need not respond to an increase in nominal demand, meaning that the effect of a monetary expansion is solely to increase the price level, at least in the long run. This proposition is expressed in the Quantity Theory of Money, which is important enough to examine in detail.

The income version of the Quantity Theory starts from the quantity equation, which is an identity, true by definition.

$$M \times V \equiv P \times Q$$

where M is the money stock, V is the income velocity of circulation, P is the aggregate price level and Q is the volume of output. This is true as an identity because V is defined as PQ divided by M, that is, as the number of times in each period that one unit of money turns over in purchasing final output. Three important further assumptions are necessary to turn this into a theory: that M is exogenous and does not change because of changes in PQ; that V is stable; and that Q is fixed in the short run.

Despite statements in many textbooks that quantity theorists assume that V is constant, this is just not true. The crucial argument is that V is a stable function of a few variables, possibly just the rate of interest, and that for the purpose of formulating monetary policy V can be predicted. Friedman and Schwartz's (1982: 204–15) view is that, although the extreme simple Quantity Theory assumption of constant velocity is incorrect, it is impressive how far this assumption took them in explaining movements in both income and the money supply. If V fell significantly as M expanded, there would be no direct link between the money stock and total nominal expenditure (nominal income), $M \times V$. In fact, Friedman (1987a) argues that the evidence is that V moves in the same direction as M, thus intensifying any monetary expansion. However, there are claims that, since the early 1970s in the industrialised countries, velocity has moved to offset some of the monetary expansion (Reading, 1989: 89–90). If V is relatively stable, M predicts total spending, $M \times V$.

How this effects the right hand side of the identity requires a further theory of how an expansion of nominal income is split between increases in real output and increases in the price level. This is an extremely complicated area of theory. Textbooks simplify by saying that Q is fixed in the short run and so all the impact is felt by P, producing the simple Quantity Theory proposition that the price level is proportionate to the money supply. However, writing as late as the 1980s, Friedman (1987a: 17) admits that a 'major unsettled issue is the short-run division of a change in nominal income between output and price. The division has varied widely over space and time and there exists no satisfactory theory that isolates the factors responsible for the variability'. This is the virtual abandonment of the Quantity Theory as a theory of the price level. It has been reduced to the relationship between money and nominal income, that is, the question of the stability of velocity or the demand for money. It is generally conceded by quantity theorists that monetary expansion has an immediate short-run effect on output, that this short run can last from three to ten years, and that the effect will begin to show up on prices with a time lag of twelve to eighteen months (Friedman, 1987a: 17). This is true of capitalist economies where there is very little or no government price control. The question of the time lag of price changes behind monetary expansion is important and will be examined for China in chapter 6. Two possibilities suggest themselves: with extensive price control there might be no price reaction at all; on the other hand, if prices are changed by planners, they may react very quickly, producing a close contemporaneous relationship between nominal demand and prices.

The quantity equation and the theory derived from it have been written down in the above form thousands of times. However, it is remarked only rarely that, given the theory derived from the identity, it is written the wrong way round. Economists usually stick to the mathematical convention that the dependent variable goes on the left hand side and the independent, explanatory, variables on the right. The Quantity Theory is always written the wrong way around in that it argues that causation runs from the left hand side (the money supply in particular) to the right (the price level in the simple Quantity Theory). There are, however, economists who read the quantity equation as it is written; they believe that the left hand side is a dependent function of the right hand side. This is true of economists in China. The criticisms of this aspect of the Quantity Theory approach by Western economists are worth reviewing here.

3.6 Criticisms of the Quantity Theory approach

Limited power to explain

One important criticism of the Quantity Theory is its relatively limited explanatory power. This is not just because there are certain historical occasions when it just has not been correct (some will be discussed below) but also because it assumes exogenous changes in the money supply. The theory starts by saying 'if there is an increase in the money supply, then this is what we expect to happen . . .'. David Hume's description of the effects of an increase in the money supply started with a 'miracle' by which every man in Britain woke up to find that 5 pounds had been put in his pocket overnight, and Friedman (1969: 4–5) supposed that helicopters dropped money freely on the population below. Admittedly, his analysis is of a 'hypothetical simple society', but assuming such unlikely means by which the money supply increases precludes analysis of the actual processes by which it does increase in a modern financial system. In seventeenth-century European economies where 'money' meant gold it was reasonable to ascribe changes in the money supply to exogenous factors such as gold discoveries, as David Hume later did. It is not appropriate for a modern economy where money is created by commercial banks, nor for the socialist system.

Furthermore, the derivation of the relationship between money and prices is based on a fundamental institutional assumption about market economies that is not true for socialist economies and, it will be argued in chapter 4, is not applicable to the Chinese economy during the period under study here. When individuals find that their nominal money balances have increased completely unexpectedly by means of this miraculous method, in a market economy they are assumed to try to reduce their balances to the demanded quantities, which have not changed. They can each do this by buying goods and services. However, as Friedman has pointed out many times (see Friedman, 1969: 175 for an example), *individuals* can reduce their excess money balances this way but the whole of society cannot. The nominal money supply will remain the same as the money stays in circulation. The only way equilibrium can be restored is if the price level eventually rises to reduce the real value of this larger nominal money supply. This assumption is not true of the socialist economic system. Increased expenditures can reduce the nominal money supply. This makes a fundamental difference to the way we must analyse changes in the economy due to excess money issue.

There is a second message of the helicopter analogy that must be dealt with here. How could there actually be an exogenous increase in the money supply in a modern real-world economy? If an eccentric miser turned philanthropist just took bundles of his own bank notes from under his bed and scattered them from a helicopter there would be no increase in the money supply. For there to be an increase there must be a net injection of money. One way in which this can actually happen in the real world is if the government increases some of its transfer payments and does not finance the expenditure through higher taxes or bond sales. Such expenditures can be called 'current grants to the private sector from the government'. They are called grants because there is not an actual transfer of money from one group to another (Surrey, 1989: 220–1). An increase in government grants to students is an example of this. The money comes into circulation as extra disposable income for the students who, presumably, spend it. The effect on total expenditure is primarily due to the extra disposable income; that is, it is the result of an increase in a *flow*. This is the first-round effect of the extra money, which is really extra income. Now, Friedman's argument has always been that such an injection will permanently increase the money stock, so there must be a second-round impact on expenditures as other people try to reduce this excessive stock. As stated above, and as will be illustrated in chapter 4, there is no presumption in China that there will be a permanent increase in the money supply equal to the increased issue of money. The secondary effect may be minor, and we should turn our attention to the primary effect of the increased *flow* of income from the government to individuals in explaining increases in expenditure, the pressure of demand and the money stock, as well as in asking how monetary planners react to the increased flows of expenditure brought about by the initial monetary issue due to changes in government policies.

A full monetary theory that examines the relationship between money and prices should include an explanation of why the money supply increases in the first place. As Friedman (1987a: 17) admits, '[t]he deeper question is why excessive monetary growth occurs'. His explanation has always been that, in fact, historical studies show that most major changes in the money supply have been exogenous to the economy. Nevertheless, there is a large critical theoretical literature, generally but not always known as Post Keynesian, that argues that the money supply is endogenous to the economy. There are two different types of argument for this;

one justification depends on the behaviour of governments, the other on the nature of the banking system.

The first can be called the political. It is argued that, although the government may technically be able to control the money supply, it in fact has political objectives that lead it to abandon monetary control in order to achieve these other objectives. For example, it is commonly argued that the British government throughout the 1950s and 1960s pursued a policy of stable interest rates rather than monetary control. This means that any shift in the demand for money has to be accommodated by an increase in supply. In addition, a policy of pegged foreign-exchange rates, which the major industrialised economies followed under the Bretton Woods system until 1971, makes the money supply endogenous, as each monetary authority has to intervene on the foreign exchange market, buying and selling its own currency to ensure a stable price for it. Another aspect of the political reasons for endogenous money sees the price level as exogenous to the model, so that it can be increased by cost-push factors such as wage increases or cost increases induced by large increases in input prices. Such explanations of world inflation became common after the oil price rises of 1973. In the face of the exogenous shock, prices rise; and if the government did not accommodate the price increases by increasing the money supply, output would fall and unemployment would rise, increasing the unpopularity of the current government. To avoid this undesirable consequence the government allows the money supply to increase.

Weintraub (1959, 1961, 1978a, 1987b and elsewhere) proposes a wage cost markup model in which the price level is proportionate to unit wage costs and price increases are accommodated by the government. The familiar expression is that

$$P = k(W/A)$$

where P is the price level, k is the markup of prices over unit wage costs, W is the average money wage and A is output per worker. Weintraub (1959: 33–43) showed that empirically k was relatively stable and was more so than velocity. The assumed direction of causation is from wage increases to price increases, followed by an accommodating money supply increase. The Quantity Theory of Money has no place for the money wage to play a role in price determination. This is because the underlying assumption is that all prices, including wages, are determined in competitive markets. All markets are in an equilibrium position 'ground out', to use Friedman's expression, by the Walrasian general-equilibrium system. The money wage is just another price. There is no means by which it could increase independently of a prior increase in the money supply. When there is such an increase in the money supply the price level rises. The real wage is assumed to be determined in the labour market, which is in equilibrium at the natural rate of unemployment. If the monetary expansion does not alter real variables, it will not alter the real wage. As the price level has risen the money wage must rise in the same proportion. When we look at the long run evidence we see that money wages, prices and the money supply do rise together, but the Quantity Theory denies that causation runs from wages to prices; it argues that causation goes from money to all prices, one of which just happens to be the money wage.

The second justification for assuming an endogenous money supply relies on more technical arguments about the nature of the banking system, not the behaviour of the government. Kaldor (1985: 17–36) presents this argument, in particular arguing that observations of relatively stable velocity are due not to a stable *demand* function for money but rather to changes in supply when there are shifts in demand. If supply did not change, velocity would change even more than it does. Rousseas (1986: 73–98) gives examples of arguments for endogeneity. A symposium of Post Keynesian views on the endogeneity of money is contained in the *Journal of Post Keynesian Economics* of Spring 1988, and the subsequent comments in the Spring 1989 issue show that even here there is no agreement on the major reasons for money endogeneity. Even economists nearer to the mainstream of analysis, such as the Nobel laureate in economics, Sir John Hicks (1977: ch. 3), stress the endogenous nature of the money supply in a credit economy; Hicks doubts the applicability of the Quantity Theory to such an economy. Moore (1988) provides the most complete attempt to justify the endogenous nature of the money supply on both theoretical and empirical grounds. This approach denies the separate existence of demand and supply schedules for money. In a credit economy where banks supply money by giving loans, buying earning assets or letting their customers draw on their unused but agreed overdraft facilities, the money supply always accommodates itself to the demand for it. Such economies are often described by Post Keynesian economists as 'overdraft economies'. Bank customers have unused overdraft facilities, which they are able to draw on when carrying out investment plans or when the need for working capital increases due to cost increases. The banks are able to secure any required reserves to back such an increase in their loans. It seems that much monetarist economic research has concentrated on the link between money stock and nominal income, that is, on the question of velocity, assuming an exogenously determined money supply. The money supply process is described by the truism of the money multiplier. Post Keynesian analysis has moved on to the detailed study of commercial bank behaviour in the modern economy. The assumption of exogenous money is appropriate for a commodity money economy but not for one with a sophisticated innovating profit-orientated commercial-banking system. Nor is it appropriate for one in which money issue results from the income-paying activities of an important state sector in a planned economy.

Although the common textbook approach to monetary analysis is to use models with an exogenous money supply, it is easy to agree with Goodhart (1987: 501) that many economists who use and teach such models readily admit that the money supply is largely endogenous. There appears to be more consensus about the exogeneity of money than there actually is. Friedman himself (1969: 179) admits that 'changes in the money stock are a consequence as well as an independent cause of changes in income and prices', but he maintains that this blurs the relationship between money and prices and does not reverse it. Supporters of the endogenous view maintain that it does reverse it. The Post Keynesian view would see both price increases and monetary expansion as functions of a third exogenous factor: increases in costs or money wages. Any complete monetary analysis for a single country should be able to explain changes in both the money supply and the price level. The impressive evidence of the close relationship between average inflation rates and monetary growth for a large sample of countries, such as that presented in Barro (1987: 164–9), tells us nothing about the direction of causation and does not help to settle this matter. The data just show that inflation and money growth do go together.

Assumption of continous equilibrium

The second major criticism of the dominant paradigm in monetary theory represented by the Quantity Theory is the assumption of continuous equilibrium between the demand and supply of money. On the basis of some impressive evidence Artis and Lewis (1981: 28) challenge this assumption but argue that their evidence does support the existence of a stable demand function for real money balances in the long run. They present a scatter diagram of money as a proportion of income, which is the inverse of velocity, plotted against the interest rate. They fit a curve to the data for the period 1920–57. Artis and Lewis are impressed by the extent to which subsequent observations for the period 1958–79 cluster around this fitted line, which they take to be a stable demand curve for money. They note that observations for the years 1973–76 lie off the curve, showing that the economy was holding more money than could be expected at prevailing interest rates and levels of income. They explain this by denying the prevalent contention held by the British Treasury, and mainstream textbook economics, that the quantity of money held is always equal to the amount demanded (p. 31). In other words, they accept the possibility of observable disequilibrium states using annual data. Only with a time lag of about four years do we see money holdings return to expected amounts in 1977. Artis and Lewis do not explain the adjustment process by which this happened. The generally held explanation of the increase in the money supply in the first place is that it resulted from the banking reforms introduced in an attempt to increase control over the money supply. In 1972 and 1973 a broad measure of the money supply (money plus quasi-money in definitions of the International Monetary Fund (IMF)) increased by 28 per cent in each year. In 1973 real output increased by 7.9 per cent, and in 1974 and 1975 the rate of inflation of consumer prices was 18 and 27 per cent respectively. Here we see a lagged reaction to monetary growth with both output and inflation responding. Initially, monetary growth produced a fall in velocity, but equilibrium was restored only with an observable lag. In Artis and Lewis's view, disequilibrium prevailed for four years. This is an important argument with some impressive evidence. A monetary buildup can reduce velocity in the short term. If this is not due to a shift in the demand for money, there must be an equilibrating response. They argue that this response took a while to occur but that in the United Kingdom it was able to take place through both output and price increases.

3.7 *Theories and evidence on income velocity of circulation*

Income velocity of circulation of money is one of the basic concepts of monetary theory, and any single-country study must examine its behaviour and account for it. The early modern formulations of the equation of exchange this century used the concept of transactions velocity. This approach starts from the medium-of-exchange function of money. Money is used to make transactions, and the total need for money depends on the total value of transactions made in any given period. Total transactions are not confined to the purchase of final output (income) but include such things as the purchase of intermediate goods, the purchase of already existing goods such as houses, and the turnover on financial markets such as the stock exchange. The 'price level' in this approach is not the price level of final output but the average price of all transactions, which is not necessarily what we want to explain. Since the 1930s, however, the equation of exchange has usually been presented in the income formulation discussed above. If the volume of transactions changes at a different rate from the flow of income, the demand for money will change along with transactions volume and the measured income velocity will change. For example, if there were a wave of takeover activity with large companies buying their suppliers, the value of transactions associated with a given volume of production would fall, so the demand for money would fall as goods would now be shipped from one branch of the larger company to another without there being any monetary payment, just an internal book-keeping settlement. Income velocity would rise as less money would be used for the same volume of output (income). The opposite would happen if there were de-mergers or if previously self-sufficient producers started marketing their output instead of consuming it themselves or bartering it without the use of money. These structural or institutional factors could account for some of the long run changes in velocity.

Emphasis is now on the income velocity, and this is usually explained on the basis of the second function of money: its role as a store of value. Holding money yields services at the cost of not being able to hold other financial or real assets with a higher yield. Friedman (1956) tries to argue that the Quantity Theory was all along a theory of the demand for money and that this was the Chicago tradition in monetary thought. Patinkin (1981a) shows that this was not the case. It is easy to see Friedman's reformulation as an extension of Keynes's liquidity preference theory of the demand for money, which theory Post Keynesians do not accept.

Anyway, the Quantity Theory requires more than just a theory of the demand for money (or velocity), which is only the left hand side of the identity. As we have seen, it requires a theory of output and prices on the right hand side. Treating money as an asset, however, leads to a consideration of two factors important in determining the demand for it: income and the rate of interest, which feature in Keynes's theory based on the earlier Cambridge (England) approach, which thought in terms of the demand for money by using the fraction k, the inverse of velocity (not Weintraub's k). Such an approach would ignore the institutional factors mentioned above and try to explain the development of velocity in terms of these two economic determinants alone.

Explaining changes in long run velocity

There exist two distinct approaches to explaining long run changes in velocity: the economic and the institutional.

Friedman and Schwartz (1963, 1982), in their justly celebrated studies, typify the economic approach, arguing that a narrow range of economic variables is sufficient to explain changes in velocity against an assumed background of constant institutional factors. Their earlier volume on the United States argues that the income elasticity of demand for real money balances is greater than 1.0. Friedman (1959) puts it at 1.8, meaning that, as incomes rise, money holdings rise more than proportionately, so velocity falls over the long term. Money is a luxury good. There are two problems with this approach. First, to many it does not seem much of an explanation to say that money is a luxury good as wine, spirits, restaurant meals and similar items are in most countries. Why should this be so? What is so special about money to make it so? Where is the theory that predicts this? These questions are particularly apposite as there is at least one alternative approach in Baumol (1952) that predicts an income elasticity of demand for money of 0.5. Although the applicability of this prediction to aggregate data has been challenged, it is consistent with the evidence. The second criticism of Friedman and Schwartz's explanation is that it is not consistent with the long run evidence. The long run pattern of velocity in the industrialised countries is U-shaped, with velocity falling until the 1930s or 1940s and then rising in the postwar period. In 1963, on the last page of their mammoth monetary study of the United States, Friedman and Schwartz made a prediction about the future development of velocity. This is particularly interesting given Friedman's methodological view that theories are instruments for making predictions, not descriptions of reality, and Schwartz's (1984: 129) view that '[t]here should not be views. There should be evidence'. They wrote that 'we expect the secular decline [of income velocity] to be resumed' (p. 700). It was not, and velocity continued to increase quite steadily until the early 1980s.

This inability of the world's leading supporters of the Quantity Theory to predict even the secular direction of change of the basic concept of their theory, let alone its rate of change, threw serious doubt on the narrow economic variable explanation of velocity. A reaction can be found in the work of Bordo and Jonung (1981, 1987), who drew on the institutional approach of Knut Wicksell in their econometric study of velocity. They argue that, up until the 1930s and 1940s in their countries (the United States, the United Kingdom, Canada, Norway and Sweden), falling velocity was the result of the monetisation of transactions and the spread of commercial banking. Rising velocity after the war was due to the emergence of money substitutes, methods of economising on cash balances, and increased economic stability. These factors are represented by proxies in their regressions. Their econometric techniques have been criticised by Muscatelli (1988) and Raj and Siklos (1988). The latter argue that the narrow economic variables (permanent income in particular) are after all sufficient to explain the pattern of velocity, and they re-estimate the functions using such variables. Friedman and Schwartz (1982) do, however, introduce the institutional factor of increasing financial sophistication in the United States to explain the period of falling velocity. They also stress the fact that in the United States, where money holdings rose (velocity fell), yields on alternatives to money rose less rapidly than in the United Kingdom, where money holdings fell (velocity rose).

To conclude, the factors likely to produce a secular change in velocity are:

1 A change in the relationship between transactions and income. If the former rises more rapidly than the latter, income velocity will fall. This could be due to monetisation of the economy or to the splitting up of enterprises into independent money-using trading units.
2 Long run changes in the interest rate or the cost of holding money, which could influence demand for money and hence velocity. Secularly rising interest rates, or the cost of holding money, would reduce the demand for money and hence increase velocity. Expectations of inflation reduce the demand for money and increase velocity. R. Weintraub (1970: 344–6) provides a theoretical model showing why velocity is a positive function of the rate of interest, and Gailliot (1973: 5.3–5.7) shows empirically that this is a clear feature in a large number of industrialised countries over a long period of time.

Explaining changes in short run velocity

The Quantity Theory approach has always insisted that velocity is stable, even in the short run. It is not a 'Will-o'-the Wisp', to use Friedman and Schwartz's (1982: 207) term. The whole thrust of much of their empirical work is to demonstrate that it is a useful concept linking money stock with the flow of expenditure. Velocity fell from favour, mainly in the United Kingdom, as a result of Keynes's rejection of the Quantity Theory as a tool of analysis. As Rousseas (1986: 30–5) shows, Keynes had denied the stable link between money income well before publishing the *General Theory of Employment, Interest, and Money* in 1936. His argument was mainly based on the case of savings deposits of businesses and of financial business deposits. He thought that other deposits and cash, mainly used for transactions purposes, *would* bear a relatively constant relationship to income. An important implication of this is that, in an economy where transactions activity dominates, such as in China, we would expect to see relatively stable income velocity. Keynes's argument that velocity could be unstable had a profound effect on British monetary analysis and on the works of Lords Kahn and Kaldor and Joan Robinson and American Post Keynesians. This influence was particularly clear at the time of the British *Report of the Committee on the Working of the Monetary System* (the Radcliffe Report) in 1959. Evidence from such Keynesians as Kaldor and Kahn led the committee to reject the concept, and Joan Robinson often referred to velocity as 'just a number'. Even in the United States a leading Keynesian such as Alvin Hansen could refer to velocity as 'a mere residual' that should be 'forced back into oblivion, where it properly belongs' (quoted from Friedman and Schwartz, 1982: 207). This was the strength of academic opinion in the 1950s that Friedman and Schwartz were reacting against.

The type of model that explains the Keynesian argument is as follows. Real expenditure factors determine real output, Q, through the multiplier, and costs, particularly wages, determine P. Nominal income, the right hand side of the equation, is thus determined independently of the money supply. Given the money supply, V follows. Velocity can take on a range of values because the demand for money is interest-elastic, according to the theory of liquidity preference. High nominal incomes produce high demand for money and high interest rates for a given money supply. These encourage people to economise on their money holdings for speculative purposes, thus freeing money for the active purpose of making expenditures. Hence, high interest rates are associated with a low ratio of money to income, just as shown in the demand-for-money approach of Artis and Lewis discussed above (page 62). If velocity is interpreted as the reciprocal of the proportion of income people wish to hold as money, the argument that demand for money determines the supply the government allows to be created in order to stabilise interest rates can be used. The Post Keynesian argument, represented by Moore (1988), could be used to argue that money supply always accommodates the demand in such circumstances. Moore's argument, based on evidence for the United States, the United Kingdom and South Africa, is that the money supply changes as a result of increased bank loans to the business sector and that these are mainly determined by firms' working capital requirements. These would increase, of course, if there were large exogenous increases in business costs.

Friedman's argument that velocity cannot be so elastic is based on the argument that it is the reciprocal of the demand for money and is not very sensitive to changes in the rate of interest. His attempts to justify this argument often go too far. He claims that the demand for money in real terms, that is, money held expressed in terms of weeks of income, is remarkably similar for a whole range of countries and is constant over time. The first argument is irrelevant to the Quantity Theory applied to one country, and Kaldor (1986: 26–36) claims to show quite easily that it is not true. Money holdings in real terms do vary considerably across countries. Moore (1985: 352) argues that Kaldor has misunderstood Friedman's claims. Friedman states that there is 'essentially the same relation between money and income' for a large number of countries. Kaldor has taken 'relation' literally to mean the proportion 'money divided by income'. Friedman could be trying to point out that the relationship is essentially of the same *type*, that is, stable and confined to a few similar determining factors. In my view Kaldor (1978: 25–6), which is an expanded version of Kaldor (1970) where he first broaches these differences with Friedman, does show an appreciation of this distinction and rejects both views.

It can be shown that the stability-of-velocity argument is not always correct either and that unexpected changes in velocity can occur, making Quantity Theory predictions of inflation completely wrong. Kaldor (1978) explicitly rejected the notion of stable velocity before velocity behaved so unpredictably in the 1980s. The results of Artis and Lewis (1981), discussed above (page 62), showed a short run fall in velocity and only subsequently its return to normality by means of inflation and real output growth. In the early 1980s there was a similar fall in velocity, but as yet no major supply-side response in either inflation or real output growth. Velocity seems to have fallen permanently. In the United States velocity of *M1* rose at a relatively steady rate of 3.4 per cent per annum over the period 1970–80. Its subsequent behaviour is described by Gordon (1987: 372) as the time when velocity 'fell off the rails', producing a 'velocity debacle' (p. 441). In the United Kingdom velocity of *£M3* fell 4 per cent per annum over the period 1980–85, leading *The Economist* (12 April 1986) to complain of 'monetary muddles'. Smith (1987: 150–1) also chronicles the rapid decline in velocity in the United Kingdom after 1980, and various views are discussed by Goodhart (1989: 316–18). Such events are completely inconsistent with the Quantity Theory assumption of stable velocity. In this case the increased money supply did not increase velocity and did not bring about an equilibrating rise in output and prices a few years later, as had the events of 1973 in the United Kingdom, discussed above (page 62). Inflation rates remained relatively low in both the United States and the United Kingdom in the 1980s.

The only way to reconcile these unexpected events with the theory ex post is to argue that there was a marked permanent shift in the demand for money. This is what Friedman (1987b: 219) does, arguing that people expected reduced inflation rates and so were willing to hold larger real money balances. Why they were prepared to change their expectations in this way at a time of rapid monetary growth and forecasts of rising inflation is not made clear in this explanation. Friedman himself, in September 1983, forecast a sharp increase in inflation by mid 1984 (Gordon, 1987: 441). The rapid monetary growth in the United Kingdom in the early 1980s provided a very clear test for the Quantity Theory. The British government spokesman in the House of Lords, Lord Cockfield, predicted an increasing rate of inflation in about two years' time. Lord Kaldor in his speeches (1983: 64) denied that such a result would follow. Clearly, the non-Quantity Theory prediction fared much better.

3.8 *Monetary developments in the Eastern European planned economies and their interpretation*

Until recently there was some degree of agreement on the monetary developments of the Eastern European planned economies, including the Soviet Union. This is no longer so, and two views can be distinguished. Using Wanless's (1985) useful categories, we can distinguish between the 'traditional' and 'new' views.

The traditional view long argued that the consumer goods markets of these economies suffered from sustained excess demand and repressed inflation. The concept of repressed inflation was originally applied to wartime market economies (see Charlesworth, 1956, for an example) but was soon extended to socialist countries including China. Jao (1967) is such an early study. Evidence cited to support this claim was the existence of queues, black markets for many state-supplied goods, the necessity to bribe shop staff to obtain goods in short supply, empty shelves, panic buying and hoarding of goods when supplies became available, and rapidly increasing household money balances in the form of cash and savings deposits. Official prices were kept relatively constant, but prices on free markets, where privately produced food is generally sold, increased as a result of excess demand.

The main consequence of repressed inflation was said to be 'forced saving', or the involuntary accumulation of unspendable money balances. This concept of forced saving differs from that found in Western economics in the writings of Wicksell, von Hayek, von Mises and others. In their concept there is a reallocation of resources that need not occur in the socialist model. Businesses borrow from the banks and buy capital goods. Money supply rises, as do prices. Those on fixed money incomes experience a fall in real income, so they reduce their expenditure (they are 'forced' to save), thus freeing resources for the business sector. In the socialist system this 'forced saving' is purely a monetary phenomenon and does not imply any reallocation of resources between consumption and investment. Households can be expected to react to this situation by making other adjustments, one of which is reducing labour supply and effort as households no longer have the motivation to continue increasing their money incomes if these cannot be converted into desired goods. A consequence of this desire is seen to be the necessity of having voluntary labour days in socialist economies, the occasional use of forced labour and, at times, strict labour discipline and antiparasite laws. A modern model of repressed inflation (Barro and Grossman, 1974) incorporates the effect of reduced labour supply into household behaviour under repressed inflation. Barro and Grossman also show that observed saving need not increase when there is repressed inflation if this reduction in desired labour supply is possible.

Adherents of the traditional view argue that excess demand for consumer goods is not just the result of the bad co-ordination of monetary and real flows but is an inevitable consequence of command planning. Taut plans are seen as the basic reason for this phenomenon. Enterprise managers hoard labour and materials because of this, paying out wages and not supplying consumer goods in the quantities and qualities consumers want. In many of his works the Hungarian economist János Kornai (1980a, 1980b, 1984) describes these economies as suffering from permanent shortages, and he builds his models of them on this assumption. Kornai's (1982) model does not incorporate money and so is not able to generate the consequences of these phenomena for monetary growth, savings, inflation and so on. Kornai (1980a: 306–9; 1986a: 33–51; 1986b) also uses the concept of the 'soft budget constraint', or the government's reluctance to bankrupt state enterprises, to explain how these enterprises are able to keep paying out money wages when not producing anything useful; losses are always covered by government subsidies. The 'soft budget constraint' concept has been applied to the situation of Chinese industrial enterprises by Naughton and is used by Chinese economists. There is no dispute that it was a feature of enterprises' position in the 1980s.

An important aspect of the 'soft budget constraint' is the belief that state enterprises have unlimited non-repayable overdraft facilities with the state bank. This implies that the insights of Post Keynesian analysis are likely to be more helpful in understanding events in China than any analysis based on assumptions of exogenous money. Gedeon (1985) seems to be the only analyst to use Post Keynesian monetary ideas in studying a socialist economy. Her analysis, however, stresses the political problems facing the government in restricting monetary growth. Such insights could be, and have been, applied to the problems facing the monetary authorities of the leading market economies. Her country is Yugoslavia, a market socialist economy that, with its system of worker co-operatives, is not likely to be a close parallel to China's economy with its greater degree of state ownership, single-bank system, pervasive administered prices and direction of much production without the use of market forces.

Some of the evidence adduced by the supporters of the traditional view was very badly misunderstood by them. Frequently, when trying to show the extent of excess household saving, they produced a ratio of current saving (an annual flow) to that year's increase in income, claiming that it showed what proportion of the increase in income could not be spent. Clearly, this ratio does nothing of the sort. Even if incomes did not rise at all, or even fell, people in any economy would continue to save some proportion of their incomes. These analysts were probably trying to compute the marginal propensity to save, which is the change in saving divided by the change in income. Portes (1977: 458–9) rightly criticises such incorrect ratios, and Asselain (1981: 21–2), specifically criticising the estimates of a J. Pavleski for the Soviet Union, comments that such an estimate 'has no relationship at all with the marginal propensity to save, and is meaningless [il n'a *aucune signification*]' (italics in the original).

Further support for the traditional view is based on the large monetary holdings in the planned socialist economies compared with household annual income. Birman and Clarke (1985) judge their estimate of this ratio for the Soviet Union of about 0.7 to be 'abnormally large' (p. 495) and consider that perhaps up to 75 per cent of savings bank deposits are forced (p. 497). Birman (1980a) earlier warned of a 'financial crisis' in the Soviet Union and, in Birman (1980b), defended his views against criticism from Pickersgill (1980). Wimberley (1981) supported Birman's views to some extent. Cassel (1990) characterises socialist inflation as 'cash-balance inflation', arguing that it is an everyday phenomenon without citing any direct evidence of excess monetary holdings in the countries he discusses. The problem with the monetary study of the Soviet Union is that the Soviet authorities have never published data on currency in circulation. Such data have to be estimated using many Soviet sources on the basis of the basic currency-planning concept: the balance of money incomes and expenditures of the population. Peebles (1981) and Birman (1981) present such estimates, and Peebles (1986b) compares them and uses them for analysis. Naughton (1986) had to use similar methods for China to estimate household money incomes, as did Qian (1988); but as will be shown in section 4.10, this is no longer necessary as the Chinese data have been published in full in a number of versions.

The new view of money in socialist countries is based on the econometric work of Portes and his associates on certain Eastern European countries for the period generally up to the mid 1970s (Portes and Winter, 1977, 1978, 1980). They claim that their results show that, at the aggregate level, planners in these countries were able, on the whole, to balance consumer demand and supply. Kornai (1982: 35) dismisses these claims as 'absurd', arguing that they do not take account of the forced substitutions people must make when their first-choice goods are not available.[3] Portes replies to his critics, including Kornai, in Portes (1989). Van Brabant (1990) compares the Portes and Kornai approaches, which he labels the 'disequilibrium school' and the 'shortage economy' respectively, showing his preference for the approach of Kornai in his conclusion. Kornai earlier criticised the Portes approach and the work of Howard, who used the Barro–Grossman disequilibrium model, in Kornai (1980a: 479). Podkaminer (1989) elaborates this criticism and concludes that no aggregate approach, whether econometric or based on any 'rule of thumb', can be used when simultaneously there are shortages and excess supplies. Although starting from an assumption of excess demand on the consumers' goods market in Poland for the period 1960–80, thus not *testing* for the existence of excess demand, Charemza and Gronicki (1988) claim that their estimates of excess demand are relatively low but not as low as those of Portes and Winter (1983). However, they do not discuss how 'low' is acceptable for determining aspects of household and planners' behaviour. Van der Lijn (1990) applies Portes and Winter methodology to East Germany for the period 1957–85 and claims that the 'dominant regime was one of macroeconomic excess supply' and that excess demand only appeared in a few years in the mid 1960s, mid 1970s and early 1980s. Within three months of the publication of this article East Germany gave up using its own currency and achieved monetary union with West Germany.

Although the econometric studies of Portes and his associates did not include the Soviet Union, Portes (1982: 364) expresses his views about that country when he writes:

> Nor is there evidence of chronic generally frustrated demand in household savings or labour supply behaviour. Savings ratios do not appear to be abnormally high, and continually rising labour participation rates suggest that people must believe there will be worthwhile ways of spending the extra family income generated by additional earners . . . For most of the period since the mid-1950s, repressed inflation cannot be verified.

Dirksen (1981) criticises Portes's earlier conclusions by specifically citing Soviet evidence, and Portes (1981) replies forcefully. Ellman (1989: 252–3), however, claims that shortages of goods worsened in the late 1970s and early 1980s and that local rationing and distribution through the workplace rather than shops became more important. Nove (1980: 252–6) cites evidence of increasing inflationary pressures and shortages in the late 1970s. Proponents of the new view often cite such estimates of the marginal propensity to save as those of Pickersgill (1976), (1980) who derived them from regressions of saving on household income. The earlier study for the period 1955–71 in the Soviet Union found a marginal propensity to save of about 6.6 per cent, which is low by international standards. Pickersgill found no evidence of rising propensities and could not accept the view of increasing repressed inflation. Peebles (1981) discusses such results and puts them into an Eastern European context.

Hartwig (1983) argues that liquid asset holdings in the Eastern European countries should not be regarded as excessive. He did this not by means of a statistical comparison with such ratios for other economies but on the logic of the situation and on Western monetary theory. His argument has two parts. One is that there are sufficient private markets in these countries for there to be an outlet for the excess money supply; this will drive up prices and provide an equilibrating mechanism, just as in a market economy. Second, he argues that the very existence of excess demand and shortages in the state sector gives rise to an *increased* demand for liquid assets, so most liquid assets will be voluntarily held. He puts the argument by saying that excess demand increases the transactions costs to consumers, who now find it necessary to hold more money. The simple way to look at it is to say that, because consumers are constantly searching for goods in short supply, they must carry with them large amounts of money to be able immediately to take advantage of their luck and clinch the bargain.[4] This is no more than Keynes's 'precautionary demand' for money elevated to a prominent position. The first of these arguments, that free markets provide an equilibrating mechanism, has been applied to China by Byrd (1987: 396). The second is implicit in some of Pickersgill's (1980) comments on Birman and is criticised by Wimberely (1981) as being a too convenient correspondence between the rate of monetary creation and the population's increased desired rate of money accumulation caused by shortages.

Howard (1976, 1979) applies the Barro and Grossman disequilibrium model to the Soviet Union. His econometric results lead him to conclude that there was sustained excess demand for consumer goods over the period 1956–72 and that household reaction to this was in accord with planners' preferences. People accumulated monetary balances and did not reduce their work effort significantly as they were coerced into working by various means. As seems true of all modern econometric work, Howard's methods have been subjected to criticism, in his case by Katz (1979) and Nissanke (1979); Howard replies to them in Howard (1979b). His methods of data construction are criticised by Rosefielde (1980) and (1981); Howard replies to these criticisms in Howard (1982), in my view successfully. Nuti (1986) surveys several studies relating to repressed inflation in Soviet-type economies, and his underlying assumption, like that of Kornai and Cassel, is that they do in fact suffer from pervasive excess demand.

The major difficulty in deciding between the traditional and new views is that all the available evidence is compatible with either view; there does not seem to be any single phenomenon (except, possibly, monetary collapse) that is consistent with only one view and hence allows us to reject the other. For example, the new view can explain queues for goods as a result of the bad management of understaffed shops (as does Portes, 1982) or of irrational prices for individual goods (as does van der Lijn, 1990: 127, fn. 8, for East Germany), and the rise in savings deposits held as just the natural consequence of rising incomes. Farrell (1989) takes this last approach, arguing that the relative money ratios (money divided by income) in the planned economies are closely correlated with the degree of economic development of these countries. He specifically criticises Birman and Clarke, arguing that a ratio of 0.7 for the Soviet Union is perfectly normal given its level of development and monetary holdings in other planned economies.

Peebles (1984b: 76) points out that there was an inverse relationship between price stability and monetary growth in a sample of Eastern European countries including the Soviet Union. Those that followed a conservative policy of aggregate retail price stability, such as the Soviet Union, East Germany and Czechoslovakia, had rapidly rising ratios of money to retail sales, whereas those where retail prices increased more, like Hungary and Poland, had less rapidly growing ratios of money to retail sales. This is consistent with the view that there is sustained excess demand in these countries as retail price increases serve both to withdraw money from circulation and to deflate the value of outstanding nominal balances. Winiecki (1985: 45–7) indicates the same empirical regularity; but as Peebles (1986a) points out, he uses only savings deposits as his measure of household liquidity. As currency holdings grow less rapidly than savings deposits their inclusion might qualify this result; but as Peebles (1986a: 88–90) shows, it is still a valid generalisation when liquidity is defined as savings deposits plus currency. Kemme (1989), discussing Peebles (1986a) and Winiecki (1985), accepts the validity of the generalisation. The non-specialist view has generally been that of the traditionalists as it has been based on observation of the state of socialist shops, particularly in the Soviet Union, and has been impressed by the extent of household money holdings there.[5]

It is difficult to judge whether marginal savings propensities or average liquidity are excessive in these countries on the basis of *external* comparisons using similar data from other countries, however similar their economic system. There is, however, an important alternative criterion that can be based on evidence *internal* to each country. Furthermore, such a criterion will allow us to explain certain macroeconomic events in each country. This approach is simply to look at macroeconomic developments and see whether planners react to them as if they were expected to lead to excessive rates of monetary accumulation. If we can establish for each country what the planners consider to be acceptable levels of liquidity, for example, then, if we can identify circumstances under which these acceptable rates are likely to be exceeded, we can expect to see some sort of reaction from planners. This view underlies the approach adopted with respect to China in chapter 6. We can even attempt to predict their reactions in these circumstances. This is important as many of the changes in such countries are the result not of spontaneous market forces but of changes made by planners.

Recent evidence has judged quite clearly between the traditional and new views of money in planned economies. The traditional view, with its hypothesis of chronic excess demand, has been supported by the financial crises of East Germany and the Soviet Union. In July 1990 East Germany gave up its own currency and adopted that of West Germany. It is hard to accept that this was due just to temporary excess demands and irrational relative prices. The Soviet Union is contemplating huge retail price increases, a confiscatory monetary reform, making the rouble convertible within two years, radical reforms to the financial system and changing to some form of market co-ordination of the economy. This constitutes the abandonment of the traditional planned-economy monetary system. These events vindicate the predictions of crisis made by Birman (1980a) and Birman and Clarke (1985). A message for China studies is that simple methodology has fared much better than the harder, more complicated methodology of the upholders of the new view.

3.9 *Monetary trends and policies in developing countries*

There is one clear empirical generalisation that can be made about monetary developments in developing countries: velocity declines over the long term. Ezekeil and Adekunde (1969), Chandavarkar (1977) and Short (1980) show this for a number of countries, and Schulze (1986) shows that this occurs in the Association of South-East Asian Nations (ASEAN) countries with the exception of the Philippines. Bordo and Jonung (1987: 101–10) show clearly that velocity declines for the postwar period for a large sample of low income and lower-middle income countries. This pattern is seen not just in the narrow measure of money (cash), holdings of which might be expected to rise as these economies are monetised (as larger proportions of output are sold for money), but also in broader measures that include bank deposits. The spread of bank branches into the countryside and the safety for money holdings they offer encourage people to hold bank deposits rather than hoards of cash, precious metals, stocks of commodities and so on. Broader measures of financial assets also increase with economic development, and this parallel development, originally established in the work of Goldsmith (1969), is accepted by economists as a near-universal feature of economic development.

Economists, however, are not in agreement about the direction of causation between these two phenomena. Drake (1980: 30–43) summarises various views, some stressing that it is financial development that promotes economic development (a view going back to Adam Smith), whereas others tend to believe that financial development follows from real economic development. Gupta (1984: 35–57) used causality tests in regressions for fourteen developing countries to try to establish the direction of causation between finance and growth. His conclusion is that every country showed evidence of the 'supply-leading phenomenon' (that is, finance promotes growth), although he does stress that 'the results should be treated with caution' (p. 57).

The general approach of theoreticians has been to build models showing how financial reforms and development can promote real economic growth. In this endeavour modern monetary development economics has undergone similar changes to modern mainstream monetary economics. Initially, in the 1950s and 1960s, the Keynesian approach dominated theory and policy formulation. This was followed by a monetarist counter-revolution, which sought a return to pre-Keynesian forms of analysis and prescription.

The Keynesian approach was influenced by the Keynesian model of income determination and the Harrod–Domar growth model, which was very much an extension of that model to the long run. This model stressed the importance of fixed capital investment in generating growth. Keynes's use of the marginal-efficiency-of-capital theory of investment led to an emphasis on low interest rates to promote fixed investment. Such investment could be financed by monetary creation and bank loans. If this caused inflation, this was no real problem as inflation also promoted economic growth. Investment financed itself by creating high incomes out of which the required saving would appear. Joan Robinson puts it forcefully by insisting: 'We cannot return to the pre-Keynesian view that savings governs investment. The essential point of Keynes's teaching remains. It is decisions about how much investment is to be made that governs the rate at which wealth will accumulate, not decisions about savings' (quoted from Thirlwall, 1974: 87).

Inflation was thought to promote growth in two ways: it redistributed income from wage earners, whose wages lagged behind rising prices, to entrepreneurs who invested the proceeds; and it redistributed funds to the government in the form of the inflation tax as people had to save more to maintain the desired value of real money balances. Thirlwall (1974) attempted to test the effect of inflation on growth for a sample of about 60 countries. Although his regression results do not reveal strong evidence for the link, he remains optimistic about the beneficial effects of a 'policy of mild inflation' of between 4 and 10 per cent (p. 234) compared with the difficulty and cost of other policies, such as taxation, in developing countries. It must be remembered that the hypothesised beneficial effect of inflation on growth is generally conceived for countries with private ownership and entrepreneurs producing for the market.

The counter-revolution in monetary development economics can be associated with the works of Shaw (1973), a book he calls 'old-fashioned', 'neo-classical' and 'monetarist' (p. vii), and McKinnon (1973), who independently developed different models that produced policy recommendations opposite to the Keynesian prescription. Although Chandler (1962: 49–51) had criticised low-interest-rate policies and Friedman (1973: 41–4) had argued that there is no link between inflation and development, Shaw and McKinnon are credited with initiating a widespread research programme aimed at developing and testing their views. The counter-revolution can be dated to the time of their works, and their views have to a great extent become a new orthodoxy in monetary development economics.

Their models are classical in form, denying many of the Keynesian assumptions. Adam Smith stressed that the way to development lay in increasing the proportion of the population working and the productivity of that workforce. The latter was probably more important than the former. Applied to finance and development, this simply implies increasing the flow of savings available for investment, increasing the efficiency with which these funds are allocated to potential borrowers and ensuring that funds go to the investment projects with the highest expected return. In Shaw and McKinnon's models saving determines investment, in the pre-Keynesian fashion, and in McKinnon's model saving *is* investment.

The required policies are high real rates of interest to encourage saving and a private profit-oriented banking system that ensures that funds are allocated with minimum administrative costs to the most efficient projects.[6]

In Shaw's model savers and investors are different people, so there is a loan market. Typically, in a developing country there is government control over nominal interest rates and probably also a high rate of inflation. This produces low or even negative real interest rates and is seen as the legacy of Keynesian policies. Shaw's analysis is, then, just the analysis of a market with price control. There will be a shortage of supply (the savings flow), which will necessitate rationing, probably involving corruption, black markets and so on. Funds will go to projects with low rates of return but political influence behind them. Increasing the real rate of interest will stimulate saving, allow a higher rate of investment, raise incomes and shift the savings function to the right, producing more funds for higher levels of investment. A typical Smithian beneficial cumulative growth process is begun. The required policies are high real rates of interest brought about by abandoning government interest-rate controls, instituting effective anti-inflationary policies and creating real commercial banks. Shaw's (1973: 82) basic diagram and analysis of what he calls 'financial repression' has been reproduced many times (see Gablis, 1977: 65; Fry, 1978: 465; Fry, 1980: 323; Ghatak, 1981: 62; and Jao, 1985: 198).

McKinnon (1973) built his model by assuming that there is self-financed investment, so there is no need for financial intermediation. Money is interest-bearing deposits. He argues that there is a positive relationship between interest rates and investment for a large range of interest rates. Investments are large compared with a typical farmer's surplus. He must accumulate funds in advance of purchasing the physical capital, a tractor or a pump or whatever. He cannot borrow from the banking system as he has no real security, but the investment will raise his income considerably. Storing any investible surplus as inventories is inefficient as storing is costly and the inventories could be damaged. If the opportunity of holding money balances with high interest rates arises, the typical farmer is assumed to hold his investible surplus in this form. Money and capital are seen as complementary assets, not as substitutes as in neoclassical analysis. High interest rates encourage saving, money holding and then investment in output-increasing physical capital.

It seems to me that this point could be made more simply by pointing out that an increase in the rate of interest reduces the current price of assets bought in the future. The law of demand states that when price falls a greater quantity will be demanded. Hence potential investors will find future capital assets cheaper in terms of today's foregone consumption, and we would expect saving, which is investment in McKinnon's model, to increase. McKinnon's analysis is more firmly bedded in the actual monetary conditions of developing countries with large agricultural populations.

McKinnon (1980: 109; 1981: 374; 1985: 188) reproduces a chart summarising his view of the bank intermediation process in a typical semi-industrial developing country. Although there may be privately-owned banks that take the population's deposits, governments impose high reserve requirements on them. The central bank thus obtains control over these funds, which it passes on to its own specialised credit agencies at low cost. They in turn lend to projects favoured by the government's development plan. Private lending by the banks is probably subject to interest rate ceilings. Such a system is condemned as 'financial repression', a term used by both McKinnon and Shaw. The general characteristics of financial repression are described by Jao (1985: 211–12).

The required cure is a policy of 'financial liberalisation', particularly the freeing of such prices as the rate of interest and the foreign exchange rate and the reduction of government control over the allocation of investible funds. Jao (1985: 212–18) describes the problems associated with adopting such policies, which must be a long drawn-out process. McKinnon (1985) himself argues that the required policies, although 'rational' (his term, p. 207) in a successfully liberalising economy, 'may be counter-productive in a repressed one'. He therefore advocates a second-best strategy of reforms as he feels that liberalisation in an economy with a continuing large fiscal deficit could be disastrous. It is important to note that McKinnon himself warns of the dangers associated with headlong liberalisation. In fact it can be shown that some of the industrialising economies of Asia, such as Japan, Korea, Taiwan and Singapore, often held up as examples of free-market export-orientated development, have had governments prepared to raise funds from the population and allocate them on favourable terms to chosen sectors of the economy. Korea's policy of increasing interest rates in 1965, Chile's policy of financial liberalisation, and to some extent certain policies in Taiwan are generally cited as examples where countries successfully reformed aspects of their financial systems and reaped the expected benefits.

The relevance of this to China is that these liberalising policies have become the recommended policies of such international organisations as the Asian Development Bank, of which China is a member. As was shown in section 2.3, the young communist government in China implemented a policy of high real rates of interest by indexing the rate of interest and the value of savings deposits and bonds in its fight against inflation. Again, on a limited scale, this policy was repeated in September 1988. This latter case may have been on the basis of suggestions by international monetary agencies, but the former certainly was not. Wang Yan (1988: 42–6), although only briefly, fully endorses the relevance of the McKinnon–Shaw approach to analysing China's financial reforms in the 1980s and its implications for further reform. Whether China's financial reforms in the 1980s can be characterised as financial liberalisation will be discussed in section 7.5.

3.10 China's monetary developments in a general perspective

By applying the dynamic form of the Quantity Theory we can gain an understanding of Chinese monetary developments in the light of the expectations suggested by the above analysis. The dynamic Quantity Theory starts from the quantity equation

$$M \times V \equiv P \times Q$$

By taking logarithms of the variables and differentiating with respect to time we obtain the relationship between the growth rates of these four variables. Fisher (1971: 133), among many others, gives the procedure. Using lower case letters for growth rates we can write

$$m + v \equiv p + q$$

That is to say, the growth rate of the nominal money supply, m, plus the growth rate of velocity, v, which together give the growth rate of nominal expenditures, must equal the rate of inflation, p, plus the growth rate of real output, q. This expression is also true by definition. It is always true. It can be rearranged to give

$$p \equiv (m - q) + v$$

The rate of inflation equals the excess of nominal money growth over the rate of real output growth plus the rate of increase of velocity; that is, it equals the excess of nominal money growth over the growth rate of the demand for real money.

If velocity grows at a constant rate and output growth does not respond to an increase in the rate of monetary growth, the dynamic Quantity Theory can be stated as the proposition that an increase in the rate of growth of the money supply by a given number of percentage points will increase the rate of inflation by the same number of percentage points. Lothian (1985) presents a recent test of this and related hypotheses for a number of Organization for Economic Cooperation and Development (OECD) countries. If velocity is constant, as assumed by the simple textbook versions of the Quantity Theory, then v is zero and so the rate of inflation equals the rate of excess monetary growth, a term that can be used to define $(m - q)$. This approximation is often used by Western economists when describing the determinants of the rate of inflation in any given economy.

In fact velocity changes. Any rate of monetary growth not justified by the increase in real output must cause either inflation or a change in velocity or both. If there is excess monetary growth and the rate of inflation is less than this figure, velocity will fall; that is, the ratio of money to income will rise. From the dynamic equation

$$m - q = p - v \qquad \text{or} \qquad m = q + p - v$$

For example, $10 - 3 = 4 - (-3)$ $\qquad$ $10 = 3 + 4 - (-3)$

The rate of excess monetary growth is 7 per cent per annum (10 − 3). This is associated with only 4 per cent annual inflation, so velocity must fall 3 per cent per annum. The 10 per cent annual growth of nominal money is absorbed by 3 per cent real growth, eroded by 4 per cent inflation and by a rise in the ratio of money to income of 3 per cent per annum. This accounts for all the observed nominal income growth. If velocity were constant, inflation would have to be 7 per cent per annum.

The extent to which excess monetary growth is translated into either open inflation or a change in velocity is a basic question of monetary theory. The equilibrium approach of Western economics assumes that the stable demand for money determines the desired rate of change of velocity, meaning that inflation must be the residual that ensures that the excess rate of growth of the nominal money supply is reduced in real terms to equal the rate of growth of real demand. In the case of the planned economies it is assumed that, if there is any excess monetary growth, the rate of inflation will be chosen by the planners to bring about a desired rate of change of velocity, which determines the change in the ratio of money to income. In an ideal situation the planners are supposed to be able to secure a rate of excess money growth that is just sufficient to produce the desired change in velocity with whatever rate of inflation they wish.

The simple Quantity Theory for capitalist economies assumes that v is close to zero, so all excess monetary growth shows up as open inflation. The extreme repressed-inflation view where p is zero would argue that all excess monetary growth has to show up as a change in velocity. Developing countries are assumed to have a high income elasticity of demand for money. This means that velocity will fall, which will absorb part of the excess monetary growth (if any), making inflation less than it would be otherwise. This is shown in the above numerical example, where velocity falls 3 per cent per annum and so the rate of inflation is only 4 per cent per annum in the face of excess monetary growth of 7 per cent per annum.

The division of excess monetary growth into either open inflation or a change in velocity is a helpful way of comparing different countries' monetary experiences and for seeing which countries China most closely resembles in this respect. Table 3.1 assembles such estimates for a number of countries representing developed capitalist countries (United Kingdom, United States, Norway, Sweden), Asian developing countries (Thailand, Philippines, Malaysia, Singapore, South Korea, Indonesia) and Eastern European planned economies (Soviet Union, Czechoslovakia, East Germany), as well as for Poland, Hungary, Yugoslavia and China. It is probably not correct to classify Hungary as a 'planned' economy as state enterprises are not subject to quantitative directive planning, and Yugoslavia is a 'market socialist' economy. We might therefore expect these two countries to show different behaviour from the planned economies.

Monetary data in the table relate to money plus quasi-money, except for the planned economies where it is currency plus savings deposits. Output growth is of *GDP* or *GNP*, except for the planned economies where it is net material product but gross material product for Yugoslavia. Inflation is given by the change in the consumer price index, except for China where it is the index of the cost of living of staff and workers. The period covered is 1960–84, except for the Soviet Union where it is 1960–78 only. Data are largely from the *International Financial Statistics Yearbook, Comecon Data 1981* and *1985*, but Peebles (1981) was used for the Soviet Union. The data are annual average growth rates in per cent per annum. As these figures represent very general trends the calculated growth rates have been rounded to the nearest whole number. The results do not mean that the developed capitalist economies had absolutely constant velocity (zero change in velocity), but this is a good first approximation. The important ratio derived from these calculations is shown in the last column; it is the ratio of open inflation to the rate of excess monetary growth.

Table 3.1 Open inflation response to excess monetary growth in selected countries

Country	Excess monetary growth $(m - q)$	Open inflation p	Change in velocity v	Inflation response $p/(m - q)$
China	5	1	−4	0.2
Poland	13	8	−5	0.6
Hungary	5	5	0	1.0
Yugoslavia	21	18	−3	0.9
Soviet Union	9	0	−9	0
Czechoslovakia	5	1	−4	0.25
East Germany	3	0	−3	0
Thailand	10	6	−4	0.6
Philippines	12	10	−2	0.8
Malaysia	12	6	−6	0.5
Singapore	6	4	−2	0.7
South Korea	24	14	−10	0.6
Indonesia	53	41	−12	0.8
United Kingdom	9	9	0	1.0
United States	6	6	0	1.0
Norway	7	7	0	1.0
Sweden	7	7	0	1.0

Source and methods: See text, page 78.

The Quantity Theory suggests that for market economies this ratio, $p/(m - q)$, should be near unity, and the repressed inflation hypothesis suggests that it should be near zero. The view that developing countries monetise during development implies that it should be somewhere between these limits. The ratio can of course exceed unity, as it does slightly for Norway, if velocity increases. Zero and unity are not the necessary fixed limits of this ratio. The data show that the countries do tend to fall into four broad groups, which can be classified as follows:

Range of $p/(m - q)$:	*Observed in:*
0.25 and less	China, Soviet Union, Czechoslovakia, East Germany
between 0.5 and 0.8	Poland, Thailand, Philippines, Malaysia, Singapore, South Korea, Indonesia
between 0.8 and 1.0	Yugoslavia
approximately 1.0	Hungary, United Kingdom, United States, Norway, Sweden

Slightly different results could be obtained using a broader measure of the money supply and different periods, but the general picture is quite robust. In the developed capitalist economies, over the long run excess monetary growth shows up almost exclusively as open inflation. This, however, does not prove anything about the direction of causation. In a number of countries, mostly the Asian developing ones, excess monetary growth shows up as both open inflation and falling velocity. This is true also of the planned economies, including China, but for these countries the picture is more extreme. Excess monetary growth produces a very limited open-inflation response, and the fall in velocity is much more than we would expect from the developing countries' experiences. Clearly, China's monetary experiences are closer to those of the planned economies. This implies that it will be fruitful to stress and use the concepts and theories developed for the analysis of monetary events in those countries in analysing monetary events in China. If the institutions, policies and concepts used by planners in China can be shown to be similar to those of the Eastern European countries, this approach will be founded on both institutional similarities and similar empirical evidence.

This way of classifying monetary experiences can be applied directly to China's experiences. Table 3.2 shows the rate of excess monetary growth and the rate of retail price inflation for the seven subperiods identified in the previous chapter. Figure 3.1 is a scatter diagram of this relationship. It shows that there is a clear positive relationship between the two variables; periods of high open inflation *are* associated with excess monetary growth. However, the rate of open inflation is consistently much less than the rate of excess monetary growth; only in period I are they approximately equal. The Quantity Theory prediction is not an accurate quantitative guide to the rate of open inflation in each subperiod. This positive relationship between excess monetary growth and open inflation will have to be accounted for in any subsequent analysis.

Table 3.3 shows annual data of the velocity of currency for the same seven subperiods. This velocity concept of national income divided by currency does not have much meaning from a behavioural point of view in the Chinese economy, but it can be used for illustrative purposes. The evidence of Table 3.2 explains these changes in velocity. From the dynamic quantity equation we can obtain an expression for the expected change in velocity:

$$v = p - (m - q)$$

If the rate of inflation is less than the rate of excess monetary growth, velocity must fall. In period I, p, at 1.1 per cent per annum, was slightly less than the rate of excess monetary growth at 1.3 per cent. Velocity should have fallen slightly, which it did, from 17.9 in 1953 to 17.2 in 1957. In periods II, V, VI and VII p was always less than the rate of excess monetary growth, so velocity fell during these periods. This was particularly noticeable in period II when the expression for v $(= p - (m - q))$ was as much as minus 19, meaning that velocity should have fallen 19 per cent per annum, which it did, falling from 16.7 in 1958 to 8.7 in 1962, at a rate of 18.4 per cent per annum. In periods III and IV both p and $(m - q)$ were negative, with the absolute value of p being less than $(m - q)$. As $v = p - (m - q)$, v must be positive; that is, velocity must rise and the ratio of money to income must fall. For example, in period III the implied value for v was 12.9 $(= -3.2 - (-16.1))$. Table 3.3 shows clearly that velocity did increase, from 11.1 in 1963 to 15.4 in 1965. Similarly, the value of v for period IV was 1.7, so velocity rose from 14.7 in 1966 to 15.6 in 1970. For the entire period 1953–85 open inflation was less than 1 per cent per annum when excess monetary growth was 2.5 per cent. The

Table 3.2 Average annual growth rates of retail prices, nominal money supply and real output, and excess monetary growth, by subperiods, China, 1953–85

(per cent per annum)

Subperiod	*p*	*m*	*q*	(*m* – *q*)
Period I	1.1	9.4	8.1	1.3
Period II	6.6	15.4	−10.2	25.6
Period III	−3.2	0.6	16.7	−16.1
Period IV	−0.5	3.9	6.1	−2.2
Period V	0.3	7.7	5.0	2.7
Period VI	2.4	14.7	8.6	6.2
Period VII	3.4	27.3	11.1	16.2
Entire period 1953–85	0.7	8.4	5.9	2.5

Source: Table IV.1. These average growth rates were calculated using semilog regressions on time for each period.

Figure 3.1 Scatter diagram of open inflation against excess monetary growth for seven subperiods

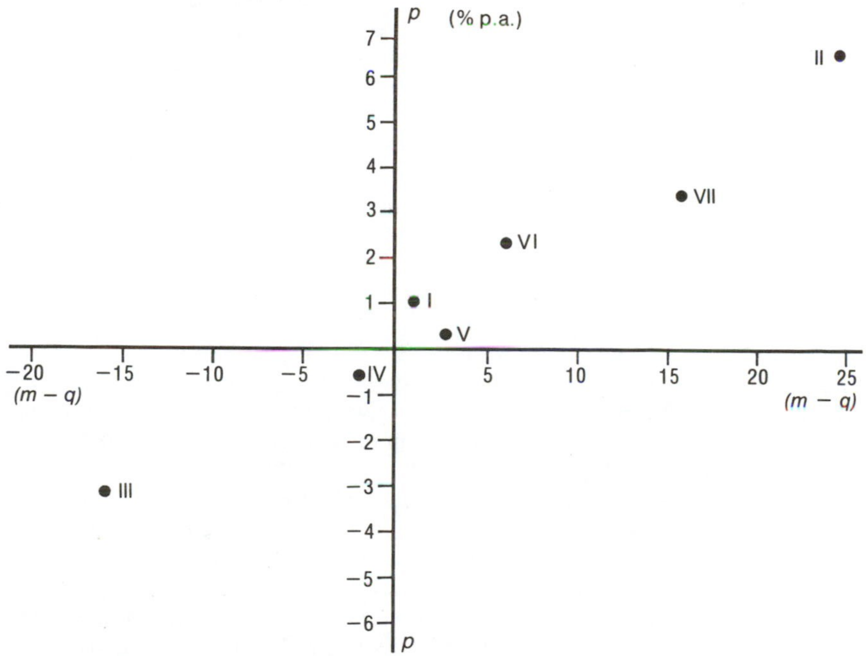

difference was minus 1.8, so velocity fell over the long run from 17.9 in 1953 to 6.9 in 1985 at an annual rate of minus 1.7 per cent.

To explain fully these changes in velocity we have to explain why there was excess monetary growth in each subperiod and why open inflation did not erode the entire amount of excess monetary growth. This requires examining the money-supply process in China to see how money can grow at a rate different from output and what institutions exist to ensure that

Table 3.3 Income velocity of currency and its inverse, China, 1953–85

Period	Year	V^a	Ratio[b] (%)	Period	Year	V^a	Ratio[b] (%)
I	1953	17.9	5.6	V	1971	15.2	6.6
	1954	18.2	5.5		1972	14.1	7.1
	1955	19.6	5.1		1973	13.9	7.2
	1956	15.4	6.5		1974	13.3	7.5
	1957	17.2	5.8		1975	13.7	7.3
II	1958	16.7	6.0	VI	1976	11.9	8.4
	1959	16.4	6.2		1977	13.5	7.4
	1960	12.7	7.9		1978	14.3	7.0
	1961	7.9	12.7		1979	12.5	8.0
	1962	8.7	11.5		1980	10.6	9.4
III	1963	11.1	9.0	VII	1981	9.9	10.1
	1964	14.5	6.9		1982	9.7	10.3
	1965	15.4	6.5		1983	8.9	11.2
IV	1966	14.7	6.8		1984	7.1	14.1
	1967	12.2	8.2		1985	6.9	14.5
	1968	10.5	9.5				
	1969	11.8	8.5				
	1970	15.6	6.4				

Notes: [a] *V* is national income in current prices divided by *CRC*. Its unit is 'times per annum'.
[b] Ratio of *CRC* to national income in current prices, per cent. It is the inverse of *V*.

open price increases are very much smaller than would be expected, given the degree of excess monetary growth.

3.11 Conclusions

Western monetary theory contains more disagreements about fundamental issues of causation and other important matters than appears from reading textbooks. Two clearly opposing views exist on the nature of the direction of causation between money and prices. Determination of the money wage and its relationship to the price level and the money supply is also very different in the two approaches, which were identified as monetarist (or conventional) and Post Keynesian. Which of these approaches is likely to help most in explaining the nature of Chinese monetary experiences depends on the nature of the institutions and policy objectives under which the Chinese monetary system works. It is not appropriate to apply blindly a particular Western approach without first ascertaining the environment in which a particular monetary system operates. Schumpeter wrote that 'Monetary relations can differ so greatly in form from epoch to epoch that it would be of no practical use to produce a general theory, which would only be limited to meaningless generalities' (quoted from Zwass 1979: 71, fn. 1). We can change 'epoch' to 'system' or possibly even 'country' and obtain a good guide for the rest of this book.

When we turn to the empirical record, Chinese monetary experiences seem more similar to those of the planned Eastern European economies than to even the developing countries where velocity also falls. Velocity falls constantly in China, and the rate of open inflation is far less than the rate of excess monetary growth. Before we can explain these empirical features in China we must establish the nature of the institutions in which these monetary and price changes occurred. This is the aim of the next chapter.

4 Institutions and policies

There are two crucial aspects of any economic system that play an important role in determining the nature of its monetary institutions and associated policies: the structure of ownership in the economy; and the co-ordinating mechanism used to guide productive units in their decisions on what to produce, how to produce it, whom to sell their output to, how to distribute their income to the contributing factors of production and so on.

A co-ordinating mechanism is the system that ensures that the output plans of all economic units are compatible with the structure of demand in the economy and the availability of the factors of production. Its aim is to ensure that final consumers get exactly the goods they want and that industrial users get the required inputs to meet their output plans. At basic level the co-ordinating mechanism ensures that for every car that the car industry plans to produce other producers know that they must produce five tyres, one engine block, one clutch, six windows, two windscreen wipers, four seats, so many spark plugs and all the other necessary components as well as all the inputs required to produce them; it also ensures that the economy has enough petrol to run the cars and adequate roads and garages in the right places. The advantages of the division of labour, specialisation and economies of scale encourage different producers to specialise in different products. They all need to know how much to produce of the required products, and what these products should be.

There are only two co-ordinating mechanisms possible for a complex modern economy that intends to grow: plan and market. A third possibility, tradition—meaning just repeating everything done in the past and allocating resources to the same uses—obviously does not lead to innovation and growth.

Assume that a socialist government owns the entire industrial sector. It appoints managers to its enterprises and funds them. The government must be responsible for telling each enterprise what it must produce. This is the essence of *planning*. A commonly used analogy, which is sometimes pushed too far, is that each state enterprise is just like a branch factory of one huge industrial enterprise covering the entire industrial sector. Each branch must have its activities planned for it by a superior 'board of managers', who in practice are the industrial ministries. They in turn are subordinate to the ruling communist party, which determines long run strategies for the development of the economy. Each enterprise is subject to a superior body that instructs it on what to produce, where to deliver the output, where its inputs will come from, what these inputs will be, the prices for its outputs and inputs, the rates of wages it must pay its workers, the extent to which it must remit profits to the government and so on. There is no need for any enterprise to have contact with any other enterprise for the purpose of ordering supplies and so on. This, in theory, is done by the planning authorities.

The claimed superiority of having a planning mechanism has generally been based on two kinds of arguments. One is that planning is cheaper than the market: enterprises do not have to waste resources searching for suppliers or convincing customers to buy their products; there is no wasteful duplication of salesmen, advertising and so on. The 'order' of planning replaces the 'anarchy' of the market. The other argument is that a unified plan can ensure the development of the economy on the lines decided by the government, whether democratically elected or not, thereby avoiding business cycles, crises and unemployment. Planning can determine more precisely the rate of investment, the allocation of investment funds to sectors of the economy to which the government gives priority and so on.

The main problem with the planning co-ordinating mechanism is that, in its extreme form, it could never possibly work. No humanly organised planning body could ever collect and distribute the incredible amount of information and orders required to co-ordinate the industrial sector of an economy. Planned economies are really administered economies. Plans cannot cover all possible products, especially products not yet invented, so they are often given to enterprises in aggregate form, as so many tonnes of steel, for example. Enterprises then have to devise ways of deciding the quantities of the different types of output to produce. The aggregate can be expressed in physical units (tonnes of steel, square metres of cloth) or in value units (so many million *yuan* of gross output). Aggregation in physical units leads to perverse enterprise behaviour (Nove, 1980: 96–100). The fact that aggregation using money is necessary presupposes prices for individual items. It is because of this that monetary units and prices must exist even in a system relying on physical allocation. The prices may play no active role in mobilising resource use, but even if only for accounting purposes they must exist. Money as a unit of account *must* exist; money as a circulating piece of paper, a means of payment, need *not* exist. Settlements could be made through a computer network. Labour could be paid in kind at the end of every working day or in non-circulating certificates that were valid only in state warehouses. Whether money as a means of exchange exists in a socialist planned economy depends on the government's decisions on how to obtain labour services and other inputs and how to distribute consumer goods. The only way to abolish money is to abolish the economic problem by abolishing scarcity; then there would be no need for money to act as a rationing device determining who gets what or as a means of material stimulation.

The planned, or rather the administered sector, of a socialist economy must obtain inputs from other sectors of the economy. If the state does not own these sectors, it cannot easily use the planning co-ordinating mechanism (that is, command) to secure them. It must induce the owners to supply the inputs. The major inputs needed by the state industrial and administrative sector are agricultural produce for state shops and industry, labour and imports. Other countries cannot be commanded to supply goods, unless they are little more than vassal states; imports have to be bought. Labour could be commanded and its allocation determined by plan. The agricultural sector could, in theory, be state owned and planned and commanded to deliver the required inputs. Farmers could be allowed to keep part of the harvest for their own consumption. How a country chooses between the command and market mechanisms for securing these inputs plays a major role in determining the extent and nature of the use of money in the economy. How these inputs were obtained by the state sector in China and retail commodities distributed will occupy the next four sections.

4.1 Agricultural inputs and prices

China has always used money to obtain agricultural inputs for state shops, state industries and export. In theory, this could have been done by the extensive use of taxes in kind with a quota put on each farm household, but it was not. From November 1953 to 1985, however, these sales to the state sector were not all voluntary as the compulsory purchase system was used to obtain grain, cotton and edible oil. Private trade in these commodities was illegal until about 1979. The commune system of 1958 to the early 1980s made state control over agricultural procurements easier, as the state set the quantities to be delivered as well as the prices it paid. This practice determined the monetary income and purchasing power of the rural sector throughout this period. Rural money incomes would increase only if the government revised its purchase prices significantly or if there was a large harvest and the government was willing and able to buy it. As late as May 1987 Chinese planners[1] were stressing how cycles in the harvest over the period 1984–86 exerted an important influence on currency issue and withdrawal and on farmers' incomes. To a great extent such variations were unpredictable, and the banking system had to accommodate them. In addition, the procurement price increases of 1979 and the introduction of the bonus price scheme changed monetary relations with the rural population considerably. The consequences of these changes for the money supply will be analysed in section 6.2.

As Oi (1989: 31, 37–8, 54–5) points out, an important consequence of the compulsory procurement system and shortages of retail goods in rural areas was that money was rarely used in the rural sector during certain long periods and little valued. As private activities were discouraged, '[s]ome peasants saw no cash income for years, a phenomenon not uncommon during the late 1960s and most of the 1970s when money-making sideline activities were discouraged and severely curtailed' (p. 37). These periods cover what has been called the Cultural Revolution in the periodisation of chapter 2 and constitute about 11 years out of the 37 years 1952–88. Not only was money not used as there was little free trade, but peasants preferred to receive grain tickets in preference to money for things they did sell. Grain tickets had more currency than money as they could buy grain whereas money could not always buy goods. Therefore, peasants 'preferred to store grain rather than money. Grain could always be exchanged for money, whereas money could not always be exchanged for grain' (pp. 54–5). In addition, the state often procured extra grain from peasants by direct exchange for scarce industrial products such as fertilisers, cloth and cooking oil. Such factors contributed to China's being one of the world's most undermonetised economies before about 1978.

4.2 Urban labour and wages

Although socialist economic institutions are supposed to help reduce the disparities between the urban and rural populations, China, just like the Soviet Union, treats these sections of the population very differently in many respects. This has an effect on the nature of money flows in China.

The urban population is mainly employed by the state in industry or commerce or as government administrative personnel. State employees are guaranteed residence rights in urban areas and social welfare provisions and housing, which are mainly provided by each worker's enterprise or unit (*danwei*). The state wage system was established by 1956 and remained basically the same until 1986. Industrial workers are paid mainly according to a nationally determined eight-grade wage scale, with seven grades being common in the construction industry (Ma, 1982a: 523). Wages in state enterprises and salaries for administrative personnel are paid monthly on the fourth day of each month; and as far as I know, this frequency has not been changed since 1951. Some joint ventures have introduced their own frequency for wage payments. I know of one Australian joint venture, for example, that pays its workers fortnightly through accounts at the local branch of the Bank of China. However, such arrangements can involve only a minute proportion of the industrial workforce, who continue to be paid monthly and in cash. In addition to the basic wage, other monetary remunerations such as bonuses and subsidies are provided at various times. Since the widespread introduction of bonuses in the 1980s, the frequency of wage payments may have changed. However, bonuses tend to be paid monthly, some are paid quarterly, and at the end of the year, around 12 December, an annual bonus is paid.

The employment system was adopted from that of the Soviet Union (Korzec and Whyte, 1986: 255; Ma, 1987: 205). Lee and Chow (1987: 179) describe it as a system of fixed employment and life tenure. The important monetary implication of this system is that the state-sector wage bill can, in theory, be controlled through the central determination of the wage rate and the planned urban workforce. Consequently, large changes in the state wage bill will result from national wage increases or unplanned increases in the labour force. Such approved increases in the wage bill are something the banking system just has to accept and adapt to. The People's Bank used to supervise enterprise wage payments and could refuse permission to an enterprise to draw cash for unauthorised wage payment. However, if there was an official wage increase, the bank had to accept it. There have been several such increases—in particular, in 1956, April 1963, 1971–72, August 1977, December 1978 and again in 1979, 1981 and 1982 (Howe, 1978: 176; Lee and Chow, 1987: 187). In 1983 enterprise reform put greater emphasis on bonuses (which had been reinstated in 1978) paid out of retained profits. The attitude to using material incentives such as piece rates and bonuses for performance in state industry has varied according to the political climate (Prybyla, 1978: 108–32). In 1978 bonuses constituted only 2.3 per cent of the total state staff and workers' wage bill, and subsidies 6.5 per cent.[2] These subsidies are really income supplements. By 1985 bonuses made up 12.9 per cent and subsidies 15.2 per cent (*Statistical Yearbook of China 1986*, pp. 573, 755).

An important point to note about the use of material incentives is this: even though wage differentials and bonuses may be used to encourage a worker to increase productivity within the enterprise or to learn new skills, such incentives have never been used to relocate labour from one enterprise to another or from one location to another. In other words, there has never been a labour market in the industrial sector in China. Workers are allocated to their jobs by state labour bureaus and very often never change them. This contrasts sharply with the case of the Soviet Union, where it is generally agreed there is much more of a labour market and workers frequently leave their jobs to seek higher wages in other enterprises (Schroeder, 1982: 12–14). In China there is very good evidence of surplus labour in state enterprises. Walder (1986: 182, 184, 216) identifies the common practice in the 1980s of state workers' taking paid sick leave and going to work in co-operative enterprises at four times their state pay.

The consequences of this urban labour remuneration system is that large changes in the purchasing power of urban residents have been due to centrally decreed increases in wages, unplanned increases in the workforce or, in the reform period, the excessive payment of bonuses. Although these constituted only 12.9 per cent of the wage bill in 1985 they were the preferred use of enterprise-retained profits in 1984 and 1985. If enterprises could get hold of money, even through bank borrowing, this was likely where a large portion of it would go. Managers received bonuses also and had an incentive to keep their workers happy using the banks' money. In addition, subsidies, at 15.2 per cent of the wage bill in 1985, were another channel for increasing urban purchasing power. An important aspect of this is that they included cost-of-living increases, so the wage bill would increase following an increase in the retail price level. Such price subsidies or allowances for urban workers are now entrenched in the system, and from 1985 statistics of staff and workers' wages include these subsidies (*Fenjinde Sishi Nian 1949–1989*: 1989, 457).

In the 1980s the urban workforce began to comprise self-employed pedlars, business people, private shop owners, privately employed servants, casual construction workers and so on, but the major source of urban purchasing power remained the state wage bill. In the early period of reform such occupations were taken up by state employees as second jobs, and in April 1982 this led to a State Council Circular on stopping workers from taking up inappropriate occupations to earn extra income (*mouqu ewai shouru*).[3] This typified the official ambivalence to private economic activity. On the one hand it provides much needed services, but on the other hand it is seen to compete with state enterprises for raw materials, power and labour. When this competition is thought to be too fierce, steps are taken to limit private activity. By the late 1980s the foreign-language Chinese press was boasting of the extent of second jobs taken on by urban workers, admitting that this was due mainly to high inflation rates and fixed wage scales for state-employed workers, who could earn much more outside the state sector using their considerable skills in such things as electronic repairs and accounting. The article 'Moonlighting craze hits China' in *Beijing Review* (no. 45, 6–12 November 1989, pp. 21–3), which is published in several foreign languages, describes the extent to which urban workers had taken on second jobs.

4.3 Foreign trade, prices and exchange rates

China's foreign trade has largely been conducted as a state monopoly through its National Trading Corporations, the number of which has varied. In 1956 there were sixteen, in 1966 there were thirteen and by 1989 there were also thirteen (Donnithorne, 1967: 324–6; *Information China*, 1989: 755–8). Hsiao (1977) discusses all aspects of China's foreign trade administration and laws for its first three decades. Economic reform during the 1980s increased the number of organisations allowed to conduct foreign trade. In addition to the specialised trade corporations mentioned above there were 23 other trade corporations under various departments of the State Council. Furthermore, local authorities were given permission to establish their own import and export companies, and many large industrial enterprises and joint ventures were allowed to trade directly.[4]

The specialised Foreign Trade Corporations are independent accounting identities, originally under the Ministry of Trade but more recently under the Ministry of Foreign Economic Relations and Trade (Riskin, 1987: 333). They purchase items for export using domestic currency and sell for foreign exchange, using this foreign exchange to buy imports for which they receive domestic currency. This system, again adopted from that of the Soviet Union and other planned economies, isolates domestic prices from world prices. The government determines the exchange rate at which these transactions occur. The Foreign Trade Corporations' profits and losses are aggregated and become part of the national budget.

In the early 1980s these foreign transactions almost certainly made losses, and the *Statistical Yearbook of China 1986* (p. 511) attributes low budget revenue from the state sector in these years to 'relatively heavy losses by foreign trade enterprises and grain enterprises'. The traditional Chinese approach to foreign trade was to set export targets in the plan and then decide on import requirements. This contrasts with what is thought to be the conventional socialist practice where the plan's implications for imports are considered first and then exports are planned so that the required imports can be realised (Ma, 1986: 13). Until 1977, before which period China's foreign trade was relatively small and slow growing, exports tended to be unprofitable and imports profitable at the existing exchange rate.

In 1981 the exchange rate for internal settlement of trade corporations' dealings was changed from US$1 = 1.5 *yuan* to US$1 = 2.8 *yuan*. This encouraged exports as it gave exporters a higher return in domestic currency. A reason for this must have been the increase in domestic prices following the agricultural price reforms of 1979. In 1979 at least 48.2 per cent of China's exports originated from the agricultural sector (*Statistical Yearbook of China 1981*, p. 358). The 1980s saw a succession of official devaluations of the *Renminbi*, the largest of which were in July 1986 and December 1989. At the time of the 1986 devaluation Chen Muhua, then president of the People's Bank of China, said that this was due to changes in China's internal prices compared with world prices (Delfs, 1986: 50), showing some appreciation of the purchasing power parity theory of exchange rate determination (Peebles, 1988: 192–3).

For analytical purposes, in the rest of this study it will be assumed that changes in the foreign exchange rate have no immediate impact on the domestic price level and that these can be explained by internal factors. With regard to the clear historical association between domestic inflation and exchange rate depreciation, it is argued that causation goes from the domestic causes to the external value of the currency. The two large official devaluations in 1986 and 1989 were in years that followed a year of the then highest rate of inflation, ignoring 1961. This supports the view taken here. No ideas of imported inflation are considered worthwhile in explaining China's domestic retail-price movements. The impact of international relations on the domestic money supply will be identified and discussed in section 4.11 below.

Like other socialist countries with a tightly controlled inconvertible currency, black-market currency transactions have occurred and attracted attention. *Pick's Currency Yearbook* has always included data of such rates, but their reliability is highly suspect. There must have been a large geographical variation in rates at any time, and the lack of any information on what other people were paying means that transactions are likely to have been carried out at rates vastly different from the ones cited, even at the same time and in the same area. As one might expect, the figures, for what they are worth, show a large depreciation of the *yuan* on these markets during 1949 and in 1962. In the latter period the figures given show a change from 8.65 *yuan* per US$1 in April 1961 to 21.25 *yuan* in June 1962.[5]

4.4 Retail sales, rationing and price policy

Apart from direct distribution by the communes, China has always relied on retail sales requiring money to distribute the fruits of their labour to workers and peasants. Since 1954 this has been supported by a complicated system of rationing, and rations have been adjusted according to the state of the economy (Donnithorne, 1967: 309–13; Cheng Chu-yuan, 1982: 204–9). Goods rationed and their amounts have varied across the country but have always covered grain, cotton cloth, edible oil and pork (Howe, 1978: 180; Solinger, 1984: 305), although pork rationing was abolished in Peking by 1979. By 1984 in Peking, only cereals, oil and luxury items remained rationed.

Butterfield (1982: 149) comments that the then rationing system was 'so Byzantine in its complexity that many Chinese themselves are at a loss to understand it', although his description is clear and informative. As Solinger (1984: 305–6) and Whyte and Parish (1984: 86–91) explain, two general methods are used. Ration tickets (*piao*) for a particular amount of the permanently rationed commodities are distributed each month on the basis of each household's certificate showing its members and their occupations. The tickets are valid for that month and have to be surrendered with the required amount of money when buying.[6] In addition, each registered resident receives a booklet each month listing commodities that are currently rationed, such as soap, sugar and bean curd (Butterfield, 1983: 150), and the item is crossed off when it is bought, again in return for money. The first permanent system is called 'planned supply' or 'unified sale' (*jihua gongying* or *tongxiao*), and the second system, introduced in the light of special local conditions of deficient supply, is called 'supply according to certificate' (*pingzheng gongying*) (Ma, 1982a: 297). Enterprises also distribute grain ration coupons to their workers (Chinn, 1980: 747–8). Enterprises are also allotted ration coupons for large industrial manufactured goods, the most important of which used to be bicycles. Cadres in the enterprises decide which workers receive the coveted coupon. The effect of this non-monetary work incentive on workers' attitudes is chronicled in Walder (1986: 172–4, 182–6), and the effect of the difficulties of shopping on people's attitudes to shopping and work and on their ability to work and study is revealed in Butterfield (1983: 151–63) and Whyte and Parish (1984: 99–100).

Rationing was the result of the communist government's desire both to establish an equitable distribution of income and to ensure that retail commodities, especially food, went to people who needed them. The rationing system has covered between 200 and 300 items at various times (Howe, 1978: 180) and been essentially an urban phenomenon (Lardy, 1983a: 167). Basic food rations were set according to the amount of physical labour required by the recipient's job. Rationing was also necessary because of the existence of excess demand for consumer goods in many years. Without rationing food would have gone to the first to arrive at the shop with enough money or sufficient connections to bribe the shop staff to favour him or her with the scarce goods. Such circumstances would have encouraged the resale of, and trade in, state-supplied commodities, encouraging 'speculation' and affecting the distribution of income. As Wan (1984: 355) reveals:

> For 19 of the years between 1950 and 1980, the availability of commodities nationally fell short of the national purchasing power, which meant that the commodity supply was lower than the demand. Even after the government took a series of measures to offset the shortage by increasing production, decreasing stockpiles and limiting government institutions and state-enterprises' purchasing of consumer goods, there were still ten years when buying power exceeded the stock of commodities.

It is interesting to note that, even after the government took these steps to reduce institutions' purchasing power and sell from its stocks (policies that have sometimes been judged by Western observers as sufficient to prevent inflationary pressures), excess demand still occurred in at least ten years. As it also occurred during the 1980s we can conclude that for about 14 out of 36 years (1950–85) there was excess demand for consumer goods even after these government reactive policies were taken. Which years were ones of excess demand and why, and what other policies planners took during these periods, will be studied in chapter 6. Without rationing, goods would have been distributed solely according to monetary purchasing power. Rationing reduces the power of money to buy goods and increases the influence of those who distribute ration coupons. Ration coupons become 'a sort of quasi money, for money alone cannot buy even a tube of toothpaste or a handkerchief' (Cheng Chu-yuan, 1982: 208). By linking access to ration coupons to the holding of a residence permit and limiting their use to certain locations (although there were national tickets for approved travellers), the system also controlled migration (Oi, 1989: 31–2). Examples of the amount of the ration are given by Durand (1965: 395–7) for the 1950s, Donnithorne (1967: 311) for the mid 1960s, and Howe (1978: 180–1), Cheng Chu-yuan (1982: 209–11) and Chinn (1980) for the 1970s.

State commerce was neglected during the 1960s and 1970s, and private trade almost completely disappeared. In 1965 the number of retail stores and shops throughout the country (881 000 or one for every 823 people) was only 45 per cent of the number in 1957 (when there was one shop for every 331 people). By 1978 the number was still only 54 per cent of the 1957 figure. In 1985 the number of retail shops was nearly four times the 1957 figure (with one shop for every 134 people). Together with the reopening and rapid expansion of urban and rural markets, and privately run service and catering establishments, the 1980s saw a huge increase in the extent of the retail trade network (Zhang Yigeng, 1983; 1984a; 1984b). By 1985 the number of units in the catering trade was 11.6 times the number in 1978 (with individually run units increasing nearly 33 times), and service trade units were 17 times as numerous (with individual units increasing 39 times) (*Statistical Yearbook of China 1986*, p. 413). Wan Zhigui (1989) provides a short summary of the development of various types of ownership forms in supplying retail goods. Soviet observers remarked on the large numbers of small shops in China during the 1950s compared with the Soviet Union, and during the 1980s one observer remarked on the much better retail situation in general in China than in the Soviet Union (Johnson, 1983: 443–5), a point also made by Bonavia (1980: 174). This was one highly visible effect of economic reform.

The odd retail-distribution practices found in China can be attributed both to Maoist asceticism and, during the reform period, to excess demand and irrational prices. This first is illustrated by the Red Guards' banning of certain undesirable products from sale and by the interesting case of light bulbs (Butterfield, 1983: 151). A new domestic light bulb could be purchased only if a used one was surrendered. The bulbs were numbered according to locality, making it quite specific which bulb had to be produced. Lost bulbs had to be reported to the police from whom a letter of explanation could be obtained. The second is illustrated by another phenomenon of the 1980s. Shop assistants would insist that in addition to the item wanted the customer had to buy some other item as well, effectively a forced tie-in sale. This practice is known as *dapei*, literally 'pairing'. Examples of pairing I have heard of are teapots and beer with colour television sets, and cheap cigarettes with good brands. The practice effectively increases the price of the desired item, helps the shop to reduce its stocks of unsaleable products, and maybe even signals to the planners and producers that people are actually willing to buy the slow items as they do eventually get sold. Shortages of goods lead the Chinese 'to go to the back door' (*zou houmen*) to obtain things in short supply (Butterfield, 1983: 135–66); the Soviet citizen obtains things 'on the left' (*nalevo*).

Retail commodities sold through state shops are sold at planned prices, which include state fixed prices (*pai jia*) and floating prices (*fudong jiage*) where the limits of the float are often set by the government. From 1962 price management was in the hands of the National Price Council (*Quanguo Wujia Weiyuanhui*), which was abolished in 1970; its work was taken over by the State Planning Commission. In August 1977 it was reconstituted as the State Price Bureau (*Guojia Wujia Zongju*). Major decisions on state retail-price changes come down from this body. Goods sold on the urban and rural markets are sold at market prices, but the government has often exercised direct control over such prices and uses its own price policy to influence market prices. For example, rationed goods are often sold at higher prices without the need of a ration ticket. This free availability of such goods puts an effective limit on the prices on free markets. Peanut oil, for example, could be had for 2.8 *yuan* a catty without a ration coupon compared to 0.85 *yuan* with such a coupon in Peking in the late 1970s (Chinn, 1980: 751–2). The implementation of State Council decrees on price control is one of the responsibilities of the State (or General, as it is sometimes translated) Administration of Industry and Commerce (*Guojia Gongshang Xingzheng Guanli Ju*), established in 1949. It was re-established in 1978 after languishing during the Cultural Revolution period (Lutz, 1983). This body and its regional offices are responsible for ensuring that goods are sold at state-determined prices where this is the appropriate method and for ensuring that free-market retail prices do not exceed state-approved limits. It encourages people to inspect local markets and to report cases of overcharging (Solinger, 1987).

Chinese price policy has undoubtedly been aimed at securing stable retail prices (Ma, 1982a: 485–8), but this does not necessarily mean frozen (*dongjie*) prices (*Jianming Jiage Cidian*, pp. 54–6). The general principles of policy have been to ensure basically stable retail prices, to narrow the gap between agricultural and industrial prices, and to create rational price differences according to quality differences and other factors. The main means of securing price stability for the urban population was the policy adopted towards the eighteen categories of commodities most important to workers and staff that took about 60 per cent of their expenditure. The prices of these commodities were strictly controlled, even during the difficult years of 1959–61; were supplied by the government through unified purchase and supply (that is, state procurement and rationing) and were subsidised (Ma, 1982a: 487; *Jianming Jiage Cidian*, p. 73). This does not mean that other retail prices were never adjusted. The *Concise Dictionary of Prices* (*Jianming Jiage Cidian*, p. 54) specifically states that an aspect of price policy during the period 1960–62 was to use high prices to withdraw currency from circulation, and section 2.5 above quoted the views of Chinese economists on the reasons for such price increases during this period. Commodities were divided into three categories (*sanlei wuzi*) and marketed under the principle of unified planning, dispersed management (*tongyi jihua, fenji guanli*) (Ma, 1982a: 293–4). The first category covered the important retail commodities such as grain, edible oil, cotton, cloth and coal, marketed by state monopoly and strictly controlled by the State Council. The second category covered such things as pigs, eggs, tea, bicycles and sewing machines, controlled by central ministries and commissions. The third category covered everything else.

From 20 August 1967 price policy was greatly simplified when the State Council and the Party Central Committee issued a decree to 'Further practise economy and make revolution, control social purchasing power, strengthen the management of funds and supplies and prices'. There was a general freezing of prices for about twelve years. This typifies the Cultural Revolution's distrust of economic incentives and signals and gave rise to the characterisation that before 1978 China followed a policy of 'low wages, high employment, low prices and low consumption' (Lin, 1989: 17). As a result it was accepted that there was a debt owed to the people because of their poor material position (*shenghuo fangmiande qianzhang*). Prices were again used for economic purposes in 1979 to discharge this debt when agricultural procurement prices were increased. Many retail price adjustments followed. The number of commodities in the first category of unified planning was reduced from 131 to 37 in 1979 and to 11 in 1982 (Wan, 1984: 374). Private trade in grain and other goods was legalised from 1979, and many commodities were procured by state commercial units at negotiated prices (*yi jia*). The government reacted to many increases in negotiated and market prices by a series of decrees on price control and tried to increase its control over prices by enforcing its official prices. The most important of such attempts were in April and December 1980 (Wang and Wang, 1982: 226–7; Wan, 1984: 400), January 1982, July 1982 and May 1983 (Ishihara, 1983: 5).

Solinger (1987) analyses the 1980 price increases and subsequent policy reactions in detail, pointing out the extent to which these price increases came as a surprise to Chinese leaders and caused problems of interpretation for economists. This is an important point. After a long period of price stability there was bound to be a problem in adjusting to the possibility of price rises. This means that reactions to events causing price rises will differ according to historical circumstances. The reactions to factors causing price rises will differ when they occur for the first time in twenty years from when they occur for the fifth year in a row. For this reason we should not expect the same quantitative reaction to the same quantitative causes. Peebles (1984a: 50; 1984c) shows that the open inflationary experience of 1980 was greater than would be expected given that year's degree of excess demand and that the inflation of 1981 was considerably less. This is consistent with the timing of the price control decree of December 1980.

This point about the possible variation in the extent of open inflation for a given degree of excess demand will be examined empirically in section 6.6.

The 1980s saw a general unchecked upward drift in the retail price level, and this gave rise to a debate about whether currency inflation would encourage economic growth or whether it would be harmful to the economy through inflation. This is a major question of monetary economics in developing economies. Chinese economists tended to stress the policy of currency stability and no inflation. Those who advocated currency inflation argued that an annual rate of 3 to 5 per cent would be a way of supplementing inadequate funds for investment. As there was a rationing system basic price stability could be preserved even though the money supply increased. The Japanese experience of credit inflation of the 1960s was cited in support of this view, and Japan was said to have achieved the 'four highs': high wages, high productivity, high profits and high accumulation (Hu and Han, 1983: 385–6). Most opposed this view, arguing that socialist China differed from capitalist economies. One aspect was that in China demand already exceeded supply, so such monetary expansion would make the situation worse and cause prices to rise. Such price increases would make planning difficult to determine and implement and not be conducive to the correct application of the law of value (Hu and Han, 1983: 386–7). Chen Wenlin (1989: 114–27) devotes a chapter to this issue, entitling it 'Inflation cannot stimulate economic growth'. He argues that attempts by other Chinese economists to use evidence from Western countries' experience to justify China's using an inflationary policy are misguided because of the different nature of the Chinese economy. One different feature he notes is that China is an economy of consumer goods shortages and overinvestment whereas Western economies usually experience excess aggregate supply and insufficient aggregate demand.

A major break in price reform policy occurred in the second half of 1984. Price reform policy changed from being one of adjusting prices to one of freeing prices (*you 'yi tiao wei zhu' zhuanbian wei 'yi fang wei zhu'*) (Chen Youping, 1989: 31). The period 1979–84 has been described as one when price adjustment was the main aspect of policy and freeing prices was just a subsidiary aspect (*yi tiao wei zhu, yi fang wei fu*). From 1985 the policy concentrated on freeing prices (*yi fang wei zhu, yi tiao wei fu*) (Zhang Chaohuang, 1989: 55). In 1985, for example, 47 per cent of social commodity retail sales were made at state-determined prices (*guojia ding jia*), 19 per cent were made at prices under state guidance (*guojia zhidao jia*), and 34 per cent were made at prices subject to market regulation (*shichang tiaojie jia*). By 1988 the proportion subject to market regulation had risen to 49.3 per cent, leaving 50.3 per cent to be state determined (28.9 per cent) or state guided (21.8 per cent) (*Zhongguo Wujia Nianjian 1989*, 351). This means that from 1985 we might expect to see a greater responsiveness of the general retail-price level to similarly strong quantitative causes of price increases. This will be examined empirically in sections 6.6 and 7.1. Despite the changes in price policy Zhang Chaohuang (1989: 56), describing the effects of the price adjustment policies of 1988, still includes withdrawing currency from circulation as one of the positive results. Institutional change had not removed this aspect of the effects of list price increases. Chen Wenlin (1989: 142 discusses the effects of the 1984 price increases. He shows that there was still an effect on government revenues of the price rises but that the largest part of the extra expenditure did not go to the government any more. He estimates that only 19 per cent went to the government. This means that a larger price rise would be necessary to bring in any given amount of extra revenue.

4.5 Retail price data

Since the publication of the *Statistical Yearbook of China* series and subsequent more specialised statistical sources, we have complete time-series data for a number of important retail price indexes. Appendix II lists the most important. Among these we have data for the general retail price index. The *Statistical Yearbooks* always state that this index is a weighted average of state list prices, negotiated prices and market prices. More precisely, it is a weighted average of planned prices (which include state-determined list prices plus floating prices, the limits of float being set by the government), negotiated prices and market prices. In 1981 these three categories constituted respectively 92.5, 3.7 and 3.8 per cent of the value of total commodity retail sales (Ling, 1982: V–349). I have never seen a clear statement of the weighting given to market prices in the general index. A vague, but recent and presumably authoritative, statement is that of a World Bank team who state that the weighting for sales through the free market 'is about 12–15%'—note the present tense (World Bank, 1990a: 35, fn. 6). Clearly, market prices constituted a very small part of the general index in 1981, much less before 1979 and no more than about 15 per cent in the late 1980s.

In addition there are available separate general indexes for list prices, list prices of consumer goods, and list price indexes for a number of separate commodity groups, with data for urban and rural areas given separately.[7] We now have complete time-series data back to 1950 of the free market price index (*jishi maoyi jiage zhishu*) of consumer goods. There is also an index of the cost of living of staff and workers, which is a weighted average of the general retail price index and an index of prices of services. This index changes very much in line with the general retail price index. Western statistical and econometric studies have tended to use the general retail price index alone as an indicator of price movements. Some Chinese studies, such as Huang (1988a), use the national income price deflator. This index is published in the International Monetary Fund's *Yearbook*. Chen Yue (1988: 62) gives the annual changes in the national income price deflator. The *Statistical Yearbooks* also publish a general index of purchasing prices of agricultural produce and of the prices of industrial products sold in the countryside. The ratio of these latter two indexes is also published; it is an important indicator of the terms of trade of the agricultural sector (Ma, 1982a: 496–7) and is commonly analysed. Tian Shanfu (1985) is just one example of such analysis. This ratio is known in Chinese as the *jiandaocha* (scissors difference), just as the term was used in the economic debates about the place of agriculture in development in the Soviet Union in the 1920s (Erlich, 1967; Nove, 1982).

The price indexes published in the *Statistical Yearbook of China* are almost certainly averages of the year's prices. Articles and speeches by officials often include references to price levels and their change for different periods within the year. Wang and Yang (1989: 9) cite monthly price indexes, so the indexes are obviously compiled on a monthly basis. *China Statistics Monthly* publishes monthly price indexes for years in the late 1980s, and *Zhongguo Jingji Nianjian*, for example (1987: V–39), also started to publish them in its review of the previous year's developments in commerce. Sometimes price indexes are quoted for nine-month periods and sometimes for end-of-year on end-of-year. The theory offered in section 6.6 would work better with end-of-year-based price indexes, but these do not seem to be available for earlier years. Aspects of the compilation of the price indexes are discussed by Ishihara (1983) and *Zhongguo Wujia Nianjian 1989* (426–9). Industrial wholesale price indexes are published but have generally not received much analysis as they have no direct impact on the population's standard of living. Interested readers are referred to Donnithorne (1967: 439–41), Chai (1987b) and Chan (1987).

4.6 Chinese money

The *Renminbi* is the sole legal currency of the People's Republic of China. Chinese economists are still debating its nature and source of value. Such old debates as whether it is backed by gold or not still continue well into the 1980s. Xiao Zhuoji (1980), Li Chonghuai (1982) and Tan Shouding (1984) represent various points of view. Chen Wenlin (1984) does us a service by discussing some of these opinions, and Hu and Han (1983: 357–82) summarise various schools of thought from the 1950s to the 1980s. The 'official' position on the value basis of the currency seems to be that written by Yi Hongren and presented in Ma (1982a: 469–70):

> The *Renminbi* is an independent and autonomous currency. The state has specified that the currency can only circulate within the country's boundaries and it is prohibited to remove it from the country. The circulation of gold, silver and foreign currencies is prohibited and this ensures that the currency does not feel the effects of changes on the international financial markets. From 1969 the *Renminbi* has been used to set prices and settle accounts in economic relations with the rest of the world.
>
> The *Renminbi* does not have a fixed gold content [*han jin liang*]. Its stability is not merely based on the continuous increase in the state's holdings of gold reserves [*huangjin chubei*] but is principally determined by the fact that the state has large holdings of commodities which it can put on the market at stable prices to guarantee the currency. Therefore, for a long period, the *Renminbi* has had a comparatively stable value.

Chen Wenlin (1984: 37) quotes Stalin's view about the value basis of Soviet currency and states that this has been quoted by many Chinese writers and has had a great influence in China. Stalin's view, hence the orthodox Soviet view, was that it is the state's ability to supply commodities at a fixed price, not state gold holdings, that guarantees the Soviet currency. Ma Yinchu and He Gaozhu have been the chief proponents of this explanation of the value basis of the *Renminbi* (Chen Wenlin, 1984:

37, 43). The same crucial point that the *Renminbi* is not officially backed by gold is made in the important economics dictionary *Jingji Da Cidian—Jinrong Juan* (1987: 23) as well as by Xue Muqiao (1982b: 117). Xue Muqiao and Li Chonghuai are the best-known representatives of the view that the Chinese currency has no connection with gold at all. The main adherents to the view that the *Renminbi* is somehow based on gold are Xu Dixin and Huang Da.

We can see that the *Renminbi*, like most of the world's major currencies, is a fiat currency; it has no intrinsic value; it is not in itself a commodity-based currency like gold or silver coins would be; and it is not convertible into gold or silver, foreign currencies or government debt at a known rate. In other words, it has no backing. The *Renminbi* is issued by the Chinese government and is pure government debt. As far as I know there has never been, nor is there, any constitutional or legal limit on the amount that can be issued. The currency is a form of credit note issued by the government. As Shubik (1987: 317) puts it, 'A dollar bill is a zero interest freely negotiable perpetuity without recourse'. This is true also of the *Renminbi* to some extent.[8] Shubik (1987: 317) defines a fiat money as 'a form of credit where the issuing party is the state and the recourse of a individual creditor is negligible against the state, but by the law of the state the fiat money must be accepted in payment to extinguish other debts'. This would be correct for a market economy, but it does not entirely accord with the case of the *Renminbi*, which in one sense is a less desirable form of currency than a 'dollar' and in another sense is more desirable. It is less desirable because the Chinese government has for many years prohibited the existence of markets on which the currency could be easily transformed into foreign currencies, gold or other precious metals, financial assets or productive assets. It is more desirable in the sense that the Chinese system is based on the belief that the individual *does* have recourse as a creditor to the state as the state supplies the population with the bulk of retail commodities. At times this supply has not been made solely in exchange for the fiat money (ration coupons were also required), but the theory of the system, as expressed in the quotation above, is that the state discharges its debt represented by the *Renminbi* banknote by supplying retail goods, ideally at constant prices and in just the quantities that people wanted. In a market economy the government of the day does not make such a guarantee, nor does it guarantee the purchasing power of the currency. When there were significant inflations in market economies the government typically seeks scapegoats in the form of greedy trade unions or monopolists who forced up prices, or speculators who forced up interest rates or sold the currency on the foreign exchange market, thus depreciating it. Such excuses are less common these days wherever monetarist ideas have been accepted, as these make excessive monetary growth the sole reason for inflation and government policy the main reason for excessive monetary growth. Governments *are* now blamed for inflation.

The *Renminbi* is a fiat money, but there is more guarantee about its value than in the case of market economies. However, there are limited opportunities in China for individuals to take their own measures to safeguard the value of their *Renminbi* holdings compared to opportunities in market economies, where individuals can easily obtain and hold foreign currencies. If Chinese planners take seriously their responsibility of backing the currency with retail supplies, as indicated in the quotation from Ma Hong's book on page 97, then we can use this to try to explain their behaviour in terms of money supply issue, retail pricing, consumption goods production and so on.

This view of the value basis of the *Renminbi* has led to various concepts of its actual nature. The famous Chinese economist Sun Yefang argued in 1959 that under a planned economy money, when used to pay wages, is really just a 'labour certificate' (*laodong quan*). It is a certificate indicating how much labour a worker has provided for society, and on the basis of the system of distribution according to labour it shows the worker's 'right' (*quan*) to a portion of the consumer goods in the state's warehouses. The state is in the position of a debtor and the worker a creditor. If such certificates were issued without a sufficient supply of consumer goods, they would just be like a creditor's certificate (*zhaiquan zhengmingshu*), that is, a labour certificate. This view was opposed by Guan Mengjiao who said that, if money were really a labour certificate, commodity production would cease to exist and so would money. Money would just be like a theatre ticket and not circulate. In fact, however, money does circulate, and workers can use it to buy things not only on free markets but also from individual producers, so Chinese money is a general equivalent of value and is money in the true sense. Zhou Jun also disagreed with Sun Yefang, arguing that only in an advanced stage of socialism could money be based on labour time and be a labour certificate. At the present stage of socialism money still has to perform a role in controlling production and distribution and so remains a means of payment and accumulation (Hu and Han, 1983: 369–71). The *Jingji Da Cidian—Jinrong Juan* (1987: 23) also briefly summarises the three different viewpoints on the value basis of the *Renminbi*.

4.7 Household financial asset choice

In the traditional socialist planned-economy model there is a very limited range of financial assets available for households to hold. There are either currency holdings or savings deposits.

Chinese policy towards private savings deposits has always been that they are 'voluntary, freely available for withdrawal, bear interest, and are confidential' (*cunkuan ziyuan, qu kuan ziyou, cunkuan you xi, wei chuhu baomi*) (Ma, 1982a: 472), and the right to their ownership has always been protected in the various Chinese constitutions. However, there have been reports of savings withdrawals' being discouraged when local cadres disapproved of the intended expenditure the savings deposits would produce. This was particularly true during the Cultural Revolution period (see Bennett, 1978: 183 for an example). Savings deposits were made more attractive by interest rate increases on 1 April 1979, 1 July 1980 and 1 April 1982, and in April and August 1985.[9] The timing of these increases will be analysed in section 6.9, and subsequent changes will be detailed in chapter 7. In addition, a longer term deposit of eight years with a higher rate was introduced in April 1982. *Renminbi* time deposits held by overseas Chinese have attracted higher rates than those of Chinese residents.

From 1982 there were available current (demand) savings deposits, six-month, one-year, three-year, five-year and eight-year term deposits, and time deposits that could be accumulated through regular instalments. There has never been a confiscatory currency reform in China. Savings deposits and currency are the liabilities of the government banking system.

Private enterprises, if allowed to exist, are of such small scale that they do not extensively issue their own debt instruments such as stocks or bonds, which households could hold and trade. This rules out a large range of privately issued financial assets. Furthermore, as Gurley (1976: 272) puts it, 'The theory and design of a socialist society are incompatible with a sophisticated financial-intermediary structure'. Such a structure would issue its own debt instruments—such as the range of deposits and financial assets offered by private banks, building societies (savings and loans associations), insurance companies and so on in a market economy—and would channel funds of surplus units to borrowers. In the socialist model this allocation of funds is mainly done by the state's accepting household deposits but, more importantly, by obtaining taxes and profits from state enterprises. These funds are then distributed to state enterprises for their investment purposes by means of the government budget or banking system. To all intents and purposes the range of assets offered by the state sector is very limited and that by the private sector virtually non-existent.

In China there are no private bank accounts that can be transferred by cheque.[10] This makes many transactions very difficult. People wishing to send money from one part of the country to another have to use the post-office money-remittances service or internal settlement through the banking system if both parties have accounts. From the mid 1980s, enterprises that were expected to obtain materials outside the system of planned distribution, where they would be paid for by cashless debits from their transfer accounts at the People's Bank of China, found that they had to use cash for such settlements. There were many stories of purchasing agents travelling the country with many tens of thousand of *yuan* in cash to make such deals.

From about 1984 fixed-term bank accounts in which a limited range of major foreign currencies could be deposited became available for Chinese citizens. Bank of China regulations governing these accounts came into effect on 20 November 1985 (see *People's Republic of China Yearbook 1986*, pp. 325–6). The *People's Republic of China Yearbook 1985* (pp. 310–12) also details regulations concerning such deposits, but their withdrawal seems to have been limited to amounts in *Renminbi* only (article 8 of the regulations). The later regulations state that foreign currency, plus earned interest, could be withdrawn.

In addition to cash and savings deposits, households could also hold government bonds. The major periods of bond issue were in 1950 (People's Victory Bonds, denominated in commodity units), during 1954–58 (National Economic Construction Bonds) and from 1981 (People's Republic of China Treasury Bonds).[11] The bond issues of the 1950s included sales to individuals and were all repaid by 1968. There was no government borrowing for the entire period 1959–79 as China adopted a policy of *Yi wu nei zhai, er wu wei zhai* (firstly, no internal debt, and secondly, no external debt) (*Zhongguo Jingji Nianjian 1988*, pp. V-25–7). This is why the propaganda articles of the mid 1970s about the stability of the currency were able to boast that China had no internal or external debt. The issues in the 1950s were for both individuals and corporates such as enterprises and organisations. Durand (1965: 285–93) details the issues in the 1950s, as do Wu (1956: 67–8, 76–85), Donnithorne (1967: 381–2) and Ma (1982a: 462). Igashiri (1985) discusses the issues in the 1980s in detail. Bonds were sold through well organised campaigns, and it is generally felt that they were bought reluctantly. Donnithorne (1967: 382) called them 'a form of forced savings'. They could be inherited and transferred but had very limited liquidity as they could not be used as currency nor sold. In 1985 limited rights for cashing in bonds at the banks were allowed, but this remained a fair way from establishing anything like a bond market or full cashability. During the period 1981–85 domestic bond sales averaged only about 3.6 per cent of total government expenditure in any year (Igarishi, 1985: 8).

In addition to government-issued debt, other financial assets emerged during the economic reform period of the 1980s but only on a very limited scale. For example, from 1982 to January 1984, 250 million *yuan*'s worth of shares in the supply and marketing co-operatives was sold to the rural population in an attempt to turn them into genuine co-operatives (Riskin, 1987: 361) or as Wan (1989: 51) puts it, turning them from being officially run (*guanban*) to being run by the people (*minban*). From mid 1984 enterprises started to issue their own stocks. These issues were often arranged and underwritten by state banks. These shares often paid a guaranteed return and a variable return dependent on performance when they were cashed in (Brotman, 1985: 22). They were for a fixed period, making them more like corporate bonds than real equities. The rate of interest paid and the eventual 'dividend' on cashing in provided a rate of return higher than that offered on savings deposits. In one writer's opinion they were among the few available assets that offered a positive real rate of interest (Engle, 1986: 36). These shares were not transferable, and the Shanghai stock exchange and other exchanges were opened on a limited scale. These purchases were mostly voluntary, but there were reports of workers being forced to 'buy' shares. This was just an easy way for enterprises to reduce current wages as they were effectively paying their workers in official money and their own pieces of paper. Such shares could be regarded as a money substitute for the enterprise although they would, presumably, have to be repaid in the future out of increased profits. Share issues expanded in 1985, probably as a result of the credit squeeze initiated after the large currency growth at the end of 1984. Enterprises could issue shares to the public to raise funds not available from the banks and by selling them to workers could reduce their wage bill.

4.8 The two spheres of monetary circulation

The traditional Chinese economic system shares with the Soviet Union and other planned economies a specific feature of its monetary system that sharply differentiates these planned economies from the widely familiar systems found in market economies. It is that monetary flows occur in two separate spheres (*lingyu*) in the economy. This feature of the Chinese monetary system was adopted from the Soviet model and became entrenched in the early 1950s as control over state-enterprise financial flows was unified by the requirement that state enterprises held deposits at the state bank. In the 'passive' non-cash sphere (*fei xianjin lintong lingyu*) state enterprises, organisations, schools, army units and so on are required to use cashless transfers through the banking system when purchases are made from each other. Such monetary transfers are necessary as each unit is subject to independent accounting so that its performance can be monitored. In this sphere money, along with prices, is merely an accounting device required by the accounting system. This name for system, '*jingji hesuan zhidu*' (economic accounting system), is a direct translation of the Soviet term '*khozraschet*', an abbreviation for '*khozyaistvennii raschet*' (economic accounting). The system was adopted directly from the Soviet Union (Kwang, 1966: 74–5). Monetary transfers passively *follow* the flow of goods within the state sector, and the offer of money plays no role in initiating or consummating economic transactions; they are supposed to be initiated by the planning mechanism. According to Dembinski (1988) it was the Polish economist Wlodzimierz Brus who first used the terms 'passive' and 'active' to describe the two aspects of money in the planned socialist system. Transfers between state units use 'passive' money, which in itself has no real ability to cause a transaction to be made. Huang (1988a: 35) identifies passive money in China as consisting of 'transfer accounts [*zhuanzhang*] of enterprises, organisations and units', which he also calls 'quasi-money' (*zhun huobi*) and later (p. 37) stresses cannot freely be transformed into currency.

In contrast to the 'passive' non-cash sphere there is the 'active' sphere (*xianjin liutong lingyu*) where cash is used. This covers all transactions between the combined state sector and the population. It consists, on the one side, of wage payments in state units, money paid for procuring agricultural products from the rural population, subsidies and interest payments on savings deposits and, on the other side, of household purchases of retail commodities from state shops, payments for services such as house rent, payments of direct taxes (if any), licence fees and depositing savings at the state bank. For such transactions money is said to be 'active' because, in theory, households can spend such cash receipts and holdings anywhere, at any time and on any item desired. Such expenditures are not subject to planning or directives as are transfers within the state sector.[12] The planning mechanism must ensure that its real plans, such as the supply of consumer goods, is compatible with the desired expenditure flows expressed in active cash expenditures. If not, household desired expenditures will not be realised.

Figure 4.1 shows how a Chinese textbook on public finance and money divides the economy into the two spheres of monetary circulation. It is clear that the individual (*geren*) receives cash from a limited number of sources. This presentation shows them as remittances from overseas Chinese (*qiao hui*), wages and other labour income from productive and other enterprises (*gongzi laodongri peifen deng shouru*), wages from organisations

Figure 4.1 Major monetary flows in the Chinese economy

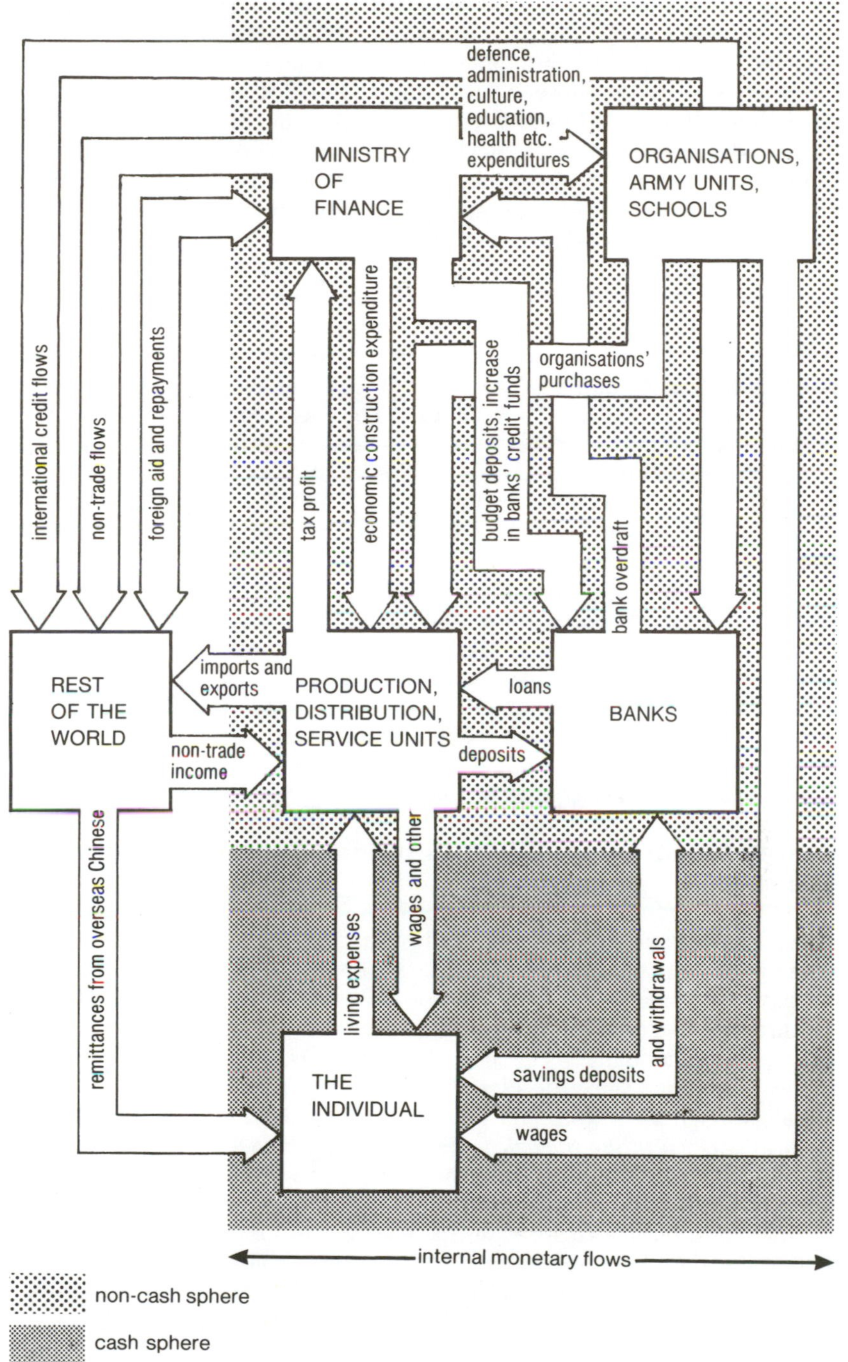

Source: Adapted from Huang et al. (1981, vol. 2: 501).

and units such as schools and army units, and the withdrawal of savings deposits. The individual makes only two forms of expenditures: living expenses (*shenghuo feiyong kaizhi*) and savings deposits in the state bank. Now this is obviously a simplified picture of Chinese monetary flows. It ignores private trade between individuals. The Soviet way of presenting these relationships specifically recognises the monetary flows between households and their consequences.[13] In the simplified world of Figure 4.1 there is no real circulation of cash; cash just gets issued in the form of wages and so on by the state sector and returns directly to it or its bank. This perhaps is how planners would like to see the role of money in the planned system, but things are a bit more complicated than this in reality.

Monetary flows within the household sector merely redistribute already existing cash between individuals and play no role in changing the amount of cash in circulation. This is the importance of this relationship between household receipts and expenditures; it determines the growth of the narrow measure of the money supply. The cash flows from production units and organisations on the one side to individuals on the other, and the reverse flows from individuals, are monitored by the banking system's cash plan. The flows between the banking system and the rest of the economy are monitored by the banking system's credit plan (Ma, 1982a: 476–9; Chai, 1981: 39–45).

It would be pleasing to be able to put monetary valuations on all these flows, but this is not possible for all of them given existing categories used in the data sources. However, it is important, and possible, to indicate the most important flows and the sources of data on them. The flows to and from what I have labelled the 'Ministry of Finance' in Figure 4.1 (the original just calls it *caizheng*, public finance) are shown in the government's budget.

The most important source of budget receipts are the taxes and profit remittances from state enterprises, mostly from state industrial enterprises. From 1980 budget revenue from all state enterprises was less than that from industrial enterprises because foreign trade corporations and grain enterprises were consistently making losses and required subsidies. The most important tax source is the industrial and commercial tax levied on state production and distribution enterprises (Ma, 1982a: 458). Since 1983 tax payments have become much more important than profit remittances because of the policy of substituting taxes for such remittances, as was discussed in section 3.10. The agricultural tax has never been an important source of revenue since the First Five-year Plan period. Chinese statistics include foreign borrowing and domestic bond sales in the category 'taxes of various kinds'. (See *Statistical Yearbook of China 1986*, pp. 511–13 for the budget revenue classifications and data.) From the flows in Figure 4.1 it appears that households do not pay taxes. Apart from licence fees and recently introduced taxes on the income of private and collective enterprises their direct tax burden is light. However, households do bear a tax burden as they generate the profits of state retail enterprises because retail prices include state taxes, thus transferring money from households to the budget via retail profits and taxes.

The major items of budget expenditure are for capital construction and for defence, administration, culture, education, health and so on. The government budget supplies state enterprises with free allocations of funds for their use for fixed investment purposes. This item is known as 'appropriations for capital construction'; it constituted 45.9 per cent of total budget expenditure in 1970, for example, and 28.8 per cent in 1985. Economic reform saw a move away from such budget allocations to the use of loans from the banking system. From 1985 such funds were to be provided as repayable loans from the Construction Bank, but some capital projects were still able to get funds from the budget (*Statistical Yearbook of China 1987*, p. 817). The flows from the budget to units for administration, national defence, culture, education, science and public health constituted 35 per cent of budget expenditure in 1985. The other expenditure items were loan repayments, pensions, institutions in commerce, industry and commerce, technical updating and trial production in enterprises, and some others. The *Statistical Yearbook of China 1986* (pp. 516–20) shows the importance of the various categories of budget expenditure. The relationship between the budget and the banking system is summarised by two parallel flows in Figure 4.1: the borrowing the government can undertake from what is really its own bank, and the transfer of budget funds to the banking system for its use.

4.9 Monetary data

On 3 July 1981 the People's Bank of China released national monetary data and stated that it would undertake to release such data regularly. This was in sharp contrast with earlier Chinese practice when currency data were regarded as a state secret (Okazaki, 1961: 1) and not published. The journal *Zhongguo Jinrong* (Chinese Finance) began to publish the balance sheet of the banking system on a quarterly basis. These tables included currency, savings deposits and various other deposits figures and were for 1979 onwards. They were the basis for tables published in *International Financial Statistics* from its October 1981 issue. The *Statistical Yearbooks* published complete time-series data of individual savings deposits from their first issue in 1982. The *Statistical Yearbook of China 1986* published an important table of the 'Sources and distribution of purchasing power of consumer goods' for 1952–85, which included data on 'cash in hand' and savings deposits that would be held by individuals and organisations. Byrd (1983: 138) published index numbers of currency in circulation for 1953–79, which could be used to construct a whole series in *yuan* amounts. (See Peebles, 1987b, for such use of these data.) Various Chinese articles contain other series, sometimes only in index number form. For example, Zheng (1986b: 37) published a series for 1952–84 of currency plus all current accounts in *yuan*. Huang (1988b: 190) published three series in *yuan* for 1952–86: currency; currency plus enterprise, organisation and units' deposits; and currency plus residents' savings deposits. Index numbers for the same series were published in Huang (1988a). Zhang Junkuo (1988a: 34) published index numbers of currency and 'broad money' for 1953–87. Western econometric work has tended to use the currency series, sometimes citing it from Chow (1987), but Chow's explanation of his source for this material (the *Statistical Yearbook*'s table of the banking system's balances) is not convincing, as this only goes back to 1979 and to 1977 for currency in circulation as published in *International Financial Statistics*. However, the compilation *Fenjinde Sishi Nian 1949–1989* (1989: 429–32) did publish the banking system's statements annually right back to 1952, and these included a complete series of currency in circulation (p. 429).

An interesting point about many Chinese sources that present data on cash and savings deposits in the context of incomes and expenditures is that the data are not labelled 'money supply' at all but rather 'surplus purchasing power' (*jieyu goumai li*)[14] or 'remaining purchasing power at the end of the year'.[15] We now have a number of monetary series for China going right back to 1952, unlike the case of the Soviet Union where currency data have never been published in postwar statistical sources. Data on certain monetary series are presented in Tables I.1 to I.4. Generally speaking, they are not collected together in Chinese sources but can be found either as a series of currency-in-circulation data in the accounts of the banking system and as savings deposits, either of households or of households and organisations, in the tables of the sources and distribution of purchasing power.

As economic reform progressed in the 1980s and, no doubt, as more statistics were published, Chinese economists started to think in terms of the relevance of broader categories of money supply than just either currency or currency plus savings deposits. As Chen Wenlin (1989: 55) notes, in Chinese economic circles there is no unanimity on which measure of money is appropriate, and he lists five concepts ranging from *M0* (currency) to *M4* (currency plus all deposits, including enterprise fixed deposits and treasury deposits and treasury bonds), making this last measure more like a liquidity concept than a money supply definition.

4.10 Changes in the money supply

We can derive two ways of looking at the change in the narrow measures of the money supply in China. Using a flow-of-funds approach adapted from Cheng (1981: appendix A) and supplementing it with a more detailed analysis of the banking system's role in monetary creation, we can obtain a reasonable understanding of the reasons for money supply changes for certain recent years.

We divide the economy into four sectors: households (H), enterprises (E), the government (G) and the banking system (B). The household sector includes all workers and agricultural producers, and the enterprise sector includes all productive enterprises and state retail shops. All variables are annual monetary flows. We identify the sources and uses of funds (both cash and non-cash) for each sector:

Sector:	*Source of funds*:	*Use of funds*:	
Government:	$T + B_G$	$= C_G + W_G + I_G + D_G$	(1)
Enterprises:	$C_H + C_G + I_G + B_E$	$= W_E + T + D_E$	(2)

$$\text{Banking:} \quad D_G + D_E + S_H + CURR = B_G + B_E \tag{3}$$
$$\text{Households:} \quad W_G + W_E = C_H + S_H + CURR \tag{4}$$

where:

T = taxes and profit remittances to the government
B = borrowing from the banking system (loans)
C = sales of retail goods and services by the state sector
W = wage payments, including bonuses and subsidies plus agricultural procurements
I = investment
D = increases in balances at the banks (deposits)
S = change in saving and other household deposits at banks
$CURR$ = the change in currency in circulation.

Subscripts indicate which sector is responsible for the flow.

From equations 3 and 4 alone we can obtain two expressions for the change in the narrow measures of the money supply. From equation 4,

$$\left.\begin{aligned} CURR + S_H &= W_G + W_E - C_H \\ \text{or} \quad CURR &= W_G + W_E - C_H - S_H \end{aligned}\right\} \quad (5)$$

The former measure ($CURR + S_H$) will be called the *narrow* measure and the latter (here labelled $CURR$) will be called the *narrowest* measure.

The increase in cash and savings deposits in any period equals household money income minus the purchase of consumer goods from the state sector. It is assumed that households pay no direct taxes. The second equation shows that the increase in currency equals household money income minus purchases of consumer goods minus the increase in household savings deposits. The change in either narrow measure of the money supply is just the difference between these two monetary flows: household money income from the combined state sector, and household expenditure with or without savings deposits. The flow of funds from households to the state sector is referred to in Chinese textbooks and articles as *xianjin huilong* (or more generally as *huobi huilong*), literally, 'money returns to the basket'.[16] As Huang (1988a: 36) puts it, there are the channels of commodity withdrawal, *shangpin huilong* (C_H above), and the credit withdrawal, *xinyong huilong* (S_H above). Other sources divide incomes and expenditures into more than just these few items. For example, Liu (1980: 168–9) divides the sources of purchasing power and the use of it each into four basic channels (*qudao*), as does the *Jianming Jinrong Cidian* (1984: 155–6). The four channels through which currency is withdrawn from circulation are through commodity withdrawal, services withdrawal, credit withdrawal (through household savings) and public financial withdrawal (through taxes). The textbook *Huobi Liutong Guanli Xue* (1985: 5–6) uses five categories on either side of the balance. Equation 5, however, captures the essence of the narrow money supply process.

From equation 3 we can obtain another expression:

$$\left.\begin{aligned} CURR + S_H &= (B_E - D_E) + (B_G - D_G) \\ \text{or} \quad CURR &= (B_E - D_E) + (B_G - D_G) - S_H \end{aligned}\right\} \quad (6)$$

The increase in the narrow measure of the money supply equals the difference between enterprise bank borrowing in any period and its new deposits, plus the difference between the government's bank borrowing and its bank deposits. Bank borrowings are loans, so we can say that the right hand side of equation 6 is enterprise net borrowing (loans minus deposits) plus government net borrowing. The right hand side therefore consists of the state-enterprise borrowing requirement plus the government borrowing requirement.

It is sometimes felt that equation 5 best describes the money supply process in the traditional planned system whereas equation 6 describes the process in a reformed system. Equation 5 visualises money actually being put into circulation at the point of receipt, mainly in the form of wages and so on, and its extinction by retail sales. To show that equations 5 and 6 are identical and that equation 6 implies equation 5, consider the following. From equation 1,

$$(B_G - D_G) = (C_G + W_G + I_G) - T$$

that is, the government's borrowing requirement equals its expenditures minus its tax revenue. From equation 2,

$$(B_E - D_E) = (W_E + T) - (C_H + C_G + I_G)$$

that is, the enterprise borrowing requirement equals expenditures minus revenue. Equation 6 is

$$\begin{aligned} CURR + S_H = (B_G - D_G) \quad &= [(C_G + W_G + I_G) - T] \\ + (B_E - D_E) \quad &+ [(W_E + T) - (C_H + C_G + I_G)] \end{aligned}$$

We must add the two right-hand-side square-bracketed expressions to obtain equation 5. In the right-hand-side top equation, for the items C_G, I_G and T the lower equation contains the same item with opposite sign. When we add the two square-bracketed equations together these items cancel each other out, leaving

$$CURR + S_H = W_G + W_E - C_H$$

which is equation 5.

In the top equation C_G and I_G are government expenditures received by enterprises and so contribute to the government's borrowing requirement, but T is the government's income from enterprises and so is a negative contributor to the government borrowing requirement. T is a required expenditure by enterprises, thus contributing to its borrowing requirement, whereas C_G and I_G are incomes from the government, reducing enterprise borrowing requirement. These flows between enterprises and the government cancel each other out, leaving the flows between the government and households (W_G) and between enterprises and households ($W_E - C_H$, where C_H is the return flow to enterprises for goods, but ultimately to the government as enterprises pay taxes) to determine the change in the narrow money supply. In this approach investment by the government (I_G) has no direct impact on narrow money growth. Only the directly money-income-forming flows in the form of W_G and W_E have this effect.

The clear implication of equation 5 for monetary policy is that wages and retail supplies must be closely controlled and balanced if excessive monetary growth is not to occur (Huang, 1988a). Equation 6 shows how imbalances between bank loans and deposits give rise to increases in the money supply, but equation 6 implies equation 5. The clear implication for a reformed system trying to use economic levers is that bank lending must be controlled as well as the government deficit, but also that controlling the elements of equation 5 will also control those of equation 6. In a reformed system the ultimate aim is to rely on indirect economic levers such as interest rates and bank reserve requirements to achieve this, but it is also clear that it could be achieved by direct administrative controls over bank loans. The main difference between equation 6 and the relevant expression for money creation in a market economy is that equation 6 does not include any bank lending to the private household or productive sector. This is a reasonable first approximation for the Chinese case. The extent of this will be discussed below. The equation also omits any reference to the foreign sector. Otherwise it includes the same two important determinants of monetary growth found in the analysis of the process in a market economy in section 3.3: the government's borrowing requirement, and lending to the productive sector. Although two separate equations for the change in the narrow money supply have been obtained, they are both correct, both must be true at all times, and both can be used. They just look at the process from two different perspectives: equation 5 from the household point of view, and equation 6 from the banks' point of view.

If we were to include enterprises' or other deposits in the money supply, we could use the same approach and show that these deposits are generated by loans from the banking system. Given the nature of the Chinese banking system, even after the reforms of 1984, there is no real limit to the extent of credit creation and the extension of loans. There is no reserve requirement on the specialised banks restricting their ability to increase loans (Chai, 1981). Huang (1988a) forcefully rejects the applicability of the money multiplier concept to the Chinese case and says that there is no limit on banks' deposit-creating ability.[17] We can point out that the only restraining factor is the amount of currency growth that the authorities are likely to tolerate as loans result in cash withdrawals by enterprises and units. It is on the basis of potential currency growth rates that we are likely to be able to understand the timing of the planners' changes in credit policy, monetary policy and other possible reactions.

4.11 Changes in the money supply: two illustrations

The real world equivalents of both equations 5 and 6 can be used. Data for equation 5 are presented in two forms in Chinese statistical sources. This information is equivalent to the 'balance of money incomes and expenditures of the population of the Soviet Union' (full data of which have never been published) and other socialist countries and plays an important part in monetary planning.[18]

Chinese sources present these flows for the purchasing power of the household sector and organisations combined in the *Statistical Yearbook of China*, starting with the 1986 issue (pp. 442–4). Here it is erroneously called 'sources and distributions of purchasing power of consumer goods'. This is incorrect as on the expenditure side retail sales include not only consumer goods but also the sale of agricultural means of production to the rural population. The Chinese term for this balance is 'sources and distribution of social purchasing power' (*shehui goumaili laiyuan he fenpei*). Aggregate data are presented in Table I.3. This purchasing power concept includes the purchasing power of households and organisations. The difference between the income and expenditure sides in any year must equal the increase in both household and organisations' holdings of unspent purchasing power, which will accumulate as their savings deposits and cash in hand (*shoucun xianjin*). In addition there is a separate balance for residents (*jumin*) showing the sources of their money incomes and expenditures (see Table I.4). The difference must equal residents' accumulation of savings deposits and cash, which must necessarily be less than cash in hand as this latter concept also includes organisations' holdings. Many income sources are given in both balances, and the figures balance exactly; that is, incomes minus expenditures in any year equal that year's increase in the relevant money holding with the single odd exception of 1979. This is quite remarkable, and it is likely that the 'other' category makes up the balance. These two balances give complete accounting explanations of why the narrow measure of the money supply changed in any year in terms of the difference between total incomes and expenditures. They do not in themselves explain what factors caused the changes in the extent of the differences between incomes and expenditures in any period. The statistical tables in the *Statistical Yearbook of China* present a larger number of income categories than are presented in equation 5.

Ma (1982a: 579–81) discusses the related concept of 'social commodity purchasing power' (*shehui shangpin goumaili*), in which expenditures on services are ignored. The concept covers the purchasing power of residents (urban and rural) and social organisations over consumer goods plus the purchasing power of rural production brigades and commune members over the means of agricultural production. This is the narrowest purchasing-power concept as it excludes services but is not limited to consumer goods. I have not seen full figures for this concept, only scattered data. (See also Zhang and Li, 1988: 71; and Liu, Chu, Han and Zheng, 1984, for a discussion of how the concept is used in planning.)

These purchasing power figures have been analysed in some prominent Chinese works. For example, Xia and Li (1987: 90–6) analyse the expansion of consumption and surplus purchasing power during the economic reform period 1976–85. Although this work is said to be by China's 'best and brightest'[19] and does make some interesting points, the analysis suffers from the old habits of not identifying sources nor defining concepts clearly. For example, Xia and Li's table 6.2 shows annual data for 'surplus purchasing power'. Familiarity with possible sources helped me to identify the source of these figures as the same source as supplied the *Statistical Yearbook of China 1986* (pp. 442–4), that is, the data contained in Table I.2, column 4, in this book. This means that surplus purchasing power is savings deposits of enterprises, units and so on plus cash in hand; that is, it is a stock at the end of each year.[20] In their next table, table 6.3, Xia and Li compare the growth of surplus purchasing power, which is a flow showing each year's accumulation of certain financial assets, with the annual growth of cash income. No sources are given. This table uses completely different data: data for *residents'* purchasing power (which their original version labels correctly in its table 4.2; see Li and Xia, 1986). These figures are presented in Table I.4 in this book. That is why the increases in surplus purchasing power in Xia and Li's table 6.3, column 2, do not equal the successive differences in their surplus purchasing power data in their table 6.2 as the reader might legitimately expect. They calculate the ratio of the growth of this latter surplus purchasing power to the annual growth of cash income (that is, residents' income). The ratio has increased considerably since 1976, from 36.7 to 91.2 per cent. They comment that 'an increasing part of the annual increase in cash income has turned into surplus purchasing power' (pp. 95–6). This ratio ($S/\Delta Y$, in Western terms) is virtually meaningless and cannot bear the interpretation placed on it. It is the same as the erroneous ratios calculated in studies of the Eastern European and Soviet economies that were mentioned and criticised in section 3.8. A little comparative knowledge might have prevented such misleading calculations.

Despite these conceptual mistakes and the confusing interchanging of anonymous data sources the work of Xia and Li is interesting in that they continue to regard monetary assets holding as 'surplus purchasing power' and to calculate the required increase in industrial and agricultural output necessary to reduce these amounts (p. 96). Their conclusion in that section is given as 'Our economy is now characterised by a striking excess of demand and oversupply' (p. 95). I regard this conclusion as unjustified in this context. Xia and Li have shown and measured excess demand of sorts, but the reference to 'oversupply' is completely unwarranted in their macroeconomic discussion. It is perfectly possible for some markets to suffer from excess demand while some show excess supply, a contention discussed in section 3.8 above, but they do not discuss this possibility. It seems like a mistranslation, and in fact it is one. In their original (Li and Xia, 1986: 96) they actually state that 'Our economy is characterised by intense excess demand and insufficient supply [*Woguo jingji biaoxianchule qiangliede xuqiu guosheng, gongji buzude tezheng*]'.[21]

Table 4.1 shows changes in certain important items on either side of the balance for the period 1952–85. It covers residents and social organisations and shows where their money came from and where it went. Certain features should be noted. Although the rural population consisted of about 80 per cent of the total population throughout this period, peasants' purchasing power never exceeded one-half of social purchasing power. The item labelled 'peasant income' in the table refers to income from the sale of products to the government and peasant service income. Purchases by urban social organisations declined slightly as a proportion of purchasing power. To get residents' purchasing power we could deduct this item from both sides. The 'other incomes' category is rather large in some years. It probably contains the statistical discrepancy that makes the whole

Table 4.1 Structure of purchasing power and expenditure, 1952–85
(selected items, selected years, per cent)

	1952	1957	1961	1970	1979	1982	1984	1985
Social purchasing power formation								
State wages	19.7	27.4	33.6	29.3	25.3	23.4	19.7	18.9
Collective wages	15.6	10.7	8.5	8.7	8.5	8.6	8.5	8.4
Peasant income	44.2	43.3	31.3	41.7	42.4	44.7	46.7	47.3
Government financial support	1.4	1.8	9.3	2.2	3.0	2.2	1.8	1.7
Agricultural loans	0.5	0	0.4	0.2	0.8	0.7	2.9	0.4
Urban social groups expenditures	7.2	7.5	7.0	5.9	6.8	6.5	6.5	6.5
Other incomes	8.2	5.8	7.8	9.1	11.0	12.2	12.6	15.5
Structure of expenditure								
Purchase of commodities	80.7	83.1	83.6	90.6	86.0	84.9	75.8	76.3
Items of cultural life	4.6	5.2	7.4	4.9	4.3	4.2	4.0	3.9
Residents' taxes	10.1	7.9	4.3	4.2	2.4	1.8	1.9	1.9
Monetary accumulation	3.3	2.5	3.5	−0.6	5.0[a]	6.6	11.7	9.7

Notes: [a] The proportion for 1979 has been calculated from the figure for the increase in money holdings, not the difference between *SPP* and *SME*.
Percentage totals do not sum to 100 as only selected important items are included.

Source: Calculated from *Statistical Yearbook of China 1986* (pp. 442–4), which contains complete data for 1952–85.

table balance. The year 1961 is remarkable for the extent of government financial support for residents, and 1984 for the large increases in net agricultural loans. Both features reflect the impact of the changes discussed in chapter 3: agricultural crisis in 1961, and banking reforms in 1984. Peasant incomes rose from 38.5 per cent of total social purchasing power in 1977 (not shown in the table) to 47.3 per cent in 1985.

On the expenditure side we can see that commodity purchases were always the most important item of expenditure, although their relative importance began to fall after 1983. This commodity purchases total is the same as the total value of retail sales, which includes the means of agricultural production, which have varied from about 18 to 12 per cent of total retail sales. Residents' taxes were always small and declined in relative significance after 1982. These taxes were mainly licence fees, not direct income taxes. The result of these declines was of course reflected in the proportion of social purchasing power remaining unspent and accumulating as cash in hand or as savings deposits. This proportion was 2.5 per cent in 1978 (not shown), but it reached 6.6 per cent in 1982 and 11.7 per cent in 1984. Full data of this important proportion, which I call the 'money accumulation rate' (Peebles, 1983), are in Table III.2.

Table 4.2 shows how purchasing power developments determined the rate of growth of the narrow money supply over the period 1979–85 when there were large increases in all items in the table. The money concept presented there is the total of savings deposits and cash in hand of residents and social organisations.

The required accounting identity underlying Table 4.2 is that *SSP* (social purchasing power) minus *SME* (realised social monetary expenditure) in any year must equal the increase in unspent purchasing power (column 3), which when added to the money holdings of the end of the previous year

Table 4.2 Social purchasing power and expenditure, 1978–85
(selected years, billion *yuan*)

Year	*SPP*	*SME*	Money accumulation (= *SPP* – *SME*)	Money holdings (end of year)
1978	176.52	172.09	4.43	48.07
1979	209.39	197.61	10.45[a]	58.52
1980	253.60	233.07	20.53	79.05
1981	274.67	255.67	19.00	98.05
1982	302.62	282.77	19.85	117.90
1983	344.06	316.89	27.17	145.07
1984	445.69	393.33	52.36	197.43
1985	564.54	509.54	55.00	252.43

Note: [a] This is the figure implied by the increase in money holdings.
Source: Table I.3.

must equal money holdings at the end of that year. As Peebles (1987a) points out, the figures for the entire period 1952–85 balance exactly with the exception of the data for 1979. For this year the implied amount of monetary accumulation is 11.78 billion *yuan* (209.39−197.61) whereas the difference between end-1979 and end-1978 money holdings is 10.45 (58.52−48.07). This discrepancy has not been corrected in subsequent versions.[22]

Before discussing the second method of presenting the increase in the money supply, as represented by equation 6, it is necessary to discuss the accounts of the banking system as these provide us with data for the loans and deposits required to use this approach. The balance sheet of the state banking sector has been published in the *Statistical Yearbook* since its first edition, dated 1981, and on a quarterly basis in various issues of the journal *Zhongguo Jinrong* (Chinese Finance). Some of the items appear in China's entry in the IMF's *International Financial Statistics*. Interestingly, the English translation of the table presents the data as being the 'bank credit receipts and payments', but the Chinese term is 'state credit receipts and payments' (*guojia xindai shouzhi qingkuang* or just *guojia xindai shouzhi* in some sources),[23] showing the identity of these two concepts (bank and state) in the Chinese system. Data comprise amounts outstanding at the end of each year (not actual receipts or loans during each year) and are available for the period after 1979 in the *Statistical Yearbooks* and, using different categories, for the period 1952–88 in *Fenjinde Sishi Nian 1949–1989* (pp. 429–31).

Data for selected years are presented in Table 4.3.[24] A better title for the table might be 'bank loans and deposits outstanding', which I have used. Banking reform in 1984 changed slightly the way the data are presented for the period 1985 onwards. The numbers down the left hand side were used in the early Chinese-language versions of the table; the English language text omits them for some reason. The letters down the right hand side are my groupings of the terms and will be used shortly. Some of the items deserve comment.

On the loans (assets) side the majority are to the state sector. Only the loans to collective and individual industrial and commercial units in urban areas, and loans to rural communes, production brigades and teams, can

Table 4.3 Bank loans and deposits outstanding, 1979–85
(selected years, end of year, billion *yuan*)

		1979	1980	1981	1982	1983	1984	1985	
1	Domestic deposits	134.004	165.864	200.558	228.714	267.641	330.561	393.648	
	Enterprise deposits	46.891	57.309	67.407	71.788	84.065	133.379	149.542	D
	Budgetary deposits	14.868	16.202	19.494	17.576	19.369	16.588	32.643	D
	Capital construction deposits	13.130	17.175	22.915	28.480	29.983	33.343	28.150	D
	Deposits of government agencies and organisations	18.488	22.945	27.488	33.143	37.839	32.346	32.576	D
	Urban savings deposits	20.256	28.249	35.414	44.733	57.258	77.662	105.781	D
	Rural deposits	20.371	23.984	27.840	32.994	39.127	37.242	44.956	D
2	Liabilities to international monetary institutions	0	3.427	5.405	5.241	5.373	6.223	7.818	*IMO*
3	Currency in circulation	26.771	34.620	39.634	43.912	52.978	79.211	98.783	*CRC*
4	Funds of banks	42.788	47.733	49.705	51.829	54.736	57.317	61.200	*F*
5	Current balance of profit-and-loss account	4.945	1.972	2.124	3.687	3.760	3.943	6.092	*F*
6	Others	7.752	8.810	7.360	8.141	4.016	22.456	21.404	*O*
	All receipts total	*216.260*	*262.426*	*304.786*	*341.524*	*388.504*	*499.711*	*588.945*	

Table 4.3 (continued)

1 Loans	203.963	241.430	276.467	305.227	343.105	441.957	536.584	
Loans to industrial production enterprises	36.309	43.158	48.735	52.672	59.709	88.409	116.508	L
Loans to industrial supply and marketing enterprises and material supply departments	24.212	23.603	24.124	23.985	26.875	30.977	38.083	L
Commercial loans	123.225	143.702	164.174	178.821	197.881	227.280	264.930	L
Equipment loans, medium and short term	0.792	5.550	8.337	15.198	19.593	28.966	43.272	L
Loans to collective and individual industrial and commercial units in urban areas	5.751	7.829	12.125	13.306	15.928	29.517	32.128	L
Loans as advance payments	0.698	0.788	0.739	0.743	0.671	0.673	0.471	L
Loans to state-owned agricultural units	0.686	0.940	1.392	1.981	2.545	5.089	5.935	L
Loans to rural communes, production brigades and teams	12.290	15.860	16.841	18.521	19.903	31.046	35.257	L
2 Gold	1.261	1.261	1.204	1.204	1.204	1.204	1.204	R
3 Foreign exchange	2.058	−0.847	6.218	14.279	18.507	18.256	9.310	R
4 Assets in international monetary institutions	0	3.604	3.874	3.791	5.731	6.644	8.694	*IMO*
5 Claims on the government	9.023	17.023	17.023	17.023	19.957	26.078	27.505	*G*
All payments total	*216.260*	*262.426*	*304.786*	*341.524*	*388.504*	*499.711*	*588.945*	

Source: *Statistical Yearbook of China 1986* (p. 530).

be considered as going to non-state enterprises. These loans expanded quite rapidly with the change in the structure of the economy and ownership. Whereas total loans outstanding in 1985 were 2.6 times their 1979 level these two categories were 5.6 and 2.9 times their 1979 levels respectively. The introduction of short- and medium-term equipment loans to enterprises by the banking system in 1979 is reflected in their rapid increase with the total outstanding in 1985 being 54.6 times the 1979 level.[25] Commercial loans remained the largest category of loans; the term 'commercial loans' represents loans to commercial units. (A Western banker on hearing the term would think of loans being made on commercial terms, not loans to the commercial sector of the economy.) The item 'claims on the government' strikes me as a bit odd. Its increase must be due to government borrowing. The data show an increase of 8 billion *yuan* in 1980. This fully accords with Xu and Chen (1984: 453) who state that '8 billion *yuan* was borrowed in bank loans' in this year. They also state that 9 billion *yuan* were borrowed in 1979, as does Zhao Dexin (1989: 423), and this is the total given for claims on the government at the end of that year, implying that the government had paid off all previous borrowing. This makes sense. However, the data show no borrowing for 1981 or 1982 when other analysts have said that there was such borrowing (see CIA, 1989: chart 8). The item 'foreign exchange', sometimes described as 'foreign exchange purchases', also seems odd. The whole logic of these accounts is that they show amounts outstanding, that is, assets and liabilities. How the stock of foreign exchange for 1980 could be negative I do not understand.

Deposits are quite straightforward although their precise coverage is not clear. One important feature is the large increase in enterprise deposits in 1984. This reflects the fact that enterprises were allowed to retain part of their profits, and they obviously had to have somewhere to hold such money. The structure of deposits changed somewhat over the period 1979–85. Enterprise deposits increased from 35 per cent of the total of domestic deposits to 38 per cent, and the deposits of government agencies fell from 13.8 per cent to 8.3 per cent. Privately held deposits (urban and rural savings deposits) increased from 30 per cent to 38.3 per cent. This meant that a greater proportion of deposits than earlier were vulnerable to withdrawal and conversion into 'active' money.

Such a balance sheet must balance. A consequence of this is that we can 'explain' (that is, 'account for') any annual change in any item or group of items as the change in the other side of the balance sheet minus the change in the side containing those items net of the items themselves. The following approach accounts for changes in currency in circulation, item 3 (left-hand-side numbers) on the receipts side, although it could also be used to explain the increase in currency plus savings deposits or any other group of deposits we might like to define as money. The 'receipts' are the deposits into the banking system and are its liabilities. The 'payments' side represents the banking system's loans outstanding, its assets. Call deposits D and loans L. The change in currency in circulation in any year must equal L minus D (net of currency). In other words, the increase in currency equals loans extended by the banking system minus new deposits received.

As one Chinese economist puts it, loans minus cash equals deposits (Li, 1986/7: 6). Loans are granted, and that part which does not accumulate as cash must have returned to the bank, or loans that do not result in deposits must have accumulated as cash. As it is put by Ma (1982a: 479): 'From the point of view of the entire country, the balance of the credit plan is identical [*shi yizhide*] with the change in the amount of currency in circulation.' Any number of groupings of items could be used to get a more detailed understanding of the factors behind the change in currency.

The letters at the right hand side of Table 4.3 represent the groupings I have chosen to use. Itemised and numbered 1 to 6 they are:

1 *D*: Domestic deposits
1 *L*: Loans outstanding
2 *G*: Claims on the government[26]
3 *R*: Gold and foreign currency reserves
4 *IMO*: Assets (net) with international monetary organisations
5 *F*: Banking system's own funds
6 *O*: Others

(Note that numbers 1 to 6 here are not correlated with left-hand-side numbers 1 to 6 in Table 4.3.) So,

$$\Delta CRC = \overset{(1)}{(L - D)} + \overset{(2)}{G} + \overset{(3)}{R} + \overset{(4)}{IMO}(\text{net}) - \overset{(5)}{F} - \overset{(6)}{O} \qquad (7)$$

where items 1 to 6 are annual increments. This shows that the annual increase in currency in circulation (ΔCRC) is dependent on a number of domestic and international factors. Equation 7 must be true arithmetically, but it tells us nothing about the reasons for the size of the various right-hand-side items. The reasons for its being true are as follows.

The basic logic of the first item ($L - D$) is that the use of funds (new loans) acts to increase domestic money and the sources of funds (new deposits) act to restrain monetary growth. An increase in loans gives their recipients the right to draw on them. If the loan is used within the state non-cash sphere, it will automatically create an equal deposit for the recipient, causing no increase in currency. If the loan is converted into cash to pay wages or bonuses or to buy agricultural produce, it will cause a cash injection. However, part of it will be spent on items supplied by the state sector, resulting in increased receipts by the supplying units (for example, shops), which deposit such funds. That part of the loan that does not give rise to an increase in deposits by its recipients (including here household savings deposits) must produce an increase in currency in circulation.

Item 2, government borrowing (G), results from the fact that the government has been unable to cover any deficit by domestic or foreign borrowing; it draws on its overdraft at the bank, and this increases currency in circulation. However, the government also holds deposits at the bank, and these can change from year to year. An increase in government deposits, for example, would offset some of that year's overdraft. Hence it is necessary to compute a net item for the government equal to the borrowing through its overdraft minus the increase in its deposits. By netting out the change in deposits this item becomes the equivalent of the item ($B_G - D_G$), government borrowing minus deposits, of equation 6. This is done in Table 4.5 but not in Table 4.4, which is presented to be compatible with Huang (1988a). I do think that this netting out is necessary, as Huang's government item is equivalent only to B_G and the offsetting item D_G is hidden in his total deposits.

Item 3, labelled *R* (reserves), represents increases in the banking system's holdings of gold and foreign currencies. These are obtained from domestic units in return for cash payments at the government-determined exchange rate or gold procurement price. If the banking system's holdings increase in any year, there must have been a corresponding payment of cash to the population. Hence, an increase in them contributes to monetary expansion and vice versa.

This also applies to the banks' net holdings at international monetary organisations (*IMO*). ($L - D$), *G*, *R* and *IMO* all represent uses of funds and so act to expand currency in circulation.

If the banking system's funds, which include its operating profits (*F*) increase, this must be because it has earned money, so obtaining existing cash from the population and reducing currency in circulation, making operating profit a negative item in equation 7. As Figure 4.1 shows, bank funds can increase as a result of outright grants from the government budget or by accumulating the operating surplus. For the period 1979–82 the successive increases in bank funds were the same as the operating profit, showing that there was no transfer of funds. For the years after 1983 the increases in funds were less than operating profit. So we can conclude that operating profit does act to withdraw currency from circulation.

Item 6, 'other' (*O*), is a residual of unknown content, and as it is on the source-of-funds side it must have a negative impact on currency creation.

Table 4.4 presents the accounting method for explaining the annual increases in currency in circulation for the period 1979–85. This method of presentation is adapted from that of Huang (1988a: 35–6). Unfortunately, his calculations for 1981 are incorrect in this version. The published actual increase in currency in circulation was 5.014 billion *yuan* (39.634 minus 34.620) whereas he gives 4.328 billion. This figure is the one obtained by adding his individual items, all of which are correct except item 1, which he gives as minus 0.343 billion when in fact it was plus 0.343 billion. The figures are correct in Huang (1988b: 192).

The 'other' item is distressingly large for some years, especially for the exceptional year of 1984 when it equalled nearly one-half of that year's increase in currency in circulation. If the original data are accurate, they imply the following. The unfunded part of the government's budget deficit that required borrowing from the banking system clearly had an important impact on currency growth in 1979 and 1980. In other years it was of little relative importance. The large increases in currency in 1984 and 1985 were accompanied by large excesses of loans over deposits, with government borrowing playing a subsidiary role in 1984 and hardly any in 1985. In 1984 loans went mainly to commercial units (no doubt because they were making losses as agricultural purchase prices exceeded retail prices), in-

Table 4.4 Explaining annual increases in currency, 1979–85
(selected years, billion *yuan*)

Year	ΔCRC	=	1 (L − D)	− +	2 G	+	3 R	+	4 IMO	−	5 F	−	6 O
1979	5.57		−1.50		9.02		0.63		0		4.92		−2.24
1980	7.849		5.607		8.0		−2.905		0.177		1.972		1.058
1981	5.014		0.343		0		7.053		−1.708		2.124		−1.450
1982	4.278		0.604		0		8.061		0.081		3.687		0.780
1983	9.066		−1.049		2.934		4.228		1.808		2.98		−4.125
1984	26.233		35.932		6.121		−0.251		0.063		2.764		12.868[a]
1985	19.572		32.540		1.427		−8.946		0.455		6.032		−1.128[a]

Note: [a] These are the figures given in Huang (1988a: 36; 1988b: 192), and they make the figures balance. However, they are not the figures one gets from the original source used here. This is a mystery. He might have used a different source.

Items 1 to 6 are identified in equation 7 in the text. Each entry is an annual increase.

Source: 1979 data calculated from data in *Fenjinde Sịshi Nian 1949–1989* (429–31); 1980–85 data calculated from *Statistical Yearbook of China 1986* (p. 530).

dustrial production enterprises, and collective and individual urban enterprises. These three categories accounted for about two-thirds of the total increase in loans made in that year. In 1985 enterprises again borrowed large amounts. The total wage bill increased 21 and 22 per cent in 1984 and 1985 respectively, when real national income increased by 13.5 and 12.3 per cent. It is argued that these bank loans financed the increase in workers' bonuses, which are said to be the priority (*youxian*) use of increased funds due to an expansion of loans to enterprises (Huang, 1988a: 37).

The interpretation of the large increase in the money supply in 1984 has caused some interesting comments by Chinese economists. In an article advocating a policy of rapid economic growth Sheng and Huang (1989/90: 46) write that 'Our country's loss of control over the money supply in 1984 demonstrates that there are serious problems in the form of our country's money supply; the loss of control meant that a large amount of money was scattered and lost outside the banking system'. The same Sheng Hong subsequently co-authored a paper (Sheng and Zou, 1990) that includes in its subtitle the phrase 'the so-called loss of control over money in 1984' (p. 75). They argue that the rapid increase in money in that year was largely justified by the increase in the monetisation of the economy and was 'very close to the increase in the demand for money and the trend of changes in this increase during the year'. Their main point is that the actual increase was not less than the increased demand, so the economy did not suffer from insufficient money supply, and that the large increase was 'one of the main reasons for the high-speed economic growth in 1984' (pp. 89–90). They do not consider any negative consequences of the rapid monetary growth.

Table 4.5 shows an alternate presentation of the same items based on a more recent data source that uses different categories and contains different data for the period after 1981. The general trends are the same. The

Table 4.5 Explaining annual increases in currency, 1979–85, using alternative data source
(selected years, billion *yuan*)

Year	ΔCRC	=	1 $(L - D)$	+	2 G	+	3 R	+	4 IMO	−	5 F	−	6 O	−	7 Bonds
1979	5.57		−5.37		12.89		0.63		0		4.92		−2.34		0
1980	7.85		6.84		6.42		−2.90		0.42		2.58		0.35		0
1981	5.01		0.88		−3.29		9.78		−1.26		2.58		−1.48		0
1982	4.28		−4.05		1.84		12.81		−0.11		5.30		0.91		0
1983	9.07		1.48		0.52		4.84		1.80		4.62		−5.05		0
1984	26.23		36.72		7.49		−0.25		0.36		5.54		12.55		0
1985	19.57		59.72		−12.44		−17.05		0.67		8.03		2.48		0.82

Note: Items are identified in equation 7 in the text. Column 2 is government borrowing net of the change in government deposits; it is not comparable with the same item in Table 4.4. Column 7 is the sale of bank bonds by the new specialised banks after 1984, which obviously withdraws currency from circulation.
Source: Calculated from data in *Fenjinde Sishi Nian 1949–1989* (pp. 429–31).

year 1985 shows the largest fall in gold and foreign exchange reserves in the period 1979–85. Table 4.4's source puts it at about 9 billion *yuan*, but the source for Table 4.5 indicates about 17 billion *yuan* as does the corresponding table in *Statistical Yearbook of China 1987* (p. 530). This no doubt reflects the policy of increased imports of consumer goods highlighted by Komiya (1989) and discussed in section 2.11. As Table 4.5 shows, this fall offset part of the huge increase in new loans over deposits. Equation 5 shows how the imported goods, when sold to households on the domestic market, reduced currency in circulation as they increased C_H and absorbed part of the increase in the wage bill (W_E in equation 5) due to the excess of new loans over deposits (item 1 in equation 7). Correspondingly, equation 7 shows how they did this by making item 3 negative. Not all of this reduction in gold and foreign exchange reserves would have been used to import consumer goods, however; some part would have been to import capital goods.

The change in foreign reserves reflects China's balance-of-payments position, which is dominated by the balance of trade. The years 1982 and 1983 saw balance-of-trade surpluses (*Statistical Yearbook of China 1987*, p. 519). As Table 4.5 shows, in these years foreign reserves increased, and this had an expansionary effect on currency in circulation via item 3. The foreign exchange would have been obtained by the government from the foreign trade corporations in exchange for *Renminbi*, thus expanding domestic money. In 1984 there was a slight deficit on the balance of trade, and in 1985 a deficit of 44.89 billion *yuan* (about US$14.9 billion) was recorded. In both these years foreign reserves fell, making item 3 negative and thus restricting the rate of currency growth. This occurred as the government had to supply the foreign trade corporations with foreign currencies in exchange for *Renminbi*, which amount exceeded the amount of *Renminbi* the foreign trade corporations required to buy goods for export. The foreign exchange reserves were used to import consumer goods, which were sold on the domestic market, increasing C_H and withdrawing currency from the hands of the population.

The impact of the balance-of-trade position on the domestic money supply is the same as that in a market economy, as explained in section 3.3. Trade surpluses tend to expand domestic money supply and trade deficits to restrict domestic money supply. This is a kind of self-regulating effect in the market economy. In the case of a balance-of-trade deficit the fall in domestic money is supposed to contract aggregate demand and to reduce the demand for imports, thus tending to correct the deficit and vice versa. Whether this occurs in China depends on the extent to which other items leading to domestic monetary creation can be restricted. Obviously, if item 1 were to remain large and positive, running down reserves could only have a temporary and minor impact in restricting domestic monetary expansion, for the reserves would run out and the potential for foreign borrowing is not limitless. Much depends on the domestic policies taken by planners; they cannot rely on textbook self-adjusting mechanisms to regulate domestic monetary growth.

Table 4.5's treatment of the government in item 2 shows a net contractionary effect on currency in circulation in 1981 and 1985. Although the government borrowed in 1985 it increased its deposits considerably, more than offsetting the new borrowing in that year.

The above analysis has concentrated on recent years as it was during this period that the narrow money stock increased dramatically. There is one period when the money stock fell, and the insights of equations 5 and 6 can account for this. In 1962 and 1963 holdings of savings deposits and cash in hand fell, and cash in hand fell also in the three years 1962–64, as did currency in circulation (see Tables I.1 to I.3). Equation 5 tells us that *SPP* must have been less than *SME* in the years 1962 and 1963. This was the case. How this was achieved was considered in the general discussion of policies in the historical sections of chapter 2. What macroeconomic forces made this possible will be shown in chapter 6. Here we can note that in 1962 *SPP* fell 10.7 per cent, mainly due to the reductions in the state wage bill of 12.3 per cent and in the purchasing power of urban social groups, which fell 19.4 per cent. Peasant income from selling products rose very slightly. Although total expenditures fell in 1962 they were greater than *SPP*, so monetary accumulation was negative. In 1963 *SPP* rose 5 per cent and total expenditures fell slightly, but *SME* remained greater than *SPP*, so money holdings fell again. In terms of equation 6, the main factors contributing to the fall in currency holdings were the fact that loans to industrial enterprises fell in 1961, 1962 and 1963 whereas the deposits of industrial enterprises rose significantly in these years. This had a contractionary effect on currency in circulation. Government deposits fell in 1962 and 1963, contributing to currency expansion, but this was offset by the excess of enterprise deposits over loans, which was negative as item 1 in equation 7 (see *Fenjinde Sishi Nian 1949–1989*, 1989: 429–32).

The impact of major policy changes aimed at reducing currency in circulation can be shown by using either equation 5 or 6 as both are always true, but equation 5, that of the household sector's balance, shows more forcefully the effects of the policies taken.

4.12 Monetary policy: objectives and tools

Whether a planned socialist economy can have a monetary policy has always been a controversial issue. Garvy (1977: 159–62) summarises Western scholars' views on Soviet monetary policy, and these have influenced Western scholars' assessments and definition of monetary policy in China. Garvy comments that it is 'more appropriate to speak of monetary strategy than of monetary policy, and assign it the role of an organic component of the planning process rather than that of an independent tool for influencing current economic activity' (p. 160). This judgement is relevant to China also. Garvy quotes Edward Ames's view that many 'nonmonetary measures' are taken on the basis of monetary analysis and are aimed at maintaining monetary equilibrium. This also is useful when considering Chinese monetary policy.

For the purposes of the present study monetary policy will be taken to embrace all actions undertaken by planners that are intended to have an effect on the quantity of narrow money and the preservation of monetary equilibrium, which is interpreted to mean achieving planners' quantitative monetary objectives. It will be argued subsequently that the relevant monetary concept is the narrowest measure of money, that is, currency. Some of these policies will not be found in discussions of monetary policy in Western countries. This is because the two systems are different and because an artificial distinction is made between monetary and fiscal policy in Western textbooks. An example of the first point is that institutions in China are such that increased nominal expenditures by households can reduce the amount of money in circulation, which is in direct opposition to the basic assumption of the Quantity Theory of Money. The second point can be illustrated by the case of bond sales. These are relegated to fiscal policy in Western textbooks. Even Hsiao (1971) regards them as such. However, if we take the definition of monetary policy proposed above, they must be considered. Bonds sales by both the government and, after 1984, the specialised banks act to restrain currency growth.

The objectives of monetary policy can be simplified to two main aims: the maintenance of price stability, and the limiting of the amount of currency in circulation to an amount consistent with price stability and economic development.[27] It will be argued in chapter 6 that these two objectives are sometimes incompatible. The correct method for assessing the required amount of currency in circulation has been debated in China since the 1950s (Hu and Han, 1983: 357–90), and various criteria have been proposed.

One proposal based required currency on the size of the wage fund as this constituted the major part of purchasing power. It was objected that this applied only to the urban population. When the entire population was considered the amount spent for agricultural purchases and the amount of rural loans had to be taken into account also.

Another proposal was that money in circulation should be compared with either the extent of government stocks of commodities or with the extent of annual commodity sales. This latter view has been expressed by many Chinese economists. Works by Liu (1981: 72–3), Shi (1982: 3), Li

(1982: 34) and Zeng (1983: 152–3), and Chen Wenlin (1989: 62–4) for example, use such ratios to assess the normality or otherwise of the amount of currency in circulation. This view follows from accepting the 'official' definition of the value basis of the *Renminbi* (quoted from Ma Hong in section 4.6). The desired ratios are based on historical experience from periods when there was reasonable price stability. From the experiences of the 1950s and 1960s a ratio of about 1:8 or 1:8.5 was considered acceptable, that is, a ratio of currency to annual retail sales of 12 to 12.5 per cent. Chen Wenlin (1989: 62–3) analyses China's monetary conditions over the period 1955–78 using this ratio. He concludes that the situation was normal or basically normal in nine years (1955–60 and 1964–66) with an unsatisfactory supply situation in the remaining years. The years 1961–62 and 1968 are described as inflationary with severe shortages and rises in some prices.

The First National Symposium on Monetary Theory (*Quanguo Shouci Huobi Lilun Taolunhui*) held in Canton (Guangzhou) in January 1981 saw many delegates accepting this method, and a ratio of 1:8.5 was proposed. In 1962 the ratio was 1:5.67, and in 1981 it was 1:6.9. As Li Chonghuai (1982: 35) and Zeng (1983: 153) argue, it would be incorrect to conclude from these ratios that the situation of 1981 was bad. There had been many changes in the economy, making a higher money ratio acceptable. They accept that economic reform had changed the demand for money. Zeng argues for recalculating the acceptable norm, fearing that, if policy were based on the old figure, a tight monetary policy might be adopted when the circumstances did not warrant it. Within a year or two of Zeng's article Chinese economists were using Western econometric techniques to estimate demand-for-money functions rather than relying on a constant ratio. Some of this work will be discussed in chapter 5.

The traditional way of showing Chinese monetary planning in textbooks uses the quantity equation framework. Here, however,

$$M = PQ/V$$

(Chai, 1981: 43; Yang, 1985: 33; Yeh, 1985: 88–90; and *Huobi Liutong Guanli Xue*, 1985: 115–16). In this approach P and Q are supposed to be planned. On the basis of the acceptable money ratio, which determines the acceptable value of V, the required increase in M could be inferred from the planned increase in Q and any planned increase in P. Most recently, Professor Wang Jiye (1989: 19–20), director of the State Planning Commission's Economic Research Institute, has revealed his way of formulating the planned increase in the money supply. Using the terms of chapter 3, and making m the *planned* rate of growth of the money supply, we can discuss his four possibilities. First, he considers what he calls the 'standard international formula used in the West', which is

$$m = q + p$$

He rejects this 'because it is tantamount to admitting inflation cannot be controlled'. Second, he considers

$$m = q$$

This ignores inflation but 'results in oversqueezing the money supply and thus restricts economic growth too much'. Third he considers,

$$m = (q + lp)$$

where lp represents what he calls 'structural price rises (i.e., commodities with state set prices)'. Fourth he considers,

$$m < (q + lp)$$

He concludes that of the four 'the last seems most appropriate for China' (p. 19). It is interesting to note that none of these formulae explicitly takes into account the likely direction of change of desired velocity, that is, the demand for money. The chosen planning criterion implies that velocity will rise naturally as the planned money-supply growth rate has been set at less than the rate of growth of demand for nominal money with constant velocity. As we saw in chapter 3, in developing countries—and one would presume also in China during market-orientated economic reforms in the countryside—the desired velocity falls in the long run as the economy is monetised. This requires a relatively higher rate of monetary growth than that given just by real growth and inflation. Wang's preferred criterion seems to be unduly restrictive. It could, however, be used to identify periods of excess monetary growth and possible reactions by planners if we were convinced that they actually used this rule of thumb.

Chen Wenlin (1989: 55–6) adapts what he calls Western central banks' method for determining money supply growth to Chinese conditions. He shows that money supply growth should equal the estimated increase in gross output value, plus the lowest rate of price increases plus the change in the demand for money due to the fall in velocity. In 1984 these three factors were 14.7, 6 and 2 per cent respectively, totalling a 22.7 per cent increase in the demand for broad money. He shows that that year's actual increase, 26.2 per cent, exceeded this amount, but his arithmetic is strange.

It is useful to keep in mind the fact that Chinese planners did consider the simple ratio of currency to retail sales when formulating policy. If we can show when this money ratio is likely to rise above the critical currency level, we can predict that there will be some sort of policy reaction.

Changing circumstances and the price rises following reform led to another criterion being offered. This was discussed at the Forum on Monetary Theory (*Huobi Lilun Zuotanhui*) held in Peking in June 1980. Some delegates proposed concentrating on the movements of the price index of the basic necessities of staff and workers to judge the monetary situation. This is similar to the Western technique that looks at movements in interest rates to judge the tightness of monetary policy, a practice often criticised as potentially misleading. It was argued in China that looking at price movements was easier and that the situation could be appraised more quickly and action taken at the right time. The obvious criticism made then was that, as China still had predominantly fixed and not floating prices, even if there were hidden (*bianxiang*) price increases this method would not reflect the true situation (Hu and Han, 1983: 383–4).

The tools of monetary policy are very simple. Equation 5 gives us the framework in the planned system. Controlling the growth of the narrow measures of the money supply implies controlling purchasing power, consisting mainly of W_E and W_G, on the one side and retail sales availability, C_H, on the other. Most existing studies of Chinese monetary policy have concentrated on how these flows can be co-ordinated to prevent excessive nominal demand and monetary growth. Such growth would increase the currency ratio and put pressure on free market prices. Prybyla (1978: 139–40) lists the possible policies. Historical studies have identified when certain measures were used, and some of the measures were identified in chapter 2. As Dong (1980: 300) puts it, balance between purchasing power and supplies can only be considered reasonable if the following three conditions are secured: the accumulation of consumer goods stocks are normal; residents' accumulation of savings deposits and cash in hand are normal; and there is basic balance between the supply of consumer goods and residents' purchasing power. This is very normative and gives no concrete definitions of what constitutes 'normal'. Ensuring basic balance between purchasing power and supplies is a means of obtaining normal narrow money growth and obtaining the objectives of monetary policy as defined above. It has consistently been pointed out that under such a system the main determinants of monetary equilibrium, W_G, W_E, and C_H are not under the control of the People's Bank of China. The bank has to be a passive reactor to the consequences of changes in these variables, be they due to deliberate policy changes (an increase in wage rates, for example), unplanned changes (an unplanned increase in the workforce) or a shortage of consumer goods (due to harvest failures perhaps). Monetary policy tended to be 'rather one-sided: it primarily aimed at contracting the money supply' (Hsiao, 1971: 207). The People's Bank could not determine the amount of money being put into circulation, so it could only follow a reactive policy of currency absorption. From a dynamic point of view currency absorption or withdrawal does not necessarily mean reducing the absolute amount of currency in circulation; it may mean adopting policies that reduce the rate of growth of currency in circulation through various means of increasing the amount of currency *huilong*. In discussions of monetary policy tools in the early 1980s Chinese economists split into those who thought that restricting bank credit would slow monetary growth and those who still emphasised the importance of policies for withdrawing money from circulation (Hu and Han, 1983: 390). It is an empirical matter as to whether monetary planners have actually managed to restrain currency issue or have had to rely on reactive policies and, if so, what these policies were.

An interesting insight into monetary planners' views of the preferred way of withdrawing currency is to be found in the comments of Hong Yuncheng, then director of the General Office of the People's Bank of China, as summarised by Li Ping (1990: 27). Hong Yuncheng noted the beneficial effects of increasing savings deposits in withdrawing currency from circulation, but this is described as 'mainly a form of recovery of currency credit, not of commodity credit, and so was inherently unstable' (p. 27). This shows a preference for commodity *huilong* over credit *huilong*. From the planners' point of view the reasons for the preference are clear although they may seem rather odd from the point of view of a Western economist. Hong likens the accumulating savings deposits to 'a tiger which had entered a cage, the door of which is left open; it can injure people at any time' (p. 27). This analogy is commonly found in Chinese descriptions of savings deposits. The planners clearly prefer to withdraw currency through commodity *huilong* as it is permanently withdrawn and becomes state revenue. It does not remain privately owned subject to withdrawal and spending as active money. Hong's view that such deposits can 'injure people' is an interesting insight into planners' psychology. The Western economist would ask who could possibly be injured. An owner of a savings deposit exercises a constitutionally protected right to obtain his or her money and then spend it on whatever is wanted, a television set, for example. The seller sells voluntarily, so both parties benefit. Who is injured? Of course, all the other potential consumers in China who do not obtain that television set are 'injured' in some way, but this is true of any purchase when there is scarcity. Planners fear that a large amount of savings deposits could be withdrawn at the same time, resulting in panic buying and widespread shortages which would disrupt their monetary planning. Thus it is the planners' planning that is injured. For analytical purposes in chapter 6, which will be concerned with planners' behaviour, it is important to remember that monetary planners seem to prefer commodity *huilong* to credit *huilong* and that one of them was still saying so in late 1989 or in 1990.

When we consider the monetary creation process from the point of view of equation 6 it is apparent that controlling monetary growth requires controlling both loans to enterprises and the government's borrowing requirement. Even after the banking reforms of 1984 it is clear that there are no effective tools for the People's Bank to be able to do this. There is virtually no limit on the amount of loans that can be created by the specialised banks (Huang 1988a), and during 1984 and 1985 such loans increased dramatically. Observers have stressed the extent to which local authorities pressure local branches to extend credit to enterprises in their own area (Tsang 1990: 230). Many bank officials have been appointed and fired by both the bank and the local authorities. Although this situation is supposed to have changed it is admitted that political and other considerations override economic ones in the granting of loans (Brotman, 1985: 19). Enterprises seemed able to obtain all the loans they wanted in order to increase worker bonuses during 1984 and 1985. Hence, the loan increases produced narrow monetary growth as they increased W_E in an unplanned manner. Equation 5 is still very useful.

An important historical aspect of monetary policy was the monetary reform of 1 March 1955. This was announced by the State Council on 21 February of that year, and a translation of the regulations is available in Okazaki (1961: 28–9). The reasons for such a reform are given by Liu (1980: 61) as follows.[28] The legacy of the Kuomintang inflation meant that prices were high and that a single *yuan* could buy nothing, so people were already used to reckoning values in units of 10 000 *yuan*, but this was very inconvenient, especially for peasants. Existing notes carried only Han Chinese writing (that is, characters), were of variable quality, and were easy to damage and forge. The monetary reform dealt with all these problems. A new set of notes was issued at the conversion rate of 10 000 old *yuan* for each new *yuan*, and all nominal values were reduced in the same proportion. The new notes bore inscriptions in Chinese characters, and Tibetan, Mongolian and Uighur (Uygur, *Weiwu'er*) scripts. Different denominations of notes were of different sizes and bore different designs, making them easily recognised by those who could not read. The exchange of old notes for new took place during March and April (Wu, 1956: 111). As Tseng and Han (1959: 107) stress, this conversion was not aimed at reducing the amount of money in circulation as was the case with the confiscatory monetary reforms in the Soviet Union and certain Eastern European countries at the end of the Second World War (Pesek, 1958). Durand (1965: 59–60) is full of praise for the way the reform was carried out, pointing out that it took place, not at the beginning of the financial year, but after the Lunar New Year holiday so that it would not complicate the huge volume of transactions at this time.

Although the intention of the currency reform was not to reduce the volume of currency in circulation such a reform was almost certain to do so. First, on learning of an impending reform people will tend to deposit currency in their bank accounts, where such sums will automatically be converted to the new unit without there being any awkward questions about the source of the money. Second, some old denomination notes will have been destroyed or badly damaged and therefore cannot be converted. Both considerations suggest that currency in circulation will fall. Tseng and Han (1959: 112) report that in China there was a large increase in savings deposits starting immediately after the announcement of the reform. In fact the amounts of all four measures of currency in circulation at the end of 1955 presented in Table I.1 were about 3 per cent lower than their end-1954 amounts, and savings deposit holdings were about 25 per cent higher. This substitution of savings deposits for currency at the time of similar non-confiscatory monetary reforms can also be found in the data for the Soviet Union (reform in January 1961) and East Germany (reform in October 1957) (Peebles, 1984c: 314).

4.13 Banking reform and the economy

The banking reforms of 1984 certainly altered the structure of the banking system. Later changes, especially from about 1986, altered its nature and functions. However, these changes did not in principle alter the working of the money supply process. The major reforms are discussed in Brotman (1985), Wilson (1986), Tam (1986), White and Bowles (1988), Bowles and White (1989) and Chang (1989).

The obvious major change was the handing over of day-to-day business to the specialised banks, especially to the Industrial and Commercial Bank of China for deposit taking and loan granting. The specialised banks were required to deposit a certain proportion of their deposits with the new central bank. This may look like the creation of a system by which the specialised banks' ability to extend loans could be controlled by the central bank, which would now use indirect levers to control the money supply, but four factors suggest that this was not so. First, such reserve requirements are probably best seen as just the way the central bank gets hold of the specialised banks' funds for itself, a process identified by McKinnon as common in developing countries and discussed in section 3.10. Second, the early years of banking reform did not show any increased ability of the central bank to control monetary growth. Indirect levers just did not exist, and the money supply process was still dominated by enterprise expansion of bonuses and wage payments with the local authorities putting pressure on branch banks to extend loans in their locality for investment projects. Third, interest rate controls were hardly used by the central bank to influence the money supply process. They were increased twice in 1985 and again in September 1988 in the face of rapidly rising inflation in this latter year. Both deposit and loan rates for enterprises and institutions were increased in 1988 in an attempt to encourage enterprises and institutions to hold deposits.[29] Fourth, when it was decided to try to restrain the rate of growth of the money supply, it was not indirect levers that were used, but administered quantitative limits on the banks' total of loans. This was done from September 1988 onwards. Such quantitative controls were, as we saw in section 3.4, a feature of British and French monetary policy and remind us just how difficult it is to control monetary growth.

There were changes in the roles of certain banks. For example, there was more competition between the specialised banks for certain forms of business (Chang, 1989), and interbank lending at negotiated rates was legalised from January 1986. The black market in foreign exchange was institutionalised in the form of swap centres, which proliferated rapidly after about 1986. At these centres units and enterprises, not individuals (except in Xiamen sometime later), could trade foreign exchange. The fact that the rate offered (a 'negotiated' rate) was much better than the official rate served as an encouragement to exporters.[30] For example, after the devaluation of June 1986 the official rate was 3.7221 *yuan* per US$1, but the market rate was between 6 and 7 *yuan* during 1988.[31]

Even through to the late 1980s banking reform had not changed the basic nature of the money supply process and the extent to which monetary growth could be controlled, nor had it changed the methods available for such attempts.

4.14 Conclusion

This chapter has described the institutional setting in which the money supply changes and why, how prices are determined and what principles of monetary and pricing policy are followed. It has shown how both domestic and international factors can affect the domestic money supply. It has quoted a monetary planner's recently expressed preference for commodity *huilong* over credit *huilong* and argued that monetary and banking reforms in the mid 1980s have not changed the nature of the money supply mechanism. The same institutional assumptions underlying equations 5 and 6 will be made when explaining monetary and price developments for the period 1952–85 in chapter 6 and for the years up to 1988 in chapter 7.

The next chapter will review important works on money and related issues published between 1964 and 1990 in search of some clues as to how we should subsequently investigate the empirical features of money and prices and related topics in China for the period 1952–85.

5 Precursors and clues

This chapter reviews the most important studies relating to money and prices in China that have appeared during the period 1964–90. Although some of these studies are not mainly concerned with monetary events in China, they are included in this review if they contain some discussion thought to be relevant to a monetary study and especially if they include any empirical examination of price or monetary data.

It must be stressed at once that many of these studies were done at a time when the amount of statistical material about the Chinese economy was very limited. Apart from the statistical work *Ten Great Years*, the English language edition of which was published in 1960, there were no official Chinese statistical yearbooks until the early 1980s and hardly any quantitative data in other sources. Many of these authors had to compile their own estimates of such basic data as the money supply, purchasing power, retail sales and price indexes. They had to do this on the basis of scanty original data scattered through Chinese journals and national and regional newspapers as well as that reported in radio broadcasts.

Another common feature of the early works included here is that they could only cover a limited number of years. This meant that the time horizon was often too short to reveal any patterns in the data. Very often the authors were forced to examine the data year by year. This does not allow the averaging of data by subperiods to search for patterns as was done in chapter 3, for example.

The following review seeks to establish the nature of the basic approach taken by each researcher and the major conclusions reached.

5.1 Studies published before 1980

Perkins (1964) and (1966)

This review concentrates on Perkins (1966, ch. 8), which was based largely on the earlier article (Perkins, 1964), as the 1966 study is more comprehensive.

This study is largely limited to the 1950s. Perkins accepts that, as there was a free consumer goods market in China except for short periods during 1955–56 and 1958–59, any inflationary pressures were able to manifest themselves in price increases rather than in the accumulation of idle cash balances. He recognises, however, that the actual published official retail price indexes might not be a full reflection of the true retail price level, including the free market price level, as it gave a heavy weight to state-supplied commodities at controlled prices.

Perkins's basic framework for analysing retail price inflation and government policy is what Peebles (1983) calls the 'purchasing power approach' as he emphasises the factors determining the amount of newly created consumer purchasing power that could be spent in the consumer goods market, the ways the authorities had of trying to control this purchasing power, and their reactive policies on the supply side of the consumer goods market when they could not fully control purchasing power developments. Perkins (1966: 159–65) bases his analysis firmly on the nature of institutions in China, arguing that there were two distinct consumer goods markets in the form of the urban and rural markets and that the authorities had control over the purchasing power developments and supplies of goods on both markets. On the urban markets purchasing power was mainly determined by the urban wage bill and the supply of goods by the availability of food supplies. On the rural markets purchasing power was determined by the extent of state purchases of agricultural supplies, and the supply of goods was mainly in the form of state-supplied industrial products.

Perkins argues that, unlike in the case of capitalist economies, the authorities had direct control over both forms of monetary purchasing power: through state wage policy and their planning of the urban labour force, in the case of the urban wage bill; and by setting procurement prices, in the case of rural purchasing power. Despite this theoretical control over both forms of purchasing power, in practice purchasing power in both forms was difficult to control. There were large unplanned increases in the urban labour force causing large unplanned increases in the urban wage bill in 1953, 1956 and 1958. The authorities were unable to reduce wages to offset this and were only able to slow down the rate of increase of purchasing power. Perkins (1966: 161) presents his own estimates of total purchasing power for the period 1950–58 and its urban and rural components for some of these years.

In the case of rural purchasing power the authorities' theoretical control was as great as in the case of urban purchasing power, but in fact they had even less control because of the need to boost sales to the state and maintain peasant incentives. Perkins makes the point that state procurements at high prices were in fact an anti-inflationary measure as they were resold at even higher prices to urban residents. This meant that such sales were able to soak up 'several billion dollars [sic] of urban and rural purchasing power more than their original purchase had created, because turnover and profits taxes raised retail prices well above the prices at which the same goods were purchased without any comparable increase in commercial wages or costs' (1966: 162). During the agricultural crisis of 1960–62 agricultural purchases fell. This increased inflationary pressure as the state no longer had the means of absorbing purchasing power, and there were large increases in free and black market prices, although Perkins does not attempt to quantify them.

Perkins argues that the remaining sources of purchasing power were more easily controlled by the authorities as this was the purchasing power of such groups as army units, schools and welfare institutions. However, their purchasing power was probably not significant. This is an important point. The significant sources of purchasing power were not easy to control whereas the insignificant ones were. Stressing the ease with which the authorities could control the purchasing power of these units misses the point that they are not very important and that the important sources were not so easily controlled.

Because the authorities could not control purchasing power developments as closely as they wished they had to rely on policies acting on the supply side of the consumer goods market for 'closing the inflationary gap' (1966: 165). Perkins argues that the authorities had a strong aversion to using price increases to reduce the imbalance between demand and supply because of their fear that price increases would remind people of the hyperinflationary conditions at the time of the collapse of the Kuomintang government.

For minor or possibly short run imbalances Perkins says that stockpiles could be reduced, but it was probable that these stockpiles were always insufficient for this purpose for any long period. A common reaction was to rely on savings drives and bond sales to absorb excessive purchasing power. Interest payments on deposits and raffles for deposit holders were positive inducements together with pressure from local cadres to buy bonds or make deposits.

In Perkins's view the 'most important measure for closing the gap, at least over the long run, was consumer taxes' (1966: 166). However, these increases in sales taxes (which were the type of consumer taxes used) could 'not stop an initial rise in prices' (as of course they were equivalent to an increase in prices) but 'could only prevent excess demand from increasing retained profits and eventually spilling onto the labour market' (1966: 168). Despite their aversion to price increases it seems that the most important policy adopted by the authorities was to raise sales taxes, which was the equivalent of raising prices. This point will be met again. It has been frequently claimed that the authorities' aversion to rekindling any memories of price increases prevented them from increasing prices at times of excess demand. Yet here is Perkins arguing that the most important measure for closing the gap was in fact increasing prices. As we saw in chapter 2, prices were raised even during the difficult years of 1959–61, so Perkins accurately identifies one of the reactive policies the authorities took after his period of study.

Although Perkins made estimates of purchasing power and had official data of retail prices and sales tax revenue he makes no attempt to link the observed increases in prices to purchasing power imbalances. This suggested link will form the basis of the theory of official retail-price changes offered in the next chapter.

Perkins's conclusion about the 1950s is that 'the situation, except perhaps during the "great leap forward", was handled about as well as it was reasonable to expect in the light of the basic goals of the regime' (1966: 173). In comparison with the industrialisation period in the Soviet Union before the Second World War, when retail prices increased many times, the extent of Chinese inflation was indeed very modest and was achieved by widespread urban and rural rationing of most basic commodities.

Jao (1967/68)

As far as I know Jao's 'exploratory paper' was the first to use the concept of repressed inflation to analyse the relationship between money and prices in China. The period studied was 1950–57. The concept of repressed inflation was adopted from Bent Hansen (1951), who develops a theoretical model of repressed inflation, and from H.K. Charlesworth (1956), who analyses the nature of inflation in postwar Britain.

Using price, output and monetary data from the works of C.M. Li (1959) (mainly for the money supply and prices) and T.C. Liu and K.C. Yeh (1965) (mainly for prices and output), Jao argues that although 'price rises seem to be under control and relatively minor' (p. 104) this was achieved because of state price control backed with rationing at a time when consumer demand was growing rapidly. The income velocity of money is said to have fallen from 16.2 in 1950 to 6.5 in 1957 although most of the decline (from 16.2 to 8.6) occurred during the period 1950–52. Jao argues that as there was no market for financial claims in China the growth in the stock of money was necessary only to meet any increasing transactions demand. This indicated that its excessive rate of growth compared with the growth of national income pointed to the existence of 'a sizeable monetary excess demand held in check only by complete controls in the commodity and factor markets' (p. 110).

Jao does not attempt to link what price changes there were to any measure of excess demand or monetary growth. He concludes that China seemed to have 'the longest repressed inflation in peacetime', suggesting that it was possibly endemic in 'a centrally administered economy dedicated to high-speed industrialisation with only limited resources' (p. 110). In both his use of excess money-stock growth rates as an indicator of repressed inflation and his comparison of China's experience with other centrally planned economies, Jao anticipates two themes found in subsequent studies of China.

Hsiao (1971)

Hsiao's book was the first full-length study of banking institutions, money and monetary policy in the People's Republic of China. Although described by its author as a mainly qualitative analysis of institutions and policy the book does contain quantitative appraisal of the effectiveness of Chinese monetary policy for the period 1953–57. The qualitative aspect of the study clearly appreciates the major peculiarities of the socialist monetary system. These are seen in the separation of the monetary sector into the active and passive spheres of monetary circulation, the limited choice of financial assets available to households, the limited role of the rate of interest in determining the amount and direction of savings flows to industry, and the essentially defensive nature of monetary policy in China as it is always trying to absorb money issue. As the main objective of monetary policy during this period is said to have been a high rate of investment and a stable price level, the target of monetary policy became the limiting of the amount of currency left in circulation so that it equalled the demand for currency. Quantitative and qualitative aspects of monetary policy are identified. The former aimed at reducing the total quantity of money; the latter was intended to reduce the liquidity of the money supply by inducing agents to hold less liquid forms of money.

Hsiao clearly appreciates the nature of inflation in a planned economy like China's when she writes:

> In a command economy such as China's, this [inflationary] pressure can manifest itself in various forms. Open inflation involves price movements, but there can be two types of prices. The official prices for items that are controlled can be changed only by the government; this type of open inflation is 'decreed'. On the other hand, there may be price changes through market adjustments, and this type of inflation is 'free'. Alternatively, the controlled prices may be frozen by the state, resulting in suppressed inflation, under which a relatively stable price level is accompanied by such familiar symptoms as rationing, waiting lines, and idle cash ready to be spent (p. 225).

This taxonomy of inflation is more acute than is to be found in many subsequent studies and in fact is better than the approach actually used by Hsiao herself in her subsequent empirical study. It implies not only the necessity of splitting inflation into its 'open' and 'suppressed' aspects (later Hsiao prefers the word 'repressed') but also the need to explain the degree of 'open' inflation actually observed. As any price index used is likely to be a weighted average of official and market prices, changes in it can be due to changes in government pricing policy (the 'decreed' aspect) or to changes in market prices (the 'free' aspect). A full explanation of open inflation must say which of these two causes predominates: Has the official index risen because of large market price increases, or is it due to revisions in official prices? Any explanation of open inflation that argues that it is due to official price changes must supply a theory of why those prices were revised. Although Hsiao determines the extent of open inflation in this period she does not really resolve this problem and presents no clear view on whether prices increased mainly because of market forces or because of government policy.

In her empirical study of the extent of inflationary pressure over the period 1953–57 Hsiao considers four possible approaches.

The first two methods, the 'price movement approach' and the 'inflationary gap approach', are those used by Liu and Yeh (1965) but are rejected by the author mainly because they either fail to show inflationary pressure in 1956 or underestimate it. From Chinese sources Hsiao has indications that 1956 was an inflationary year, so she rejects any quantitative measure of inflation that fails to show this.

The next possible method discussed is the 'purchasing power approach', which involves comparing some measure of effective monetary demand and available supply. Hsiao tries out this method using data of social purchasing power and social commodity retail sales. The former is divided by the latter with the belief that a resulting index of 100 indicates that there is equilibrium, an index of more than 100 indicates inflationary pressure and an index of less than 100 indicates deflationary pressure (appendix F). As the index shows 'heavy deflation' for 1953, whereas other indexes suggest inflation, and only mild inflation for 1956 when there was said to be inflationary pressures, this approach is rejected. Hsiao understands fully why her treatment of the purchasing power approach produces such odd results. All she has done is to compare ex post expenditure with total incomes. Any ex ante excess demand might have produced price increases. Hsiao writes 'would have driven up prices', forgetting the need to provide an explanation of why prices increased. Open inflation would not be identified using this approach. Furthermore, her approach fails to consider the fact that there must be a gap between money incomes and expenditures in any year in order to produce the planned increase in the household sector's holdings of narrow money. The vital question is how big this gap should be. These important failings in her treatment of the purchasing power approach make her conclusion that the approach is 'sterile' somewhat premature.

The fourth method used to measure inflationary pressure is the 'currency supply approach', which is the same as that of Jao, under which an index of currency growth is compared with an index of retail sales in constant prices.

Hsiao had to estimate her own currency series for the period 1949–57 from scattered Chinese data. Although her estimate of the growth of currency in circulation over the period 1953–57 of 34 per cent corresponds with that shown by the recently available official data of 33.3 per cent, her series shows a very different annual growth path from that implied by the recent data. For example, her data show a slight fall from end-1953 to end-1954 whereas the modern data show an increase. Her data show an increase from end-1954 to end-1955 whereas the modern data show a fall. (See Table I.1 for the modern data for confirmation of this point.) These differences are sufficient to explain some of the odd features of her estimates.

Hsiao's approach is to take the end of 1952 as the base period and to compile an index of total inflation by deflating the index of currency growth by the index of retail sales at constant 1952 prices. Then the currency index is deflated by retail sales at current prices (as this will account for the open inflation), and the resulting index is labelled 'repressed inflation'.

Hsiao recognises the strong assumptions necessary: that 1952 was a normal year in the sense that money holdings stood at their desired ratio to retail sales, and that there were no changes in factors that might lead people to want to change their desired money holdings. These assumptions are the same as saying that the rate of growth of desired nominal expenditure is the same as the rate of growth of currency in circulation because the velocity of circulation of currency has remained stable, and that the desired velocity can be identified from the 1952 observation. The resulting index of total inflation shows continuing inflationary pressure, which is put at about 3.5 per cent per annum, and this is split almost equally into open inflation and repressed inflation. The index of total inflation shows increases in 1953 and 1956 as expected from qualitative evidence in Chinese sources, and this gives added weight to the figures in her view.

The major weakness of this approach is that because it had to be limited to so few years there is no clear explanation of why total inflation was split between open inflation and repressed inflation in a given ratio in any year. Furthermore, there is no consistent explanation of why there was open inflation. Was it due primarily to official price increases (which is implied for the 1957 observation), or was it mainly due to free inflation (which is implied for the 1953 observation by the use of the phrase 'prices soared' on p. 237). This shortcoming is probably due to the shortness of the period studied and the fact that it covers the transition from the existence of relatively free agricultural markets to the introduction of compulsory purchases, state supply in urban areas, rationing, price control and the socialisation of commerce in general.

Donnithorne (1974) and (1978)

Donnithorne (1978) is a revision and update of Donnithorne (1974), and both articles are descriptive but helpful discussions of the nature of inflation in China given the relative lack of statistics available at the time when Donnithorne was writing.

Donnithorne makes the important point that Chinese price statistics generally show the trend in only officially controlled prices and fail to indicate what was happening to the prices of the about 30 per cent of retail commodities that were subject to less stringent price control. The indexes, then, do not give any indication of changes in free market prices. The divergence between free market and official prices is said to have been striking at times.

The fact that there was rationing of various commodities and price control from 1953 indicates to Donnithorne that there was in fact excess demand throughout the period since then (1978: 3). Although there was excess demand and despite the fact that 'the state controls prices and has a monopoly of most forms of trade, it could in theory soak up excess purchasing power by raising the tax on consumer goods', the desire for price stability is thought to have taken precedence even at times of inflationary pressure (1974: 21–2). This argument is found also in Wang (1980) and will be examined empirically in chapter 6.

Donnithorne discusses reasons for official price stability, which are found mainly in the strict national budgetary policy and the nature of investment. Donnithorne says that the policy aim of securing a small budget surplus was a success except in the 'disaster years of 1960–62 and possibly during the cultural revolution' (1974: 7). During the First Five-year Plan period investments were mainly in large-scale slow-maturing projects, but the inflationary potential of this was reduced by relying on loans from the Soviet Union and other communist countries to maintain an import surplus. The end of the First Five-year Plan period saw decentralisation of control over consumer goods industries to local authorities and the end of foreign loans. The central government could not afford to implement large-scale investment projects, so from 1958 to 1972 investment was mainly financed by local authorities and agricultural collectives, which at first invested unwisely in duplicating small iron and steel furnaces and water conservancy schemes. Together with the collapse of national income after the Great Leap Forward this large investment drive produced marked inflationary pressure. After 1962 investment decisions were left mainly in the hands of local authorities, but these adopted a reasonable policy of small scale and high-yielding projects leaving large scale projects to the military. Donnithorne argues that after 1972 the need for large-scale nationally funded projects revived and that these were financed again by foreign loans. She concludes that the inflationary effects of large scale investment in China have always been dealt with by foreign loans.

Wages policy, Donnithorne says, also played a role in controlling inflationary pressures. Administrative means had to be substituted for market signals in allocating labour. She argues that the switch to non-material labour incentives in 1957–58 was a reaction to the inflationary pressures caused by the wage reform of 1956.

Donnithorne's discussion of the banking system's role in controlling inflation emphasises the familiar point that the People's Bank does not really have much control over the extent of credit granted to enterprises and ultimately over the amount of currency put into circulation. This means that the bank's anti-inflationary policy has to be confined to the supply side of the consumer market. Donnithorne identifies two policies. First, the bank puts pressure on enterprises to liquidate inventories, which will reduce their need for working capital and push finished goods onto the consumer goods market. Second, savings drives act as a means of absorbing household currency holdings and reducing their liquidity. Although savings are supposed to be made voluntarily there is usually a high degree of political and social pressure put on people to save. Furthermore, obstacles have been put in the way of depositors wishing to withdraw part of their savings deposits. No references are given for the latter, but as we saw in section 4.7 such pressures were observed during the Cultural Revolution period. Donnithorne argues that planners can control the wage bill more successfully than they can the total of agricultural payments.

Despite a tendency to see every policy solely as an anti-inflationary policy (the switch to non-material incentives in 1958 is a good example, and paying wages at the end of each month is another) Donnithorne's papers make some interesting and important points. Two in particular can and will be examined empirically:

1 Is it true that even at times of inflationary pressure increases in official prices were not used to absorb excess purchasing power?
2 Is it true that over the long period it has proved easier to control urban purchasing power than rural purchasing power?

Wang (1980)

Wang's book is a very detailed study of a large amount of statistical information on retail prices from a microeconomic standpoint. It is thus difficult to derive from it any clear propositions about planners' likely policies towards retail prices at times of macroeconomic imbalances. A chapter is devoted to the macroeconomic policies behind long-run price stability, but Wang's primary conclusion is that although these have been helpful 'the factor most responsible for the stability of official retail prices has been the specific price policy and pricing practice adopted by the Chinese. These have, to a great extent been carried out with the help of rationing, subsidies, and substantially higher prices in the nonsocialist market' (p. 127).

My interpretation of Wang's view on the importance of macroeconomic factors in explaining changes in the aggregate retail price index (and this includes the noticeable increases in the early 1980s, after Wang's study was published) is based on the above quotation and on the following argument. Wang writes that in maintaining the principles of price stability:

> . . . the price authorities appear to believe that any excess demand can be reduced to a desirable level or eliminated in due course, while retail prices are kept basically stable. They may also fear that any upward price adjustments for key commodities in years of economic crisis might lead to some degree of inflation, even if macroeconomic policies are anti-inflationary, because prices once raised, are difficult to push down when economic conditions improve later (pp. 94–5).

My interpretation of these quotations is that they suggest that when there is excess demand planners will *not* increase prices. Two observations contradict this proposition. First, in the difficult period of 1960–62 official prices of many state-supplied commodities *were* raised. These official price increases were subsequently reversed, and the aggregate price index was reduced to its earlier levels. As shown in chapter 2, the motive for raising some of these prices was to withdraw currency from circulation. Second, if we were to accept Wang's conclusion for the period before 1980, we would have to argue that all these principles and policies were soon abandoned as imbalances emerged in the 1980s and retail prices were increased. This phenomenon caused two seasoned observers, Chen and Hou, referred to in chapter 2, to ask why planners were increasing prices and contributing to inflation. It is my view that, if we did accept Wang's conclusion, we would not expect to observe significant price increases in the 1980s. Taking a longer view than Wang could we see that there were official price increases in the early 1960s, which were later reversed, and that there were subsequent official price increases throughout the 1980s. This suggests that price increases have been used at times of excess demand (if we can confirm that there was in fact excess demand during these periods) and that the search for a link at the macroeconomic level between demand imbalances and official price changes might be a fruitful task. This search will be undertaken in the next chapter.

Wang introduces his concluding chapter by stating that the 'problem of Chinese economic policy and price stability (or changes) is complicated and controversial' (p. 127). I think that this overstates the degree of controversy existing at the time when Wang wrote, although disagreements emerged later with the arrival of the significant price increases of the 1980s. Before the late 1970s many China specialists stressed the achievement of price stability in China, and this can be seen in the articles of Tsakok (1979) and Schran (1977). Only Swamy (1969) seems to have been prepared to argue that official Chinese data for the 1950s were misleading and that there were considerable price increases then. Wang challenges his claims (pp. 6–9).

5.2 *Studies published after 1980*

Chai (1981)

Chai's article was one of the first English-language articles to take advantage of the increased flow of Chinese language textbooks on money, banking and related topics. It is mainly concerned with institutional change and reform up to 1981 but does contain a small empirical section aimed at showing that 'the Bank's control over household money through the cash plan appears rather inadequate as more money than consumers' goods is constantly being fed into the economy as measured by the increase of the value of retail sales volume at constant prices' (p. 44). Indexes of cash in circulation and savings deposits suggested to Chai that the total money supply index (defined as the sum of these two items) increased by 85.3 per cent over the period 1978–80 whereas retail sales at constant prices increased only 25 per cent (p. 45).

The main conclusion of the paper is that the banking reforms of the period 1979–80 threatened the authorities' ability to maintain price stability, so a retreat from various reforms was adopted towards the end of 1980. This retreat involved dropping plans for increasing enterprise autonomy in fixing prices, reintroducing state price control, and forbidding local authorities and enterprises to use their own funds and bank credits for decentralised investment. Limitations on the amount of credit available for short- and medium-term fixed investment were imposed, such credit was to be supervised more closely, and the principle that credit be granted on the basis of the plan was reimposed. Chai concludes that by 1981 the banking system in China had reverted to being similar to the traditional Soviet-type system 'with minor modifications' (p. 50).

Hsiao (1982) and (1984)

These two works can be taken together as Hsiao (1982), an article, is updated slightly in Hsiao (1984), a short book containing more detailed statistics. The period covered is from 1979 to end-1981 although the book does present a comparison with the events of the 1950s on the basis of the statistics of Hsiao (1971). There is a year-by-year discussion of the inflation of the period 1979–81 in both works.

Hsiao (1982) identifies the main changes in banking operations in the following areas. The introduction of medium- and short-term equipment loans in 1979 is seen as a marked departure from previous practice under which bank loans to industrial enterprises were only to provide working capital for temporary and seasonal needs. Investment was financed from budget allocations. Under the new system loans could be granted for up to five years and were intended for light industry to renovate existing equipment and raise production levels quickly. They were not intended to be used for large scale investment or building new plant. The loans were to be repaid from enterprises' retained profits, depreciation funds and fixed asset tax.

After 1979 the People's Bank began to extend loans to urban co-operatives and individuals, something rarely done before 1979 but now necessary because of the development of small urban co-operatives and individual entrepreneurs, generally providing services such as transport and repairs.

Because enterprise reform allowed enterprises to retain part of their profits and depreciation funds and to decide on the use of these funds themselves the banking system had to respond in two ways: it allowed enterprises to grant credit to one another; and it introduced bank deposits in which enterprises could hold the funds they were now allowed to retain. These accounts were known as trust deposits. In addition, the People's Bank undertook to invest enterprises' funds according to the directions of the deposit holder, thus acting as a financial investment agent for the enterprise.

Hsiao sees another important change in banking policy in the attitude towards interest rates. Formerly, holders of bank deposits would receive one of only two interest rates: one rate for current savings accounts and one for fixed savings accounts. There was a similar uniformity in interest rates charged on loans, with all industrial and commercial enterprises paying the same loan rate no matter the duration of the loan, its purpose, whether repayment was overdue, or the nature of ownership of the enterprise. The major changes were the introduction of a variety of different savings deposits available to households and different interest rates. Loan rates were increased and differentiated according to the length of the loan and its purpose. Furthermore, the People's Bank could now levy surcharges on overdue loans.

The empirical analysis of inflation over the period 1979–81 is identical in both of Hsiao's studies (see 1982: 471–5; and 1984: 82–5). This means that her later treatment did not take advantage of the significantly increased amount of statistical information on money and prices available after 1981. Hsiao seems to have been unaware of the fact that monetary and cost-of-living data for the years after 1977 started appearing in *International Financial Statistics* of the International Monetary Fund (IMF) from October 1981. Furthermore, much price data and information on savings deposits appeared in the *Statistical Yearbook of China 1981* published in October 1982. This means that Hsiao's statistical basis for examining inflation is very scanty with, for example, only one year's increase in the cost of living identified for the period 1979–82 and three years' data for retail price increases (p. 83). This may explain why inflation is taken to be synonymous with an increase in currency in circulation and there is no attempt to explain why prices were increased during this period or whether there might have been a shift in the demand for money.

Hsiao sees a change in policy towards inflation control occurring in this period. She identifies the inflation of 1979 with the 17 billion *yuan* budget deficit that required bank loans to the government totalling 9 billion *yuan*. Currency in circulation, Hsiao says, did not increase significantly because of the increase in supplies of consumer goods and because of increases in rural and urban savings deposits and the deposits of enterprises, local governments and public organs. The monetary policy used to combat inflation is said to be the 'traditional and passive one of currency absorption' (1982: 473; 1984: 82). In 1980, Hsiao says, the situation was different because of the large increase in basic investment due to a failure in state budgetary policy to limit investment to within planned amounts and due to an increase in basic construction financed outside the state budget using funds from enterprises, local governments, banks and foreign loans. Hsiao argues that currency in circulation in this year, unlike in the previous year, increased substantially. In fact currency in circulation in 1980 rose about 29 per cent over the previous year, whereas the figure for 1979 was about 26 per cent higher than the previous year's. These are not significantly different rates of increase, although they are both large. Hsiao argues that the government was afraid that an inflationary psychology would develop, so a different set of policies was adopted. These included bond sales to enterprises and local governments together with requests to local authorities to lend 7 billion *yuan* to the central government. In addition, Hsiao says, the State Council issued a decree in February 1981 aimed at reasserting central control over money supply by giving the Bank greater power to withhold or recall bank loans and to ensure that loans were used for productive purposes. The Bank was allowed greater power in changing interest rates on loans and deposits within prescribed limits. Hsiao sees the first two policies (bond sales and loans to the central government) as belonging to the realm of fiscal policy as they were aimed at removing surplus funds already in the hands of enterprises. The third policy (increased bank powers) is identified as monetary policy proper as it tried to control the extent of monetary creation through loans to enterprises. Hsiao judges these policies to have been a success because the budget deficit in 1981 was lower and the rate of retail price inflation fell. Despite this, further measures for controlling retail prices were announced in early 1982, and further bond sales, to individuals as well as organisations, were made.

Many of the quantitative statements and conclusions of Hsiao (1984) cannot really be accepted because of the faulty statistics on which they are based. In particular, the data for currency in circulation before 1979 are suspect as these are based on reported rates of increase for various years. These rates of increase are applied to the absolute figure for 1957 derived in Hsiao (1971). The result is that all subsequent figures are larger than the figures officially published in China today. The rate of growth of Hsiao's currency data is about right, but the absolute values are too large. The series for non-state-sector bank deposits (1984: 42–2), painstakingly assembled from a large number of separate sources, must be judged inferior to the complete savings deposit data available from various issues of the *Statistical Yearbook of China*.

The visual representation of the money supply series in (1984: charts IV and V) is extremely misleading. Generally, data were available to Hsiao only for the periods 1953–57 and 1979–81 (and for a few intervening years for currency in circulation). Even though these figures are inaccurate in themselves they are presented in a most misleading way. The periods for which no data were available are represented in a time series graph by a space of a fraction of a centimetre when the true scale requires a space several times larger. Moreover, the data points for, say 1964, are extended to the right, even though no data are reported, so they seem to meet a line extended backwards and downwards from 1979, which is the next year for which there are data. This makes it look as if there was continued rapid growth of currency in circulation after 1964 until 1979. If the 1979 observation were plotted in its true position in relation to the horizontal time axis, it would not show such a rapid rate of increase. Readers of Hsiao (1984) are warned not to draw the intended conclusions about the speed of monetary growth over the intervening period without first examining the graphs very carefully.

Byrd (1983)

Byrd's book was the first English-language study of reform in China's banking system, and it concentrates on the period 1978–82. Although it contains copious statistics and was, as far as I know, the first English-language publication to contain statistics on currency in circulation in China for the period 1953–76 (although in index number form), the analysis is almost entirely descriptive in nature. Some interesting and relevant points and propositions do emerge, however. The two most important of these concern Byrd's view of the way banking reform can increase the inflationary potential in the economy, and whether there was an increase in repressed inflation in this early reform period.

Byrd argues that the traditional assumption of socialist monetary theory, that currency is the sole determinant of inflationary pressure, is incorrect and that in fact the overall liquidity position of state enterprises is the most important determinant. During a period of banking reform and decentralisation banks become able to increase considerably their loans to state enterprises. In fact, Byrd argues, with a decentralised banking system the old policy of encouraging savings deposits as a means of controlling inflation will actually increase the banks' ability to extend credit to any borrower. This will lead to an 'increase [in] inflationary pressures, in that the purchasing power that economic units perceive as being available to them will exceed the quantity of goods and materials by a greater margin than before' (p. 74). Byrd believes that decentralisation of the power to grant loans to local branch banks means that the typical money-creation multiplier of Western monetary theory will become the mechanism by which the money supply (defined broadly as currency in circulation plus enterprise bank deposits) will be created.

For any local branch of the banking system extending a loan to an enterprise in its area, there are two ways in which that loan, when it is used, will *not* result in a similar increase in deposits at other branches in the same local network: if the proceeds of the loan are used to make cash payments such as wages or agricultural procurements; and if the enterprise has to make payments for supplies from other enterprises in different regions. Apart from these two leakages out of the local branch network any loan extended will result in a new deposit in the network and allow a further loan to be made.

Byrd's numerical example assumes that the proportion of any loan extended by the local bank that returns to it as a future deposit is 0.8. If the bank receives a new deposit of 100 units, it can extend a loan of 100, which will increase its deposits by 80, allowing it to extend a further loan of 80, which will increase deposits by 64, allowing a further loan of 64, and so on. The total amount of loans the bank can create on the basis of the 100 unit deposit is 500 units, and its deposits would rise by 400 units. The difference is the amount of credit extended that does not return to this local network. Assume that it is all currency in circulation. If the original increase in deposits were due to the withdrawal of cash from circulation, the amount of currency in circulation would remain unchanged, but the total money supply (including bank deposits held by enterprises) would increase considerably. If the proportion of any loan that returns to the bank as future deposits is x, the multiplier effect on total loans of a unit increase in deposits will be $1/(1 - x)$, which is 5 units in the above simple example. Byrd's important conclusion is that, if decentralisation creates institutions in which this loan expansion multiplier works, the traditional policy of encouraging savings deposits will make possible even greater inflationary expansion of loans. This is because such policies will increase the value of x and hence the multiplier. Byrd (p. 74) estimates x as about 0.78 for 1980, giving a multiplier of 4.53 at the national level with much greater multipliers being found in different provinces.

Byrd recognises that there was 'significant inflation in retail prices' from 1979 (p. 84), which he links to certain features of the economic reforms until about 1982. He challenges the Chinese argument that central budget deficits are the primary cause of increases in currency issue and, by implication, of retail price inflation. Two features of the reforms are stressed by Byrd. First, the increased stress on enterprise profitability made them more willing to try to 'manipulate' prices (p. 85). Second, enterprises were allowed to retain greater proportions of their profits; this increased the 'moneyness' of bank deposits and allowed them to be used freely by enterprises, thus contributing to the demand for commodities and exerting inflationary pressure on the consumer goods market. Byrd estimates that bank credit was as important as the state budget deficit in its contribution to inflationary money creation.

Despite significant changes in the economic system due to reform Byrd sees little change in the nature of anti-inflationary policy, which concentrates on withdrawing currency from circulation. The policies he identifies are:

1 quantitative controls on credit;
2 policies to increase individual financial saving;
3 policies to increase the production of light-industrial consumer goods and services;
4 increased procurements of agricultural produce for sale to the urban population;
5 control over cash transactions and reserves of units in the state sector; and
6 a balanced budget, with any surplus frozen.

In addition he cites the strict administrative control over prices as a policy but points out that such a policy does not tackle the causes of inflationary pressure.

Byrd argues that policies aimed at encouraging households to hold savings deposits rather than currency are not likely to reduce demand for commodities. The fourth policy cited above is also thought not to be viable any more as a result of the change in relative procurement and retail prices of agricultural products. Previously the state could procure produce at low price for resale in processed form at higher prices, withdrawing currency from circulation. Now many of the procurement agencies must pay higher prices, thus making losses, which are subsidised, and this results in more currency being issued in rural areas than is withdrawn in urban areas.

Byrd's view is that increasing individual savings are not a sign of repressed inflation and, generally speaking, are held voluntarily. This is the opposite view to that of Travers (1985: 126–7) who sees the increases in urban savings deposits and cash holdings as involuntary. In urban areas in order to buy the increasing supplies of consumer durables, which in the absence of consumer credit required cash savings. The fact that the free market price index is said not to have increased substantially in the period 1978–81 is taken by Byrd as evidence that there could not have been frustrated purchasing power, which, he argues, would have contributed to rapidly rising free-market prices (p. 92). In addition, policies to increase the attractiveness of savings deposits, such as higher interest rates, better banking services and the restoration of confidentiality for customers, are cited as arguments to explain increasing individual savings deposits.

Li (1985)

Li's study of the demand for money starts with some interesting evidence that we described in chapter 2 and that Li never really explains. A time series graph for the period 1953–82 of the annual rates of change of national income and gross industrial and agricultural product, together with the annual growth of cash, quite clearly shows an inverse relationship. This is particularly clear for the following three periods: 1958–61, when output growth rates fell markedly and became negative while cash growth rates rose; 1961–65, when output growth increased and cash growth rates fell and became negative; and 1966–68, when output growth fell and cash growth increased. The pattern is even clearer in the case of individual years, such as 1975 and 1978, when output growth increased and cash growth fell. Li performs correlation analysis for cash growth rates against seven indicators of supply availability, including the two mentioned above, and obtains negative coefficients for national income, gross industrial and agricultural output, and gross agricultural output. The few positive coefficients are insignificant.

Li is perplexed by this finding that there is no positive correspondence between output growth and cash growth on an annual basis, and she proposes that there must be a lag in the determination of money supply behind output change. She investigates this by a series of regressions for the period 1963–82 of cash against output variables for the current year and the two previous years, obtaining a consistent pattern of positive coefficients for the current year, Y_t, and the year before the previous one, Y_{t-2}, but negative coefficients for the previous year, Y_{t-1}. The negative impact of output growth on cash in the next year is found to be interesting, and Li offers some possible explanations, the most interesting of which is as follows. It is argued that China is characterised by excess consumer demand, so expansions of output can withdraw cash from circulation, but this apparently involves a one-year lag before the increased output provides the extra consumer goods, which is favourable for the recall of money from circulation (*you li yu huilong huobi*, p. 44). The variables shown to have greatest effect in withdrawing cash in the next year are national income, then light industry and agriculture with the least effect being shown by heavy industry.

Li's paper provides some interesting insights into the negative impact of output growth on cash growth rates, and these were established initially by Li on the basis of a synchronous relationship. This provides a useful clue in the subsequent analysis of the determinants of cash circulation.

Wang (1985)

Wang's study is concerned with understanding why the increase in the money supply in 1984 was so large, especially after a period in which it had been admitted that monetary growth was excessive. Wang refutes the argument that rapid economic development after 1979 was a consequence of rapid monetary growth and tries to formulate a quantitative rule for future monetary growth. The ratio of average annual monetary growth of 10.9 per cent during the period 1953–83 to output growth at 8 per cent for the same period is shown to be 1.363, which is modified by omitting the Great Leap Forward and the Cultural Revolution to produce a ratio of 1.33. This is rounded up to 1.35, which is said to be the same as the ratio found in developed industrialised countries (p. 72). On the basis of planned output growth of 8.8 per cent per annum to the year 2000 Wang proposes an annual planned rate of monetary growth of 11 to 12 per cent. This is to be achieved by stricter use of the new system of bank reserve ratios created at the time of the banking system reform of 1984, and by use of the rediscount rate to increase the cost of loans from the newly established independent banks. Wang recognises, however, that as these banks are still state banks they are virtually obliged to provide loans to all enterprises. In addition, administrative controls will be necessary to limit monetary growth.

Zheng (1986a) and (1986b)

These two articles are remarkable for the fact that Zheng[1] provides two completely contradictory arguments concerning the long run trend of velocity in China using essentially similar evidence.

Zheng (1986a) is concerned with the phenomenon that money supply grows faster than national income. There are said to be many different opinions in China as to what constitutes money, with the old view that it was only currency being replaced by the new view that bank deposits should be included. Zheng chooses a relatively broad concept consisting of cash in circulation, the deposits of enterprises, institutions and organisations, basic construction deposits plus rural collective deposits. Over the period 1952–84 the growth of this monetary aggregate averaged 1.55 times the growth of output with the ratio reaching 1.72 for 1980–84 (1986a: 63). For a number of capitalist countries monetary growth has outstripped output growth. Because monetary growth exceeded output growth during prosperous periods in China and because this seems to be a general phenomenon in developed countries, Zheng concludes that it is a completely normal phenomenon. If true, this means that velocity would show a long run decline.

Although quite happy to see the rate of growth of money exceeding that of output Zheng goes on to show that in 1984 the actual amount of currency issue was 3.3 times greater than the planned amount, that is, an actual increase, which he gives as 26.2 billion *yuan* against a planned amount of only 8.0 billion *yuan* (1986a: 65). He argues that although a part of this excess was due to the expansion in the consumption fund in 1984 a large part was simply due to the fact that actual real output growth and retail sales growth were about twice the planned rate.

Zheng (1986b) seeks to contradict the conventional wisdom and the implication of Zheng (1986a) by arguing that there is a law of progressively increasing velocity that applies to China. He summarises the views of Friedman and Schwartz, Marx, Fisher, Pigou and Keynes to show that there is no real theoretical consensus as to how velocity should develop in the long run. He cites Friedman and Schwartz's (1963) evidence for the long run decline in velocity in the United States over the period 1867–60. He then cites postwar evidence from the United States, the United Kingdom, France and India that shows a progressive increase in velocity in all countries. On the basis of this evidence he concludes that there is a law of increasing velocity that has general application (1986b: 36).

In investigating this phenomenon in China Zheng rejects the common way of measuring velocity as annual retail sales divided by currency at the end of the year in favour of total product of society divided by cash in circulation plus bank demand deposits. He tabulates this velocity for the period 1952–84, commenting on the periods when it fell (1954–58, 1961–62, 1966–68 and 1980–84) and when it rose (1963–65, 1969–70 and 1977–79). There are, Zheng says, no common factors lying behind the periods of decline in velocity. He argues that the periods of increase in velocity were all periods of economic recovery. In spite of his own table 5 (1986b: 37), which shows the long run decline in velocity from 10.95 in 1952 to 4.72 in 1984, he maintains that there is a law that velocity tends to increase gradually under normal economic circumstances and will fall only under special circumstances. He claims that China's history supports, not refutes, the law of progressively increasing velocity (1986b: 33).

The conclusion of Zheng (1986b) seems very weak especially in the face of the contradictory evidence presented. The change of heart might have been due to an article by Zhang Yutang (1986a), which criticises both Zheng (1986a) and Zhou Cequn (1986). Both the latter argue that there is a law of excess monetary growth that applies to China just as much as to the developed countries where it can be observed. Zhou (1986: 31) calls this phenomenon 'the tendency of advanced [*chaoqian*] or accelerated [*jiasu*] increase in the money supply'. He derives it on the basis of evidence from five industrialised countries and shows that it can be observed in modern China as well. He argues that it is a necessary and healthy sign but is unable to put any quantitative limits on it.

Zhang Yutang (1986a) criticises those who argue for the greater increase in money supply, citing evidence from fifteen capitalist countries that money supply does not grow at a greater rate in all of them (it is true in only three of his chosen countries). He argues that the sole effect of high monetary growth will be high inflation and cites some data from five capitalist countries to illustrate this. Zhang rejects the tendency of greater monetary growth as an objective law (p. 75) and says that it can never be China's policy.

Li Shuhe (1987) also entered the debate between Zheng and Zhang with a more detailed study that uses a number of velocity concepts that tend to show a steady decline in velocity (p. 43). This decline was marked for the period 1952–61, after which time velocity increased until about 1966 before falling until 1968; thereafter it fluctuated slightly until rising in 1979 and then showing a progressive decline afterwards. Li goes on to look at seasonal fluctuations in velocity but does not reach a firm conclusion about the long run trend in velocity. Li also comments that his conclusions are different from those of Zhang Yutang (1986a).

Zhang Yutang (1986b), however, is another study that shows declining velocity in China, measuring it as total product of society divided by cash plus demand deposits. Zhang cites comparative evidence from West Germany, Japan, Singapore and South Korea (p. 28) to show that in the early stage of their modern economic development velocity fell particularly quickly and then under normal economic development continued to fall at a slower rate. Zhang's explanation for the fall in velocity in China includes the fact of increasing monetisation of the economy and the consequences of high investment ratios. The latter requires the previous accumulation of monetary reserves, thus entailing a fall in velocity (p. 29). This is quite a sophisticated argument concerning developing countries, made familiar in the works of McKinnon and referred to in chapter 3. Zhang concludes by arguing that the rate of decline of velocity during the First Five-year Plan period should be taken as the norm for future monetary planning.

Li (1986) does not really come down on one side or another in the debate about whether the long run trend of velocity in China is one of increase or decrease. He argues that forecasting the future trend in velocity requires knowledge of the long run phase it is in, the stage of its cyclical fluctuation it is in, as well as a consideration of possible abnormal influences (p. 6).

Chen and Hou (1986)

This paper concentrates on inflation in China during the period 1979–83 and tries to quantify its true extent. Chen and Hou start by rejecting the national income deflator as an indicator of inflation because it is too narrowly based as it is only drawn up for the material production sectors of the economy and because it values agricultural produce at procurement prices, not at retail prices. They argue that the official indexes, particularly the retail price and cost-of-living indexes, are likely to underestimate the true extent of open inflation because they use out-of-date weights from the 1950s. Since then the share of retail sales made at market prices has 'increased greatly' (p. 814), and these prices have risen faster than the other price categories, that is, list prices and negotiated prices. They argue that 'the price indexes compiled by the State Statistical Bureau. . .principally reflect the movements in the government-fixed prices' (p. 817). This is a very important point, which leads Chen and Hou to raise the following trenchant question: 'But why did the government raise prices and hence contribute to inflation, especially in the past few years?' (p. 817). This clearly means that any explanation of price changes will have to be an explanation of planners' retail pricing behaviour as it cannot rely on arguing that market price changes were large enough to account for most of the change in any retail price index. This point will be discussed again in the review of Chow (1987) below.

In analysing the nature of inflation in China during this period Chen and Hou argue that the concept of 'suppressed inflation' is relevant. Using the simple Quantity Theory framework ($MV = PT$) they assume that V is constant and T is under planners' control; hence changes in M (currency) will not cause PT (retail sales) to change to the same degree. In inflationary periods M tends to grow faster than PT; 'the discrepancy reflects suppressed inflation' (p. 822).

What they do is to modify the approach used by Hsiao (1982, 1984) discussed above and simply compare the growth rate of currency with that of retail sales in constant prices. The year 1978 is taken as base year. Their procedure differs from that of Hsiao in that they compute all variables as changes over the previous year. Hence a figure showing the percentage increase in currency (19.1 per cent in 1979) is converted to a link index (1.191) and divided by the link index obtained for growth of retail sales in constant prices (which is 1.137 as real retail sales grew 13.7 per cent over the previous year). The resulting index of 1.047 (1.191 divided by 1.137) is converted into a simple percentage increase, 4.7, and labelled 'total inflation'. The actual rate of open inflation (which is derived from the general retail price index and was 2.0 per cent in 1979) is subtracted from 'total inflation' and the remainder is labelled 'suppressed inflation', here being 2.7. These are all treated as changes in the two aspects of inflation (open and suppressed) over the previous year. However, Chen and Hou make no attempt to explain what determines whether total inflation in any year will show up as open inflation or suppressed inflation. These proportions vary considerably. For example, their estimates imply that in 1980 open inflation, at 6.0 per cent, was 71 per cent of 'total inflation', at 8.5 per cent, whereas in 1981 open inflation, at 2.4 per cent, was only 20 per cent of 'total inflation', at 12.2 per cent (p. 823).

Having quantified these three measures of inflation so precisely Chen and Hou then devote three pages to explaining why the measures are not correct, because, as they admit, the assumption that velocity is constant is not likely to be correct during this period. They discuss a variety of factors likely to change the demand for currency, and hence velocity, without any clear conclusion about whether desired velocity is likely to have risen or fallen during the period 1979–83. It seems, however, that on balance they believe that the demand for money is likely to have increased during this period mainly due to four factors: decentralisation; the rapid growth of rural free markets; the increase in autonomy of state and collective enterprises, which allowed these enterprises to hold larger sums of cash; and the increased hoardings of cash in preference to savings deposits, especially in rural areas. This discussion is marred by their not clearly distinguishing between the demand for money, that is, desired velocity, and what actually happened to velocity in this period. Clearly, velocity fell, and that in fact is what their 'suppressed inflation' index identifies. If all of the change in velocity were due to a shift in the demand function for money, there would be no 'suppressed inflation' at all. On balance, Chen and Hou conclude, their estimate of 'suppressed inflation' is likely to be an overestimate because there was a shift in the demand for money function, but they make no attempt to say by how much their actual figures overstate its extent.

Chen and Hou's analysis of government policy to control inflation stresses policies to boost the production of consumer goods and to control the growth of currency. This latter involves balancing the state budget and 'perhaps the most significant, short-term measure was to encourage, urban and rural residents to increase their savings deposits' (p. 830). Savings campaigns and interest rate increases were used. Consumer goods supplies were encouraged by the policy of favouring the agricultural sector after 1979 and the policy of providing medium- and short-term equipment loans for light industry to use for modernising and renovating plants and equipment.

This summary of anti-inflation policies is similar in emphasis to Byrd's, summarised above, but with a tendency to interpret every policy primarily as an anti-inflationary policy rather than simply as a policy to raise production and living standards.

Nambu (1985) uses a similar approach to derive three indexes of inflation ('open', 'suppressed' and 'overall') for the period 1978–84 but gives no clear description of the precise method used.

Feltenstein and Farhadian (1987)

The empirical starting point for this paper is the evidence of a large increase in the broad money supply in China 'over the past several years'. Broad money is defined by them as currency in circulation plus household time and savings deposits. Feltenstein and Farhadian show graphically that this series has increased much faster than the rates of increase in real *GNP* and open inflation would lead one to expect. From end-1978 to end-1984 broad money increased by 268 per cent while the consumer price index only rose 20 per cent. They take the deteriorating trade balance as evidence of strong demand pressure and assume throughout the paper that there was sustained excess demand on the consumer goods market and repressed inflation.

The two questions Feltenstein and Farhadian seek to answer are: What determines the rate of growth of broad money supply in China, and what is the extent of repressed inflation? On the basis of the nature of the sphere of cash circulation in China they derive an expression for the increase in broad money, showing it to be a positive function of the state wage bill, agricultural procurements, the current account of the balance of payments and the state budget deficit. They estimate this equation econometrically using annual data for the period 1954–83, concluding that as all coefficients are significant at the 5 per cent level, except the current account, changes in broad money are reasonably well explained (p. 148). One conclusion they come to is that, because the coefficient of the procurement variable is larger than the wage bill variable, increased agricultural procurements have a larger expansionary effect on the money supply than extra wage payments. They state that 'a higher proportion of payments for farm procurements appear to be monetized than are public sector wage payments', explaining this as 'perhaps reflecting the different expenditures on retail goods from these sources of income' (p. 148). This is an important finding, which will be investigated in the following chapter, and it could of course be an important explanation of the rapid increase in broad money after 1979 because of the large expansion of agricultural procurements resulting from agricultural reform. Their finding that the current account has no identifiable impact on monetary expansion is also of interest, given the discussion in section 4.11 showing that it is but one element of several influencing the increase in narrow money. These questions will be taken up again empirically in chapters 6 and 7.

Feltenstein and Farhadian's procedure for estimating the degree of repressed inflation is to ask what implicit price level (virtual prices) would induce households to hold the large amounts of nominal money they are observed to hold. These excess holdings are assumed by them to be the result of shortages on the consumer goods market. This true rate of inflation is unobservable but is assumed to be the rate perceived by households in determining their desired money balances. They estimate that households perceive the true rate of inflation to be 2.5 times higher than the official rate. They also conclude that households adapt their expectations of inflation relatively slowly as households only revise their expected rate of inflation upwards by less than half of the excess of the actual true rate of inflation over the true rate expected in the previous period. This seems reasonable to Feltenstein and Farhadian as households would not have much experience of changing prices. Their estimate of the income elasticity of demand for real money balances is 1.373.

Feltenstein, Lebow and van Wijnbergen (1990)

These authors investigate savings behaviour using the same 'virtual prices' concept used in Feltenstein and Farhadian (1987). They compare regression results for the period 1955–83 for four types of savings equations estimated by using both the official cost-of-living index and their estimated virtual price level to deflate nominal values. The virtual price index is estimated so that the divergence of the unobserved virtual price index from the official index is a positive function of the excess of the rate of growth of nominal money supply over the rate of growth of the value of retail sales (their equation 16). This is a simple quantity theory formulation of what the true price level should be. They argue that the results for all savings functions are better, as well as being stable after 1979, when the virtual price index is used for deflation rather than the official index. This indicates that households do perceive the true price level to be higher than the official level because of repressed inflation. The authors compute a virtual real rate of interest and find that a measure of consumption (taken as real retail sales) is significantly negatively related to the real rate of interest, meaning that saving is encouraged by high real rates of interest. They state that this has rarely been demonstrated empirically in other studies. They further show that 'consumption' is not related to expected inflation, implying that nominal interest rates have an impact in encouraging saving. They had to use 'consumption' rather than saving in these regressions as they preferred a log formulation and the savings flow was negative in some years.

There are some problems in interpreting these results because of the nature of the data used. The authors study only the period 1955–83 and rely on Byrd (1983) and *International Financial Statistics* for monetary data. No data are presented in the paper. They say that no series of disposable income is available and so estimate it as retail sales plus the savings variable (p. 244). This is both incorrect and unnecessary. Disposable income is approximately equal to retail sales plus the annual accumulation of *both* savings deposits and currency. Furthermore, there have been available for a number of years complete data of household monetary incomes that could be used to estimate a series of disposable incomes. In fact, as was shown in section 4.11, these data are part of a balance that allows us to account for changes in savings deposits and holdings of cash in hand. The authors use retail sales for their consumption measure but do not make it clear whether they have deducted the sales of agricultural means of production from this total. This is obviously not an item of consumption, and as it has varied as a proportion of total retail sales the trend in consumption may not be accurately proxied by the trend in total retail sales. As the authors do not publish any data it is not possible to be clear about the coverage of their 'consumption' variable.

The claimed relationship between savings and real interest rates is open to question. The virtual real rate of interest is a positive function of the virtual price level, which in turn is a positive function of the excess of the rate of growth of money over retail sales. Now this money measure consists mainly of savings deposits, so when money grows rapidly real interest rates are high, but by definition savings will be high as well. The relationship observed could just be the result of the fact that rapid savings growth generates a high estimate of virtual real interest rates. The authors question the ability of the model to explain events after 1983 when there were rapid increases in cash balances, a fact that is 'leading to an initial indication that there continues to be monetary overhang and repressed savings [sic]' (p. 248).

Chow (1987)

Chow's paper is important for two reasons: it analyses annual data for the period 1952–83, and it uses the simple Quantity Theory of Money as a framework for discovering the relationship between money and prices in China. The main variables used are as follows. Money is defined as currency in circulation, the source of which data is something of a mystery as the source given by Chow (p. 323) (that is, *Statistical Yearbook of China*'s table entitled 'Bank credit receipts and payments'—no volume or page numbers are given) has never presented full time series of this important series. The income measure used is real national income available (y), which can be obtained by deflating the readily available series of nominal national income available by the implicit price deflator obtained by comparing the series of nominal and real national income. National income available is equal to national income (net material product, of course) plus imports minus exports, plus the statistical discrepancy. The price index used is the general index of retail prices. Now this index is predominantly of state-controlled list prices, an argument we have seen accepted by Chen and Hou (1986), discussed above. However, Chow assumes that the Quantity Theory 'could still provide a good explanation of the general price level if the remaining uncontrolled prices were able to adjust sufficiently' (p. 322).

Chow's first step is to regress the real money supply as defined above on real income, obtaining an income elasticity of demand for real money balances of 1.162, an estimate whose confidence limits do not embrace 1, thus 'contradicting the quantity theory' (p. 325).

The simplest possible form of the theory is tested by regressing the natural logarithm of the price level (P) on the natural logarithm of the ratio of money to real income (M/y) to obtain the following result for the period 1952–83 (p. 325):

$$\ln P = \underset{(0.0567)}{0.9445} + \underset{(0.0229)}{0.2687} \ln (M/y) \qquad R^2 = 0.8217,\ s = 0.0363,\ DW = 1.003,\ n = 32$$

Standard errors of the estimates are in brackets, R^2 is the coefficient of determination, s is the standard error of the regression, and DW is the Durbin–Watson statistic. These are the only test statistics Chow reports.

Chow concludes that 'the ratio M/y does provide a good explanation of the price level, P, as the quantity theory predicts' (p. 325) because the t-statistic of the ratio (11.76) is high, as is the coefficient of determination. However, he comments that as the slope coefficient is 'only 0.2687 and very much below unity' it is 'contradicting the quantity theory' (p. 325). In other words, the results show a statistically significant but quantitatively unimportant relationship and one that is well below that expected on the basis of the Quantity Theory. This should be no surprise as the price index used contains such a large proportion of controlled prices, the purpose of price control being precisely to prevent prices from rising in line with any increase in the money ratio.

Chow goes on to estimate equations explaining the annual changes in the same price index, using the change in the money ratio (and later the lagged value of the change in the money ratio, which he drops, however). He concludes that there is evidence of a long run relationship between ln P

and ln (M/y) as suggested by the Quantity Theory, but as we have seen this relationship is not very important quantitatively and is very far from the predicted proportionality of the simple Quantity Theory.

Chow rejects the hypothesis that the total wage bill affects the price level, because when it is added to a simple regression of ln P on ln (M/y) it produces a statistically significant but small coefficient (elasticity of only 0.043). He also concludes that the relationship remained stable after 1979 and uses the equation to predict a price level of 161.27 for 1984 (the actual figure was 160.00). Chow concludes that 'the quantity theory of money provides a useful starting point in constructing a model to explain the index of retail prices in China' (p. 332). We can accept this conclusion by pointing out the limitations of the theory. First, no attempt is made to show that actual free-market prices changed sufficiently to produce the observed changes in the general retail price index. If state-controlled list prices were an important element of the price index (which they undoubtedly were) and if they were changed (which is not investigated by Chow), a completely different theory must be constructed. This must be a theory to explain why *list* prices were changed. Second, no attempt is made to explain why the money ratio changed. This is similar to the use of the Quantity Theory in market economies where reasons for changes in the money supply are not integrated into the model. If the money supply is largely endogenous, it cannot be taken as exogenous nor assumed to be an initiating cause of the price increases. A more complete approach would try to explain both monetary growth and the associated price increases. What Chow has done is to establish that there is a weak association between the money ratio and the price level, but he has not really provided an explanation of why the money ratio changes nor, more importantly, of exactly why prices change.

Perkins (1988: 624) quotes Chow's results approvingly, even citing an unpublished but forthcoming paper of Chow's that obtains a slope coefficient of only 0.127 for the regression of first differences of natural logarithms of prices and the money ratio. He concludes that '[m]uch more work is required before we have a reliable model for analyzing China's inflationary experience' (p. 624).

Naughton (1986) and (1987)

This brief review will concentrate on Naughton's 1987 paper although reference to the 1986 dissertation will be necessary as it contains many of the time series and estimates underlying the 1987 paper.

The main aim of Naughton (1987) is to examine the change in the financial relationship between the three major sectors (the government, households and enterprises) during the modern reform period of 1979–85 when there were changes in both government fiscal policy and in the economic environment faced by households and enterprises. The government budget became expansionary by running large deficits, and enterprises were given greater freedom of operation at the same time as households were allowed to follow private economic activities. The necessary response to the increase in government dissaving (the budget deficit) was obviously that enterprises and households had to increase their saving. Using a consolidated balance sheet for the banking sector Naughton (1987: 340–41) shows that, whereas in 1978 about 50 per cent of bank liabilities were held by the government, the government's increased holdings over the period 1978–83 amounted to only 10 per cent, with households holding 49 per cent of the increase and enterprises 40 per cent. Naughton notes a large change in household saving behaviour that necessarily accompanied this sector's increased holdings of bank liabilities in the form of currency and savings deposits.

He estimates a household saving function for the period 1957–78 of the Houthakker–Taylor form where the increment in money holdings (ΔM_t) is made a function of the increment in total incomes and of the predicted value of savings for the previous period. The method of estimating household incomes is described in Naughton's earlier dissertation (1986: appendixes A, B and D, pp. 11–17), which also gives the saving equation (1986: 55). This function implies an average saving rate (in financial assets) of only 2.4 per cent of household money income for the period 1970–78. The equation is used to predict the saving rate for the period 1980–83. Together with estimates of reasonable amounts of household monetary accumulation expected to result from the reforms, an expected value for the saving rate of 5 to 6 per cent of income is expected. In fact the recorded rate for the period 1980–83 was 10 per cent (1987: 344).[2]

Naughton asks whether this large shift in the saving function is evidence of 'forced saving' or whether it represents a desired response to the changing economic environment. He argues that it represents a desired response and likens it to the similar large changes in household saving that occurred in Taiwan in the 1960s. He cites four supporting pieces of evidence for the view that there was no increased shortage of consumer goods in the early 1980s nor forced saving: that the number of goods formally rationed after 1978 declined; that free market prices did not rise more rapidly than state prices; that consumption goods inventories increased; and that most of the increased household assets holdings were in the form of savings deposits. He argues that, if there had been increasing shortages, people would have held more currency as a sort of precautionary balance to maximise their likelihood of obtaining goods in short supply when they came across them. He argues that the only evidence that savings might have been forced is the increase in the savings rate itself, but there is no further supporting evidence for this. Households now had greater opportunities for both consumption and investment in household production, and these increased opportunities led to increased saving.

For the pre-reform period of 1956–78 Naughton (1986) does show that household saving rates did respond to imbalances on the consumer goods market. He does this by associating them with an index of shortage, which he constructed by comparing household demand for consumer goods with available supply. This last set of data is from a series that Naughton describes as a 'remarkable data set' that has 'no parallel in any other CPE [centrally planned economy]' (1986: 105). Household demand is identified as money income (estimated as actual purchases plus monetary accumulation, as no purchasing power data were available then) adjusted for desired saving, which is estimated from the saving function discussed above. The absolute gap between available supply and household demand is presented as a percentage of household demand for the period 1956–78. This variable, labelled 'shortfall', is then used as an additional explanatory variable in regressions of the accumulation of monetary assets by households. A significant dependence is found for currency accumulation and the accumulation of savings deposits. As the implication is that the supply shortfall does result in a net increase in household money holdings Naughton accepts this as evidence of 'forced' saving. However, he interprets the increased currency holdings as a necessary adjustment to a situation of intensified shortage, not as evidence of 'forced saving *per se*' (1986: 111).

Naughton also uses his index of shortage to explain fluctuations in investment, arguing that it is the only leading indicator of changes in investment. Other candidates, such as agricultural production and energy supplies, failed to predict changes in investment. The equation he reports for the period 1956–78 for the percentage change in fixed investment (dI_f/I_f) regressed against a time trend (t) and the index of shortage of the previous year (X_{t-1}) is

$$\underset{}{dI_f/I_f} = \underset{(16.49)}{52.76} - \underset{(0.89)}{1.04t} - \underset{(0.05)}{0.21\ X_{t-1}} \qquad R^2 = 0.4679$$

He interprets this as showing that planners have responded to conditions on the consumer goods market when determining investment, showing their willingness to reduce investment when consumer goods are in short supply. This is the equation reported in Naughton (1987: 342). However, the nearest equation to this that actually appears in Naughton (1986: 168), which he cites as its source, is

$$dI_f/I_f = \underset{(3.20)}{52.76} - \underset{(1.17)}{1.04t} - \underset{(4.08)}{0.21\ (X_{t-1})^2} \qquad R^2 = 0.4679,\quad F = 8.35$$

where $(X_{t-1})^2$ appears to be the square of the shortage indicator (labelled S in this source), which was used in the estimates of household saving. In Naughton (1986: 168) the coefficient of X_{t-1} is minus 4.57 (at least I think that it is on the photocopy I obtained) with a t-statistic of 3.76.[3] If it is, it gives stronger support to Naughton's interpretation.

However, Naughton's dependent variable is not necessarily a good indicator of changes in planners' attitudes towards investment versus consumption, which is how he interprets his results. In certain years investment fell simply because income fell. Even if planners maintained an unchanged attitude to investment and kept it at the same percentage of national income, investment would still be reduced. Some of these years of negative income growth followed years of excess demand or shortage, thus producing the effect captured in Naughton's regression. A better indicator of changing attitudes to investment would be obtained by examining investment as a proportion of income and how this proportion was changed as a result of excess demand on the consumer goods market. This will be done in section 6.8.

Naughton (1987) spends less time analysing the changes in enterprise saving behaviour and enterprises' holdings of financial assets than he spends on households because, as he rightly notes, no comparable theory of enterprise saving is available. He concludes that the changed saving behaviour of both households and enterprises are voluntary responses to the new economic environment created by economic reform and provide a 'breathing space' for reform by not creating sustained excess demand (1987: 349).[4] He also recognises the fact that macroeconomic management has become much more difficult in China because of the planners' difficulty in interpreting data becoming available to them. For example, what is the correct volume of currency needed in the new circumstances? Naughton's conclusion is that economic reform has meant that consumer goods availability is no longer the factor limiting economic growth (energy and foreign exchange availability are now the limiting factors) and that the future success of the reform process will depend on policy makers' ability to understand the major changes in economic behaviour brought about by the reform.

Portes and Santorum (1987)

In this technical paper Portes and Santorum seek to do two things: to test whether the money supply in China has been exogenously determined by the government or is endogenous to the economic system; and to compare the results from a number of studies that have tried to assess the degree of imbalance on the consumer goods market. The first question is answered by the conclusion that 'our results do cast substantial doubt on whether M_0 or M_2 (especially the latter) could reasonably be viewed as exogenous' (p. 361). (M_0 is currency, and M_2 is currency plus personal savings deposits; see p. 370.)

Portes and Santorum compare the results of a number of models, including Feltenstein and Farhadian (1987) and Naughton (1986), reviewed above, that estimate the degree of excess demand on the consumer goods market. They conclude that all models give a similar picture of excess demand for the years 1956–58, 1960, 1964, 1967, 1971, 1976 and 1980–83, which periods correspond with the Great Leap Forward, the Cultural Revolution (at least the beginning of it), 'the stormy year of Mao's death, and the economic reforms' (p. 369). They 'conjecture that in years like 1961–62, for example, the open inflation was sufficient to eliminate excess demand within the period' (pp. 369–70). None of the indicators produced by the models suggest that excess demand dominated the entire period, and they all suggest that there was excess demand during the reform period of 1979–83, although this cannot be concluded from Naughton (1986) because his shortage index extends only to 1978.

He, Duan and Yuan (1987)

This paper studies the reasons for inflation in the period after 1979 and tests some of the authors' views using simple but interesting econometrics.

The authors argue that the fundamental cause of the modern inflation is the new enterprise system. In the pre-reform system where all enterprise profits were collected by the budget, central control could ensure the macroeconomic balance between consumption and investment and control wages. Now that enterprises are allowed to retain much of their profits there is no mechanism at the enterprise level for ensuring balance between consumption and investment. In fact, the authors argue, the decentralisation of power to enterprises leads them to attempt to expand both investment and the consumption levels of their workers. This latter is done by increasing bonus payments to workers, which can increase their purchasing power even though basic wages may be controlled. Furthermore, attempts to reform the irrational wage structure lead to increases in the average wage. Enterprises now devote a much greater proportion of their investment funds to non-productive construction and residential housing. These tendencies to increasing non-productive investment as well as increasing workers' money incomes through higher bonuses ensure the expansion of purchasing power and the slower growth of available consumer goods.

The authors go on to test this view using regression analysis. They compute an index of the excess of consumer demand over available supply. Demand is estimated as residents' and groups' actual expenditure on consumer goods and expenditure on cultural life and services, plus net fixed investment, plus the increase in enterprise liquidity, plus exports and purchases by foreign residents. The total of these items is called 'pressure of aggregate demand' (*zong xuqiu yayi*, p. 24). Supply is estimated as national income plus imports and capital outflow minus consumption by peasants. Demand is expressed as a percentage of estimated supply for the period 1981–85 and is represented by D/S. This is used as the explanatory variable for the annual increases in the general retail price index for the period 1982–86. A one-year lag of price increases after demand pressure is used. The price index is expressed in the form of each year's price level as a percentage of the previous year's level, producing the regression result

$$P_t = 42.18 + 0.58\ (D/S)_{t-1} \qquad r = 0.945$$

where r is the correlation coefficient. There were only five observations.

The authors stress that one of the consequences of the emerging gap between demand and supply is that the money supply will increase. Increases in the money supply are seen as consequences of demand imbalances, not as an independent cause of price increases. The authors do investigate the association of money supply increases and inflation for the period 1979–86. Their independent variables are the general retail price index and the cost-of-living index, and these are regressed on the rate of increase of cash (*xianjin*) and money (*huobi*) respectively. High correlation coefficients are reported. However, the regression equations they report cannot be obtained from the data in the form in which they are presented and from the authors' description of the procedures used, although similar correlation coefficients can be obtained.

This paper is important because of its insistence that changes in the money supply are not independent causes of price increases but are themselves a consequence of demand imbalances caused by the nature of enterprise reform.

Xu and Huang (1987)

The empirical section of Xu and Huang's paper is an attempt to quantify the extent of excess money issue in China. Having charted the extent of the increase in the ratio of money to income over the period 1952–86 Xu and Huang reveal the People's Bank of China's formula for planning the required increase of money in circulation. This sets the increase in the money supply as equal to the real rate of economic growth plus the sustainable (*ke cheng shou*) rate of inflation minus the rate of decline in the velocity of circulation (p. 19). (If the rate of change of velocity is negative, subtracting this produces a positive number, thus increasing the required rate of increase in the money supply.)

Xu and Huang define money in a very broad way as cash plus enterprise and organisations' deposits, that is, total deposits minus fiscal deposits (p. 18). The formula is used on the historical data to establish the required increase in money supply, which is then compared with the actual increase for each year of the period 1952–86. The calculations are charted and show excess money issue in a number of years, particularly for the early 1960s and the modern reform period, especially in 1981, 1984 and 1986 (p. 19).

Xu and Huang admit that this method is very rough, and they propose using regression analysis to determine money demand. Using a double-logarithm regression of money on the price level, real income and an indicator of the extent of international trade, they obtain an income elasticity of demand for money of 1.32. They use this to calculate the required annual increase in the money supply and compare it with each year's actual increase. This is done for the period 1953–86, showing excess money issue in 22 years. They admit that the reform period has probably increased the demand for money, making this method unreliable. They re-estimate the equation for the period 1978–86, obtaining an income elasticity of 1.95. They recompute the required demand for this period, producing estimates of excess money issue in 1979, 1981, 1984 and 1986 (p. 21). The estimate for 1984 is the lowest of the four, which is quite surprising given the extent of money issue in that year.

The implication of Xu and Huang's work is that the reform process had increased the demand for money sufficiently to justify most of the money issue in 1984 given the high rate of growth and the increase in prices. They argue, however, that increasing commercialisation and monetisation of the economy has not been sufficient to justify this excessive monetary growth and support this argument by reference to the high rates of inflation in the years 1984–86 (p. 21). They also argue that there is a very close correlation between monetary growth per unit of output and the price level over the entire period 1952–86. They argue that the principal cause of inflation is excess monetary growth. In the past this did not cause open inflation because of extensive price control, and even though this price control has been relaxed in recent years this relaxation has only been partial. They still believe that excess demand will result in forced saving and excess monetary holdings as well as open inflation despite the reforms, and they use their data to compute the amount of forced saving accumulated over the period 1984–86 as 160 billion *yuan* (p. 22). They conclude by discussing some necessary reforms of the banking system.

Qian (1988)

This is an econometric study of national, urban and rural household saving for the period 1955–85. Although Qian uses Chinese data many assumptions and adjustments to the data had to be made in order to provide the required time series of disposable income, expenditure and financial asset accumulation.

The whole study is based on the assumption that there was no change in the degree of repressed inflation during the entire period, and, as Qian recognises (pp. 622–3), he is unable to conclude whether the observed increased household saving rates were due to voluntary behaviour or disequilibrium in the consumer goods market. His framework is

$$MV/PQ = s$$

where s represents an index of shortage or repressed inflation when it exceeds unity. His assumption is the extreme one that s is constant, so increases in M are exactly offset by the decline in V (on a voluntary basis); this means that there is an increase in the demand for money, which is achieved by higher saving rates (pp. 599–600). This approach is firmly rooted in the Quantity Theory approach, where desired expenditure is correlated with the money stock. Qian makes no attempt to investigate whether desired expenditure did grow at the same rate as output (PQ) throughout the period 1955–85 and what the consequences were for saving behaviour and other observable variables such as prices. He does remark that before 1979 household saving seemed to increase only when transitory income rose (p. 611), which could be interpreted as the result of households' inability to spend the unexpected (and perhaps unplanned) short-run increase in income. This is an implication of Naughton (1986) for the period before 1978.

Qian's main results are that saving behaviour supports the Keynesian absolute-income hypothesis, not the Friedman permanent-income hypothesis. He claims that there was a major shift in saving behaviour after 1979 with the marginal propensity to save for urban residents increasing from 0.04 to 0.26 after 1979.

Huang (1988a) and (1988b)

These are important studies for a number of reasons. Huang (1988a) is a journal article based on the longer work (1988b), which is a chapter in a book. They present the same arguments. Emphasis in this review will be placed on the more easily obtainable (1988a). Huang's arguments about reasons for changes in the money supply over the period 1980–85 were used and discussed in section 4.10, and Huang (1988b) was referred to in section 4.9.

Huang attempts to explain the increases in monetary aggregates, assesses the extent of excess money supply and briefly attempts an analysis of the consequences of this excessive monetary growth. Although one can disagree with certain aspects of the approach (especially the way variables are processed before being used in the regressions) the study is nevertheless orderly, logical and enquiring. Huang stresses the differences between changes made under the former planned system, under which changes in the narrow measure of the money supply were just the difference between household incomes and expenditures (1988a: 36), and changes brought about by the process of reform. These reforms, however, have left the specialised banks with no real control over the money supply; in fact they have unrestricted power to increase it. The soft budget constraint exists (*ruan yusuan yueshu*), and money just 'leaks' from enterprises in the state non-cash sector, which uses bank transfers (*zhuan zhang fangshi*), into household incomes in the form of worker bonuses.

Huang uses regression analysis to obtain income elasticities of demand for money of 1.02 (currency), 1.15 (currency plus enterprise, organisation and units' deposits) and 1.26 (currency plus residents' savings deposits) for the period 1952–86. As the observations for the 'unstable period of disturbances' of 1960–69 are outliers they are omitted from further regressions, and elasticities of 1.16, 1.57 and 1.68 respectively are obtained for the same three measures of the money supply for the pooled observations of 1952–56 and 1970–86 (1988a: 39). Why the years 1957–59 are also omitted is not explained. (I have a feeling that the book chapter has been edited down for the journal article.) These elasticity estimates are used in the subsequent analysis. Huang also obtains higher estimates for the period 1978–86. For example, the income elasticity of demand for currency is put at 2.15 from a regression in which the share of international trade in national income is added as an explanatory variable. The explanation offered is that an important reason for the rise in this elasticity is the lag in the reform of the financial system and its relative underdevelopment in China. The pooled regression results are used to generate actual amounts of money demanded (in index number form) for the entire period. After these figures have been compared with the actual increase in the money supply Huang notes that supply exceeded demand in the vast majority of years (1988a: 40).

The institutional reasons given for this are novel and interesting. Huang starts from the insights of the Harrod–Domar growth model in which the growth rate of output equals the saving rate divided by the capital–output ratio. In capitalist economies causation goes from the saving rate to investment to growth. Huang states that in China the opposite is true, with the government determining the desired growth rate, then the required investment rate, then working out how to generate enough saving.[5] The interest rate is controlled and so can play no part in regulating saving. There are three ways of making up any deficiency in the amount of investment funds: an increased budget deficit, which might involve an overdraft at the bank, foreign loans or issuing money. There will be a nominal constraint on the size of the budget deficit the government can get away with, and a firm real constraint on the amount it can borrow from abroad. However, printing money has no such constraints as it is:

> . . . completely concealed, dispersed in character, difficult to perceive and, furthermore, corresponds with the increased nominal demand for money. So we can say that printing money is the most convenient option. A majority of

> the governments of developing countries frequently use such a method to achieve their development goals but its consequences, however, are just great disturbances [*judade bodong*] for the economy. Our country is no exception. Issuing money becomes a means of helping the state fulfil its very ambitious and wild [*xiongxin bobode*] growth plans and this causes the supply of money regularly [*jingchang*] to exceed the demand for money (1988a: 42).

Huang concludes by trying to identify the adjustment mechanism to the large increases in the money supply. He again denies that the rate of interest can play any role in this adjustment. From our discussion of Western monetary theory in chapter 3 we know that the remaining factors must be prices and velocity. Huang knows this too and investigates their changes. He uses the national-income price deflator as his indicator of inflation. He argues that its behaviour falls into four periods: 1952–60, when it was basically stable; 1961–70, when it saw great changes; 1971–76, when it was most stable; and after 1977, when there was a constant upward trend. He uses regression analysis to show the dependence of this price index on the differences between actual money supply and his estimate of demand and on the differences between actual and desired velocities (1988a: 26). He also shows how velocity fell considerably.

While admitting that monetisation did increase the demand for money he still firmly argues that modern China shows symptoms of forced saving (*qiangzhixing chuxu*) and hidden inflation (*yinbixing tonghuo pengzhang*). Huang is really saying that the household sector has been pushed off any demand curve for money and is holding excessive monetary balances. As we saw in section 3.6, this possibility is admitted by Artis and Lewis even for a market economy where the adjustment of prices and output to increases in money holdings is slow and there are short-run disequilibrium monetary holdings. An implication of Huang's findings is that, if prices and output are made responsive to monetary excess demand by continuing economic reform, such an adjustment would be possible in China and we would expect rapid output growth with high inflation.

Chen (1989)

Chen's article is an application of advanced econometric techniques for determining the causality relationships between various measures of the money supply on the one hand and indicators of economic performance, such as nominal income, the budget deficit, the trade deficit and 'total inflation', on the other. The technique used is Bayesian vector autoregression (BVAR). Each variable is regressed on past values of itself and the other four variables (income, budget, trade deficit and total inflation). The number of past years used (three) and other a priori statistical limits imposed on the data are not derived from any economic theory or common sense but are chosen solely as the ones that minimise the prediction error of the equations.

Results are presented for the three measures of the money supply, but they suggest that the narrow measure of currency, here labelled M_0[6], is a more appropriate measure of the money supply for policy purposes as it is more sensitive to macroeconomic variables (p. 319). This has always been argued to be the case in the few previous studies of money in China. The causality results imply that there is bidirectional causality between currency and nominal income, currency and the budget deficit, and currency and the trade deficit, and unidirectional causality from currency to 'total inflation'. Chen also claims that as the statistical results show unidirectional causality from inflation to the trade deficit this implies that the 'central authorities have tried to offset part of the excess demand in the consumer goods market by importing more consumer goods' (p. 322). This interpretation has also been common in the literature; it is argued by Komija (1989) and was discussed in section 2.10.

It is interesting to note that Chen attributes the trade deficits to the importation of consumer goods without even showing this to be the case, and also that the central authorities are said to be behind the imports, not decentralised enterprises. Centralised allocation still seems to be responsive to monetary conditions. The study covers the period 1951–85, so Chen presumably believes this to have been the case throughout this period. Someone who believed that economic reform had transformed China into a more market-like economy would not explain this relationship in such words. He or she would probably just say that excess demand, fuelled by excessive monetary growth, always causes inflation, a current account deficit and exchange rate depreciation (all of which were observed in China during the mid 1980s). Invoking the actions of the central authorities to explain the current account deficit shows that Chen basically still thinks in terms of the planned allocation model.

Hsu (1989)

Hsu's book is a study of reforms to China's foreign trade system. It is relevant to this book as Hsu has a theory he seeks to test, namely, the proposition that China's increasing involvement in foreign trade has caused severe imbalances on domestic markets. He seeks to test this by linking an indicator of imbalance on the domestic consumer goods market to the volume of foreign trade. He therefore needs a quantitative indicator of domestic imbalance. He discusses the purchasing power imbalance concepts of Peebles (1983; 1986b) but does not think that this is suitable for his purposes. He therefore adopts a variant that he calls *Z* and describes as 'the index of real purchasing power imbalance' (p. 164). He defines it as the percentage increase in money incomes minus the percentage increase in money expenditures. It is thus the difference between two nominal variables. Hsu calls it 'real' because he feels that it is independent of the rate of inflation. In fact the expenditure side already includes any changes in retail prices, so this indicator cannot be used to explain anything at all. It is an unnecessarily complicated indicator of imbalance. Obviously, if incomes grow more rapidly than realised expenditures, the proportion of incomes remaining unspent must rise. Such a measure (*m* in Peebles, 1983) could have been computed and used as an indicator. Increases in *m* can only be interpreted as indicators of imbalance if one assumes that there is permanent excess demand for consumer goods and its rise does not reflect voluntary behaviour but supply-side constrained consumption, and hence excess savings.

Hsu links average values of his Z indicator for various subperiods and claims that it is high for periods of high trade growth and negative for the other (p. 166). He measures trade growth on the basis of total trade volume and makes Z the dependent variable. This ignores the clear historical episodes when imports were increased in response to developments on domestic markets (in the early 1960s and in 1985 in particular), meaning that imports are the dependent variable and domestic imbalances are an explanatory variable of changes in trade volume.

5.3 Conclusions

The studies reviewed in this chapter suggest some clues with which to proceed to an analysis for the entire period 1952–85. Perkins (1964; 1966) uses purchasing power concepts to highlight the flows of money onto and out of the consumer goods market. As we have data for such flows and as Chinese planners are concerned about them we must follow this approach to the question. Donnithorne (1974) argues that it might be easier to control urban purchasing power rather than rural. Feltenstein and Farhadian (1987) argue that rural purchasing-power increases contribute more to monetary growth than do urban and that the current account had no significant impact on monetary expansion before 1983. Hsiao (1971) reminds us that the general retail price index changes either because planners change official prices or because market prices change. This distinction must be kept in mind. Chen and Hou (1986) ask why the government has increased prices in the 1980s. Chow (1987) shows us that there is a weak association between the money ratio and the price level. We must explain this. He, Duan and Yuan (1987) suggest that there may be a time lag between price increases and monetary growth, as does Li (1985). Hsiao (1971; 1984) and Yeh (1985) remind us that the People's Bank of China does not have much control over currency issue and always has to resort to reactive policies. Huang (1988a) argues the same lack of control for the specialised banks after 1984. Portes and Santorum (1987) suggest that currency may be endogenous. Anyway, we have to explain why it changes. Huang (1988a) shows that adjustment to rapid nominal money growth is both higher prices and lower velocity. He does not investigate whether there is any affect on interest rates nor why.

Armed with such clues and an understanding of the institutional environment in which money is issued and recalled and prices are determined we can proceed to an investigation of monetary growth and price changes for the period 1952–85. This is the subject of the next chapter.

6 Theory and evidence

This chapter analyses the principal empirical features of money, prices and other variables connected with monetary changes mainly over the period 1953–85. The analysis is based on a set of characterisations of the Chinese economy which were discussed in chapter 4 and are assumed to be correct for this entire period. The main assumptions are:

1. The principal source of urban purchasing power is the state wage bill (including bonuses) and that of rural purchasing power is state agricultural procurements.
2. The bulk of retail sales are made by the state sector.
3. Retail supplies emanate principally from state industrial production and agricultural procurements.
4. List price changes are the main cause of changes in the general retail price index.
5. The foreign exchange rate and world prices have no impact on the domestic price level.

Furthermore, it is assumed:

6. Planners act to prevent any rapid increase in the ratio of currency in circulation to total retail sales; they prefer commodity *huilong* to any other method.

Whether such assumptions are approximately true to the nature of the economy will be tested if we can show that they lead to a consistent explanation of why the money supply changed, discover the relationship between money and retail prices, and show what other policy reactions were taken in the light of monetary developments.

6.1 Changes in the narrow money supply

This section examines reasons for changes in the narrow measures of the money supply. It asks the simple questions: Where did the money come from, where did it go, and how much did people accumulate in various years? The analysis is non-theoretical; that is, it is descriptive and imposes no theory on the data. Changes in the narrow measures are explained using the identity derived in chapter 4 showing that annual changes in household monetary holdings must equal the difference between monetary purchasing power and realised expenditures. No theory is offered of the reasons for the size of each year's accumulation. For example, it may be shown that in a certain year nominal purchasing power increased rapidly but expenditures did not, so producing a large increase in money holdings. Some readers will rationalise this as due to households' perceiving the income increase as transitory and not permanent, so households naturally voluntarily increased their savings rate and not their rate of consumption. Other readers will see this, and look for supporting evidence, as the result of an uncoordinated increase in money incomes (possibly an unplanned increase) when there was no corresponding increase in consumer good supplies.

Figure 6.1 shows the development of social purchasing power (*SPP*) and total social monetary expenditure (*SME*) in the top panel. The difference in these series, shown in the second panel, is the annual increase in the economy's holdings of cash in hand (*CH*) plus savings deposits (*SD*). The data are in Table I.3. Part of this increase will be currency in circulation (*CRC*), and its annual changes are shown in the lowest panel. A similar analysis using the data of Table I.4 could be made, accounting for the increase in residents' monetary holdings. The conclusions are the same.

It is obvious that the experiences after 1978 are very different from those of the previous 26 years. They will be discussed separately later. For the period before 1978 we can identify periods of above- and below-average monetary growth using two criteria. The first just identifies years in which the absolute changes were significantly above or below the average for the period 1953–77. The second is based on the proportion of *SPP* not spent and hence accumulating as monetary assets. This proportion, labelled *m*, is presented in Table III.2. Table 6.1 identifies the different periods.

Short periods of relatively rapid monetary growth were followed by usually shorter periods of slower monetary growth. The periods of rapid monetary growth became longer in the early 1970s. The years 1953 and 1956 have long been identified as inflationary years (Hsiao, 1971); both experienced large increases in the state wage bill. The period 1958–61 saw large increases in the state wage bill during 1958–60 and in rural incomes during 1958–59. Total realised expenditures fell in 1961, 1962 and 1963. Rural incomes fell markedly in 1960–61, as agricultural production began to collapse and procurement volume fell, and the state wage bill fell in 1961, 1962 and 1963. These early falls were not as large as the fall in expenditure, so monetary holdings rose markedly, especially in 1958–61. Money holdings fell in 1962 and 1963.

During the period 1965–68 rural incomes rose in 1965 and 1966 and then the state wage bill continued to rise in 1967 and 1968 even though real national income fell. In 1968 *SPP* was reduced, and in 1969 and 1970 *SPP* grew at a slower rate than real national income. The years 1969 and 1970 saw reductions in monetary holdings. The early 1970s saw *SPP* growing more rapidly than real national income, and monetary accumulation became more rapid. In 1955, 1962–64 and 1969–70 when monetary growth was slow, and even negative in some years, *SPP* grew less rapidly than real national income. It seems that in periods when real national income growth is slow, or negative (1960–61, 1967–68, 1976), we observe relatively rapid monetary growth. This is suggestive, implying that slow output

Figure 6.1 Changes in measures of the narrow money supply, 1953–85

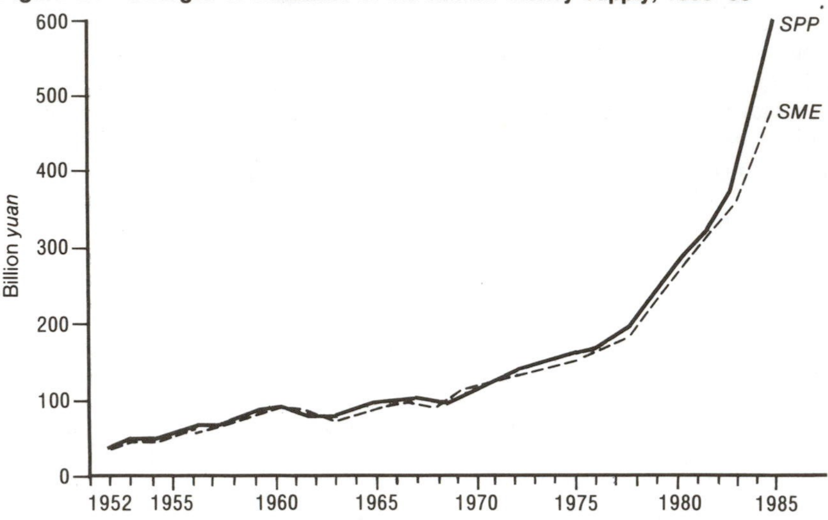

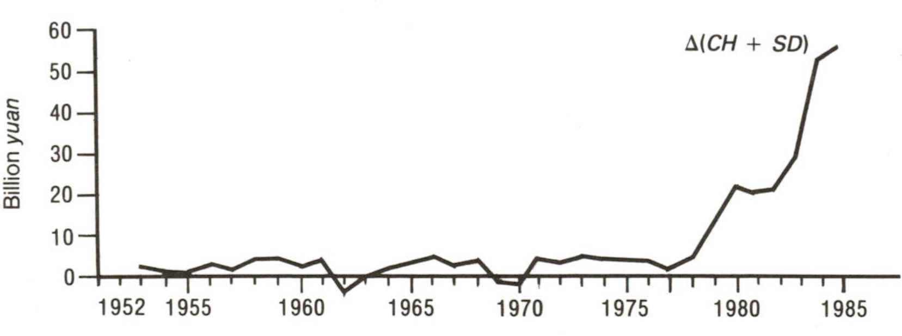

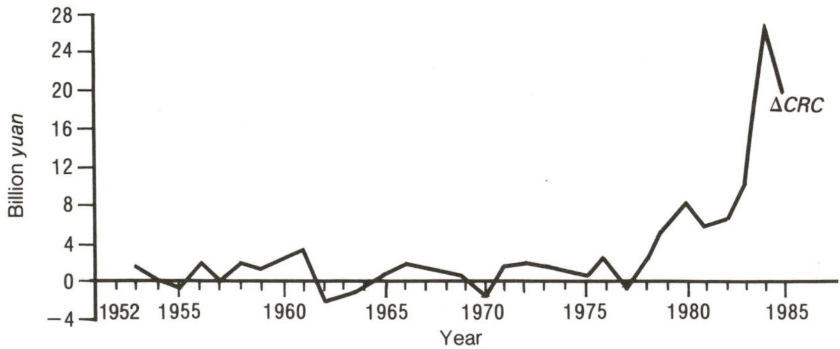

Table 6.1 Differences in monetary growth, 1953–77

Based on absolute change							
Above average			1956 1958–61		1965–68		1971–76
Below average		1954–55		1962–64[a]		1969–70[a]	
Based on proportion remaining unspent							
Above average	1953		1956–61		1965–68		1971–75
Below average		1954–55		1962–64		1969–70	

Note: [a] 1962–63 and 1969–70 were negative.
Source: Data in Tables I.3 and III.2.

growth may reduce the volume of retail supplies and hence the volume of commodity *huilong*, C_H, in equation 5 of chapter 4. It also suggests why we observe the inverse relationship between real output growth and currency in circulation. The exogenous falls in real output, although they are associated to some extent with falls in purchasing power, reduce C_H; hence money that is issued as *SPP* stays in circulation.

The annual increases in money holdings after 1978 are spectacular as is the growth of *SPP* and *SME*. Special factors associated with the rural reforms of 1979 and the urban ones of 1983 and after were responsible for the large increases in *SPP* during the 1980s. These changes were imposed on the banking system, and there was very little it could do to control the growth of the narrow measures of the money supply. This might even have been the unexpected consequences of some of the rural price reforms, as will be suggested shortly. First it will be useful to identify the major components of the annual increases in *SPP* for this period. In other words: Where did the money come from?

6.2 *Purchasing power developments, 1978–85*

Table 6.2 shows the annual absolute increases in *SPP* for the period 1978–85 and the proportions of these increases represented by the state wage bill (*SWB*), farmers' income from selling products (*FIP*), and farmers' service income (*FIS*). These three categories on average made up at least two-thirds of the increases in *SPP* during this period. Certain expectations are borne out. The major increases in agricultural procurement price occurred in late 1979. In that year and particularly in 1980 the increase in *SPP* was especially large, with 57.3 per cent of the increase going to the rural sector compared with only 39 per cent of the increase in 1975 and none of it at all in 1976 when rural incomes fell. Except for 1980 the rural population received at least 56 per cent of the increases in *SPP* over the period 1979–83.

The agricultural reforms created a situation for the rural population under which it could only expect rapidly rising incomes as it sold output to the state procurement agencies. Whether the monetary consequences of the agricultural price reforms were fully understood and anticipated in 1979 is an interesting question. Whether they were or not does not matter for the consequence of them was rapidly increasing rural purchasing

Table 6.2 Components of the increases in *SPP*, 1978–85

Year	*ΔSPP* (billion *yuan*)	% of *ΔSPP*		
		SWB	*FIP*	*FIS*
1978	18.34	23.4	35.6	13.3
1979	32.87	18.4	49.0	8.3
1980	44.21	22.3	34.3	9.2
1981	21.07	15.3	46.8	12.4
1982	26.15	18.5	45.3	11.2
1983	41.44	9.5	44.4	13.8
1984	101.63	12.6	40.0	7.9
1985	118.85	15.9	38.2	15.5

Source: Calculated from *Statistical Yearbook of China 1986* (pp. 442–4).

power. The main cause of this was the nature of the procurement system used. The government increased the basic quota procurement price but also increased the bonus price it was willing to pay for any output sold to it in excess of the quota amount. The new higher above-quota bonuses were set at 50 per cent for grain and oil-bearing crops and at 30 per cent for cotton.[1] The government was willing to buy any output offered to it until it dropped this policy in 1985.

This bonus price system and government willingness to buy any quantity established a very odd demand curve facing each agricultural producer, which is shown in the left hand panel of Figure 6.2. For all amounts up to the quota amount, q, the average and marginal price is P_q, but for above-quota sales the marginal price is aP, where a is the bonus factor, being 1.5 for grain, for example. This produces a very odd average-price curve, labelled AP, for units sold to the government in excess of the quota. AP is the weighted average of the two prices P_q and aP, where the weights are the proportions of total sales sold at each price. As long as the quota amount remains fixed, then as sales increase the proportion sold at the bonus price increases, so the average price must rise. This phenomenon is known as 'price perversity' (Wyzan, 1985). Farmers cannot loose by expanding output as long as the government has enough money to pay them. In a market economy rapidly rising sales would depress prices and, as demand tends to be inelastic, incomes also. Chinese farmers were put in a position where they could increase sales and prices at the same time. It is no wonder that rural purchasing power rose so rapidly.

Although we cannot be certain that the aggregate demand curve for the entire crop was exactly the same as that in Figure 6.2, this is very likely. The right hand panel of Figure 6.2 shows what happened to the average price paid for grain over the period 1979–83 as sales increased enormously. Grain sales rose 70.5 per cent and average price by 18.7 per cent. For cotton the increase in sales was 120 per cent and the average price rose 27.7 per cent (Peebles, 1985: 47–51). As the pattern for grain shows, in the early years small increases in sales brought about large average-price increases, and the later years larger year-to-year increases in sales brought about relatively smaller increases in average price, in conformity with the general shape of AP in the theoretical part of Figure 6.2.[2]

Figure 6.2 Effect of procurement policies on agricultural prices, 1979–83

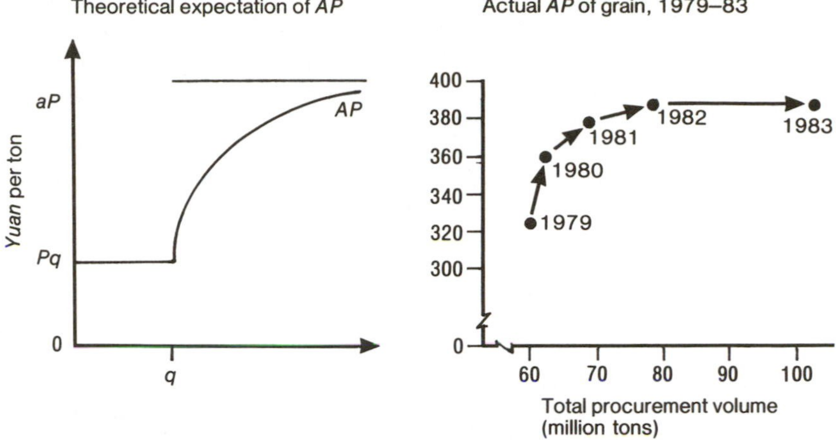

This case study shows how one aspect of agricultural reform had a major, possibly unanticipated, monetary consequence in which the banking system could really do nothing to restrain the amount paid out to farmers. It had to rely on reactive policies. One central government response was to raise state urban and rural retail prices of these commodities. The retail price remained below the rising procurement price, however, so subsidies increased. In 1978 price subsidies on a selection of consumer goods totalled 5.56 billion *yuan*, which was 5 per cent of total budgetary expenditures, while in 1983 these subsidies totalled 26.952 billion *yuan*, which was 20.8 per cent of budget expenditure, a proportion maintained in 1985 (*Statistical Yearbook of China 1986*, pp. 509, 525). Such an inversion of procurement over retail price resulted in a net injection of currency into circulation of course.

Although planners were obviously trying to stimulate agricultural output by offering material incentives, in the form of generalised purchasing power, which is what money is, they also offered less general forms of material incentive but ones that they must have felt were more attractive to farmers than state-issued money. This shows the continuing limited role of money in rural areas and its usefulness to farmers. During the late 1970s and early 1980s a whole series of encouragement sales programmes (*jiang shou*) were used to encourage sales of cash crops, grain, cotton and other crops to the state (Sicular, 1988: 685–8, 705). Farmers were variously promised fixed amounts of scarce fertilisers or grain supplies, or the right to buy scarce commodities in return for sales to the state. In 1986 this system worked by means of procurement agencies' giving farmers coupons entitling them to various supplies when they signed contracts for grain supply (Ash, 1988: 549). These coupons thus become money substitutes as they were a means of payment although they had a very restricted range of purchasing power.

Chinese economists recognise that even in the 1980s changes in agricultural production could still have a major impact on currency developments. High yield years usually lead to a large increase in currency in circulation and low yield years to a small increase.[3] This is generally borne out by the data in Table 6.2. Low yield years were 1980, 1981 and 1985, and high yield years 1982, 1983 and 1984—unexpectedly in the case of 1984 as it is thought that yields follow a cycle of two years high and then two years low. Although 1980 was a low yield year, *SPP* grew rapidly, probably due to the price increases of the previous year, and the rate of currency growth (29.3 per cent) was higher than in the previous year. In 1981, the next low-yield year, *SPP* growth was less than half that of the previous year and the rate of currency growth was only 14.5 per cent, again about half the rate of the previous year. The high yield years 1982 and 1983 saw larger *SPP* increases, and currency growth rates also rose in 1983. The increase in *SPP* in 1984 was the then largest at 101.63 billion *yuan* (29.5 per cent), and currency growth rose to 49.5 per cent. In 1984 agricultural loans and down-payments were 4.8 times their rate in 1983 (*Statistical Yearbook of China 1986*, p. 443), contributing to the rural sector's monetary receipts. The year 1985, seen as a bad agricultural year by Chinese economists, did, however, produce the largest-ever increase in *SPP* but only a 24.7 per cent increase in currency in circulation. The rural sector still received 53 per cent of the increase in *SPP*.

The urban and banking reforms, bank lending and the bonus explosion in 1984 and 1985 did not reduce the importance of the rural sector in causing increases in *SPP*. The events of the 1980s tend to confirm Chinese economists' view that increases in rural purchasing power tend to produce high rates of growth of currency, a point made also in the econometric study by Feltenstein and Farhadian (1987: 148) discussed in chapter 5.

6.3 Changes in per capita money holdings

During the periods of rapid currency growth the distribution of the resulting money changed somewhat. An important question is: Where did the money go, and why? Table 6.3 shows per capita holdings for selected years around the periods when there were marked changes in national currency holdings. These years showed significant changes in urban and rural per capita holdings.[4] In 1961 urban cash holdings and savings deposits fell whereas rural cash holdings nearly doubled and rural savings deposits increased slightly. Rural cash holdings rose from being 33.9 per cent of urban in 1960 to 73.8 per cent in 1961.

How did this redistribution come about? Two views suggest themselves in the light of what we know about the history of this period. One, which we can call the 'trade' view, would expect to see an increase in the nominal value of rural sales to the urban population, a resulting transfer of cash and an increased need for it in rural areas. This would produce an increase in the transactions demand in rural areas. The alternative view, which we can call 'repressed inflation', would see these increased holdings as simply due to the inability of the rural population to spend a large part of its income at a time of intensified shortages. Both effects seem to have been working at different times. In 1961, urban and rural retail purchases fell 9.3 and 21.5 per cent respectively (*Statistical Yearbook of China 1986*,

Table 6.3 Per capita narrow money holdings, 1952–83
(selected years)

Year	Urban (*yuan*)		Rural (*yuan*)		Rural/urban (%)	
	Cash	Savings deposits	Cash	Savings deposits	Cash	Savings deposits
1952	7.3 (41.2)	10.4	3.2	n.a.	43.8	n.a.
1957	9.0 (25.5)	26.3	5.6 (80.0)	1.4	62.2	5.3
1958	14.0 (32.8)	28.7	6.6 (64.1)	3.7	47.1	12.9
1959	14.3 (29.1)	34.9	6.6 (62.9)	3.9	46.2	11.2
1960	21.8 (36.9)	37.2	7.4 (71.8)	2.9	33.9	7.8
1961	19.1 (37.7)	31.6	14.1 (82.5)	3.0	73.8	9.5
1962	17.9 (39.1)	27.9	11.5 (87.1)	1.7	64.2	6.1
1963	16.4 (34.8)	30.7	8.7 (82.9)	1.8	53.0	5.9
1968	23.2 (32.3)	48.6	11.6 (82.9)	2.4	50.0	4.9
1970	16.3 (26.2)	45.9	10.8 (83.1)	2.2	66.3	4.8
1975	23.1 (23.0)	77.3	13.7 (75.3)	4.5	61.4	5.8
1977	19.4 (19.5)	80.0	14.2 (70.6)	5.9	73.2	7.4
1978	20.7 (18.7)	90.0	15.2 (68.5)	7.0	73.4	7.8
1979	24.1 (17.6)	113.2	19.2 (66.2)	9.8	79.7	8.6
1980	30.8 (16.6)	154.9	24.8 (63.1)	14.5	80.5	9.4
1981	36.2 (16.1)	188.4	29.7 (58.8)	20.8	82.0	11.0
1982	39.6 (14.5)	233.0	34.1 (55.2)	27.7	86.1	11.9
1983	48.3 (14.2)	292.1	41.9 (52.1)	38.5	86.7	13.2

Note: Figures in brackets denote the percentage of total monetary holdings held in the form of cash.
Source: Table I.6.

p. 445). In 1960 farmers' sales of agricultural produce to the non-agricultural population increased by 129 per cent in nominal terms, and in 1961 by 275 per cent (*Zhongguo Maoyi Wujia Tongji Ziliao 1952–83*, p. 64). This must have produced a large cash flow from urban to rural areas. In 1962 and 1963 these sales fell by 10 and 28.5 per cent respectively. In the two same years, while urban retail purchases were falling along with urban incomes, rural retail purchases rose 11.3 and 4.9 per cent respectively. Both factors would tend to reduce rural money holdings, and both cash holdings and savings deposits in rural areas fell in 1962; cash holdings continued to fall until 1964. Rural trade with the urban population continued to fall until 1977, and rural cash holdings compared with urban continued to fall also. The year 1970 seems an exception when the ratio rose. In this year national cash holdings fell but urban holdings fell by a greater amount than rural, thus increasing the rural ratio. How national cash holdings were able to fall in 1970 will be explained in section 6.7.

The agricultural reforms after 1978 saw the revival of rural and rural–urban trade, and the ratio of rural to urban cash holdings began to rise, no doubt due to the increased need for cash for transactions purposes. The ratio of average rural household incomes to urban incomes rose also. Household survey data do not permit full comparisons for the important years during this period. They suggest that the ratio of per capita rural household income to urban rose from 48.9 per cent in 1981 to 61.2 per cent in 1983 (*Statistical Yearbook of China 1986*, pp. 576–83). This would account for some of the increase in rural savings deposits and their rise from a ratio of 9.4 per cent of urban in 1980 to 13.2 per cent in 1983.

The form in which monetary holdings were held changed considerably. The proportion of urban per capita money holdings held as cash (the cash ratio) fell from 41.2 per cent in 1952 to 14.2 per cent in 1983. In 1958, 1960 and 1961 this process was reversed temporarily when the cash ratio rose. As we have seen, in these last two years rural–urban trade increased significantly. It was also a period of rapidly increasing free-market prices, so it is natural to expect that people tried to get out of savings deposits and into goods. The rural cash ratio fell from 80 per cent in 1957 to 52.1 per cent in 1983. In the years 1960–62 the cash ratio rose, which was the time of increased rural–urban trade. The spread of rural banking facilities no doubt played a role in encouraging rural savings deposits rather than cash holdings. In 1981, for example, there were 2020 savings bank offices of the rural credit co-operative network, 5476 by 1984 and 7557 by 1985 (*Statistical Yearbook of China 1986*, p. 529).[5] It is impossible to separate all the different factors influencing household choice between cash holdings and savings deposits by means of the simple methods used here.

6.4 Seasonal variations in currency holdings

It has long been recognised that the agricultural nature of the Chinese economy is responsible for the seasonal variations in the volume of currency in circulation (Donnithorne, 1967: 416; Naughton, 1986: 32–5; Li Chengrui, 1986: 55 and 1986/7: 6–7). There tends to be a net outflow from the banks to the public in the second half of each year and a net inflow into the banks in the first half. Peak currency holdings occur in December and January, which is the end of the Chinese Lunar Year, and the lowest holdings are in May and June. This is described as 'two high points with a low in between' (*liang tou gao zhongjian di*).[6] The population tends to make many expenditures in the first half of the year connected with such festivals as the New Year festival (*Yuandan*), the Spring festival (*Chunjie*) and May Day (*Wuyi*). The spring planting and the three major summer jobs of planting, harvesting and field management (*sanxia*) also lead to increased expenditures and a net inflow into the banks as agricultural procurement payments are low. From June and right through the autumn crops are procured, so currency is put into circulation.[7]

This means that year-end figures exaggerate average currency holdings. Figure 6.3 shows the pattern of quarterly currency holdings by graphing the end of each quarter's currency holdings as an index of the end of the previous year's amount.[8] On average, end-of-year figures were 14.9 per cent higher than each year's average holdings. One might expect high yield years to show a higher-than-average excess end-of-year holding and vice versa as more money would have been paid out to buy that year's crop. Generally, the opposite is true; low yield years such as 1980, 1981 and 1985 had year-end excesses of 23.1, 16.4, and 17.6 per cent respectively, that is, above-average excesses, while high yield years such as 1982 and 1983 had year-end excesses of 13.5 and 14.4 per cent respectively, that is, below-average excesses. The year 1984, a high yield year, had an excess of 33 per cent, way above average. The pattern is the same if we compare end-of-year holdings with that year's midyear holdings (end-quarter II's figure). There are also seasonal fluctuations in the savings deposits of various branches of the economy.[9]

Non-agricultural Chinese societies show a marked seasonal variation in the demand for currency related to similar factors. In Hong Kong, for example, there is an increased demand for currency in the first two months of each year, the time of the Lunar New Year festival. The currency is used to buy presents, settle debts and make cash gifts to children (*lai see*, in Cantonese). This increases the public's currency ratio and reduces the money multiplier discussed in section 3.4. The Hong Kong banks anticipate such a seasonal increase in cash demand and accommodate it so there is no disruption to the money supply process (Peebles, 1988: 150–2).[10]

6.5 Money and prices: the Quantity Theory again

Chow (1987) uses the Quantity Theory approach to this important question for the period 1952–83. This section continues this analysis in a number of ways. First, we update the simple regressions of the general retail price index (P) on the money ratio (M/y) for the period 1952–85 and use corrected data for currency in 1952. Second, we analyse the market price index separately. Third, we allow for the fact that end-of-year currency data exaggerate that year's average holdings.

For the period 1952–85 the regression results are

$$\ln P = \underset{(0.0398)}{0.9489} + \underset{(0.01625)}{0.2690} \ln (M/y) \qquad R^2 = 0.8954,\ s = 0.0326,\ DW = 1.3083,\ n = 34$$

The price index has a base of 1.00 for 1950 to make comparison with Chow's results easier. The explanatory variable is the same as his, updated to 1985 using the method he describes in the text. Chow's slope coefficient is 0.2687, the same as the above (0.2690) to the third decimal place.[11] A 1 per cent increase in the money ratio is associated with only a 0.269 per cent increase in the general retail price level. There is nothing here to make us change our mind about the results; the slope coefficient remains very low.[12]

Using first differences of the logarithms for 1953–85 to try to correct for the evident positive serial correlation yields

$$\Delta \ln P = \underset{(0.02573)}{0.0080} + \underset{(0.0048)}{0.1294}\, \Delta \ln (M/y) \qquad R^2 = 0.4493,\ s = 0.0268,\ DW = 1.8105,\ n = 33$$

Chow's slope coefficient is 0.1266. The higher Durbin–Watson statistic (1.8105) is an improvement. However, the numerical size of the slope coefficient remains low (0.1294).

Figure 6.3 Seasonal variations in currency in circulation, 1979–85

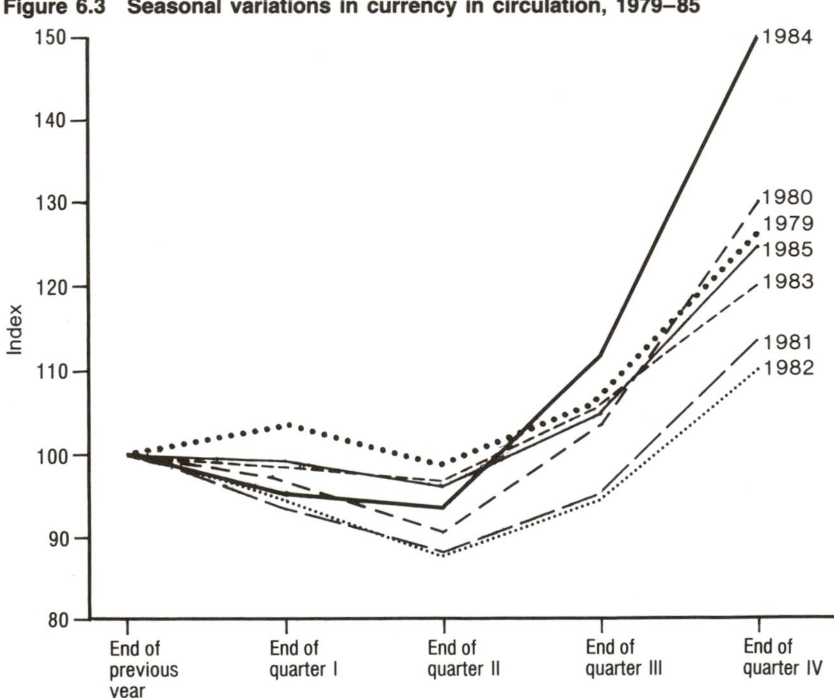

As end-of-year currency holdings tend to overstate average holdings and as the price index is an average for the year, the Quantity Theory might be expected to produce better results if each year's average currency holdings were used to calculate the money ratio. Here, each year's currency figure is taken as the simple average of its own end-of-year figure and the previous year's end-of-year figure. When this is done the regressions for 1953–85 produce a slope coefficient of 0.2753 for the general retail price index, slightly higher than the result obtained above but not sufficiently different to justify any change of mind about its poor performance.

Chow limits his regressions to the controlled general retail price index whereas the whole logic of the Quantity Theory is that market prices will respond to changes in the money ratio. Hence, it might be instructive to perform such a regression. The following equations show the results for 1952–85 using the market price index (*MP*) and the same explanatory variable:

$$\ln MP = \underset{(0.2555)}{2.8764} + \underset{(0.1042)}{0.8881} \ln (M/y) \qquad \begin{aligned} R^2 &= 0.6941 \\ s &= 0.2090 \\ DW &= 0.7579 \\ n &= 34 \end{aligned}$$

For the first differences of the logarithms for 1953–85 the results are

$$\Delta \ln MP = \underset{(-0.277)}{-0.0091} + \underset{(0.1756)}{0.9853} \, \Delta \ln (M/y) \qquad \begin{aligned} R^2 &= 0.5038 \\ s &= 0.1830 \\ DW &= 2.5474 \\ n &= 33 \end{aligned}$$

This shows a significant association between the money ratio and the market price index. The slope coefficient (0.9853) is not significantly different from unity, as would be expected from the result for a market economy with the assumption of no rationing and no price control. The slope coefficient on the basis of average currency holdings is 0.9320.

For the case of China, however, we would not necessarily expect a coefficient of unity. Intuition suggests that the market price index will be more responsive to an increase in the money ratio in an economy where there is rationing and price control for the bulk of retail sales and where the market price index covers a very limited range of goods for most of the period under study. The common view is that there will be a large spillover from the state sector onto a very narrow free market, driving prices up more than proportionately. Regression results just produce average relationship for the entire sample period; they do not necessarily give good predictions of changes in individual years. For example, in 1961 the money ratio rose 89.5 per cent, but the market price index rose 260 per cent. If we applied a coefficient of approximately unity for predicting this, the actual outcome would be hopelessly underestimated. Xue Muqiao (1982a: 69) must have had this idea in mind when he discusses the price consequences of the agricultural collapse of the early 1960s, writing: 'When money supply doubled, prices in farmers' markets had to increase from three to four to five to six times.' The money supply did not double, but the money ratio nearly did. Free market prices in 1961 were just over four times their

1959 level. Tobin and Houthakker (1951) have established theoretically that rationing increases the income elasticity of demand for non-rationed goods. This provides a theoretical reason for expecting a larger increase in demand for free market goods, the spillover effect, and larger-than-proportional price increases.

We might expect the Quantity Theory to perform better in the modern reform period when both currency in circulation and prices did increase more markedly and more prices were freed from state control. For the period 1977–85 the result is

$$\ln P = \underset{(0.0518)}{0.9560} + \underset{(0.0243)}{0.2624} \ln (M/y) \qquad R^2 = 0.9434 \quad s = 0.0212 \quad DW = 2.680 \quad n = 9$$

The observations show less variance and a better fit, but the slope coefficient has not increased. Even in the reform period price control kept the quantitative relationship between the general retail price index and the money ratio very low. This should not be a surprise as this is what price control is intended to do and list prices are an important component of the general retail price index.

6.6 *Money and prices: an alternative explanation*

The Quantity Theory is not consistent with China's actual economic institutions, nor does it explain why the money ratio changed—in particular, why the money supply changed. Any alternative approach must rectify these deficiencies and, I feel, must have the following characteristics. It must be:

1 consistent with actual institutions in China;
2 consistent with what Chinese economists say happens in their economy;
3 consistent with the evidence; and
4 able to be illustrated using the simplest of techniques without resorting to overelaborate processing of the original annual data of prices, money and other related variables.

An alternative explanation can be built up on the following assumptions, which result from chapter 4's coverage of China's economic institution and policies:

1 Planners wish to maintain an acceptable ratio of currency in circulation to annual retail sales.
2 Planners also wish to maintain general stability of the price level, including the free-market price level.
3 The narrow measure of the money supply rises more rapidly when the gap between purchasing power and realised expenditures rises.
4 As is well recognised, this gap could be narrowed by increasing state list prices.
5 Such increases restrain the rate of growth of unspent purchasing power.
6 Such increases also increase the nominal value of retail sales, thus

reducing the ratio of remaining unspent purchasing power to retail sales.

When would planners be likely to increase list prices?

Figure 6.4(a) shows the situation in the consumer goods market facing monetary planners. The amount of purchasing power paid out each year is *SPP*. Out of that flow households are assumed either to buy consumer goods supplied by the state C_1 at state list prices (*LP*) or to accumulate monetary assets (currency and savings deposits) in the form of unspent purchasing power. The proportion of *SPP* not spent on consumer goods and hence leading to the accumulation of monetary assets can be called the 'money accumulation rate' (Peebles, 1983: 95). Assume that households wish to accumulate a fixed proportion of *SPP* in monetary assets and that planners are happy to let them do so. This proportion is labelled m^*. This means that desired aggregate consumption expenditure is $(1 - m^*)$ *SPP* and will grow at the same rate as *SPP*. Aggregate consumer demand is represented by the rectangular hyperbola labelled $(1 - m^*)$ *SPP*. If consumer goods supply equals C_1, the list price level can be LP_1, ensuring that *VRS*, the value of retail sales, is just sufficient to withdraw the required proportion m^* of *SPP* through commodity *huilong*. Planners' assumed objectives are realised.

If *SPP* grows at a rate greater than available supplies, planners face a dilemma. In Figure 6.4(a) *SPP* is assumed to grow by 20 per cent, thus increasing demand to $(1 - m^*)$ *SPP* (1.20), and there is no increase in consumer goods supplies. This can be called a situation of purchasing power *imbalance*. In order to maintain a constant price level, consumer goods supplies would need to increase by 20 per cent also. This would would be a situation of purchasing power *balance*.

In the situation where supplies do not grow and planners do not increase prices, there will be excess demand for consumer goods to the extent of *AB* in quantity; but more importantly, consumers will find that they cannot realise a part of their desired expenditures equal to the rectangle $ACLP_2LP_1$, and this will show up as unspent purchasing power and as an observed value of m greater than m^*. Realised purchasing power will equal the value of retail sales, *VRS*. This unspent purchasing power will produce excessive growth in the narrow measures of the money supply.

Planners can, however, restrict this excessive monetary growth by increasing list prices over the range LP_1 to LP_2, producing a tradeoff between price stability and monetary accumulation. If they leave list prices constant (that is, $\text{pd}LP = 0$), m will take on some large value equal to m_{max} in Figure 6.4(b). As they increase prices by different amounts over the range LP_1 to LP_2, m will fall in such a way that, if $\text{pd}LP = 20$, m will equal m^*. This tradeoff, described in Peebles (1986b), is shown in Figure 6.4b and is labelled *AC*. Planners can choose any combination of price increases and money accumulation rates over this range by choosing any rate of list price increases between 0 and 20. Once pd*LP* is chosen, m follows under conditions of excess demand. Generally, it has been argued, planners can increase list prices to reduce the quantitative gap between excess demand and available supply; but as this argument shows, the real

Figure 6.4 Planners' reactions to purchasing power imbalances

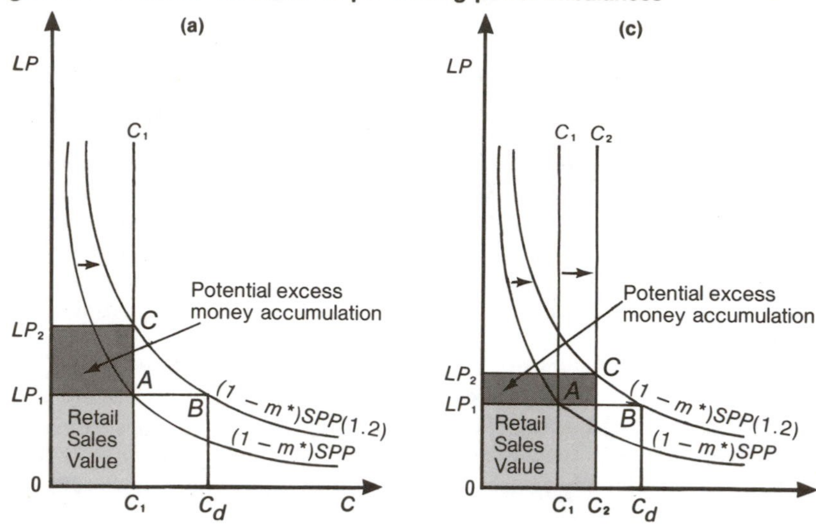

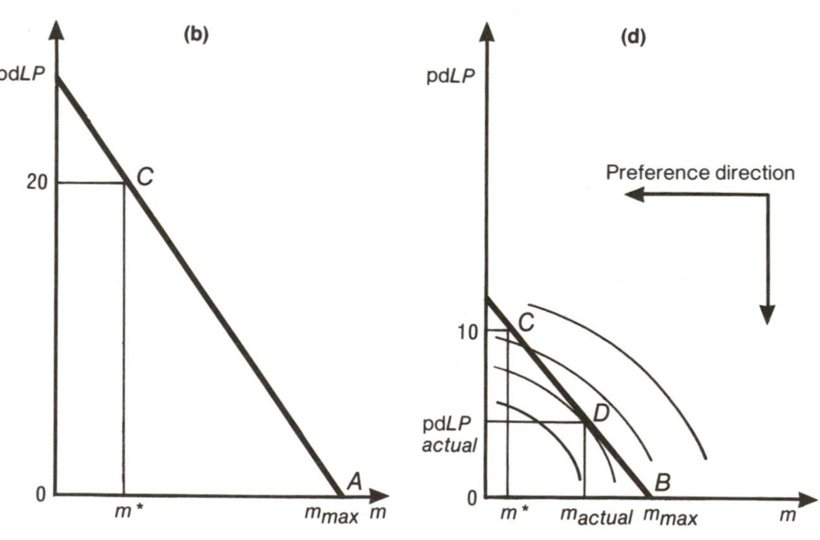

consequence of increasing list prices is to restrict the rate of growth of unspent purchasing power by using commodity *huilong* to increase the sales value of a given volume of consumer goods. Planners' activities in the consumer goods market determine the extent of narrow monetary growth, given the nature of the Chinese monetary-supply process discussed in section 4.10.

Figure 6.4(c) shows the situation where pd*SPP* is 20 and consumer goods supplies grow by 10 per cent. Even with constant prices, *VRS* will rise, but not by as much as nominal demand. The tradeoff between price stability and monetary accumulation is shown in Figure 6.4(d). Obviously, the necessary increase in list prices in order to maintain monetary accumulation at rate m^* is less than the increase shown in Figure 6.4(a) because the extent of imbalance is less.

I hypothesise that in circumstances of positive *PPI* planners do increase list prices to restrain excess monetary growth, but that the extent of list price increases chosen is less than the maximum rate necessary to keep m constant.[13] Figure 6.4(d) represents planners' preferences in a formal textbook way, showing their indifference curves. Their preferences are for zero or low open inflation and low values of m, preferably m^*. In circumstances of *PPI* they cannot obtain both objectives and face the tradeoff shown along line *BC*. I assume that they do not choose a corner solution of either pd*LP* equal to zero (and m equal to m_{max}) at point *B*, or m equal to m^* (and pd*LP* equal to the maximum rate) at point *C*. In this diagram they are shown to choose point *D*. The implication of this is that, whenever there is positive *PPI*, there will be list price increases (and hence increases in the general retail price level), higher values of m, and excess narrow monetary growth. When there is purchasing power balance or negative *PPI*, planners can leave list prices unchanged or even reduce them while securing acceptable values of m and acceptable rates of narrow monetary growth.

This analysis also implies the possible use of other policies to restrict excess monetary growth in the face of *PPI*. Increasing sales from government stocks and importing consumer goods are other ways of restricting the gap between desired and realised expenditures. Increasing interest rates will increase households' desired value of m^*, which means that aggregate demand will grow less rapidly than pd*SPP* and produce a smaller degree of imbalance given any increase in consumer goods supplies. Households will also be more willing to hold their unspent balances as savings deposits rather than currency in these circumstances. In the following analysis these two possible policy reactions to imbalances are regarded as secondary; they are not sufficient in themselves to deal with any significant levels of *PPI*.

PPI is defined as pd*SPP* minus pd*RNI*, where the growth rate of real output is taken as proxy for the growth of consumer goods supplies. This is a strict test of the view that list price increases are the main policy response to imbalances as it ignores all policies that can ensure that consumer goods supplies grow at rates different from total output.

There are two ways of testing the view that list prices are increased when there is positive *PPI* and vice versa: the qualitative and the quantitative tests. The qualitative test just looks for a coincidence of positive *PPI* and list price increases and vice versa. Frequent observations of positive *PPI* and list price reductions, or negative *PPI* and list price increases, would contradict the proposition. The qualitative test does not look for any quantitative association between the *size* of *PPI* and the extent of list price increases (pd*LP*). This is what the quantitative test does. The quantitative test is both more strict and more generous than the qualitative test. It is more strict because it requires such a positive correlation between *PPI* and pd*LP*. There is no reason to believe that there would be such a relationship. In the case of China it is not automatic that similar degrees of *PPI* in different decades produced the same annual values of pd*LP*; attitudes to price changes have varied considerably during the four-decade period covered. If some sort of quantitative relationship does exist, this will add considerable extra support to the hypothesis. The quantitative test is more generous because there could be a large number of observations of negative *PPI* and positive pd*LP*, for example, offset by some quantitatively large positive *PPI* and pd*LP*, which would still produce positive correlation coefficients. The following uses both tests.

Figure 6.5(a) shows a scatter diagram of pd*LP* against *PPI* for the entire period 1953–85. Observations supporting the proposition would lie in the northeastern and southwestern quadrants, as do 22 of them. Some of the observations are of very small *PPI* and pd*LP*. Such changes in the list price index could be due to changes in one or two price categories and not really be part of any macroeconomic monetary policy. Figure 6.5(b) shows all those observations of pd*LP* which are equal to or greater than plus or minus 1 and so identifies significant changes in the aggregate list price index. There are seventeen observations, only three of which fall in the wrong quadrants: 1957 and 1962, when there was a negative *PPI* and list prices were increased; and 1971, when there was a positive *PPI* and list prices were reduced. Three wrong observations out of seventeen is not a significant number. Even using a crude measure of excess demand (*PPI*) and annual data, the qualitative test produces reasonable results; when there was positive *PPI* list prices were increased, and negative *PPI* was associated with list price reductions at the aggregate level.

This finding contradicts the proposition of Wang Tong-eng (1980: 94–5) who argued that at times of excess demand planners would not increase prices because of the fear of inflation and because they would not be able to reduce them subsequently. As we have seen, this is precisely what they did in the early 1960s when list prices were increased during 1961–62, only to be reduced during 1963–67. The significant price increases occurring from 1979 can be seen as part of this pattern of responding to large positive *PPI* by increasing list prices. List prices were hardly ever increased during the period 1963–78, not because planners froze prices irrespective of the state of excess demand, here *PPI*, but because the *PPI* indicator was generally well controlled.[14] Even in years such as 1956, when the aggregate list price index did not rise, contrary to what we would expect from the existence of positive *PPI* for this year, there were some increases in list prices of certain categories of goods such as clothes,

Figure 6.5 Scatter diagram of pd*LP* on *PPI*, 1953–85

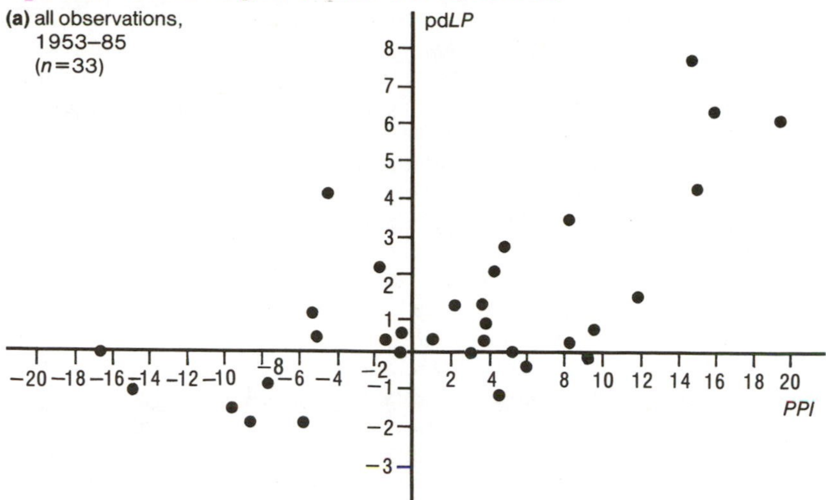

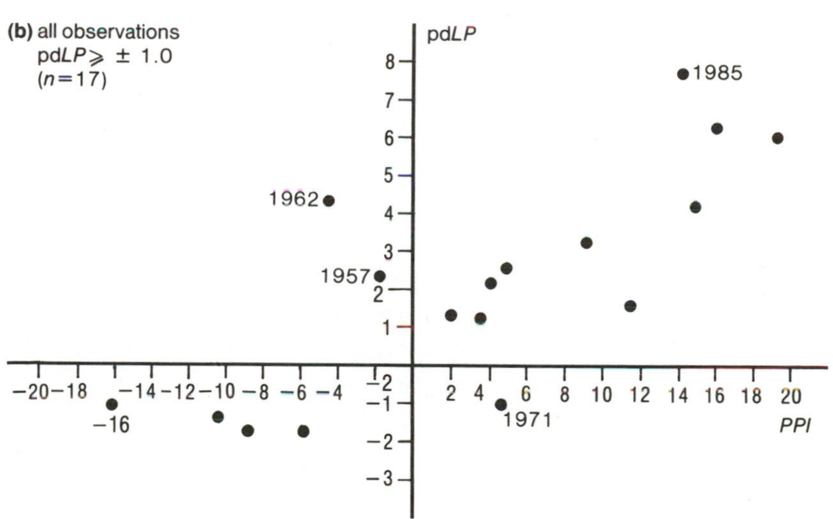

fresh vegetables and consumer goods (*Zhongguo Maoyi Wujia Tongji Ziliao 1952–83*, pp. 374–5). There was a price reaction even though it did not show up in the aggregate index.

The three years that are exceptions to the simple view can be explained reasonably satisfactorily. The year 1957 followed a year of large *PPI*. Restraining policies were adopted in 1956, but price rises were not considered until after September 1956 and not implemented until 1957. Zhang Chaohuang (1989: 54) states that the imbalances were recognised during 1956, but the party decided to implement a price freeze in the second part of 1956 to stop price rises temporarily. Perkins (1966: 172–3) had recognised this slow policy response to the 1956 situation. The restraining policies had the effect of reducing *PPI* for 1957 but of increasing prices in that year as a result of the high *PPI* in 1956. The year 1962 can probably be best explained by noting how crude the measure of *PPI* is as an indicator of supply availability. National income fell 6.5 per cent, but *SPP* fell 10.7 per cent, producing a negative *PPI*. As *SPP* includes organisations' purchasing power, this could have been the result of the usual policies of freezing organisations' funds. Residents' purchasing power, however, fell only 5.7 per cent, producing an alternative *PPI* (see Table III.1) that is just positive. In addition, 1962 followed three years of high positive *PPI* and rapid currency growth, and we might expect the list price increases to reflect the policies identified in section 2.6 to deal with this situation. In 1971 *PPI* was positive, but the list price index was reduced by 1 per cent, just qualifying it for inclusion as a significant price change. The year 1971 followed two years of very large negative *PPI* and so can be seen as a continuation of the policy of price reductions that occurred in those years, seemingly irrespective of changes in the purchasing power situation in 1971.[15]

The quantitative tests can be made by simple linear regression of pd*LP* on *PPI*. For all 33 observations for 1953–85 the result is[16]

$$\begin{array}{lr} \text{pd}LP = \underset{(0.3219)}{0.7747} + \underset{(0.0373)}{0.1796}\ PPI & R^2 = 0.4285 \\ & s = 1.7952 \\ & DW = 1.3478 \\ & n = 33 \end{array}$$

and for the seventeen observations it is

$$\begin{array}{lr} \text{pd}LP = \underset{(0.4756)}{1.3402} + \underset{(0.0465)}{0.2371}\ PPI & R^2 = 0.6336 \\ & s = 1.8522 \\ & DW = 1.9544 \\ & n = 17 \end{array}$$

The scatter diagrams in Figure 6.5 show that there was a close positive correlation, but that different degrees of list price increases occurred at the time of similar degrees of *PPI* in different years and that list prices were not increased in some years of positive *PPI*. It can be seen that the list price increase in 1985 was larger than could be expected from the average response. The resulting higher increases in the general retail price index cannot be attributed solely to the effects of freeing prices in the second stage of price reform discussed in section 4.4.

List price increases continued to have an important effect on the general retail price index. Because list prices are such an important element of the general retail price index (*P*), increases in this index were significantly correlated with *PPI*. For the entire period 1953–85

$$\text{pd}P = \underset{(0.5224)}{0.8372} + \underset{(0.0604)}{0.2780}\, PPI \qquad R^2 = 0.4057,\ s = 2.9128,\ DW = 1.7347,\ n = 33$$

The above method of presentation can easily be translated into words. Planners monitor the growth of purchasing power during the year and take the growth of real national income as an approximate indicator of retail supply availability. When purchasing power is growing more rapidly than real income, apart from undertaking policies aimed at reducing the rate of growth of purchasing power and boosting consumer goods supplies, planners increase retail list prices. As these are an important constituent of the general retail price index this latter index also rises.[17] The reason for increasing list prices is to restrain the growth of unspent purchasing power, that is, the narrow measure of the money supply.

The above theory answers Chen and Hou's (1986) question as to why the government increased retail prices in the 1980s. Zhang Yigeng (1985: 30) even goes so far as to calculate the required extra expenditure made necessary by retail price increases. Given China's institutions, much of this extra expenditure became government budget revenue and was withdrawn from circulation.

In the period 1953–85 there were twenty years of positive *PPI*, a figure not too different from that implied by Wan Dianwu (1984: 355). A different opinion is given by Wan Zhigui (1989: 51) who maintains that there was equilibrium (*pingheng*) or basically equilibrium between consumer goods supplies (*huoyuan*) and purchasing power (*goumaili*) for 26 years out of the 37 years 1952–88. The present *PPI* measure of imbalance, however, suggests a different frequency of excess demand.

The extent of retail list price increases in years of positive *PPI* have not been sufficient to restrain the growth of the ratio of currency to retail sales. Out of the nineteen years of positive *PPI* that occurred during 1954–85 there were seventeen in which the ratio of currency in circulation to annual retail sales increased. In both the two other years the ratio remained unchanged (when the ratio is taken to the nearest whole number). List price increases prevented these increases in the ratio from being larger but did not prevent them entirely. Out of the thirteen years of negative *PPI* the same ratio fell in nine, remained unchanged in one and increased in three. This shows that changes in the narrow money ratio are reasonably well explained by the state of *PPI*. Positive *PPI* is associated with list price increases, currency growth *and* increases in the narrow money ratio. This means that there is a positive association between the narrow money ratio and the price level, as revealed in the Quantity Theory approach, but the present theory explains *why* there is such a relationship and that it is not a causative relationship going from the money stock to prices.

Out of the twenty years of positive *PPI* the market price index of consumer goods rose in sixteen, falling in the three years 1971, 1979 and 1984 and remaining unchanged in 1968. This positive association is another reason why the general retail price index rose at times of positive *PPI*.

Certain other questions suggest themselves: Why was there positive *PPI* in certain periods? Which list prices were increased? Can we call such increases inflation? What is the relationship between *PPI* and narrow monetary growth? The twenty years of positive *PPI* were 1953–54, 1956, 1959–61, 1967–68, 1971–74, 1976 and 1979–85.[18] Positive *PPI* in these years occurred as a result of both nominal changes and real changes. Reductions in real national income in 1959–61, 1967–68 and 1976 obviously contributed to this even though purchasing power fell slightly in some of these years. These unexpected exogenous output shocks caused the imbalances. In contrast, positive *PPI* emerged in years when real output was growing rapidly but nominal changes brought about a much larger increase in *SPP*. The wage increases of 1953 and 1956 increased *SPP* in these years. The high accumulation rate, unplanned increases in the workforce and increased wage bill in the early 1970s produced the imbalances then. After 1979 virtually all nominal variables increased considerably and boosted *SPP*. Both agricultural purchasing prices and state wages were increased, as were workers' and staff subsidies, leading to the marked imbalances then. Purchasing power balance was mainly achieved during the period 1962–78 with the exceptions noted above. This was done by strict nominal wage control and virtually unchanged agricultural procurement prices. There is no neat way to ascribe the occurrence of *PPI* to one overriding factor throughout the period.

The whole logic of the above theory is that list prices of goods in excess demand will be increased, due to their having a high income elasticity of demand when nominal incomes rise, as will the prices of goods that are price-inelastic. The extent of the list price increases is not an accurate indicator of the extent to which such price increases can increase government revenue and withdraw currency from circulation. Figure 6.6 shows the example of a good in excess demand. It is delivered to the state retail network at a price of 1 *yuan*. There is a 0.20 *yuan* markup to cover retail profit and commercial tax. Under the pre-reform system virtually all of this would have been remitted to the budget. In the face of rapidly growing purchasing power planners increase list prices by 10 per cent. Sales do not fall, so budget revenue increases 60 per cent (from 0.2 *yuan* per unit to 0.32 *yuan* per unit) by this 10 per cent price increase. Even under the reformed system under which the retail enterprise is allowed to keep, say, 45 per cent of the markup, budget tax revenue still rises in the same proportion. Such list price increases are a powerful way of increasing revenue from goods in excess demand.

Examining the various categories of list price indexes in years when the aggregate list price index was increased does not reveal any consistent pattern. However, the category of 'cigarettes, wine and tea' showed the most significant increases in years when the overall list price index increased. Such increases were used in 1961 and were continued right until 1964. These increases became a common feature of the increases in list

Figure 6.6 Effect on state revenue of increasing list prices

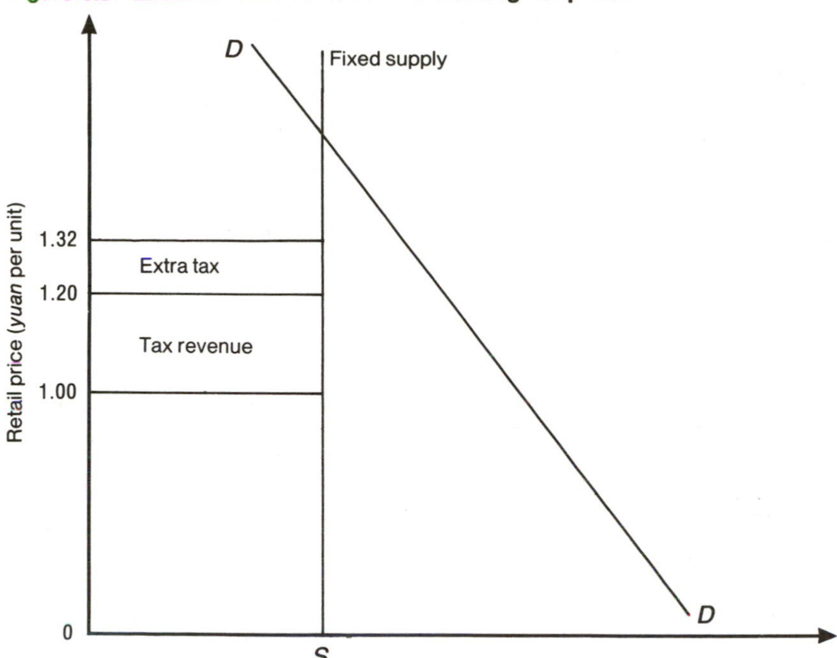

prices in the 1980s, with this category rising 16.5 per cent in 1982 alone, as shown in section 2.10. In the years 1981–83 the quantities of tea, alcohol (*jiu*) and cigarettes sold increased by 14, 77 and 26 per cent respectively in each year, but total expenditures on them rose 26, 117 and 67 per cent respectively. In 1962 and 1963, although the quantity of wine consumed rose only 3.5 per cent in each year, expenditure on it rose 50 and 13 per cent in each year.[19] In 1962 tea consumption fell, but expenditure on it remained constant. This illustrates how list price increases are able to increase expenditures more rapidly than sales volume growth. List food prices were also increased in the 1960 episode of significant increases in the overall list price index, as were manufactured goods prices. *Zhongguo Maoyi Wujia Tongji Ziliao 1952–83* (pp. 94–5, 374–5) provides the sales volume, expenditures and list price indexes for a more detailed analysis. As McLure and Thirsk (1978: 501–2) show, virtually all studies of price elasticity of demand for cigarettes and liquor in the West indicate very low own-price elasticity. This is why governments tax these products so much; demand falls very little as prices rise, so revenue is boosted. This is not proof that such products are in inelastic demand in China, but it is suggestive. Anyway, the government did increase these prices, which is what we would expect if demand were inelastic.

Were these list price increases equivalent to inflation? Most Western economists, I think, would say that they were not. This is especially the case if they were increases in list prices from below-market clearing levels to somewhere nearer the equilibrium price, as shown in Figure 6.6. They would be seen as a necessary means of correcting the distorting effects of government price control. Chinese economists would probably agree, and some of them tend to reserve the phrase 'inflation' for the situation when market prices rise. An increase in the general price index not accompanied by an increase in free market prices would not be described as inflationary by these economists. They distinguish the following four cases when the general retail price index (P) can be seen to increase:

Direction of change			
P	*LP*	*MP*	*Interpretation*[20]
+	0	+	Inflation
+	+	+	Inflation
+	+	0	Balance
+	+	−	Retrenchment

This suggests that classifying *all* the observed changes in the general retail list price index according to these two components might be a useful way of identifying the extent to which there was inflation in these price changes.[21] Such a classification obtains the nine categories: shown in Table 6.4. If we take the first two categories as representing inflationary increases in the general retail price index, such increases occurred in 48 per cent of the years under study. If we add the three years in which market prices rose but were offset by list price reductions, inflationary years made up 58 per cent of the total. Market prices fell in twelve of the years, and in six of these the general retail price index rose because list prices were increased. The first category shows that in only two years of market price increases were there no list price increases (1974 and 1975); that is, in only two years out of 33 were increases in market prices the sole reason for increases in the general price level. The seventh category shows that there were three years when list prices were reduced when market prices rose (1965–67). If we take market price increases to be an indicator of inflation, then in only five years out of nineteen of inflation did planners not increase list prices. These years were at the beginning and towards the end of the Cultural Revolution period. This may lead readers to formulate the proposition that list price increases generally follow market price increases. But why did market prices increase? Out of the 23 years of general price increases there were 21 in which list prices were increased. Market prices rose in sixteen of these 23 years. This again shows that list price increases, not market price increases, were the main reason for increases in the general price index.

The relationship between *PPI* and the extent of narrow monetary growth is important. Any explanation of money and prices in China, and their association, must provide a reason for different rates of monetary growth. On a qualitative basis it has already been shown that in the years of positive *PPI* the currency ratio rose. The interpretation offered here is that this is a causative association; positive *PPI* results in large increases in unspent purchasing power. As years of positive *PPI* were also years of increases in the general retail price index, we observe a positive relationship between the currency ratio and the general retail price index. However, the relationship is not one of cause and effect; both are the

Table 6.4 Price changes by type of price, 1953–85

P	*LP*	*MP*	Observed in	Frequency
+	0	+	1974, 1975	2
+	+	+	1953, 1954, 1957–59, 1960–61, 1973, 1976, 1980–85	14
+	+	0	1968	1
+	+	–	1955, 1962, 1977–79, 1984	6
–	–	–	1963–64, 1969	3
–	–	0	1970	1
–	–	+	1965–67	3
–	+	–	1971, 1972	2
0	0	–	1956	1
				n = 33

consequence of positive *PPI*. The positive association between the annual percentage rate of growth of *CRC* and *PPI* is quite clear, as shown in the following result for the period 1953–85:

$$\text{pd}CRC = \underset{(2.2624)}{9.9981} + \underset{(0.2618)}{1.2603}\ PPI \qquad R^2 = 0.4278,\ s = 12.6154,\ DW = 2.1445,\ n = 33$$

The greater the extent of *PPI* in any year, the greater the rate of growth of currency.

This can be shown to be true also for the seven subperiods of chapter 2. Figure 6.7 shows a scatter diagram of the average annual growth rates of various variables for each of the seven subperiods, where *ppi* is the average annual rate of growth of *SPP* minus that of real national income, *lp* is the average annual rate of increase in list prices, and *crc* is the average annual rate of growth of currency in circulation (see Table IV.1 for the data). Note that *crc* is plotted against an inverted scale. There is clearly a good positive relationship between both *lp* and *crc* and *ppi*. Such periods as II and VII with high *ppi* saw rapid currency growth and high average list price increases. Periods such as III and IV, when *ppi* was negative, saw list price reductions and average and moderate rates of currency growth. Periods such as I, V and VI fall in the middle of the range of observations of *ppi* and therefore of *lp* and *crc*. This explains why we observe a positive relationship between currency growth and price increases; they are both positive functions of something else. *PPI* has been treated as the exogenous variable (itself determined by exogenous uncoordinated changes in nominal purchasing power and real income) and list price increases as the reaction. These are not sufficient to restrain monetary growth completely, so monetary growth is positively correlated with *ppi*.

Because list prices exert a dominant effect on the general retail price index, the average rates of change in this index are also explained by the average values of *ppi* for these subperiods:

$$p = 0.6443 + 0.4234\,ppi \qquad R^2 = 0.850$$
$$(0.5213) \quad (0.0796) \qquad s = 1.3208$$
$$DW = 1.523$$
$$n = 7$$

Figure 6.7 Scatter diagram of *lp* and *crc* on *ppi* for seven subperiods

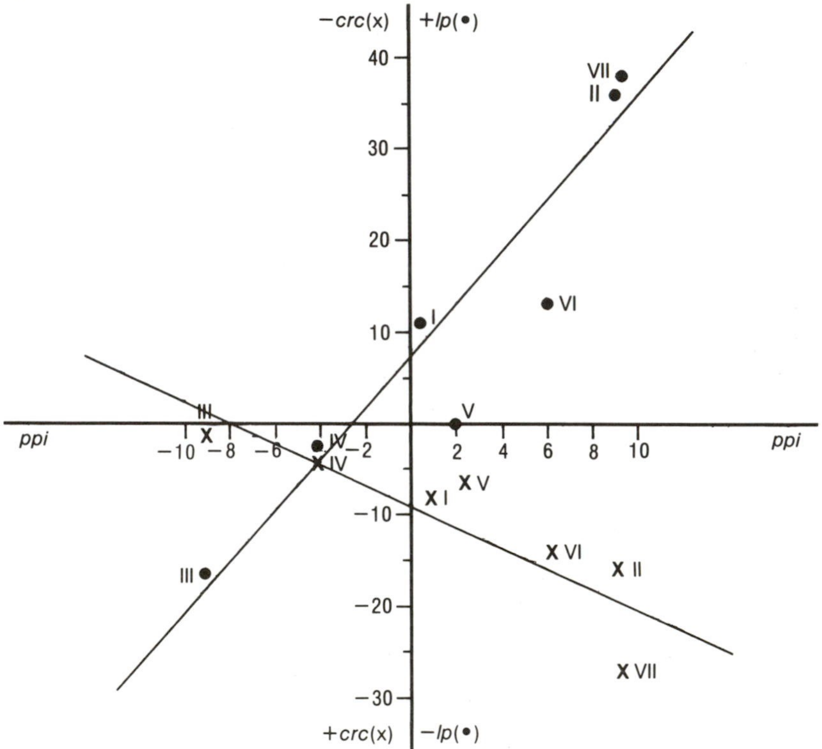

6.7 The alternative theory: an alternative presentation

The above form of presentation was chosen as it is easily put into words to describe the planners' reactions to *PPI* in a dynamic context. Its clear implication is that, when the ratio of *SPP* to real income rises, list prices will be increased. We would therefore expect to see a clear positive association between the ratio of *SPP* to real national income and the retail price index. This is accepted as a possibility by Chow (1987: 331) when he adds the wage bill (just one element of *SPP*) to a regression equation including the money ratio. This is not really a fair test of the view that purchasing power developments exert a more important effect on the price level than the money ratio. This view should be examined independently and directly.

Figure 6.8 shows an index of the ratio of *SPP* to real national income (1952 = 100) for the period 1952–85 in the top section and the general

Figure 6.8 ***SPP* ratio, price index, budget and changes in currency in circulation, 1952–85**

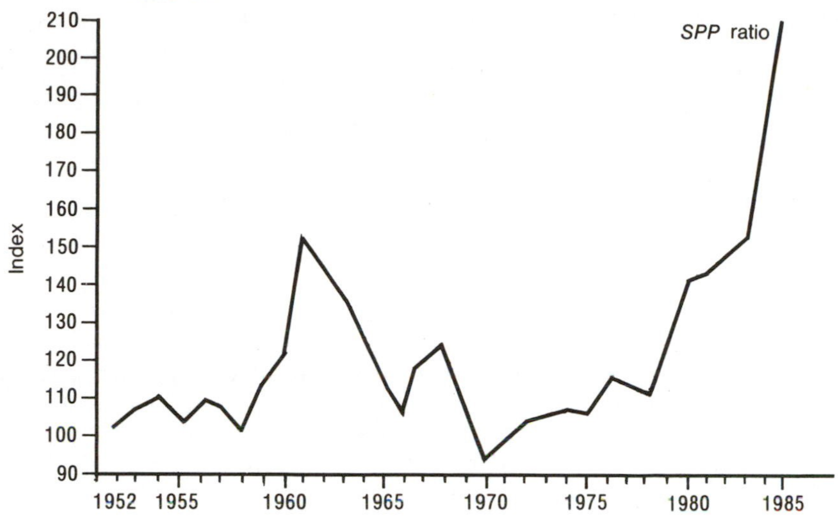

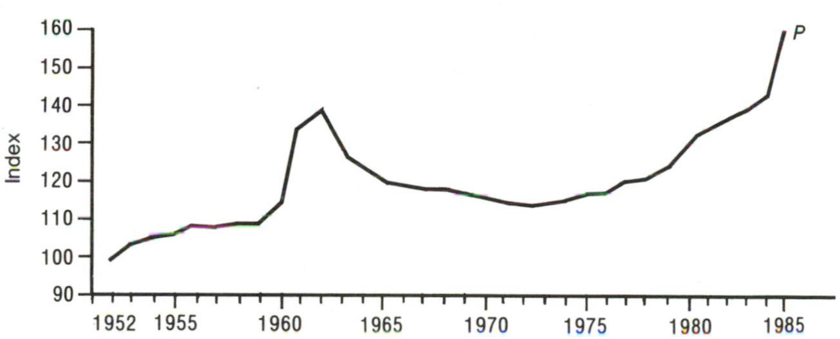

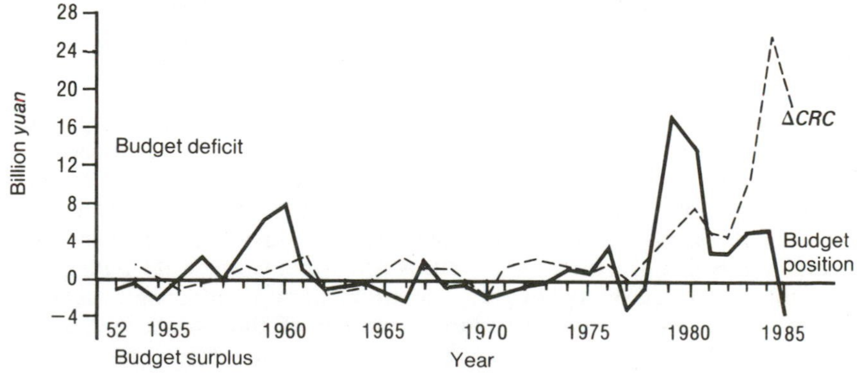

retail price index (1950 = 100) in the middle section. There is clearly a close positive association between them, as we would expect. When the ratio rises so does the price index and vice versa.[22] As we have seen, this is mainly due to the fact that the list price index is increased at times of positive *PPI*, which here shows itself as a rise in the ratio of *SPP* to real national income.

The quantitative relationship between the general retail price index and the *SPP* ratio is

$$\ln P = \underset{(0.0124)}{0.2023} + \underset{(0.0483)}{0.4929} \ln (SPP/RNI) \qquad R^2 = 0.7652, \; s = 0.0488, \; DW = 0.3810, \; n = 34$$

Even in the presence of positive serial correlation the coefficients remain unbiased estimates. This shows that a 1 per cent increase in the *SPP* ratio leads to a 0.49 per cent increase in the general retail price index. This coefficient is 81 per cent larger than that of the money ratio, 0.27, obtained by Chow (1987) and in section 6.5. A regression using the Cochrane–Orcutt procedure allowing for first-order serial correlation provides a satisfactory regression with an R^2 of 0.9333 and a *t*-statistic on the slope of 6.31.

The possibility that list prices are increased with a time lag is confirmed by the positive effect of the previous year's *SPP* ratio on the general retail price index in the following result for 1953–85:

$$\ln P = \underset{(0.0119)}{0.2037} + \underset{(0.0966)}{0.2954} \ln (SPP/RNI) + \underset{(0.1093)}{0.2288} \ln (SPP/RNI)_{-1}$$

$$R^2 = 0.7968, \; s = 0.0443, \; F[2, 30] = 58.82, \; DW = 0.3045, \; n = 33$$

Again, a regression using the Cochrane–Orcutt procedure and assuming first-order serial correlation provides a satisfactory result with both slopes having *t*-statistics in excess of 3, R^2 of 0.9461 and $F[3, 28]$ of 163.94.

We can put this equation into words that are fully compatible with Chinese institutions and highlight the nature of the assumptions about which are the exogenous variables in this explanation. The following is a stylised description of the economy that accounts for this relationship. Imagine the economy as one large state-run company that sells its output to the population. Transactions between its branches (state enterprises) do not use cash; they are just internal accounting settlements. The banking system is the 'firm's' wages and accounts department. The state budget is its profit and loss account. The 'firm', a virtual monopsonist, has to obtain inputs such as labour and agricultural goods from the population using cash. *SPP* is an indicator of the cash costs to the 'firm' of obtaining these inputs, and the ratio of *SPP* to *RNI* is an indicator of cash cost per unit of output.[23] The explanation of the previous section looked at this ratio as an indicator of excess demand and as the potential cause of monetary growth. Here we can see it also as an indicator of unit cash costs and an indicator of losses to the 'firm'. If this ratio rises, then, ceteris paribus, the state industrial 'firm' will make losses unless it increases its prices, which in China are state list prices. Hence we have been able to show that the price level is a function of this cost ratio. Recall Weintraub's wage cost markup theory of the price level

$$P = k(W/A)$$

If we multiply the numerator and denominator of the right hand side of the equation by the labour force, we get an expression for the general retail price index as a function of the total wage bill divided by total output. This is what we see is the case for China. The cost increases are often the result of the 'firm's' own actions. Sometimes they are a result of the fall in A, but the very action of increasing W (*SPP* in the Chinese context) is to increase automatically the issuance of currency. If prices rise, increased wage subsidies will increase *SPP* and money issue even further. A general wage rise in a capitalist country does not automatically increase the money supply according to the assumptions of the Quantity Theory approach, but this is an argument about the true nature of the money supply process used by Post Keynesian economists. In the Chinese context an increase in the *SPP* ratio ensures that most of the extra currency issue remains in circulation because C_H does not rise sufficiently to withdraw all the extra issue; nor do the increases in list prices that are undertaken as part of monetary policy.

The other aspects of this analogy are obvious. When the 'firm's' unit cost ratio rises it will make temporary losses, which it recoups by increasing its prices. These losses show up in the state budget deficit. An individual firm making losses in a capitalist society could go on trading if it could convince its workers and suppliers to accept its own money in place of the legal money it cannot obtain from its customers. This is just what the Chinese 'firm' does. It issues its own currency printed by its own accounts department (the People's Bank of China), forbids any other currency to circulate and continues to accept tax payments only in its own currency. The capitalist society firm could continue to trade by issuing promissory notes to be repaid when business improved. The Chinese 'firm' issues government bonds. This is why we see increases in the budget deficit and increasing currency issue at times of large increases in the *SPP* ratio. They, similarly, are consequences of the occurrence of *PPI*, not independent causes of price increases.

Figure 6.8 shows these relationships. Causation goes from the top section to the lower sections and can be explained on the basis of the institutions described in chapter 4.[24] Events since 1956 are broadly compatible with the explanation of the links between these variables offered above. *PPI* emerges as a result of uncoordinated changes in *SPP* and real output, leading planners to resort to list price increases in most years. Imbalances cause budget deficits and increases in *CRC*. In the 34 years 1952–85 there were budget deficits in fifteen years, namely, 1956, 1958–61, 1967, 1974–76 and all the years after 1979 except 1985. In these fifteen years of deficits *PPI* was positive in all except 1958 and 1975. In the years when the budget showed surplus after each of these periods of deficits (that is, in 1957, 1962, 1968, 1977 and 1985), *PPI* became negative in three and fell in the other two. This shows that *PPI* developments were quite closely connected with the state of the budget.

In 1956 the *SPP* ratio increased. There were list price increases for some items but the aggregate index did not rise, so a budget deficit emerged after five years of surpluses and currency growth increased significantly. The government sold from stocks, which fell 6.5 per cent (*Zhongguo Tongji Nianjian 1989*, p. 618). This shows a preference for a policy of sales from stocks and purchasing power reductions over a policy of list price increases in this year. In five later years, four of them years of positive *PPI*, the government sold from its stocks of commodities. In 1957 the *SPP* ratio fell (that is, *PPI* was negative), prices were increased (a year late because of the policy lag), a budget surplus was achieved, and *CRC* actually fell. After 1958 the *SPP* ratio rose steadily to peak in 1961. List prices were increased in every year and by a record amount in 1961. Government stocks of commodities were reduced in 1961 and 1962. Budget deficits existed for 1958–61, and currency increases were large in 1958–61. In 1962 the *SPP* ratio fell but remained high, prices were still increased, the budget deficit became a slight surplus, and *CRC* fell considerably. The year 1962 saw negative *PPI* following three years of large positive *PPI*. The government seems to have been committed to continuing policies of higher list prices, sales from government stocks, imports and reductions in the accumulation rate. This is why 1962 stands out as an anomaly; it had negative *PPI* but experienced all the reactive policies taken in years of positive *PPI*.

Thereafter the *SPP* ratio was reduced steadily until 1966. Over this period prices were reduced and there were budget surpluses, even in 1966. Currency growth was moderate until 1966. In 1967 the *SPP* ratio rose sharply and again in 1968. There was no reaction in the form of list price increases, but stocks were reduced in 1967. There was a budget deficit in 1967, and currency growth remained high. Although the *SPP* ratio peaked in 1968 and there were no price increases a budget surplus was achieved. In 1969 and 1970 the *SPP* ratio fell, prices were reduced, and budget surpluses were achieved. In 1971 the *SPP* ratio began to rise steadily until 1976. Currency increases occurred in 1971–75, although there were budget surpluses until 1974 when there were deficits in 1974 and 1975.[25] In 1976 there was a sharp rise in the *SPP* ratio, there was a very small price reaction, the budget deficit increased 500 per cent, and currency growth increased also. In this year stocks of retail goods fell, indicating that this policy was also being used to deal with the emerging excess demand (*Zhongguo Tongji Nianjian 1989*, p. 618). In 1977 and 1978 the *SPP* ratio was reduced and budget surpluses were achieved; *CRC* fell in 1977. In 1979 there was a sharp increase in the *SPP* ratio, list prices were increased by the largest amount since 1962, a huge budget deficit emerged, and currency growth increased. Again, in 1980 the *SPP* ratio increased, list prices were increased significantly, the budget remained in deficit, and currency growth increased.

In 1981–83 the *SPP* ratio increased at a slower rate and the budget deficit fell, as did the rate of currency growth. In 1984 and 1985 the *SPP* ratio increased markedly, as did the rate of currency growth. In 1984 retail stocks were reduced again, indicating that they were also being used to deal with the situation (*Zhongguo Tongji Nianjian 1989*, p. 618). In 1985 the general retail price index recorded its largest increase since 1961, and the State Council issued a number of directives aimed at dealing with this problem.[26] The budget remained in deficit until 1985 when a surplus was achieved, but only for that single year. It is in the years after 1983 that the relatively close relationship between the budget deficit and currency growth breaks down. Before that, as Figure 6.8 shows, they tended to move together, except for 1961 and 1966. After 1983 the moderate increase in the deficit in 1984 was associated with a very high and substantially increased rate of currency growth; and although surplus was achieved in 1985 and the currency growth rate did fall, it remained very high. The *SPP* ratio rose because agricultural procurement prices rose. As retail prices remained below the procurement price, procurement agencies made losses, which were a drain on the budget and put currency into circulation. After 1979 retail prices rose. The foreign trade corporations would have had to obtain output for export at higher domestic prices. Without a change in the domestic settlement rate for foreign exchange earnings, which did occur in 1981, they would have made losses, which they did. This was a drain on the budget, as were the increased household subsidies required because of the increases in retail prices.[27]

The above explanation of the determination of the general retail price level has made it a function of the money costs of producing national income. It has been well remarked that the Soviet or Stalinist approach to economic development regards food and labour as necessary inputs into the state economy for the purpose of producing steel. Food output is not in itself regarded as an important indicator of economic development, which concentrates on heavy industrialisation. During a conversation I once had with a Chinese student he remarked that the Chinese retail price level is determined by the price of grain. There are two interpretations of this. One is that retail grain prices, as they enter into the composition of the general retail price index, must have an impact on the general index. The second interpretation, which is consistent with the above approach, is that it is the procurement price of grain that exerts a dominant effect on the retail price level. We have seen that when agricultural procurement prices were increased *SPP* rose markedly. The years of marked increases in the grain procurement price index were 1961–62, 1966, 1976, and 1979 and after.[28] These were all years of sharp increases in the *SPP* ratio. The subsequent increases in retail prices also led to further increases in wages, thus increasing the *SPP* ratio even more. Wage increases and falls in national income are of course the other factors that can change the *SPP* ratio dramatically.

The coincidence of changes in the grain procurement price index and the general retail price index is clearly shown in a recent graphical history of the Chinese economy.[29] That agricultural procurement prices should influence the general retail price index in a predominantly agricultural country would not have surprised a British classical political economist of the early nineteenth century. David Ricardo's view of the economy (1817,

1819, 1821) gave the agricultural sector a dominant influence over the rate of profit in industry and the price level. In his model, as nominal food prices rose because agricultural output was subject to diminishing returns, money wages would rise to maintain the constant real wage, increasing nominal wage costs throughout the economy and thus leading to an increase in the general price level. Increases in the prices of goods not consumed by workers would not have this effect in Ricardo's model.

This effect seems to be at work in China also; food prices increase costs and wages (via the institution of subsidies for rising food prices) and hence the *SPP* ratio. Changes in procurement prices are not the sole reason for changes in the *SPP* ratio, however, and it would be wrong to push this effect to a dominant position although it has played an important role at times of large changes in the general retail price level.

6.8 Further reactions to purchasing power imbalances: changes in investment

As we saw in chapter 5, it has commonly been said that a consistent reaction to demand imbalances in China has been reductions in investment. We also commented that Naughton's (1986, 1987) linking of the rate of change of investment to the previous year's extent of shortage is not a really satisfactory way of identifying changes in policy towards investment. What we need to do is to examine changes in the accumulation rate in the light of the extent of *PPI*. If we accept that a one-year lag of investment behind demand imbalances is appropriate, we must expect a year of positive *PPI* to be followed by one of a reduction in the accumulation rate. Years of negative *PPI* should be followed by constant or increased accumulation rates. Out of the twenty years of positive *PPI* over the period 1953–85 ten were followed by reductions in the accumulation rate and ten by increases. Out of the thirteen years of negative *PPI* ten were followed by increases in the accumulation rate and three reductions. (See Tables II.2 and III.2 for the data.) Hence, in cases of positive *PPI* it was equally probable that the accumulation rate would be increased in the following year as that it would be reduced. Naughton's regressions, showing a negative association between the rate of change of investment, not the accumulation rate, and his shortage indicator are for the period 1956–78. In the present sample ten extra years are included, five of which were years of positive *PPI* followed by an increase in the accumulation rate. This analysis is qualitative and does not use regressions as that technique would discount some of the exceptions noted here. There seems to have been a change in the attitude towards accumulation in the period after 1981. In the four years 1981–84 positive *PPI* was followed by increases in the accumulation rate. It was only in 1986 that the accumulation rate was reduced following a year of positive *PPI*.

Figure 6.9 shows two scatter diagrams of data for the seven subperiods used above. The top section shows the average rate of change of investment in nominal terms (*i*) plotted against each period's measure of *PPI*, and the lower section shows the average rate of change of the accumula-

Figure 6.9 Scatter diagram of *i* and *acc* against *ppi* for seven subperiods

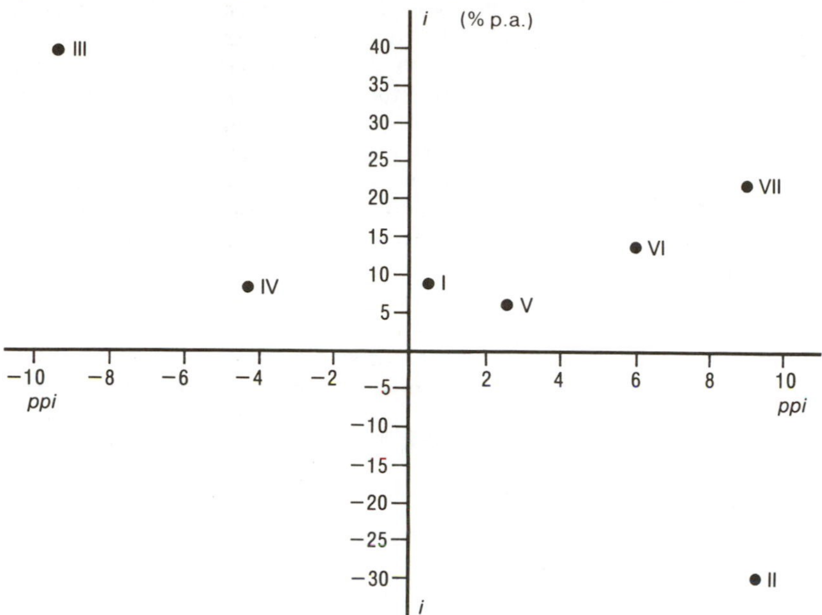

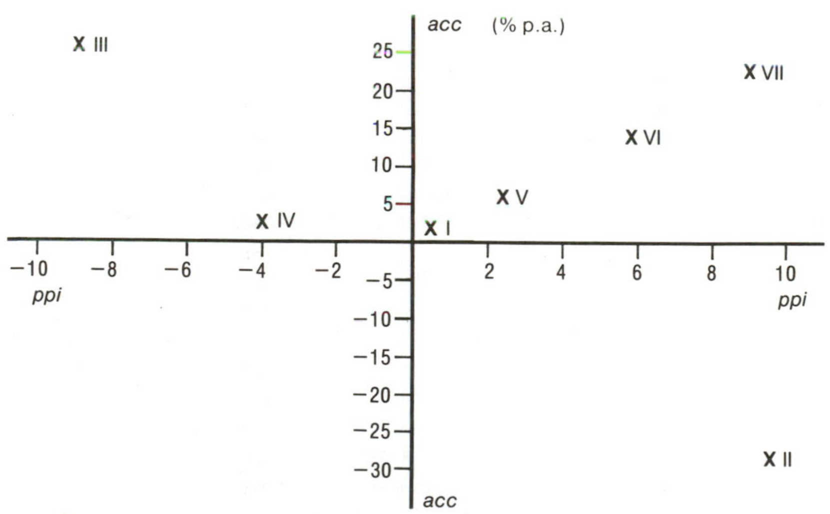

tion rate (*acc*) plotted against each period's average *PPI*. The plots suggest negative association for periods I to IV and then a positive association taking over in periods V and VII.[30] They dispose of the view that rapid investment growth is associated with demand imbalances for the entire period, and it is more reasonable to interpret the association as the response of planners' investment policies to demand imbalances, as Naughton does. In period I *PPI* was moderately positive, and investment and the accumulation rate were increased slightly. In period II the huge positive *PPI* was associated with reductions in investment and the accumulation rate. In the period of recovery, period III, negative *PPI* was achieved, and investment and the accumulation rate were increased rapidly. In period IV negative *PPI* was maintained, and investment and the accumulation rate were increased again. In periods V to VII successively larger degrees of positive *PPI* were associated with successively more rapid rates of growth of investment and increases in the accumulation rate. In these periods planners do not seem to have been able to respond to the increasing degrees of imbalance by reducing the accumulation rate.

6.9 Further reactions to purchasing power imbalances: interest rate increases and bond sales

Hsiao (1971) proposes that one aspect of Chinese reactive monetary policy was to reduce the liquidity of household monetary assets by encouraging households to hold such assets as savings deposits rather than cash. We can examine this proposition for the period after 1978 as interest rates on savings deposits were increased a number of times. To do this we can invoke a concept I find quite helpful: 'savings propensity'. This must not be confused with either the average or marginal propensity to save of Western macroeconomics. In the Chinese context it is not universally accepted that the rate of saving by households in the form of total monetary accumulation is purely voluntary; hence it would be inappropriate to call any such proportion a 'propensity'. However, it is reasonable to assume that the proportion of any increase in monetary assets going to either cash accumulation or savings deposits does reflect the wishes of households or units. The proportion of total monetary accumulation in any year taking the form of the accumulation of savings deposits will be called the 'savings propensity'.

This proportion is governed by the usual economic factors such as units' and households' preference for future consumption versus present consumption and the real rate of interest. In an economy such as China's there is the additional factor of changes in expectations about the safety of savings deposits. An expectation of a policy of freezing personal deposits (as units' deposits have been at various times) would obviously change households' willingness to accumulate savings deposits. An additional factor, common to all countries, is the desire to conceal monetary holdings from the authorities.[31] This would have increased during the 1980s as economic reform allowed people to earn more money through private economic activity. The desire to avoid possible taxes, and changes in tax laws and the force with which they are likely to be implemented, may cause fluctuations in the savings propensity.

We might expect planners to monitor the savings propensity and to react when it falls. During the period 1971–75 the savings propensity averaged 62 per cent for residents and 70 per cent for all accumulators of savings deposits. (These proportions can be obtained from Tables I.4 and I.3 respectively.) In 1976 this proportion fell to 51 per cent for residents and only 30 per cent for all accumulators. This was the year of the large increase in *PPI* remarked upon above. On 28 October that year savings deposits of all units, not households, were frozen.[32] In the following year the savings propensity rose to well over 100 per cent for both groups as they reduced their cash holdings but continued to accumulate savings deposits. In 1978 the ratio was 70 per cent for both categories of accumulators, back to its average for immediately before 1976. In April 1979 interest rates were increased with effect from 1 April. The savings propensity fell in that year. This was the year when private markets were being opened up, and this would have increased the demand for cash for transactions purposes. Interest rates were again increased in April 1980, and the savings propensity increased in 1981. The propensity increased again in 1982, a year when interest rates were again increased with effect from 1 April, but the savings propensity fell in 1983. On the previous two occasions of increased interest rates the savings propensity increased in the following year, but it did not for the 1982 interest rate increases. The decisions to increase interest rates were probably taken towards the end of the year previous to that in which they were increased. For example, the April 1982 increase was approved by the State Council on the recommendation of the People's Bank of China on 23 December 1981.[33] (See also Jin, 1987; and *Zhongguo Jinrong*, no. 2, 1982, pp. 5–6.)

In 1981 Treasury Bonds were issued but allocated only to local governments, units and so on, not individuals (*Beijing Review*, no. 7, 15 February 1982, p. 7). From 1982 individuals were expected to take up at least half of each year's Treasury Bond issue. The bonds were to be repaid after five years in five one-yearly instalments. The 1985 bond issue was to be repaid in full in the sixth year after its issue.[34] These repayments show up in the government budget for 1986 in the item 'repaid capital with interest in [sic] government domestic bonds', amounting to 0.798 billion *yuan*, in respect, I presume, to the issue of 4.866 billion *yuan* of bonds in 1981, which are not shown separately in the accounts for that year (*Statistical Yearbook of China 1987*, p. 558).[35] The repayment of bonds adds an extra item to the income side of the sources and distribution of purchasing power of the population in addition to their higher interest receipts from the government. This obvious point is made by Chen Yige (1990: 53) who sees it as a further reason for continuing budget deficits. The repayments item was very small in 1986 but could be expected to increase steadily as repayments for each successive year's bond issue five years earlier had to be added to the repayments of earlier issues. Interest rates on savings deposits were increased twice in 1985, in April and August (*People's Republic of China Yearbook 1986*, p. 324; Tam, 1987: 101).

There does not seem to be a clear association between changes in the savings propensity and decisions to increase savings-deposit interest rates. As household liquidity rose, however, nominal interest rates were increased. It is hard to be precise about the real interest rate being offered, as this variable in its ex ante aspect requires calculation of the expected rate of interest. Suffice it to say that by 1985, when the annual rate on one-year fixed deposits was 6.84 per cent from April and 7.20 per cent from August,[36] the rate of increase in general retail prices for that year was 8.8 per cent. We could expect households to seek other forms of holding their financial wealth than savings deposits. All they had were government bonds, paying about 9 per cent for individuals and 5 per cent for organisations, shares in companies, if they could obtain such shares when these were first issued as there were no secondary markets on which these could be bought, foreign currencies and commodities.

6.10 Conclusions

This chapter has tried to show the forces determining the rate of growth of the narrow money supply, the relationship between currency in circulation and the retail price level, and certain reactions by planners to what I have called purchasing power imbalances. I have linked both the growth of narrow money and changes in the retail price level to these purchasing power imbalances, arguing that both are a consequence of such imbalances. Changes in the narrow money supply are not a separate independent cause of price increases. Planners have been assumed to monitor the extent of emerging imbalances during each year and to increase state list prices when imbalances were positive. This contributed to increases in the general retail price level. These price increases were never sufficient entirely to absorb potentially excessive monetary growth, so the narrow money supply increased in years of increased prices. In addition I have shown how government budget deficits also are associated with purchasing power imbalances. They also are not an independent cause of price increases or money supply growth; they come about because of the imbalances. These imbalances cannot be attributed to a single overriding cause; they result from a breakdown in the co-ordination between nominal and real factors in the economy. Sometimes this breakdown was caused by nominal factors, and sometimes by real.

The explanation offered here is essentially monetary,[37] but it does not take the money stock as an indicator of demand pressure. The money stock and its growth are a consequence of monetary demand imbalances, which can be directly identified from data of monetary and real flows in the Chinese economy—flows, moreover, that are an important tool of Chinese monetary planning. Another difference in the above approach is that it is accepted that household monetary holdings can exceed desired levels because of the lack of adjustment in prices and interest rates. An implication of this is that, if prices were freed in such an environment, they could rise significantly. What happened in the Chinese economy after 1985, when price reform proceeded to the freeing of more prices, will be taken up in the next chapter.

7 Comparisons and conclusions

This chapter makes a series of comparisons of the events in China after 1985 with those in earlier years on the basis of the ideas used and patterns revealed in the previous chapter. It also makes some international comparisons in the light of China's economic reforms of the 1980s. It offers some conclusions drawn from the entire study.

7.1 Main economic events, 1986–88

Before looking at the main monetary developments in these three years it is possible to make some statements about what we are likely to see. We know that banking reform was instituted in 1984 and continued afterwards. This produced a large increase in currency in circulation in 1984. Another aspect of the reforms that continued was the freeing of many retail prices, especially in 1985 and in 1987. By 1986 about 34 per cent of total retail sales value was made at market prices, but this category included negotiated and floating prices with ceilings fixed by the government (Kueh, 1990: 103–4). This left 47 per cent of retail sales to be marketed at state prices. In addition, a greater proportion of retail supplies came from private traders. For example, by 1988 the proportion of total retail sales made by individual traders and peasants selling to the non-agricultural population was 25.8 per cent; in 1984 the proportion was only 14.6 per cent (*Fenjinde Sishi Nian 1949–1989*, 1989: 397).

In industry the two-track price system meant that increases in demand were transmitted to enterprises by means of higher prices, which they now had an incentive to respond to as bonuses were linked to profit. It is reasonable to assume that the simple textbook output multiplier might apply during the period 1986–88 as industrial reform had created a more elastic aggregate supply curve rather than the completely price-inelastic supply curve of a planned system. In short, we can expect an increase in nominal demand to have had an impact on both retail prices (which were being decontrolled) and on output (as enterprises were being encouraged to market larger parts of their output outside the plan).

The actual response of output and prices to an increase in nominal demand is an extremely complicated part of macroeconomic theory even for the most studied economies of the world. As we saw in section 3.5, Friedman's view is that there is no accepted theory on this matter for capitalist economies. The way increased nominal demand is transmitted into either open inflation or real growth in a market economy depends on the way inflationary expectations are formed and adapted and on the extent to which nominal variables can be renegotiated during the inflation.[1] We have, however, seen one case very similar to the period being considered here: the banking reform in the United Kingdom in 1972, which caused a large increase in the nominal money supply. The immediate short-run reaction was a large increase in real money holdings, followed by an increase in real output in the next year and very high rates of inflation during the next two years. We have seen how Huang (1988a) has argued that the monetary buildup in China in the mid 1980s did not bring about the necessary equilibrating changes in interest rates or prices. This is similar to the British case mentioned above when, according to Artis and Lewis, the economy was pushed off its money demand curve. We can expect to see an equilibrating (or partially equilibrating) adjustment in China involving both real output growth and price increases, possibly with the real output growth preceding the higher inflation rates.

Table 7.1 presents the main economic indicators for the years 1986–88. To some extent they support the expectations suggested above. Real growth rates of national income and industrial output remained high but were lower than in 1984 and 1985. Only in 1988 did real growth in industry equal the high rate achieved in 1985. There were many reports of capacity constraints on industrial output growth at this time, such as energy and transport bottlenecks. These must have played a role in restraining real output growth. Initially, the rate of open inflation in 1986 and 1987 fell below the record rate of 1985, but in 1988 it reached its highest recorded annual rate of 18.5 per cent. Monetary buildup during 1984 and 1985 did not produce a noticeably higher rate of inflation within the following two years. However, the *PPI* indicator remained closely correlated with retail price developments.

It was in 1988 that the Chinese population really became inflation-conscious. There had been serious indicators during 1987 (the market price index of consumer goods, mainly foodstuffs, rose 16.3 per cent in this year), and retail rationing was reintroduced for pork, eggs and other food products in several cities (Ling, 1988). Many food prices were decontrolled during the first half of 1988 (especially from 15 May), and this contributed to the large rise in the general retail price index in this year. The urban food price index rose 25.2 per cent and fresh vegetable prices 31.7 per cent (*Fenjinde Sishi Nian 1949–1989*, 1989: 408). In August there were runs on the banks, and reports of panic buying throughout the country became common. One familiar policy response was to increase food subsidies for urban residents, and these were given for six important food items. By September 1988 a whole new policy had been adopted. Interest rates on savings deposits were increased for the first time since 1985, and some deposits were guaranteed in real terms. A strict credit policy was introduced under which the specialised banks had to reduce the amount of loans outstanding to below the previous month's level, and many investment projects were halted and suspended (Li Ping, 1989: 16). Attempts were made to reduce the budget deficit significantly. This austerity programme was to have dramatic effects on the performance of the economy in 1989, but these events will not be covered here.[2]

Table 7.1 Main economic indicators, 1986–88
(percentage increase over previous year except columns 5 and 6)

Year	*RNI*	*IND*	*AGR*	*VRS*	*ACC*	*B*	*CRC*	*P*	*MP*
1986	7.7	9.6	3.0	15.0	34.7	−7.06	23.3	6.0	8.1
1987	10.2	13.0	4.5	17.6	34.2	−7.96	19.4	7.3	16.3
1988	11.1	17.4	2.3	27.8	34.1	−8.05	46.7	18.5	30.3

Source: Calculated from data in *Fenjinde Sishi Nian 1949–1989* (1989: 341–2, 405, 413, 423, 429).

One thing is very clear from the data of Table 7.1: banking reform did not improve the ability of the banking system to control the rate of growth of currency in circulation. In 1988 it grew 46.7 per cent, almost equivalent to its record increase in 1984 and well above the planned rate of 15 to 16 per cent. Its average growth rate over the period 1986–88 was 32.3 per cent per annum at a time when real national income was growing at 10.6 per cent per annum. The excess money growth rate ($m - q$), at 21.7, was higher than that in period VII, 16.2 per cent, but lower than the 25.6 per cent of period II (Table IV.1).

Why the money supply increased so rapidly during 1988 is an interesting question, to which the anonymous commentator of the *China News Analysis* of 1 December 1989[3] offers a quasi-political explanation. He notes that there was a relatively more conservative leadership in power and that the monetary performance of 1987 had been quite good. Why was the policy reversed? The commentator sees it as a result of Li Peng's political tactics in allowing a disapproved sector of the economy (the banking system, referred to as the 'enemy' by the commentator) to behave as it liked in a situation of tension solely for the purpose of later discrediting its actions. In the subsequent credit squeeze Li Peng ensured that sectors of the economy with which he had ties were ensured credit funds, whereas earlier credit squeezes under Zhao Ziyang had restricted credit to all sectors.

Table 7.2 shows the money supply process during this period to help identify the factors responsible for each year's increase in currency in circulation. The source and method of presentation is the same as in Table 4.5. As can be seen, the government's impact on currency growth was evident in 1986 and 1987 as the government both borrowed and ran down its deposits. The excess of new loans over deposits to the productive sector remained the dominant reason for increases in currency in this period as it was numerically larger than the government item.

7.2 *Two ways of explaining open inflation, 1980–88*

Here we examine whether continuing economic reform in the 1980s changed the nature of the relationship between demand imbalances, open inflation and monetary growth proposed in the previous chapter.

Table 7.3 shows the rate of open inflation for the years 1979–88 and two simple measures of excess demand on the consumer goods market. Column 2 shows the rate of excess monetary growth, which is simply pd*CRC*

Table 7.2 Explaining increases in currency in circulation, 1986–88
(billion *yuan*)

Year	ΔCRC =	1 (L – D) +	2 G +	3 R +	4 IMO –	5 F –	6 O –	7 Bonds
1986	23.06	53.85	15.19	−5.5	−3.19	9.54	25.89	1.86
1987	23.61	27.49	14.94	9.4	1.87	12.22	14.69	3.18
1988	67.95[a]	57.41	9.76	2.63	3.29	12.29	−3.25	1.70

Notes: [a] Columns 2 to 7 account for an increase of only 62.35 billion *yuan*. This is because the items given in this source for the use of funds in 1988 (p. 431) add to only 1148.53 billion *yuan* whereas the total is given as 1154.13 billion *yuan*. This accounts for the 5.6 billion *yuan* difference between the identified change in currency and the actual increase.

Item 2 is government borrowing net of the change in its deposits as in Table 4.5.

Item 7 is the sale of bank bonds by the specialised banks, which started in 1985. See Table 4.5.

Source: Calculated from data in *Fenjinde Sishi Nian 1949–1989* (1989: 429–31).

Table 7.3 Variations in open inflation response, 1980–88

Year	pd*P*	Excess money growth[a]	Ratio[b] (%)	*PPI*	Ratio[c] (%)	pd*CRC*
1979	2.0	19.3	10.4	11.6	17.2	26.3
1980	6.0	22.9	26.2	14.7	40.8	29.3
1981	2.4	9.6	25.0	3.4	70.6	14.5
1982	1.9	2.5	76.0	1.9	100.0	10.8
1983	1.5	10.9	13.8	3.9	38.5	20.7
1984	2.8	36.0	7.8	16.0	17.5	49.5
1985	8.8	12.2	72.1	14.4	61.1	24.7
1986	6.0	15.6	38.5	13.1	45.8	23.3
1987	7.3	8.2	89.0	9.2	79.4	19.4
1988	18.5	35.6	52.0	15.7	117.8	46.7

Note: [a] Excess money growth (or monetary indicator of excess demand) is pd*CRC* minus pd*RNI*.
[b] Ratio of rate of open inflation to the monetary indicator of excess demand.
[c] Ratio of rate of open inflation to purchasing power indicator (*PPI*).

Sources: Tables 2.6, 2.7 and III.2; and calculated from data in *Fenjinde Sishi Nian 1949–1989* (1989: 406, 429), *Lishide Xiongbian* (1989: 436), *Statistical Yearbook of China 1987* (p. 480) and *Zhongguo Tongji Nianjian 1989* (p. 599). There are problems with the comparability of the data after 1985. See note 16.

minus pd*RNI*; this will be called the 'monetary indicator of excess demand'. Column 4 shows *PPI* (the purchasing power imbalance concept of chapter 6); this will be called the 'purchasing power indicator'. Column 3 shows the ratio of each year's rate of open inflation to the monetary indicator of excess demand, and column 5 shows the same as a ratio to *PPI*. An important question is the extent to which these ratios changed as a result of continuing price decontrol. As price reform continued we might expect a similar degree of excess demand to have produced a greater open-inflation response, identified by the ratios presented in Table 7.3. As can be seen, the 1979 ratio was quite low. The ratios from both indicators show similar year-to-year changes in the extent of the open inflation response, with the exception of 1981 when they move in opposite directions. They imply a lower price response in 1983 and 1984 and higher responses after 1984, given each year's excess demand. This makes sense in the light of the timing of the major price-decontrol measures adopted in the 1980s.

A further important issue is the extent to which each measure of excess demand is associated with open inflation. The respective ratios give some indication of this. The monetary indicator ratio displays greater variance than the purchasing power indicator ratio, showing that the former is a less reliable indicator of the likely rate of open inflation in any year for any given extent of excess monetary growth.[4] The year 1988 was an exceptional year in the extent of its rate of open inflation; it was the only year in this study in which pd*P* exceeded *PPI*. The relationships implied by the *PPI* approach hold up best for the years up to and including 1987. This is confirmed by the following. (Results for the period 1980–87 are given in brackets; results given first are for 1980–88.) The simple correlation coefficient between the excess money growth rate and pd*P* on a contemporaneous basis is 0.512 (0.011), whereas that between pd*P* and *PPI* is 0.602 (0.641). This confirms that the *PPI* indicator is slightly more closely associated with the annual rate of open inflation than the excess money growth rate, and very much more closely associated for the period 1980–87 when there was hardly any relationship between excess monetary growth and open inflation. This is also true if pd*CRC* is used as an indicator of monetary growth; its correlation coefficient with pd*P* is only 0.524 (0.078). Including the year 1988 improves the performance of the monetary indicators, but the *PPI* approach still has a relatively close association with open inflation on an annual basis.

The reasons for the relatively weak association between the monetary indicators of excess demand and open inflation are clearly explained by the alternative *PPI* theory offered here. A high ratio of open inflation to *PPI* will act to withdraw a lot of currency from circulation, thus tending to produce an inverse relationship between open inflation and monetary growth. Two years clearly show this: 1982 and 1984. In 1984, as we have seen, there was high *PPI* and marked excess monetary growth, and a relatively low open-inflation response. Because the open-inflation response to the high degree of *PPI* was so low, monetary growth was so large. In contrast, in 1982 there was a low degree of *PPI* but a full open-inflation response, and so very little excess currency growth. The 1982 case is a perfect numerical example of the foundation of the theory proposed in chapter 6. If pd*P* equals *PPI*, then *m* (the proportion of *SPP* remaining unspent) will remain constant and monetary growth will be reasonable.[5] In fact, in 1982 *m* fell from 6.9 per cent to 6.6 per cent (Table III.2), remaining constant if we take the numbers to the nearest whole number, and the ratio of *CRC* to *VRS* rose from 16.9 per cent to 17.1 per cent (Table I.5), also remaining constant in whole number terms. In 1985 and 1987 there were also relatively high open-inflation responses, each producing lower rates of monetary growth than on average and than in the previous year. This is confirmed to be a general feature of the 1980s by the correlation coefficient between pd*CRC* and pd*P*/*PPI*, which is minus 0.172 for the period 1980–88 and minus 0.838 for 1980–87. Clearly, this inverse association is strongest for the period 1980–87. With so few observations, adding an exceptional year like 1988 can change the coefficients considerably.

In other words, when there is a high ratio of open inflation to *PPI*, there is a relatively moderate degree of currency growth. When there is a relatively small inflation response, there is a high degree of currency growth. Price control in the face of a given degree of *PPI* will result in a greater extent of monetary growth. This is explained by the assumption underlying the *PPI* theory that list prices are increased to withdraw currency from circulation. Here they quite clearly continued to restrain monetary growth even in the changed circumstances of the 1980s. Attempting to reverse the direction of causality implied by the *PPI* theory requires an answer to the question: Why did years of rapid and excess currency growth produce a low rate of inflation and vice versa, given each year's degree of currency growth?

7.3 *A further test of the* PPI *theory for the 1980s*

This test takes the form of running the regression of the general price level on both the money ratio and the *SPP* ratio to see which produces the largest effect. Such an approach is likely to be an improvement over the detailed examination of each year's case, as was done above, as some of the exceptional observations get ironed out. The approach also serves to examine whether both ratios still show some clear relationship during the 1980s, a period during which there was continuing reform in retail price determination and some large increases in currency in circulation.

Using the Quantity Theory approach to explain the general retail price index we obtain the following for the years 1978–88:

$$\ln P = \underset{(0.0818)}{5.9588} + \underset{(0.0337)}{0.3588} \ln (CRC/RNI) \qquad \begin{aligned} R^2 &= 0.9263 \\ s &= 0.0472 \\ DW &= 0.8227 \\ n &= 11 \end{aligned}$$

whereas the result for the *SPP* ratio is

$$\ln P = \underset{(0.0341)}{5.4537} + \underset{(0.0566)}{0.6357} \ln (SPP/RNI) \qquad \begin{aligned} R^2 &= 0.9334 \\ s &= 0.0449 \\ DW &= 0.8143 \\ n &= 11 \end{aligned}$$

It can be seen that the coefficient of ln (*SPP*/*RNI*) is much higher than that of ln (*CRC*/*RNI*). The results indicate that a 1 per cent increase in the ratio of *CRC* to *RNI* is associated with only a 0.36 per cent increase in the general retail price index, compared with a 0.64 per cent increase caused by a 1 per cent increase in the *SPP* ratio. The latter coefficient is 77 per cent higher than the former. Each of these coefficients is larger than those obtained in chapter 6 for the period 1952–85, where the coefficients were 0.27 for the money ratio (see note 11 in chapter 6) and 0.49 for the *SPP* ratio. This indicates a slightly higher degree of responsiveness of the general retail price index to indicators of excess demand during the 1980s, which is no surprise given the continuing process of price reform and, we assume, an increased weighting for free market prices in the general retail price index.

Furthermore, the annual absolute increases in *CRC* are closely positively associated with the *SPP* ratio, as implied by the view that occurrences of *PPI* cause both retail price increases and narrow monetary growth. For the period 1978–88,

$$\Delta CRC = -47.7509 + 110.4186\ (SPP/RNI) \qquad R^2 = 0.7728$$
$$(12.1588) \quad (19.9572) \qquad s = 9.5093$$
$$DW = 1.7481$$
$$n = 11$$

Increases in the *SPP* ratio are associated with both increases in the general retail price level *and* increases in the absolute amount of currency in circulation on an annual basis. This is why there is a contemporaneous relationship between increases in *CRC* and the retail price level. Because of this the money ratio (*CRC*/*RNI*) is also closely associated with the *SPP* ratio, with the correlation coefficient for the period 1978–88 being 0.994. The whole logic of the explanation offered here is that causation goes from the *SPP* ratio to both the price level and the money ratio. The money ratio is not an independent determining variable; it is a consequence. This shows that in the 1980s the purchasing power approach remained a good explanation of changes in the general retail price index and currency in circulation.

It might be thought that during the 1980s, when many retail prices were being decontrolled and free markets were spreading, the simple Quantity Theory might have come into its own, in the sense that the slope coefficient of the market price index might have approached unity, as predicted for a market economy and as expected by Chow (1987) for the general retail price index. The following results show that it did not:

$$\ln MP = 6.9261 + 0.5168 \ln (CRC/RNI) \qquad R^2 = 0.8357$$
$$(0.1852) \quad (0.0764) \qquad s = 0.1069$$
$$DW = 0.8221$$
$$n = 11$$

A year like 1984 stands out as one when there was a large increase in the amount of currency in circulation, by 50 per cent, and no increase in *MP*. Even the total market price index, which includes privately sold means of agricultural production, increased only 0.3 per cent in that year (*Fenjinde Sishi Nian 1949–1989*, 1989: 413). However, the association between market prices and the *SPP* ratio is greater:

$$\ln MP = 6.1988 + 0.9161 \ln (SPP/RNI) \qquad R^2 = 0.8429$$
$$(0.0794) \quad (0.1318) \qquad s = 0.1046$$
$$DW = 0.7873$$
$$n = 11$$

The market price index has a much greater relationship with the *SPP* ratio than with the money ratio, even during a period of price decontrol.

Another way of showing that prices were more closely associated with demand conditions in the 1980s can be shown using the dynamic Quantity Theory approach described in section 3.11. Its basic proposition is that an increase in the rate of growth of the money supply by so many percentage points will, ceteris paribus, increase the rate of inflation by the same number of percentage points. In a market economy it is also said to increase the nominal rate of interest by the same number of percentage points via the Fisher effect (Friedman, 1987; Lucas, 1980), but this proposition will not be investigated here. The proposition is usually applied to average annual growth rates over a number of years to discount short run effects on the real variables. We can take into account the increase in the rate of growth of real output in China in the late 1980s by examining the rate of excess monetary growth $(m - q)$, which was discussed in chapter 3. Over the period 1981–85 this was 16.2 per cent and the average annual rate of inflation was 3.4 per cent, that is, 21 per cent of $(m - q)$. Over the period 1986–88 excess monetary growth was 21.7 per cent. If the responsiveness of retail prices was the same as in period VII, we would expect to see open inflation at about 4.6 per cent per annum; in fact, however, it was at the much higher rate of 12.8 per cent per annum. This indicates that price reform led to higher rates of inflation on average than in earlier years when price control was more prevalent. The rate of open inflation remained lower than the extent of excess monetary growth, indicating that velocity would continue to fall and the money ratios to rise, but that now velocity would fall at a slower rate than before when there was a smaller price response.

There were two opposing forces influencing the direction of change of velocity. As was shown in section 3.7, Western monetary theory would expect a fall in velocity if the volume of transactions was growing more rapidly than income. It would also expect a rise in velocity if interest rates were rising. Both factors were occurring in China in the 1980s. It is not easy to show that the economy was monetising rapidly in the 1980s, but it is reasonable to assume that this was the case. This would have increased the demand for currency for transactions purposes. Nominal interest rates increased throughout the 1980s. We would expect people to substitute interest-bearing savings deposits for currency. This factor did not increase velocity, but it did lead households and organisations to hold relatively more savings deposits compared to currency as interest rates rose. In 1978 savings deposits constituted 64.3 per cent of household and organisations' total monetary holdings $(SD + CH)$. At end-1988, after successive interest rate increases and the increase and limited indexation of September 1988, the proportion was 69.2 per cent. It peaked at 72.6 per cent at the end of 1987 (*Zhongguo Tongji Nianjian 1989*, pp. 598–9). This substitution of interest-bearing savings deposits for currency is what we would expect during a period of rising interest rates. However, it did not result in an increase in the measured velocity taken as *VRS/CRC*. This is what we would expect in a market economy. However, in China in the 1980s currency holdings grew more rapidly than *VRS*, even though they represented a smaller proportion of total narrow money holdings, so observed velocity continued to fall. As shown above, velocity, as implied by the relationship between $(m - q)$ and p, fell more slowly than before.

The greater responsiveness of open inflation to excess demand is also shown by the ratio p*dP/PPI* of Table 7.3 (column 5), which is generally higher for the years after 1984. Of course, the argument of this book is that it is the *PPI* indicator that best explains open inflation via list price increases, not the rate of excess monetary growth. One reason the average rate of open inflation was so high for the period 1986–88 was the 18.5 per cent increase in 1988, an important component of which was the 30.3 per cent increase in market prices of consumer goods.

The movements in the *PPI* indicator shown in Table 7.3 reflect the different causes of currency growth in the 1980s. The first wave of large imbalances during 1979 and 1980 can be ascribed to increases in rural purchasing power resulting from procurement price increases. As grain procurement agencies had to buy at higher prices than those at which they were allowed to sell they required government budget subsidies. This is why in the early 1980s there was an association between the increased budget deficit in 1979 and 1980 and currency growth. This was shown to be the case in Table 4.5. The second wave of large purchasing power imbalances was after 1984. They were associated with urban reforms. The budget deficit was less in these years, yet currency growth rates were much higher in such years as 1984 and 1988 than earlier. The imbalances were primarily associated not with the deficit, as Table 4.5 shows, but with the excess of loans over new deposits to enterprises, and these funds came from the banking system, not the budget. The factors that caused differing degrees of *PPI* directly caused variations in currency growth and open inflation during the 1980s as well as budget deficits in the early 1980s.

The *PPI* indicator of excess demand was shown in chapter 6 to be associated with such monetary phenomena as open price increases, currency growth, and budget deficits on a qualitative basis for the period 1953–85 on the basis of historical narrative. Table 7.4 summarises the simple quantitative relationships between *PPI* and such variables of interest for the periods 1953–85 and 1953–88. Such correlations can hide some of the exceptions noted in the historical discussion of chapter 6, but they do provide evidence on whether there is a general significant linear association of the kind expected by the arguments underlying the *PPI* approach. The results are given for the two periods to see whether the events of the years 1986–88 tend to strengthen or weaken any relationship that holds good for the period 1953–85. Generally speaking, the important relationships are closer for the period 1953–88. *PPI* has clear significant positive correlations with the annual percentage increases in retail prices (pd*P*), currency in circulation (pd*CRC*), the annual absolute increase in cash in hand plus savings deposits, $\Delta(SD + CH)$, as well as the proportion of purchasing power remaining unspent (*m*). There are significant negative correlations with the two indicators of changes in investment in the following year (pd*i* and dif*acc*). This shows that planners reduced investment in years following years of high *PPI* and vice versa. The budget position is significantly negatively correlated with *PPI* on a contemporaneous basis. This shows that years of high *PPI* had small budget surpluses or, more generally, had significant budget deficits. This was established in the narrative historical sections of chapter 6, but the relationship can be shown to hold good in a quantitative sense. There is also a clear negative correlation between *PPI* and the balance-of-trade position, showing that years of high *PPI* tended to be years of trade deficits and vice versa.

Table 7.4 Correlations between *PPI* and selected variables

	1953–88, $n = 36$		1953–85, $n = 33$	
Variable	Correlation with *PPI*	t^{b}	Correlation with *PPI*	t^{b}
pd*CRC*	0.685	5.48	0.653	4.81
$\Delta(SD + CH)$	0.502	3.23	0.516	3.51
m	0.585	4.02	0.636	4.80
pd*P*	0.666	5.21	0.643	4.67
pd*i*[a]	−0.408	−2.57	−0.422	−2.59
dif*acc*[a]	−0.386	−2.40	−0.392	−2.37
Budget	−0.536	−3.70	−0.469	−2.96
Balance of trade	−0.447	−2.91	−0.318	−1.87

Note: [a] pd*i* is the percentage change in nominal investment in the following year, and diff*acc* is the difference in the accumulation rate in the following year. Hence these correlations are for 1953–87 only.
[b] *t*-statistics in excess of 2 in absolute value show a correlation significantly different from zero at the 5 per cent level, and those in excess of 2.75 show significance at the 1 per cent level.

These correlations imply an interesting cross-correlation: that between the balance of trade and the rate of growth of *CRC*. In section 4.11 it was shown that a balance-of-trade deficit would in itself tend to reduce currency growth and vice versa. If this were the dominant element in the money supply process, there would be a positive correlation between balance of trade and currency growth. In fact there is a significant negative correlation ($r = -0.336$, $t = -2.08$, $n = 36$). This shows that the self-equilibrating balance-of-trade effect was outweighed by all the other currency-increasing elements of the money supply process. Of course, the main years of large positive *PPI* and balance-of-trade deficits were in the 1980s when there was rapid currency growth, producing this negative association between the balance of trade and currency growth. This result reflects Feltenstein and Farhadian's (1987: 148) finding for the period 1954–83 of a statistically insignificant positive effect of the current account on broad money growth. Here there is a significant negative relationship because I have been able to add the subsequent observations in the 1980s of balance-of-trade deficits and rapid currency growth.

There is one final correlation worth mentioning: that between the budget deficit and pd*CRC* ($r = -0.483$, $t = -3.22$, $n = 36$). This supports those who argue that budget deficits are associated with rapid monetary growth. The present approach argues, however, that both budget deficits and currency growth are the results of *PPI*.

The above simple quantitative analysis provides further support for the historical narrative of chapter 6 and shows that the relationships identified there hold up for the period until 1988. High values of *PPI* were associated on an annual basis with rapid currency and broader monetary growth, open inflation, budget deficits and reductions in investment in the following year.

By the late 1980s the Chinese population had experienced nearly ten years of rising retail prices, a phenomenon they had not experienced during the previous twenty years. By 1988 inflation-induced behaviour such as bank runs and panic buying was observed. One last comparative question is the extent to which this inflationary experience changed the general relationship between monetary growth and open inflation and hence the rate of change of velocity. We have seen that price reform from the mid 1980s onwards increased the rate of open inflation given the extent of excess demand. How did this alter the nature of velocity change compared with other inflationary socialist countries?

Table 7.5 shows excess monetary growth and open inflation for a few selected countries. It is clear that the inflationary socialist countries of Poland and Yugoslavia are radically different from China in their monetary relations. In both countries the rate of open inflation is very high and exceeds the rate of excess monetary growth. This means that velocity is rising, contributing to the high rate of open inflation. In China this has not occurred, although the rate of decline of velocity is less than it was previously, which is just the same as saying that the rate of open inflation is higher than previously for any given rate of excess monetary growth. Inflationary psychology has not changed the general point that the rate of open inflation in China is less than the rate of excess monetary growth.

7.4 Agricultural procurement reform and the seasonality of CRC

From the beginning of 1985 the government did not guarantee to buy all agricultural output offered to it in excess of the contracted amounts. Producers had to market this themselves on the free markets. As we saw in section 6.4, the government procurement system had a clear effect on seasonal variations in *CRC* during the early 1980s. Government purchases of the harvest towards the end of the year inject currency into the economy. Household purchases related to festivals at the beginning of the year and farmers' purchases for the summer sowing reduce *CRC* in the middle of the year. The government's reduced role in agricultural purchases after 1985 might be expected to have reduced the seasonality in *CRC*. Now a larger part of the harvest would be sold among the population on private markets. This trade would use existing currency stocks, and there would be less net injection of currency into circulation via government procurements.

Figure 7.1 repeats Figure 6.3 for the years 1986–88. In the first two years there does not seem to have been much difference. The midyear low points are just about as deep as those for earlier years. However, the low point of 1988 hardly exists, and its end-of-year peak is as high as the 1984 record peak. Each of the years 1986–88 shows successively less reduction in midyear currency holdings. This is some support for the view that seasonal variations in end-of-quarter currency holdings are becoming less pronounced. In 1988 there seems to have been hardly any midyear currency *huilong* and a huge net injection of currency in the third and fourth quarters.

Table 7.5 Velocity change in selected countries
(per cent per annum)

Country	$(m - q)$	p	Change in velocity	Period
United Kingdom	13	9	Decline	1976–87
United States	5	7	Increase	1976–87
Poland	16	29	Increase	1980–86
Hungary	9	7	Decline	1976–86
Yugoslavia	29	38	Increase	1976–86
China	10	4	Decline	1976–87

Source: Calculated from data in *International Financial Statistics Yearbook 1988* (passim.) using a narrow measure of the money supply.

Figure 7.1 Seasonal variations in currency in circulation, 1986–88

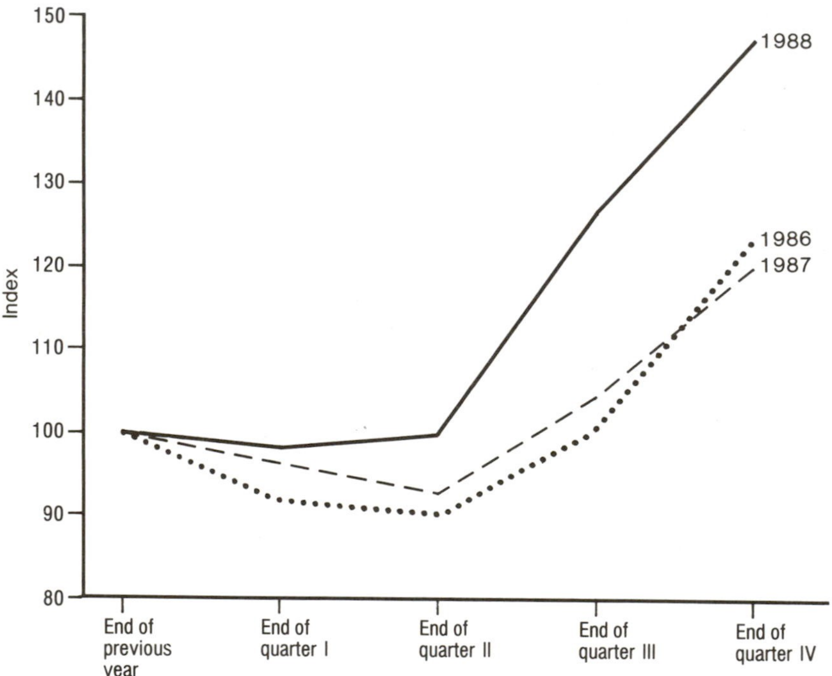

7.5 China's monetary situation: 1988 and 1978 compared

China's Maoist development strategy implied a very limited role for money in the economy: the agricultural sector was under the command system; international trade was of very little importance; material incentives were used to a very limited extent for motivating workers; and the required high accumulation rate was maintained by allocations through the state budget and materials allocation system. China has been described as 'probably one of the least monetised economies in the world before 1978' (Wang Yan, 1988: 28).

The new approach to development adopted at end-1978 implied that money would become more important in the economy. Farmers were offered higher prices as incentives, and the higher incomes were backed by changes in real resource flows. Urban and rural markets flourished. Bonuses were introduced for workers, and enterprises were allowed to retain more of their profits. These monetary incentives were aimed at increasing the efficiency of the workforce to ensure that growth came from higher productivity, not just from greater quantities of capital and labour. Sales outside the plan at market prices were allowed. Investment funds were allocated more by the banking system at a positive nominal rate of interest, and loans were expected to be repaid. International trade increased in importance. To derive the greatest possible benefit from this it became important that producers understood where their comparative advantage lay. This could be brought home to them by allowing them to trade and to compete for foreign exchange without any preferential treatment. The implied necessity for a foreign exchange market where the most efficient producers could obtain and sell foreign exchange at the best price was met by the establishment of the foreign-exchange swap centres.

This greater reliance on prices and monetary incentives obviously had an effect on money and related variables. This section reviews the main quantitative changes the reform process brought about by comparing the values of certain variables in 1988 and 1978.

By 1988 the general retail price level had risen 73 per cent over its 1978 level, with the urban price level rising 90 per cent and the rural 61 per cent. These differences reflect the new policy attempt to improve the terms of trade of the agricultural sector. The cost of living of staff and workers increased 89 per cent. Despite these increases, real incomes on average increased. For example, the nominal average wage of staff and workers increased 184 per cent, producing a 51 per cent increase in the real wage if it is deflated by the cost-of-living index.[6] The nominal value of retail sales in 1988 was 4.8 times its 1978 level. Of course, these averages conceal the wide variations in changes in real living standards in urban areas. Many state-employed skilled workers, administrative personnel and teachers found the continuing inflation of the 1980s eroding most of their official nominal incomes, hence the 'moonlighting craze' of the late 1980s and, in the view of certain analysts, some of the worker support for the student pro-democracy movement of April–June 1989.

The use of monetary incentives for farmers and workers, together with the banking system's inability to control credit, caused the large purchasing-power imbalances of the 1980s and as a consequence a huge increase in currency in circulation. By end-88 the nominal amount of currency in circulation was 10.1 times its 1978 level. Currency in circulation rose from being 13.6 per cent of a year's retail sales value to 28.7 per cent at end-88. This currency growth, together with most of the increase in the retail price level, was, in the view of the theory offered in chapter 6, the direct consequence of the extensive purchasing-power imbalances of the 1980s. Another reaction to these imbalances was the sale of government bonds. By September 1988 the total amount outstanding had reached about 90 billion *yuan* according to an official statement.[7] This amount was about 19 per cent of total monetary asset holdings (currency and savings deposits). Together with the increased savings-deposit holdings, these bonds would become another medium through which increasing amounts of currency would in the future be injected into circulation as interest was paid on them and bonds were redeemed. A pro-reform Chinese economist could see these bond holdings as the necessary raw material for establishing a network of secondary markets for financial assets.

The greater extent of household monetary-asset accumulation was associated with the larger proportion of purchasing power remaining unspent. In 1978 about 3.3 per cent of that year's total residents' incomes remained unspent, and in 1984 (the year of rapid monetary growth) the figure was 15.8 per cent (see Table III.1). For households and organisations taken together the proportion of *SPP* remaining unspent in 1978 was 2.5 per cent; in 1984 it was 11.7 per cent, and by 1988 it was 13.1 per cent (see Table III.2 and original data in *Zhongguo Tongji Nianjian 1989*, p. 599). By 1988 an official source was quantifying the extent of excess demand on the consumer goods market very much in terms of the *PPI* concept of chapter 6. It points out the differences between the growth of social aggregate demand and that of aggregate supply and then identifies the resulting extent of imbalance between demand and supply (*gongxu chalü*).[8] This concept, like *PPI*, is presumably an ex ante indicator of excess demand. The proportions of purchasing power remaining unspent cited above are ex post results of demand imbalances. They are also open to interpretation as voluntary increases in saving propensities brought about by what are thought to be temporary increases in current incomes.

The fact that money accumulation was more rapid meant that currency and savings deposit liabilities of the banking system increased markedly. In 1978 currency and savings deposits were 11.3 and 8.3 per cent respectively of the banking system's total liabilities. By the end of 1988 these proportions had risen to 18.5 and 23.0 per cent respectively, that is, from about 20 per cent in total to almost 42 per cent. Although the proportion of savings deposits that was fixed deposits rose from 61 per cent in 1978 to nearly 75 per cent in 1988, this represented a large increase in the amount of active money that could be withdrawn at will by the population—a situation that Lian (1990) sees as very dangerous for the prospect of securing balance on the consumer goods market, reflecting Hong Yuncheng's concept of the tiger in the open cage. Towards the end of the 1980s a further complication enters into the definition of household monetary holdings. In the pre-reform system nearly all currency was held by households. This was true of most savings deposits also. Enterprise reform meant that households were allowed to retain part of their earnings, which they were supposed to hold in bank accounts. This would, however, allow their holdings to be monitored. A phenomenon that occurred in the late 1980s was the transfer of enterprise deposits into personal savings deposits held in the name of a company official. The increases in interest rates on personal savings deposits in September 1988 might have contributed to this switching, as well as the desire for hiding enterprise liquid-asset holdings.[9]

The banking system was obtaining more of its funds from the population in the form of currency issue and their savings deposits. It was expected to channel these funds to efficient productive enterprises. By the end of 1988 the total of the banking system's outstanding loans was 5.7 times the 1978 level. It can be seen that industrial production enterprises and the agricultural sector were given a greater proportion of new loans as their amounts outstanding increased to 5.9 and 7.0 times their 1978 levels respectively. The loans outstanding to material supply and marketing undertakings and commercial enterprises increased to only 2.4 and 3.7 times their 1978 levels respectively. The increasing importance of the banking system in channelling funds to enterprises for fixed investment, rather than their obtaining such funds through budgetary grants, is shown by the fact that the amounts outstanding on this account in 1988 were 197 times their 1979 levels, the first year in which they were used.

Corresponding to the increased flow of investment funds from household savings, bank loans for fixed investment and enterprise-retained profits there was a marked reduction in the flows of national income going to the government budget. In 1978 total budget income was about 37 per cent of national income, but by 1988 it had fallen to about 22 per cent. This would be a remarkably low figure for any economy.[10] Some sources cite an even lower figure of about 19 per cent, probably obtained by deducting domestic and foreign loans from budget income.[11] A government budget deficit means of course that the government is not a net saver in the economy. These figures present the picture of an economy where most of the country's saving–investment flow was now coming through the banking system via household savings deposits and bank loans, directly from enterprise-retained profits, and possibly through household-to-household loans, self-financed investment by individual entrepreneurs and share issues. A World Bank team estimated that in 1978 about 51 per cent of Chinese investment funds came from the central government, 34 per cent from enterprises and local governments and 15 per cent from households. By 1985 these proportions had changed to 23, 32 and 46 per cent respectively, thereby trebling the significance of the household sector in generating savings.[12]

The intention of the reform programme became enshrined in the announcement of the Twelfth Party Congress of September 1982 that it was planned to quadruple real output by the end of the century. The year 1980 is conventionally taken as the starting point of this programme. In simple terms this means doubling real output by 1990 and then redoubling it by the year 2000. In aggregate terms the first stage was completed by 1988 when real national income reached 2.1 times its 1980 level. The earlier Maoist development priorities were to some extent retained despite the radical agricultural-reform programme of the early 1980s. Agricultural output in 1988 was only 1.7 times its 1980 level whereas industrial output was 2.4 times that level.

Chinese economic reform captured world attention and by the late 1980s had progressed further than most economists thought possible in the early 1980s. Relying on the problems encountered by earlier Eastern European reforms, and noting that there was no clear Chinese blueprint for comprehensive reform, most seemed to think that radical change was unlikely. A major question about the modern Chinese economy is: To what extent did all the disparate reforms of the 1980s change the nature and operation of the economy? Various views stress that the reforms after 1986, in particular the two-tier pricing system and the continuing use of contracts and free marketing in agriculture, turned the economy into something much more like a market economy than could be expected. I feel that economists connected with the World Bank tend to take this view. On the other hand some economists, such as Chai (1987a) and Kueh (1989; 1990), see the Chinese economy of the late 1980s merely as a modified version of the Maoist model, with a few private markets added to a system where state allocation and control over the large and medium scale enterprises dominate. Most of these arguments are based on describing institutional changes. One side will cite the percentage of major products directly marketed by enterprises at free or floating prices and argue that as this is a large proportion the market mechanism dominates; the other side cites similar figures claiming that these are not large proportions. The mere identification of these proportions and other institutional changes is not sufficient in itself to tell us whether the reforms have fundamentally changed the way the Chinese macroeconomy behaves. The only way to settle this important question is to look at *behaviour*, not at institutions alone. Here we can examine financial and monetary behaviour in the late 1980s to see whether it corresponds with the behaviour of a market-type economy or is understandable in terms of the behaviour of a command-type system.

To start with, some observable changes were clearly due to the marketisation of some aspects of the economy. Price reform made retail prices more responsive to aggregate demand and contributed to some of the inflation of the late 1980s. However, price reform in itself cannot be held responsible for inflation. Although most of us living today have experienced only an inflationary economic environment, inflation is not a universal phenomenon of market economies, and there have been prolonged periods of price deflation and relative price stability. Price reform in China was introduced into an economy that had marked and continuing excess demand. If there initially had been excess demand on the consumer goods market, a one-off increase in the aggregate price level could have removed it and reduced money holdings to acceptable levels in terms of units of retail sales. However, throughout the 1980s the indicators of excess demand used in this study suggest persistent excess demand, which led to list price increases and later in the 1980s to considerable free-market price increases. It is a general feature of price decontrol in planned economies that such price liberalisation does result in higher inflation rates. A Soviet view is that 'inflation and all of its negative consequences *invariably* accompanies economic reform in socialist countries' because '[a]ll evils rooted in the economic model of bureaucratic socialism have now come into the open' (Solnsteva, 1990: 91) (italics added and text corrected).

Vietnam, however, has been claimed to be an exception to this generalisation, with widespread price liberalisation during 1988 and 1989 being accompanied by rapidly falling inflation rates and an appreciating currency (Wood, 1989; *Asian Development Outlook 1990*, pp. 123–4). This is said to have been achieved by combining very strict fiscal and monetary restraint with the price liberalisation programme and increasing interest rates dramatically, which are said to have reached 100 per cent per annum in *real terms* (Wood, 1989: 565–6). If this example can be substantiated with better data and shown to be a permanent effect, this exception to the general pattern of price liberalisation and higher inflation serves to emphasise the importance of monetary and fiscal policy in restraining aggregate demand. China is unlikely to want to 'learn from Vietnam'.[13] The Vietnamese policies are an example of orthodox fiscal and monetary restraint coupled with very high real interest rates, as recommended by the McKinnon–Shaw views discussed in section 3.9 and proposed for China by Wang Yan (1988: 45).

So why was there sustained excess monetary demand? Inflation exists in market economies, so was it further evidence that China had become more like a market economy? Is it explained by a market process or by the nature of the command system? Was it due to central bank incompetence, which is Friedman's usual explanation of why monetarist policies have not been successfully implemented in major market economies? The first relevant observation is that during the Cultural Revolution period, despite certain claims to the contrary, monetary affairs were handled reasonably well. There was aggregate price stability and there was not excess monetary issue. However, during this period very little use was made of money, prices, monetary incentives, specialisation and trade, and there was hardly any improvement in living standards. Only official propagandists trumpeted price stability and freedom from debt. It was this approach to development that was abandoned in December 1978, but this abandonment does not necessarily mean that the structure of the entire economy was changed to that of a market economy. The use of monetary incentives and decentralisation of certain monetary functions to enterprises and specialised banks followed in the mid 1980s. However, these innovations were introduced into an economy that basically retained the important aspects of the command system, and this fact contributed to the monetary mismanagement of the 1980s.

Two fundamental features of the command system have produced the recent monetary behaviour: the fact that the state continues to own most of the significant branches of the industrial economy and markets the bulk of retail sales; and the fact that the banking system is not a truly independent system but remains under government control. Each of these features can be considered in turn.

The fact that the government runs many enterprises means that it is ultimately responsible for subsidising them when they make losses. The fact that the government continues to sell important commodities at controlled prices means that subsidies are required to keep retail prices below procurement prices. Both these factors contribute to the budget deficit and are a means of injecting currency into circulation. A marketisation of the economy would see the private sector producing and marketing most output without any need for government money-creating subsidies. Unprofitable enterprises would be allowed to go bankrupt and their assets transferred to private users who could at least cover costs. Workers would be free to reallocate themselves according to wage differentials established by competing enterprises. Because this type of property reform has not gone very far in China the nature of the monetary process has not changed from that found under the command economy, and it cannot be admitted that a market economy has been established.

Similarly, when we turn our attention to the banking system we can see that reforms there have not removed the implications of the command system from our understanding of its behaviour. In theory, the banking reforms were supposed to allow the People's Bank of China to control the specialised banks and to carry out monetary policy using indirect 'economic levers'. When we remember the tools of monetary policy available in a market economy we can see that essentially there are only four: open market operations; interest rate policy; reserve requirements on the specialised banks; and quantitative limits on bank lending. The first three are 'economic levers'.

Open market operations cannot really be used in China as there are no extensive public holdings of government bonds and bills the quantity of which the monetary authorities could change by open market purchases, and there is no network of secondary markets on which a government broker could operate such a policy.

Interest rate policy, a prime example of an 'economic lever' and a market price, has been used in China during the reform period. However, it has probably had little effect on enterprise borrowing as rates have remained low. There might have been an effect on households' willingness to hold savings deposits at various times, but by the late 1980s the real interest rate was almost certainly negative. Government bonds were allocated to holders administratively in late 1988, not sold, so we can conclude that the interest rate offered on them was not an acceptable market rate. A whole range of interest rates were applied to loans to different sectors of the economy, with favoured sectors obtaining cheaper loans. If other prices were rational (and this was not the case in China, so this policy might have been used to offset these irrationalities), then differential loan interest rates obviously led to misallocation of resources, on a strict economic interpretation. Multiple interest rates and different prices for different users are of course a feature of command systems that would not exist in market systems where at least in theory everyone faces the same price and this establishes allocative efficiency.

With regard to the third 'economic lever' designated above, the specialised banks were required to hold reserves with the central bank in China, and it might appear that by this means the central bank could control the specialised banks' ability to increase loans. An obvious point is that the central bank seems not to have been able to do this. Currency growth rates far exceeded real growth rates and, as shown in various sections above, exceeded planned rates in certain years in the 1980s. As was shown in chapter 3, failure to hit monetary targets has been a feature of many market economies recently, but this similarity does not mean that China is like a market economy.[14] It cannot meet its monetary plans for its own institutional reasons, which are very different from those of a market economy. Bowles and White (1989: 487–8) come to a similar conclusion and write that, 'If the intention of the banking reforms has been to harden enterprise credit constraints by increasing the autonomy and commercial orientation of the banks, the evidence to date, after eight years of reform, suggests that this has not been realised. In fact, the credit constraint may have become softer.' They argue that the new central bank has very weak control over the specialised banks, which tend to approve all applications for loans made to them regardless of profitability,[15] and that enterprises still strive to build up excess inventories financed through bank loans. The banks take no role in bankrupting unprofitable state enterprises, which can continue production with bank loans being supplied to cover their losses. White and Bowles (1988) present similar views. Wang Yan (1988) agrees with these negative characteristics of financial reform, stating that 'State banks have to finance state-owned enterprises running at losses' (p. 40) and that 'China's central bank (the People's Bank) lacks policy instruments for macroeconomic management and control of the money supply' (p. 41). For similar views see Tsang (1990: 228–34).

When a restrictive credit policy was finally adopted in September 1988 there was very little recourse to 'economic levers' (although interest rates were increased), and the main tool of policy was quantitative limits on bank lending. Although quantitative limits have been used in certain market economies, they are an obvious feature of the command and allocative mentality that does not like to leave resource allocation to market forces.

We can see that the main reason behind rapid monetary growth in the 1980s was the policy of introducing monetary incentives and the consequent active monetary flows into an essentially unreformed command system. Very little 'market discipline' was used in the allocation of bank loans. All the bad aspects of the old system led to monetary growth. The 'soft budget constraint', enterprise desire to pay bonuses and hoard scarce materials and the necessity of price subsidies all contributed to the desire for money creation at a time when the central bank had no effective means of stopping it. Political pressures on it from all levels to extend loans ensured that it did just that, a fact stressed by Xu and Huang (1987: 22–3).

From the point of view of monetary and financial behaviour it can be concluded that the Chinese economy did not become a market economy and that the retained pre-reform ownership system and distribution mechanism were responsible for monetary growth in the 1980s. The discipline of the market was not used in the financial sector. The obvious market elements in the reformed economy were largely confined to commercial and industrial sectors in the form of the dual-pricing system, and to the agricultural sector.

7.6 *Conclusions*

These conclusions relate only to the analytical aspects of this book. They do not review the facts of money and prices in China, which can be found in chapter 2; nor do they review the nature of money and the money supply process in China, which can be found in chapter 4. Instead they concentrate on the approach taken in analysing money in China: its nature, the reasons for taking it and the type of evidence that supports it.

A basic theme of this book is that the Quantity Theory is an inappropriate mental framework for thinking about the relationship between money and prices in China. (Many economists think that it is an inadequate framework for thinking about money in market economies also.) The institutional features of the Chinese economy do not accord with the basic assumptions of this theory. First, increased nominal expenditures can reduce the narrow money supply. Chinese monetary planners know this and use this as part of their money planning. Second, the money wage, and other variables determining nominal income, are not just impassively determined in a competitive market, thus adjusting to prior exogenous money changes. The determinants of nominal purchasing power (wages and agricultural purchase prices) are, in theory, subject to government control; they remain principally government determined. Monetary control is supposed to be exercised by control over incomes. When the government delegated some control over part of the wage bill in the form of bonuses, it lost control over developments in the state wage bill. These changes in money incomes are the means by which new monetary issue takes place. Historically, the main changes in purchasing power can be explained as the result of deliberate government policies, of unexpected increases in the labour force or, in the reformed economy, of increases in enterprise use of bonus payments. Another important institutional feature of the Chinese economy is that large increases in purchasing power automatically bring about a large increase in currency issue. Increases in the state wage bill and state procurements cause extra currency to be issued. This is not admitted as possible in the Quantity Theory framework, which assumes that the nominal money supply is exogenously determined and would not change in such circumstances.

The explanation of the relationship between the price level and the money supply offered above is monetarist in nature. The price level is increased because there is too much money *issue*, identified by the *flows* of purchasing power onto the consumer goods market. These flows also explain the observed increases in the money stock. Another monetarist aspect is that Chinese planners are concerned about the quantity of currency in circulation compared with available retail supplies. This has been used to explain their behaviour whenever there was excess money issue. The fact that Chinese monetary planners think that maintaining a desired ratio of currency to sales is important does not make the Quantity Theory a helpful way of thinking about why the money supply changes in China or what policies monetary planners actually take to achieve their 'monetarist' objective.

Given these institutional features of the Chinese economy, the simple approach taken here has been to concentrate on purchasing power developments as the prime determinant of currency growth and retail price changes. The ability to co-ordinate purchasing power growth with retail supply availability generally leads to reasonable monetary growth and stable retail prices. This is possible under the command system when monetary incentives are hardly used; there is widespread wage and price control and strict supervision of the banking system. Such a system existed in China from about 1956 to 1978. China seems to have been able to control purchasing power developments under its version of the command system in a way that the traditional interpretation of the monetary affairs of planned economies says could not be achieved in the Eastern European and Soviet variants. However, the traditional command system was not conducive to economic growth in China and was the system that allowed completely unrealistic and overambitious development plans to produce the economic disasters of the years 1960–62.

Under this system real output grew, but living standards stagnated. At various times, even under the command system, there were short term imbalances between purchasing power developments and supply availability. These came about for different reasons at different times. In the period 1959–61 the imbalances were due to the collapse of output, as were the less marked imbalances of 1967, 1968 and 1976. Rapid monetary growth, budget deficits and open price rises occurred with the introduction of economic reforms after 1978. After the adoption of monetary incentives, first in agriculture and secondly in industry, the imbalances of the 1980s were due to purchasing power's continually growing more rapidly than real retail-supply availability. There was no single overriding cause of these imbalances; history is more complicated and less neat than economic models can allow for. During these periods of purchasing power imbalance there was a monetary system under which the banking system could not refuse to allow nominal variables to increase. Increases in nominal purchasing power were invariably accompanied by unrestrained currency issue and the granting of loans to state enterprises and procurement units.

In the face of purchasing power imbalances monetary planners reacted with some consistent policies. It has been argued that they consistently used commodity *huilong* to restrain the rate of growth of unspent purchasing power, that is, narrow money. They did this by increasing the list prices of certain state-supplied goods in the early period of 1960–62. This policy was extensively documented in chapter 2 and explained in chapter 4. It has been argued here that list price increases became a general feature of policy in the 1980s. Planners were faced with sustained excess demand for the first time in nearly twenty years, so it was natural for them to resort to policies they had used before. Increases in list prices raised the general retail price index. These price increases were always less than the extent of purchasing power imbalance, except in 1988. This means that positive purchasing power imbalances produced relatively rapid monetary growth. This is why years of high open inflation were also years of rapid currency growth and increases in the ratio of currency to income. There was no causative relationship between growth in the monetary stock and open inflation; they were both the consequences of purchasing power imbalances.

Both qualitative historical evidence and quantitative evidence have been provided to show that purchasing power imbalances were associated with both open inflation and currency growth, both on an annual basis and for seven subperiods. The quantitative relationships held good for the entire period 1952–88.

These purchasing power imbalances were also associated with budget deficits. This has been shown on the basis of both qualitative and quantitative evidence. Institutional reasons for expecting such a link have been adduced. A main theme of this book is that money supply changes and budget deficits are not independent primary causes of open price increases; they are all consequences of purchasing power imbalances, which are themselves the result of different factors at different historical periods. To select either monetary growth as an explanation of price increases, as Quantity Theorists would do, or to select budget deficits as the explanation of both monetary growth and price increases, as some Quantity Theorists would do, would oversimplify the nature of their interrelationship and their dependence on purchasing power imbalances. Statistical evidence can be provided to show that there is an association between, say, monetary growth and open inflation, or budget deficits and open inflation, but this in itself is no real reflection of the more complex nature of the actual relationship between money and prices in China. The whole logic of the approach taken here is that purchasing power imbalances are the primary exogenous change to which the monetary sector, and particularly monetary planners, have to react. Monetary change itself is one of the consequences of these imbalances; it cannot be taken as the prime exogenous initiating cause of the other changes.

Various other reactions to purchasing power imbalances have been discussed and shown to have been used. Interest rate increases were used to reduce the liquidity of household financial assets, as were bond sales. Consumer goods imports were used at the time of the most marked imbalances in 1960–62 and in the mid 1980s: food imports on the first occasion, electronic goods on the second. Sales from stocks of retail goods occurred in 1956, 1961, 1962, 1976 and 1984. Investment was reduced following years of purchasing power imbalances. Some of these reactions were clearly 'non-monetary' from the point of view of Western monetary economics; but as discussed in section 4.12, socialist economies do resort to policies for monetary purposes even though they do not use monetary tools to accomplish this. Historically, the timing of certain shifts in policy, such as rapidly increasing food imports in the early 1960s, reducing investment, cutting social purchasing power, selling bonds and increasing interest rates, can be shown to be dependent on the nature of purchasing power developments in the economy.

Economic historians have ascribed great significance to monetary problems in playing a role in the fall of great empires. Over long periods of time, too much money and its debasement cause inflation and popular discontent; too little causes falling prices, stagnation and discontent. I am sure that upholders of the traditional view of money in planned economies (sustained excess demand, repressed inflation and monetary overhang—see section 3.8) will argue that much of the popular wave of protest against the planned economic systems of the Soviet Union and Eastern Europe during 1989 and 1990 was to no little extent due to monetary mismanagement in these countries. China has a system similar to theirs in important respects: the currency is a pure fiat issue without legislative restraint on the amount of its issue; the bulk of the economy is state owned; the state sector is the main source of currency issue; and there is very little market discipline for enterprises, banks and workers. China seems to have avoided the problems of the other planned economies. Monetary buildup, deficits and price rises in the 1980s were accompanied by economic growth and increases in the supply of consumer goods. When inflation rates, particularly those of free market goods, soared during 1988, administrative measures were taken to restrict monetary growth, but these produced a recession in the economy. The Chinese Communist Party seems to have survived the problems caused by both the inflation and the policy-induced recession brought about to cure it. I make no predictions about what will happen in China.

Finally, here is a word or two about some themes of monetary economics and Chinese institutions that have not featured in this book. I have not presented any original statistical estimates of money demand functions. We have all the required data for this, and it is easy to do. I do not think that the results would tell us anything more significant about the money supply process than is revealed in chapter 4, nor have I used statistical methods to search for a few simple reasons for money supply growth. This follows from the basic message of the *PPI* approach, which in itself explains in a simple way why there is monetary growth. The message is that imbalances are caused by different factors in different periods; it is unlikely that a single cause of monetary growth could be found for the entire period, just as a single cause of *PPI* cannot be found. The results of the analysis of chapters 4 and 7 are that loans to the state sector exert a dominant effect on monetary expansion, with the budget deficit showing an effect also. The trade balance does not play an equilibrating role in the money supply process.

Generally, Chinese economists estimate money demand functions for two purposes. The first is to provide some sort of guide for formulating money supply targets. Income elasticities of demand are estimated and then chosen from periods of relative monetary stability and real growth for calculating a reasonable ratio between monetary growth and real growth. The second purpose is to compare actual monetary stocks with the implied demanded amounts as revealed by regressions of money on the important demand-determining factors. As the regressions are just averages of the relationship over the whole period studied, there are bound to be periods when actual holdings exceeded the amount implied from the demand equations. This is the approach of Huang (1988a). In itself this is not interesting unless it can be shown that there were consistent reactions to these differences between actual and desired money holdings.

Another topic not pursued here has been the empirical definition of the money supply in China. This would just require the use of successively broader measures of money to see which provided the best association between 'money' and some variable of interest, such as the price level. I have confined my attention to the very narrow measure of 'money', currency in circulation, for the institutional reasons given in chapter 4 and for the reason that the important study by Chow (1987) also does so. In order to study retail price and monetary developments currency in circulation is the appropriate concept for China. If full marketisation and decentralisation of the Chinese economy were to occur under a future reforming leadership, money would become everywhere active. Broader measures of the money supply, those including enterprise deposits, for example, would become more relevant to any monetary study of such a possible future Chinese economy.

I have not tackled the question of whether there was sustained repressed inflation in China in the 1980s. As we have seen, some Chinese economists such as Xu and Huang (1987) and Huang (1988a), together with Travers (1985), argue that economic reform *was* associated with repressed inflation and forced saving. On the other hand Byrd (1983) and Naughton (1987) argue that this was not the case and that the required variables were free to adjust to ensure equilibrium monetary holdings. The World Bank Report *China: Macroeconomic Stability and Industrial Growth under Decentralized Socialism* (1990: 106–9) examines the question of the voluntariness of household saving but does not reach a clear conclusion. This book has been about explaining behaviour, not measuring such things as the extent of excess money holdings. For this it was just necessary to show how planners would react to excess demand, that excess demand did occur in certain periods and that in fact planners did react to excess demand in the manner expected of them. Their reactions were not sufficient to restrain monetary growth completely, and monetary targets were exceeded during the 1980s. Free-market price increases, transactions growth and interest rate increases might have been sufficient to induce households to hold the resulting extra nominal money as both higher cash-transactions balances and voluntary savings deposits. However, it is not necessary to say whether this was the case if one just wants to explain why there was excess monetary growth in the first place—why planners increased list prices, interest rates, imported consumer goods, cut back investment and so on. To argue that there is a monetary overhang, as the result of sustained repressed inflation in the 1980s, would require a statement about how the economy would behave if there were such an overhang, evidence that it does so behave and evidence that it would not so behave if there were not such an overhang. I know of no simple aspect of macroeconomic behaviour in China that could be investigated to see which of these two views is correct. This is why there has been so much controversy about the existence or extent of repressed inflation in other command economies. We must observe how Chinese planners behave in the future to gain any clues about their view on this matter.

An aspect of the economic history of China during this period not covered in detail in this book is the nature of monetary policy formulation and the political and administrative roles of, and conflicts between, all the organisations that have a part in influencing (I cannot write 'determining') the money supply, interest rates, the exchange rate, retail prices and so on. For the purposes of this study it was necessary first to make some simplifying assumptions about how planners would behave in certain circumstances and then to show that certain variables did actually behave in a way consistent with the assumptions about planners' behaviour over the entire period under study. To show the policy reaction to various problems in detail, with all the attendant policy debates and political disagreement, is both beyond my desires and abilities. Of course, the Quantity Theory approach has no place for institutional discussions, except for the assumption that the general retail price index is dominated by the free-market price index in China. The approach's other assumptions are just those of the theory as applied to a market economy and assumed to be relevant to China also. The Quantity Theory attempts to be applicable to all systems and so sees no need for a detailed description of institutions in any particular country under study. It is based on the trans-systemic assumptions that money is exogenous, that there is a stable demand for real money balances and that prices are flexible. These assumptions are not entirely relevant to China.

Such policy decisions as those taken in response to the 1980 price increases, or the reasons for, and debates about, the 1986 and 1989 devaluations and their extent, would be interesting studies in themselves. This has not been done here. The methodology of this book has been to show when certain policy reactions were made and that these are understandable on the basis of a few assumptions about planners' monetary objectives and the actual institutions of the Chinese economy. It is necessary to bring planners into the story as they do play a role in determining many of the important nominal variables in the Chinese economy, such as the retail price level, the level and structure of interest rates and the exchange rate. The extent to which their policies have been narrowly economic and rational, given their goals, is not discussed here although it would be an important topic for research. The extent of arbitrary political decisions and power play has not been isolated. Did Li Peng deliberately let the banking system overexpand the money supply so that he could later discredit it and enhance his power by selectively granting credits during the squeeze that followed? That is the type of question I have not tried to answer in this largely empirical study. If that really was the case, it shows that the Chinese banking system is not immune from political decisions and that there was continuing pressure on it to expand the money supply. When the restraining influence of government policy and possible control was temporarily removed the money supply expanded rapidly to meet the ever-present demand for loans.

There are many untouched topics relating to money in China. China's historical experiences in creating its independent monetary system, similar to that of the planned economies, after the hyperinflation of the twelve years of war, and its particular ways of trying to operate this system, are an important episode in the world's long history of using money. This book has done no more than scratch a small part of the surface of this subject. The study of money in non-market economies is in its infancy. Given the way the economies of Eastern Europe and the Soviet Union are changing it may not have a very long adulthood. For the case of China it is not likely that there will be major changes in the nature of its economic system as there have been in East Germany, for example. In the case of China we have many statistical data for the study of its modern monetary experiences, mostly at an aggregate level, and some interesting and significant recent events. For the reader interested in following up some of the issues raised in this book appendix V presents a short reading list arranged by topic, and the other appendixes and the list of references contain statistical sources where many monetary data can now be found.

Appendixes

Contents

Note: While every endeavour has been taken to ensure the accuracy of the following data and the interpretation of their coverage, serious potential users are recommended to consult the original sources cited in the table notes.

Appendix I Chinese monetary data

Table I.1 Narrow measures of the money supply (currency)
(end of year, billion *yuan*)

Year	*CHR*	*CH*	*CRC*	CRC_2
1952	2.20	2.20	2.75[a]	2.75
1953	3.15	3.15	3.96	3.94
1954	3.31	3.32	4.12	4.12
1955	3.21	3.25	4.01	4.03
1956	4.28	4.43	5.70	5.73
1957	4.02	4.29	5.28	5.28
1958	5.21	5.66	6.76	6.78
1959	5.49	6.11	7.50	7.51
1960	6.89	7.54	9.61	9.59
1961	9.87	10.62	12.57	12.57
1962	8.47	9.13	10.67	10.65
1963	6.92	7.52	8.98	8.99
1964	5.96	6.54	8.03	8.00
1965	6.84	7.47	9.08	9.08
1966	8.70	9.40	10.83	10.85
1967	9.80	10.50	12.20	12.19
1968	10.60	11.40	13.41	13.41
1969	10.90	11.70	13.73	13.71
1970	9.76	10.27	12.36	12.36
1971	10.54	11.09	13.63	13.62
1972	11.66	12.28	15.10	15.12
1973	12.84	13.52	16.64	16.61
1974	13.60	14.32	17.64	17.66
1975	14.05	14.79	18.27	18.26
1976	14.96	16.49	20.38	20.40
1977	14.34	15.81	19.54	19.54
1978	15.55	17.14	21.20	21.20
1979	19.62	21.58	26.771	26.77
1980	25.56	28.12	34.620	34.62
1981	30.96	33.29	39.634	39.63
1982	35.66	37.33	43.912	43.91
1983	44.32	45.82	52.978	52.98
1984	—	65.93	79.211	79.21
1985	—	82.00	98.783	98.78

Definitions and sources:

CHR: Cash in hand of residents (*Zhongguo Maoyi Wujia Tongji Ziliao 1952–83*, p. 16).

CH: Cash in hand: 1952–83 from *Zhongguo Maoyi Wujia Tongji Ziliao 1952–83* (p. 8); 1952–85 from *Statistical Yearbook of China 1986* (p. 444) and *Zhongguo Tongji Nianjian 1986* (p. 526).

CRC: Currency in circulation: 1977–78 from IMF *International Financial Statistics Yearbook 1986* (p. 275); 1979–85 from *Statistical Yearbook of China 1986* (p. 530); 1953–76 derived from index numbers of currency in circulation at the end of the year with a 1957 base taken from Byrd (1983: 138). The original source is *Jinrong Yanjiu* (Financial Research), no. 4, 1981.

CRC_2: *Fenjinde Sishi Nian 1949–1989* (1989: 429). See also Huang Xu (1988b: 190) for similar but not identical data.

Notes: [a] The 1952 figure is from Huang (1988a: 41), which presents different index numbers of currency in circulation for the period 1952–86 with a 1952 base. Zhang Junkuo (1988: 34) gives index numbers of currency showing the 1953 figure as 1.432727 times the 1952 figure, the same increase as given in Huang (1988a). The implied figure from both sources for 1952 (2.75 billion *yuan*) is a lot less than that in Chow (1987: 324) of 3.855 billion *yuan*.

In the text and in all regressions the series of currency in circulation is labelled *CRC* for simplicity. The data used are the series CRC_2 in Table I.1.

Table I.2 Savings deposit data
(end of year, billion *yuan*)

Year	*SDR*	*SD*	(*SDR* + *CHR*)	(*SD* + *CH*)
1952	0.86	0.86	3.06	3.06
1953	1.23	1.33	4.38	4.48
1954	1.59	1.86	4.90	5.18
1955	1.99	2.30	5.20	5.55
1956	2.67	3.04	6.95	7.47
1957	3.52	4.58	7.54	8.87
1958	5.52	6.29	10.73	11.95
1959	6.83	9.55	12.32	15.66
1960	6.63	10.10	13.52	17.64
1961	5.54	9.54	15.41	20.16
1962	4.11	6.30	12.58	15.43
1963	4.57	7.02	11.49	14.54
1964	5.55	9.04	11.51	15.58
1965	6.52	10.24	13.36	17.71
1966	7.23	12.06	15.93	21.46
1967	7.39	12.91	17.19	23.41
1968	7.83	14.56	18.43	25.96
1969	7.59	13.94	18.49	25.64
1970	7.95	14.78	17.71	25.05
1971	9.03	16.68	19.57	27.77
1972	10.52	17.65	22.18	29.93
1973	12.12	20.14	24.96	33.66
1974	13.65	22.92	27.25	37.24
1975	14.96	25.15	29.01	39.94
1976	15.91	25.89	30.87	42.38
1977	18.16	27.83	32.50	43.64
1978	21.06	30.93	36.61	48.07
1979	28.10	36.94	47.72	58.52
1980	39.95	50.93	65.51	79.05
1981	52.37	64.76	83.33	98.05
1982	67.54	80.57	103.20	117.90
1983	89.25	99.25	133.57	145.07
1984	121.47	131.50	185.79	197.43
1985	162.26	170.43	242.79	252.43

Definitions and sources:

SDR: Savings deposits held by residents: 1952–83 from *Zhongguo Maoyi Wujia Tongji Ziliao* (p. 16); 1984–85 from *Fenjinde Sishi Nian 1949–1989* (p. 459).

SD: Savings deposits held by residents, enterprises, organisations, army units and so on: 1952–83 from *Zhongguo Maoyi Wujia Tongji Ziliao* (p. 8); 1952–85 from *Statistical Yearbook of China 1986* (p. 444) and *Zhongguo Tongji Nianjian 1986* (p. 526).

(*SDR* + *CHR*): Residents' holdings of monetary assets, that is, residents' savings deposits plus residents' cash in hand: 1952–83 from *Zhongguo Maoyi Wujia Tongji Ziliao* (p. 15); 1984–85 calculated by adding annual data of monetary accumulation of residents from Song and Zhang (1986: 25). Although these data are labelled 'saving' (*chuxu*) they correspond to 'total monetary accumulation' of residents as defined in Table I.4 below.

(*SD* + *CH*): Total holdings of monetary assets by residents, enterprises, organisations, army units and so on, that is, total savings deposits plus total cash in hand: 1952–83 from *Zhongguo Maoyi Wujia Tongji Ziliao* (p. 8); 1952–1985 from *Statistical Yearbook of China 1986* (p. 444) and *Zhongguo Tongji Nianjian 1986* (p. 526).

Table I.3 Social commodity purchasing power, expenditure and monetary accumulation
(billion *yuan*)

			Total monetary accumulation		
			Increase in		
Year	*SPP*	*SME*	*CH*	*SD*	Total
1952	34.24	33.12	—	—	1.12
1953	41.82	40.40	0.95	0.47	1.42
1954	45.87	45.17	0.17	0.53	0.70
1955	46.44	46.07	−0.07	0.44	0.37
1956	55.56	53.64	1.18	0.74	1.92
1957	57.05	55.65	−0.14	1.54	1.40
1958	66.71	63.63	1.37	1.71	3.08
1959	78.48	74.77	0.45	3.26	3.71
1960	81.10	79.12	1.43	0.55	1.98
1961	72.71	70.19	3.08	−0.56	2.52
1962	64.96	69.69	−1.49	−3.24	−4.73
1963	68.21	69.10	−1.61	0.72	−0.89
1964	73.70	72.66	−0.98	2.02	1.04
1965	78.97	76.84	0.93	1.20	2.13
1966	86.55	82.80	1.93	1.82	3.75
1967	87.86	85.91	1.10	0.85	1.95
1968	85.28	82.73	0.90	1.65	2.55
1969	88.83	89.15	0.30	−0.62	−0.32
1970	94.66	95.25	−1.43	0.84	−0.59
1971	105.49	102.77	0.82	1.90	2.72
1972	114.59	112.43	1.19	0.97	2.16
1973	125.10	121.37	1.24	2.49	3.73
1974	130.84	127.26	0.80	2.78	3.58
1975	141.05	138.35	0.47	2.23	2.70
1976	148.70	146.26	1.70	0.74	2.44
1977	158.18	156.92	−0.68	1.94	1.26
1978	176.52	172.09	1.33	3.10	4.43
1979	209.39	197.61	4.44	6.01	10.45
1980	253.60	233.07	6.54	13.99	20.53
1981	274.67	255.67	5.17	13.83	19.00
1982	302.62	282.77	4.04	15.81	19.85
1983	344.06	316.89	8.49	18.73	27.17
1984	445.69	393.33	20.11	32.25	52.36
1985	564.54	509.54	16.07	38.93	55.00

Definitions:

SPP: Social (commodity) purchasing power.

SME: Social (commodity) monetary expenditures.

Total monetary accumulation equals the increase in society's holdings of cash and savings deposits and is the difference between *SPP* and *SME* with the exception of the data for 1979. All three sources cited below give exactly the same figures, which are incompatible with this necessary accounting identity. The difference between *SPP* and *SME* for 1979 totals 11.78 whereas the total of monetary accumulation is 10.45.

CH: Cash in hand (see Table I.1).

SD: Savings deposits held by residents, enterprises, organisations, army units and so on (see Table I.2).

Sources: *Statistical Yearbook of China 1986* (pp. 442–4), *Zhongguo Tongji Nianjian 1986* (pp. 524–6) and *Zhongguo Maoyi Wujia Tongji Ziliao* (pp. 5–8).

Table I.4 Residents' total monetary incomes, expenditure and monetary accumulation
(billion *yuan*)

			Monetary accumulation		
			Increase in		
Year	*MIR*	*MER*	*CHR*	*SDR*	Total
1952	26.93	25.81	0.81	0.31	1.12
1953	32.90	31.58	0.95	0.37	1.32
1954	35.24	34.72	0.16	0.36	0.52
1955	35.82	35.52	−0.10	0.40	0.30
1956	42.46	40.71	1.07	0.68	1.75
1957	44.10	43.51	−0.26	0.85	0.59
1958	49.95	46.76	1.19	2.00	3.19
1959	54.77	53.18	0.28	1.31	1.59
1960	57.59	56.39	1.40	−0.20	1.20
1961	56.06	54.17	2.98	−1.09	1.89
1962	52.89	55.72	−1.40	−1.43	−2.83
1963	54.09	55.18	−1.55	0.46	−1.09
1964	57.26	57.24	−0.96	0.98	0.02
1965	61.04	59.19	0.88	0.97	1.85
1966	65.05	62.48	1.86	0.71	2.57
1967	67.42	66.16	1.10	0.16	1.26
1968	65.19	63.95	0.80	0.44	1.24
1969	68.08	68.02	0.30	−0.24	0.06
1970	71.01	71.79	−1.14	0.36	−0.78
1971	76.80	74.94	0.78	1.08	1.86
1972	84.20	81.59	1.12	1.49	2.61
1973	90.10	87.32	1.18	1.60	2.78
1974	94.88	92.59	0.76	1.53	2.29
1975	100.97	99.21	0.45	1.31	1.76
1976	106.04	104.18	0.91	0.95	1.86
1977	113.68	112.05	−0.62	2.25	1.63
1978	125.41	121.30	1.21	2.90	4.11
1979	152.23	141.12	4.07	7.04	11.11
1980	189.99	172.20	5.94	11.85	17.79
1981	209.06	191.24	5.40	12.42	17.82
1982	230.62	210.75	4.70	15.17	19.87
1983	263.91	233.54	8.66	21.71	30.37
1984	330.73	278.51	—	—	52.22
1985	396.20	339.20	—	—	57.00

Definitions and sources:

MIR: Total monetary incomes of residents: 1952–83 from *Zhongguo Maoyi Wujia Tongji Ziliao* (p. 10); 1984–85 from Song and Zhang (1986: 25).

MER: Total monetary expenditures of residents: 1952–83 from *Zhongguo Maoyi Wujia Tongji Ziliao* (p. 13); 1984–85 calculated as column 1 minus column 5.

The annual increases in monetary holdings are the differences between successive end-of-year data of residents' total monetary holdings and are fully compatible with the given data for *MIR* and *MER*; that is, *MIR* minus *MER* equals the identifiable amount of monetary accumulation with no exceptions. The figures for 1979 balance exactly, whereas those of society's money incomes and expenditures do not. See notes to Table I.3.

CHR: Cash in hand of residents (see Table I.1).

SDR: Savings deposits held by residents (see Table I.2).

Increases in *CHR*, *SDR* and their total were calculated as the differences between end-of-year holdings of these assets from *Zhongguo Maoyi Wujia Tongji Ziliao* (pp. 15–16) except for the data for 1952, which can be calculated for residents as the tables give monetary holdings at the beginning of each year including 1952. See *Zhongguo Maoyi Wujia Tongji Ziliao* (pp. 9–10). This is not the case for society's purchasing power as only data for end-1952 are given.

Total monetary accumulation for 1984–85 is from Song and Zhang (1986: 25) where it is labelled 'saving' (*chuxu*), but it is equal to total monetary accumulation as defined above for all other years.

Table I.5 Major monetary ratios
(each monetary magnitude expressed as a percentage of the annual value of retail sales (*VRS*))

Year	*CHR*	*CH*	*CRC*	(*SDR* + *CHR*)	(*SD* + *CH*)	*M1*
1952	7.9	7.9	9.9	11.1	11.1	33.5
1953	9.1	9.1	11.4	12.6	12.9	31.6
1954	8.7	8.7	10.8	12.9	13.6	33.2
1955	8.2	8.3	10.2	13.3	14.2	34.5
1956	9.3	9.6	12.4	15.1	16.2	34.9
1957	8.5	9.0	11.1	15.9	18.7	37.3
1958	9.5	10.3	12.3	19.6	21.8	51.4
1959	8.6	9.6	11.8	19.3	24.5	55.6
1960	9.9	10.8	13.8	19.4	25.3	53.3
1961	16.2	17.5	20.7	25.4	33.2	68.6
1962	14.0	15.1	17.7	20.8	25.5	71.0
1963	11.4	12.4	14.9	19.0	24.1	69.2
1964	9.3	10.2	12.6	18.0	24.4	63.6
1965	10.2	11.1	13.5	19.9	26.4	68.9
1966	11.9	12.8	14.8	21.7	29.3	74.0
1967	12.7	13.6	15.8	22.3	30.4	76.8
1968	14.4	15.5	18.2	25.0	35.2	85.1
1969	13.6	14.6	17.1	23.1	32.0	80.1
1970	11.4	12.0	14.4	20.6	29.2	73.4
1971	11.3	11.9	14.7	21.1	29.9	75.3
1972	11.4	12.0	14.8	21.7	29.2	68.7
1973	11.6	12.2	15.0	22.6	30.4	73.6
1974	11.7	12.3	15.2	23.4	32.0	74.7
1975	11.1	11.6	14.4	22.8	31.4	73.3
1976	11.2	12.3	15.2	23.0	31.6	75.2
1977	10.0	11.0	13.6	22.7	30.5	71.3
1978	10.0	11.0	13.6	23.5	30.8	66.9
1979	10.9	12.0	14.9	26.5	32.5	65.4
1980	11.9	13.1	16.2	30.6	36.9	67.4
1981	13.2	14.2	16.9	35.5	41.7	71.6
1982	13.9	14.5	17.1	40.2	45.9	81.8
1983	15.6	16.1	18.6	46.9	50.9	74.4
1984	—	19.5	23.5	55.0	58.5	80.5
1985	—	19.0	22.9	56.4	58.6	—

Definitions and sources:

CHR: Residents' cash in hand (see Table I.1).

CH: Cash in hand (see Table I.1).

CRC: Currency in circulation (see Table I.1).

(*SDR* + *CHR*): Residents' holdings of monetary assets (see Table I.2).

(*SD* + *CH*): Total holdings of monetary assets (see Table I.2).

M1 equals currency in circulation plus all current accounts; precise coverage is not clear (Zheng, 1986b: 37).

VRS: Value of retail sales (see Table II.2).

Table I.6 Residents' per capita holdings of cash in hand and savings deposits, 1952–83
(end of year, *yuan*)

	National		Urban		Rural	
Year	Cash	Savings deposits	Cash	Savings deposits	Cash	Savings deposits
1952	3.8	1.5	7.3	10.4	3.2	—
1953	5.3	2.1	8.0	14.0	4.9	—
1954	5.5	2.6	8.8	15.5	4.9	0.3
1955	5.3	3.2	8.4	18.1	4.6	0.6
1956	6.9	4.2	9.0	22.4	6.4	0.8
1957	6.3	5.4	9.0	26.3	5.6	1.4
1958	7.9	8.4	14.0	28.7	6.6	3.7
1959	8.1	10.2	14.3	34.9	6.6	3.9
1960	10.4	10.0	21.8	37.2	7.4	2.9
1961	15.0	8.4	19.1	31.6	14.1	3.0
1962	12.6	6.1	17.9	27.9	11.5	1.7
1963	10.0	6.6	16.4	30.7	8.7	1.8
1964	8.4	7.9	14.6	38.4	7.2	1.8
1965	9.4	8.9	15.9	42.2	8.1	2.1
1966	11.6	9.7	19.1	46.0	10.1	2.4
1967	12.8	9.7	22.3	48.6	11.0	2.2
1968	13.4	10.0	23.2	48.6	11.6	2.4
1969	13.5	9.4	24.1	48.2	11.5	2.2
1970	11.7	9.6	16.3	45.9	10.8	2.2
1971	12.4	10.6	17.7	52.3	11.3	2.4
1972	13.3	12.1	19.7	60.3	12.2	2.7
1973	14.4	13.6	22.4	65.4	12.9	3.6
1974	15.0	15.0	23.3	72.5	13.4	4.0
1975	15.2	16.2	23.1	77.3	13.7	4.5
1976	15.9	17.0	25.2	78.8	14.1	4.7
1977	15.1	19.1	19.4	80.0	14.2	5.9
1978	16.1	21.9	20.7	90.0	15.2	7.0
1979	20.1	28.8	24.1	113.2	19.2	9.8
1980	25.9	40.4	30.8	154.9	24.8	14.5
1981	30.9	52.3	36.2	188.4	29.7	20.8
1982	35.1	66.5	39.6	233.0	34.1	27.7
1983	43.1	86.9	48.3	292.1	41.9	38.5

Source: *Zhongguo Maoyi Wujia Tongji Ziliao* (pp. 22–3).

Table I.7 Monetary data published by the International Monetary Fund
(selected years, end of period, billion *yuan*)

Year/quarter	*CRC*	*QM*	*M*
1977	19.54	27.83	58.01
1978	21.21	30.93	58.04
1979 I	21.90	26.31	58.71
1979 II	20.87	28.26	56.55
1979 III	22.56	30.59	60.14
1979 IV	26.77	40.63	73.66
1980 I	26.15	35.56	68.66
1980 II	24.32	36.52	68.70
1980 III	27.43	39.83	75.20
1980 IV	34.62	52.23	91.93
1981 I	32.56	46.56	88.31
1981 II	30.64	47.57	86.83
1981 III	33.32	50.51	92.12
1981 IV	39.63	63.25	107.04
1982 I	37.79	57.86	102.14
1982 II	35.25	59.58	97.56
1982 III	37.74	63.31	102.95
1982 IV	43.91	77.73	115.70
1983 I	43.33	71.64	113.13
1983 II	42.20	73.17	113.52
1983 III	46.73	78.82	119.73
1983 IV	52.98	96.39	137.05
1984 I	51.12	90.86	132.82
1984 II	49.10	91.75	131.01
1984 III	58.72	97.55	152.10
1984 IV	79.21	114.91	212.59
1985 I	78.76	118.06	216.96
1985 II	75.75	122.90	201.24
1985 III	82.71	131.10	218.29
1985 IV	98.78	150.74	248.32

Definitions:

CRC: Currency in circulation.

QM: Quasi-money, equals savings and term deposits held by households.

M: Money, equals currency in circulation and demand deposits held by enterprises.

These definitions were provided by the director of the Bureau of Statistics of the International Monetary Fund (IMF).

Sources: IMF, *International Financial Statistics*, October 1982 (pp. 120–1), November 1985 (pp. 152–3) and October 1986 (pp. 160–1). The IMF also publishes the following series:

Capital Construction Deposits, which are the deposits of the People's Construction Bank of China that were redeposited at the People's Bank of China when the Construction Bank was not included in the monetary survey, that is, up to end-1985. From 1986 the Construction Bank was consolidated in the monetary survey, and deposits at the Construction Bank are included in money from 1986.

Government deposits, which are the budgetary deposits of the central government and deposits of government organisations.

The item 'other items' is a residual.

Data for subsequent years can be found in these IMF sources.

Appendix II Retail prices and sales

Table II.1 Major retail price indexes
(1952 = 100)

Year	*P*	*CP*	*CLI*	*LP*	*LPC*	*LPIR*	*MP*
1953	103.4	102.2	105.1	103.2	103.1	98.6	103.9
1954	105.8	104.6	106.6	105.5	105.4	100.5	106.3
1955	106.9	107.0	106.9	106.3	106.3	102.0	106.1
1956	106.9	107.5	106.8	106.3	106.6	101.0	105.9
1957	108.5	108.6	109.6	108.6	109.1	102.2	108.9
1958	108.8	108.8	108.4	108.8	109.6	101.5	117.5
1959	109.7	109.8	108.7	109.5	110.1	102.5	119.0
1960	113.1	114.0	113.4	112.5	113.7	105.3	136.6
1961	131.5	133.7	129.3	119.4	119.9	110.5	491.8
1962	136.5	137.3	134.2	124.3	124.6	115.4	319.6
1963	128.4	128.5	126.3	122.2	122.4	114.2	241.2
1964	123.7	124.4	121.7	120.1	121.6	112.0	167.8
1965	120.4	122.0	120.2	118.4	119.5	107.9	173.2
1966	120.0	122.9	118.8	117.6	119.1	104.8	175.3
1967	119.1	122.0	118.0	117.5	119.0	104.0	178.2
1968	119.2	122.8	118.2	117.6	119.2	103.7	178.2
1969	117.9	121.8	119.3	116.3	118.4	102.2	178.1
1970	117.6	121.6	119.3	116.2	118.3	102.0	178.1
1971	116.7	123.3	119.2	115.0	118.0	100.5	193.8
1972	116.5	123.0	119.5	114.8	117.9	99.9	209.6
1973	117.2	125.1	119.6	114.9	118.0	99.9	220.7
1974	117.8	125.2	120.4	114.9	118.3	99.9	224.8
1975	118.0	126.2	120.9	114.9	118.3	99.9	233.8
1976	118.3	126.6	121.3	115.0	118.4	100.0	243.1
1977	120.8	130.5	124.5	115.1	118.5	100.1	237.2
1978	121.6	132.4	125.4	115.4	118.8	100.1	221.6
1979	124.0	135.2	127.8	117.1	120.7	100.2	211.6
1980	131.4	144.7	137.4	122.3	127.0	101.0	215.8
1981	134.6	148.5	140.8	123.9	128.5	102.0	228.3
1982	137.2	151.4	143.6	125.5	130.0	103.6	235.8
1983	139.3	153.2	146.5	126.5	130.5	104.6	245.7
1984	143.2	155.8	150.4	134.6	138.4	107.9	244.7
1985	155.8	170.4	168.4	145.1	149.9	111.4	286.8

Definitions and sources:

P: General retail price index (*quan shehui lingshou wujia zong zhishu*), which is a weighted average of list prices, negotiated prices and market prices: 1952–83 from *Zhongguo Maoyi Wujia Tongji Ziliao* (p. 370); 1984–85 chain linked from *Statistical Yearbook of China 1986* (p. 536).

CP: General retail price index of consumer goods: 1952–83 from *Zhongguo Maoyi Wujia Tongji Ziliao* (p. 370); 1952–85 from *China Trade and Price Statistics* (p. 90).

CLI: Cost-of-living index for workers and staff: recalculated to a 1952 base from the data of annual increases in *Statistical Yearbook of China 1986* (p. 535).

LP: National retail list price index (*quan guo lingshou paijia zong zhishu*): 1952–83 from *Zhongguo Maoyi Wujia Tongji Ziliao* (p. 376); 1952–85 from *China Trade and Price Statistics* (p. 96).

LPC: National retail list price index of consumer goods: 1952–83 from *Zhongguo Maoyi Wujia Tongji Ziliao* (p. 376); 1952–85 from *China Trade and Price Statistics* (p. 96).

LPIR: General index of retail list prices of industrial products sold in rural areas: 1952–82 from *Statistical Yearbook of China 1983* (p. 455); 1983–85 from *Statistical Yearbook of China 1986* (p. 536). The series has been recalculated to a 1952 base as these sources use a 1950 base. In the 1983 *Statistical Yearbook* the series is clearly labelled as referring to 'list prices', but this is omitted from its title in subsequent editions although the data remain the same.

MP: Price index of consumer goods sold on free markets (*Jishi Maoyi Jiage Zhishu*): 1952–83 from *Zhongguo Maoyi Wujia Tongji Ziliao* (p. 395); 1952–85 from *China Trade and Price Statistics* (p. 112) and selected years in *Statistical Yearbook of China 1987* (p. 580).

Table II.2 Indicators of retail sales and output

Year	*VRS* (billion *yuan*)	*NI* (billion *yuan*)	*RNI* index (1952 = 100)	Consumption rate, *c* (%)	Accumulation rate, *a* (%)
1952	27.68	60.7	100.0	78.6	21.4
1953	34.80	72.7	114.0	76.9	23.1
1954	38.11	76.5	120.6	74.5	25.5
1955	39.22	80.7	128.3	77.1	22.9
1956	46.10	88.8	146.4	75.6	24.4
1957	47.42	93.5	153.0	75.1	24.9
1958	54.80	111.7	186.7	66.1	33.9
1959	63.80	127.4	202.1	56.2	43.8
1960	69.69	126.4	199.2	60.4	39.6
1961	60.77	101.3	140.0	80.8	19.2
1962	60.40	94.8	130.9	89.6	10.4
1963	60.45	104.7	144.9	82.5	17.5
1964	63.82	118.4	168.8	77.8	22.2
1965	67.03	134.7	197.5	72.9	27.1
1966	73.28	153.5	231.0	69.4	30.6
1967	77.05	142.8	214.3	78.7	21.3
1968	73.73	140.9	200.4	78.9	21.1
1969	80.15	153.7	239.1	76.8	23.2
1970	85.80	187.6	294.7	67.1	32.9
1971	92.92	200.8	315.3	65.9	34.1
1972	102.33	205.2	324.5	68.4	31.6
1973	110.67	225.2	351.4	67.1	32.9
1974	116.36	229.1	355.2	67.7	32.3
1975	127.11	245.1	384.7	66.1	33.9
1976	133.94	242.4	374.4	69.1	30.9
1977	143.28	257.3	403.6	67.7	32.3
1978	155.86	297.5	453.2	63.5	36.5
1979	180.00	335.6	484.9	65.4	34.6
1980	214.00	369.6	515.9	68.5	31.5
1981	235.00	390.5	541.2	71.7	28.3
1982	257.00	429.0	586.1	71.2	28.8
1983	284.94	477.9	643.5	70.3	29.7
1984	337.64	566.1	730.5	68.8	31.2
1985	430.50	727.3	820.2	66.3	33.7

Definitions:

VRS: Value of retail sales at current prices.

NI: National income available at current prices, which differs from national income due to the difference between imports and exports and to the statistical discrepancy.

RNI: Real national income; index of national income in comparable prices.

Consumption rate: Proportion of consumption in national income, including personal and public consumption.

Accumulation rate: Proportion of investment in national income, including net fixed productive investment and net non-productive investment (which includes residential buildings and accumulation of stocks of consumer goods held by industrial enterprises or commercial departments).

Source: *Statistical Yearbook of China 1986* (p. 41 for *RNI*; p. 49 for *NI*, consumption rate and accumulation rate; p. 445 for *VRS*).

Appendix III Indicators of purchasing power imbalance and its consequences

Table III.1 Purchasing power imbalance (narrow concept)
(percentage increase over previous year except for columns 3 and 4)

Year	pd*MIR*	pd*RNI*	PPI_r	m_r (%)	pd*LPC*
1953	22.2	14.0	8.2	4.0	3.1
1954	7.1	5.8	1.3	1.5	2.2
1955	1.6	6.4	−4.8	0.1	0.9
1956	18.5	14.1	4.4	4.1	0.3
1957	3.9	4.5	−0.6	1.3	2.3
1958	13.3	22.0	−8.7	6.4	0.5
1959	9.6	8.2	1.4	2.9	0.5
1960	5.1	−1.4	6.5	2.1	3.3
1961	−2.7	−29.7	27.0	3.4	5.5
1962	−5.7	−6.5	0.8	−5.4	3.9
1963	2.3	10.7	−8.4	−2.0	−1.8
1964	5.9	16.5	−10.6	0.03	−0.7
1965	15.7	17.0	−1.3	3.0	−1.7
1966	6.6	17.0	−10.4	4.0	−0.3
1967	3.6	−7.2	10.8	1.9	−0.1
1968	−3.3	−6.5	3.2	1.9	0.2
1969	4.4	19.3	−14.9	0.1	−0.7
1970	4.3	23.3	−19.0	−1.1	−0.1
1971	8.2	7.0	1.2	2.4	−0.3
1972	9.6	2.9	6.7	3.1	−0.1
1973	7.0	8.3	−1.3	3.1	0.1
1974	5.3	1.1	4.2	2.4	0.3
1975	6.4	8.3	−1.9	1.7	0
1976	5.0	−2.7	7.7	1.8	0.1
1977	7.2	7.8	−0.6	1.4	0.1
1978	10.3	12.3	−2.0	3.3	0.3
1979	21.4	7.0	14.4	7.3	1.6
1980	24.8	6.4	18.4	9.4	5.2
1981	10.0	4.9	5.1	8.5	1.2
1982	10.3	8.3	2.0	8.6	1.4
1983	14.4	9.8	4.6	11.5	0.4
1984	25.3	13.5	11.8	15.8	6.1
1985	19.8	12.3	7.5	14.4	8.3

Definitions and sources:
pd*MIR*: Calculated from Table I.4.
pd*RNI*: Calculated from Table II.2.
PPI_r equals pd*MIR* minus pd*RNI* (*r* is for 'residents').
m_r: Monetary accumulation expressed as a percentage of *MIR*.
pd*LPC*: Calculated from Table II.1.

Table III.2 Purchasing power imbalance (broad concept)

Year	pd*SPP*	*PPI*	*m*	pd*LP*	*SPP* ratio (1952 = 100)
1953	22.1	8.1	3.4	3.2	107.1
1954	9.7	3.9	1.5	2.2	111.1
1955	1.2	−5.2	0.8	0.8	105.7
1956	19.6	5.5	3.5	0	110.8
1957	2.7	−1.8	2.5	2.2	108.9
1958	16.9	−5.1	4.6	0.2	104.4
1959	17.6	9.4	4.7	0.6	113.4
1960	2.9	4.3	2.4	2.7	118.9
1961	−10.3	19.4	3.5	6.1	151.7
1962	−10.7	−4.2	−7.3	4.1	144.9
1963	5.0	−5.7	−1.3	−1.7	137.5
1964	8.0	−8.5	1.4	−1.7	127.5
1965	7.2	−9.8	2.7	−1.4	116.8
1966	9.6	−7.4	4.3	−0.8	109.4
1967	1.5	8.7	2.2	−0.1	119.7
1968	−2.9	3.6	3.0	0.1	124.3
1969	4.2	−15.1	−0.4	−1.1	108.5
1970	6.6	−16.7	−0.6	−0.1	93.8
1971	11.4	4.4	2.6	−1.0	97.7
1972	8.6	5.7	1.9	−0.2	103.1
1973	9.2	0.9	3.0	0.1	104.0
1974	4.6	3.5	2.7	0	107.6
1975	7.8	−0.5	1.9	0	107.1
1976	5.4	8.1	1.6	0.1	116.0
1977	6.4	−1.4	0.8	0.1	114.5
1978	11.6	−0.7	2.5	0.3	113.8
1979	18.6	11.6	5.0	1.5	126.1
1980	21.1	14.7	8.1	4.4	143.6
1981	8.3	3.4	6.9	1.3	148.2
1982	10.2	1.9	6.6	1.3	150.8
1983	13.7	3.9	7.9	0.8	156.2
1984	29.5	16.0	11.7	6.4[a]	178.2
1985	26.7	14.4	9.7	7.8	201.0

Definitions and sources:

pd*SPP*: Calculated from Table I.3.

PPI: equals pd*SPP* minus pd*RNI* (given in Table III.1).

m: Calculated as total monetary accumulation, that is, Δ (*CH* + *SD*), expressed as a percentage of *SPP*.

pd*LP*: Calculated from Table II.1.

SPP ratio equals *SPP* divided by *RNI*, turned into an index with 1950 = 100.

Note: [a] This is the increase implied by the original source, *China Trade and Price Statistics* (p. 96). In addition, *Statistical Yearbook of China 1985* (p. 532) gives the 1984 index as 150.3 (1950 = 100) and *Statistical Yearbook of China 1984* (p. 429) gives the 1983 index as 141.4 (1950 = 100). These are the same as *China Trade and Price Statistics* (p. 94). They imply a pd*LP* for 1984 of over 6 per cent. However, *Statistical Yearbook of China 1985* (p. 533) gives the 1984 figure as 102.7 per cent of the 1983 figure. This increase of 2.7 per cent in list prices makes more sense given the fact that the general retail price index increased only 2.8 per cent in 1984. Unfortunately, I cannot reconcile this increase with that clearly implied by the three indexes in *China Trade and Price Statistics* (pp. 94–98), which all imply an increase in list prices (the tables are clearly labelled as so) of more than 6 per cent in 1984.

Appendix IV Variables by subperiods

Table IV.1 Variables by subperiods: average annual increase
(per cent per annum)

Subperiod	$(m - q)$	p	lp	ppi	crc	i	acc
Period I	1.3	1.1	1.1	0.4	9.4	7.9	1.1
Period II	25.6	6.6	3.6	8.9	15.4	−31.2	−27.3
Period III	−16.1	−3.2	−1.6	−9.1	0.6	41.2	24.4
Period IV	−2.2	−0.5	−0.3	−4.2	3.9	7.3	2.3
Period V	2.7	0.3	0	2.4	7.7	5.3	0.1
Period VI	6.1	2.4	1.4	5.8	14.7	13.0	1.1
Period VII	16.2	3.4	3.9	9.0	27.3	21.5	4.4

Sources: Calculated from data in Tables I.1, II.1 and III.2 and from *Statistical Yearbook of China 1986* (p. 49).

Appendix V Selected references by topic

Economic history and economic reform
Liu and Wu (1986); Riskin (1987); Yu (1984); Lin and Chao (1983); Reynolds (1987) and (1988); Zhao Dexin (1988) and his second volume (1989); Feuchtwang and Hussain (1983); World Bank (1990a) and (1990b).

Institutions
Donnithorne (1967); Howe (1978); Prybyla (1978); World Bank (1983); Ma (1982a); *Economy* (1984); *Cambridge Encyclopedia of China* (1982); *Information China* (1989: vol. 2).

Money
Tseng and Han (1959); Miyashita (1966); Hsiao (1971) and (1984); *World Currency Yearbook 1984* (ed. P. Cowitt); *Pick's Currency Yearbook: A History of Chinese Currency (16th Century BC – 20th Century AD)*; Qian and Guo (1985); *Jingji Da Cidian—Jinrong Juan* (1987); *Xiandai Shiyong Jinrong Cidian* (1987); Ma (1982a).

Banking institutions and their reform
Hsiao (1971) and (1984); Samansky (1981); Byrd (1983); Lee (1985); DeWulf (1985); DeWulf and Goldsbrough (1986); Brotman (1985); Tam (1986) and (1987); Wilson (1986); Zhou and Zhu (1987); White and Bowles (1988); Bowles and White (1989); Chang (1989); Donnithorne (1989); Tsang (1990).

Monetary data
International Financial Statistics (monthly and yearbook); *Statistical Yearbook of China*; Byrd (1983); *Zhongguo Jinrong* (Chinese Finance); Huang (1988b); Zhang Junkuo (1988); *Fenjinde Sishi Nian 1949–1989* (1989: 429–30).

Prices and price data
Jianming Jiage Cidian; Ma (1982a); *Statistical Yearbook of China; Zhongguo Wujia Tongji Nianjian 1988; Zhongguo Wujia Nianjian 1989; Zhongguo Maoyi Wujia Tongji Ziliao 1952–83* (1984); *Fenjinde Sishi Nian 1949–1989* (1989: 405–16); *Zhongguo Tongji Nianjian 1989* (pp. 687–716); *Zhongguo Tongji Yuebao* (China Statistics Monthly Report); *China Monthly Statistics*.

Econometric and statistical studies
Chow (1987); Feltenstein and Farhadian (1987); Portes and Santorum (1987); Huang (1988a) and (1988b); Chen Chien-Hsun (1989); Feltenstein, Lebow and van Wijnbergen (1990).

Chronologies and reports of events
Beijing Review; Far Eastern Economic Review; Issues and Studies; The China Business Review; The China Quarterly; Jiushi Niandai (The Nineties); *Lishide Xiongbian: A Sketch of Chinese Economy 1949–1988* (1989: 325–437); Sherer (1978–85).

Endnotes

Chapter 1

1 Zhang Junkuo (1988b: 29) does in fact present estimates of Chinese *GDP* for the entire period 1952–86 using World Bank methods.

2 Katz (1979) and Nissanke (1979) are critical of Howard, Muscatteli (1988) criticises Bordo and Jonung (1987), and Raj and Siklos (1988) also criticise Bordo and Jonung (1981; 1987). As well as in many reviews, Friedman and Schwartz (1982) has been severely criticised on econometric grounds by Hendry and Ericsson (1983) who, using Friedman and Schwartz's own data, re-estimated many equations and came to the opposite conclusions.

3 See *Lishide Xiongbian: Zhongguo Jingji 1949–1989 Nian Sumiao: A Sketch of Chinese Economy* (1989: 436), which compares the rate of growth of aggregate social demand (*shehui xong xuqiu*) with that of available supply and presents an index of excess demand (*gongxu chalü*). The former indicator is remarkably similar to the one used in chapter 6 to identify excess demand and planners' reactions to such demand imbalances. See also *Zhongguo Jingji Nianjian 1984* (p. IV-18) for a similar analysis of the excess demand problem of 1983. This source specifically uses the growth rate of purchasing power (*goumaili*) compared with the growth of supply but gives no absolute figures. Li Ping (1990: 24) gives figures of what are clearly the *gongxu chalü* for 1983–88.

4 I might have chosen a better term but I appear to be stuck with it. Gardner (1988: 39) applies the concept, citing it from Peebles (1986b). Hsu (1989) also has adopted it.

5 See 'Retrenchment and economic growth' (1989).

Chapter 2

1 Chinese national income data use the socialist method of material accounting. A better term for national income (*guomin shouru*) in China would be net material product as, following the conventions adopted from the Soviet Union, it covers only the net ('newly created') output of the five sectors of material production: agriculture, industry, construction, transport and commerce. It thus omits all service sector output such as administration, education and health, and personal services such as entertainment, laundries and bath-houses. It is a 'net' concept in the sense that it has had all intermediate material consumption deducted from total product of society (*shehui zong chan zhi*), which is just the sum of total (gross output) of the same five material sectors of production. This latter concept is guilty of double counting in terms of Western conventions. Another national-income concept used subsequently is that of national income available. This refers to the 'final income of material production sectors and non-material production sectors and of individuals after national income produced is distributed and redistributed in society'. It equals national income produced plus the balance of trade surplus and

the statistical discrepancy. See *Statistical Yearbook of China 1986* (pp. 735–6).

2 Briefly, the two different views can be summarised as follows. A monetarist view that believes that 'money matters' would argue that causation goes from exogenous changes in money to the change in output. For example, Milton Friedman (1968: 3) blames the American Federal Reserve Board for allowing a sharp reduction in the monetary base, which caused the fall in the money supply. An alternative view represented by Kaldor (1970; 1978) argues that the fall in the nominal money supply was a consequence of the fall in real output, which was caused by real factors in the economy. See also Temin (1976). Kaldor (1978: 16–17) and others have argued that Friedman's and Schwartz's own data (their 1963: 803–4) show an increase in the monetary base, not a fall.

3 Mao Zedong's views on financial policies in the liberated areas are contained in Watson (1980: 59–250).

4 This document is translated in Liu and Wu (1984: 509–18).

5 On Taiwan, which reverted to Chinese sovereignty in November 1945 and which had a separate currency unit and was occupied by the Kuomintang army, there was also a hyperinflation, with prices rising at about one-third of the rate of those on the mainland. A stabilisation programme was adopted in June 1949, and this is said to have contributed to price stability by 1952, even though the government was unable to cut its budget deficit substantially (Maniken and Woodward, 1989).

6 Chang (1958) presents a map (opposite p. 386) showing the different currency areas.

7 This document is translated in Liu and Wu (1986: 501–8).

8 A legacy of the inflation was that prices were in very large units although they were stable. The highest note issued was the 50 000 *yuan* note of 1950. See *A History of Chinese Currency* (p. 192). This made accounting tedious, and people were used to dividing all prices by 10 000 (*yi wan*) for convenience (Liu, 1980: 61). This problem was rectified in March 1955. See section 4.12.

9 This and many subsequent statements of fact in the historical narrative are taken from Liu and Wu (1986).

10 In Chinese terminology 'grain' refers to a large number of crops. It covers 'all types of grain such as rice, wheat, corn, sorghum, millet and other miscellaneous grains, as well as tuber crops [such as potato and sweet potato] and soybean' (*Statistical Yearbook of China 1986*, p. 743). It thus includes the staples of both the south, rice, and the north, wheat.

11 Chinese statisticians compute real constant-price variables (those in comparable, that is, *kebi* prices) using different base-year prices for different periods. The base years used are 1952, 1957, 1970 and 1980. See *Statistical Yearbook of China 1986* (p. 737).

12 Chow's explanation is this. Under the compulsory purchase scheme that operated from November 1953 farmers could easily see the losses they bore by having to supply the state at state-determined prices. This was because there were alternative opportunities for the use of their land and other resources open to them. One way to prevent farmers from realising the extent to which they were making losses on government-decreed output was to abolish the right to follow all these alternatives, so rural land and labour markets were abolished by the establishment of the communes. The communes would still pay out wages and buy inputs, so there were prices and costs, but there was no mechanism for the communes to compute the true opportunity costs of doing what the planners

told them as the alternative uses were not valued at true prices. Communes could receive money incomes just sufficient to meet their money outlays, but such incomes and costs were economically meaningless.

13 The actual statistical series that I have taken to represent social purchasing power was 16 per cent lower in 1963 than in 1960. This shows that the time series I have adopted to represent *SPP* must be the one Chinese economists use, but do not identify, when they refer to *SPP* developments.

14 A Red Guard poster listed the amount of money looted between August and September 1966. As a Hong Kong analyst of this report comments, the amount of Chinese currency listed, at 482.8 billion *yuan*, must be a misprint. It could not have been anything like that amount. See *China News Analysis*, no. 677 (p. 3).

15 See *China News Analysis*, no. 644 (pp. 4, 648).

16 According to Wan (1984: 396) commercial departments lost 2 billion *yuan* between March and September 1979 on sales of pork, beef, mutton and eggs. Such losses would show up as both deficit items in the budget and increases in currency in circulation as these units were paying out more than they received for the same products, the opposite effect from that envisioned by Chen Yun in 1950. *Statistical Yearbook of China 1986* (p. 525) shows subsidies on selected consumer goods in 1979 to be 13.602 billion *yuan* compared with 5.56 billion *yuan* in the previous year.

17 If market and list prices only were weighted to get the general retail price index, these figures suggest a weight of 76 per cent for list prices and 24 per cent for market prices. This latter weight is much too high compared with the proportion of retail sales likely to have been sold at market prices.

18 Some such moves in early 1979 seem to have been spontaneous (Lu, 1984: 20), and others were observed and encouraged by Zhao Ziyang and Wan Li in Sichuan and Anhui provinces respectively.

19 See the important *Circular of the Central Committee of the Communist Party of China Concerning Rural Work in 1984* of 1 January 1984. This document is reproduced in Liu and Wu (1986: 656–71).

20 See the *Circular* cited in note 19 (Liu and Wu, 1986: 657) for restrictions on the completely free leasing of land, and p. 658 for restrictions on the use of land for housebuilding.

21 As one farmer reported, he was not sure how long the new policies would last, but if he built a house he would at least have that if policies were changed (Lu, 1984e: 25).

22 Retail sales data by source included these co-operatives in the state sector until 1983. Thereafter they come under the co-operative description. See *Statistical Yearbook of China 1986* (p. 414). Riskin (1986: 356, 374, fn. 23) says that these co-operatives were state organs until denationalisation.

23 He cannot be certain because he does not know whether the definition of rural retail sales was changed in line with the change in the definition of the urban population in 1984.

24 See *Decision of the Central Committee of the Communist Party of China on Reform of the Economic Structure* (1984). It is also reproduced in Liu and Wu (1986: 672–700).

25 See *Decision* cited in note 24 (Hong Kong edition, p. 14) and Liu and Wu (1986: 683).

26 See 'Banking reform favours centralization' (1984), an interview with Lu Peijian, president of the People's Bank of China.

27 The price increases for 1980 are puzzling. List prices increased 4.4 per cent and market prices 2 per cent (*China Trade and Price Statistics*, 1987: 94, 112), yet the general retail price index, which is a weighted average of these and negotiated prices, increased by 6 per cent (p. 89).
28 I quote from the version published in Liu and Wu (1986: 467–9).
29 All budget figures cited include domestic and foreign loans as items of revenue.
30 These figures are those compiled by the General Administration of Customs and became official data for publication in statistical yearbooks from 1980 in place of the earlier data from the Ministry of Foreign Economic Relations and Trade. See Hishida (1984) for details of the difference in coverage.
31 In *pinyin* '*huilong*' means recalling currency to the bank. Komiya is arguing that the sale of imports was able to do this. The concept of *huobi huilong* (withdrawing currency) and its importance will be discussed in section 4.8.
32 *Renmin Ribao* (People's Daily), 13 October 1958 (p. 7). See also *China News Analysis*, no. 993, 14 March 1975. Zhang Chunqiao was a prominent leftist and member of the 'gang of four'. He produced the report on the revision of the Chinese Constitution in 1975 as well as a famous article in *Hong Qi* (*Red Flag*), reproduced as Chang (1975).
33 I owe this information to reading an unpublished paper by Dr Borge Bakken of the Department of Sociology, University of Oslo. His sources are *Zhongguo Jiaoyubao* (*Chinese Education Journal*), 12/11, 1985 (p. 4) and *Renmin Jiaoyu* (*People's Education*), no. 3, 1985 (p. 35).
34 *China Trade and Price Statistics* (1987: 82, 94–5, 100–1, 106–7, 112).
35 See *Statistical Yearbook of China 1986* for the figure for 1985 and the 1985 volume (p. 559) and for data for calculating the increase in 1984 (p. 554).
36 The period is 1954–85, and the significance level chosen was 5 per cent.

Chapter 3

1 Gowland (1984: 7) states that the United Kingdom, for example, does not include foreigners' holdings of the domestic money supply in its definitions whereas the United States does, and that the United Kingdom does include government money holdings in some definitions of the money supply whereas the United States omits them from all. There are about 30 different money-supply concepts published in the United States.
2 Although Chrystal shows the long-run stable growth trend of the velocity of *M0* a fellow monetarist, Congdon (1989: 72–3), argues that this is no evidence of causation and that in fact causation goes from the economy to *M0* and not, as Chrystal is arguing, from *M0* to the economy.
3 An interesting early contribution on this point about the macroeconomic and microeconomic aspects of balance between demand and supply is that of Frederick Engels (1978: 12–15). In criticising Rodbertus's view that, if a planned economy used labour tokens, paying them out according to labour input, then aggregate demand would exactly equal available supply, Engels asked what mechanism there would be to ensure that the supplies of all the different commodities were forthcoming in amounts just equal to the demand for them. He answers his own question by saying that in an economy of independent producers the only possible mechanism is competition and a price system, so trial and error on the part of suppliers, and the resulting profits and losses, make them learn what is wanted and what is not. Interestingly, the edition of Marx from which this pro-market

argument is taken (and it predates and is similar to the arguments about the information-bearing nature of prices in a market economy of von Hayek and Friedman) was published in China in 1978. I wonder whether anyone read it with this connection in mind.

4 The chronic problem of shortages of certain consumer goods, especially foodstuffs, and the resulting behaviour of consumers have added to the Russian language. The colloquial word for a stringbag (which can be easily carried around in order to cope with fortuitous discoveries of rare supplies) is *avos'ka*, derived from the adverb *avos'*, meaning 'just in case'. Hartwig's argument is that large amounts of money are held and carried around 'just in case'.

5 See, for an example, 'Roubles, roubles', *The Economist*, 17 June 1989 (pp. 11–12), which puts household monetary asset holdings at more than one year's retail sales value, an increase on the ratio earlier identified by Birman and Clarke (1985). The traditionalists' view is further supported by such things as significant devaluations of the currency, such as have occurred in Poland and occurred in the Soviet Union in late 1989, and the wave of popular protests and complaints about chronic shortages of consumer goods. I wonder how the new view will explain these phenomena. By the beginning of 1990 Soviet economists were debating the necessity of policies (such as a confiscatory currency reform or a gold-backed rouble), which suggests that *they* believed that there was a serious financial problem whatever outside observers said. Kincade and Thomson (1990) cite some of their views. East Germany achieved monetary unity with West Germany on 1 July 1990 as a prelude for political and economic unity. The new view has to supply valid reasons to counter the traditional view's argument that the East German and Soviet Union currencies were becoming worthless to explain why East Germany was so keen to abandon its own currency and the Soviet Union to abandon virtually all the features of the traditional monetary system.

6 Banks increase investment by reducing the transactions costs involved in getting lenders and borrowers together. They thus offer a higher deposit rate to savers and lenders and a lower lending rate to investors, so increasing the flow of investment. *World Development Report 1989* (p. 30) summarises this familiar argument.

Chapter 4

1 They were those at the Macroeconomic Research Office, Economic Structural Reform Research Institute of China. A translation of their analysis is published as 'An analysis of the economic situation in 1986', *Chinese Economic Studies*, vol. 21, no. 3, Spring 1988 (pp. 3–23). See pp. 9–11 in particular.

2 In 1978 about 200 kinds of subsidies were paid out (Ma, 1982a: 525–6). They covered a whole range of items but included the grain and subsidiary food price subsidies and food subsidies for the *Hui* (Muslim) minority people.

3 See *Lishide Xiongbian: A Sketch of Chinese Economy 1949–1988* (p. 406).

4 *Information China* (1989: 762) lists some of them.

5 See *Pick's Currency Yearbook 1955* and *1964–65*. The data for the 1949 hyperinflation period are likely to be more representative than data for 1962 when China was effectively closed to outside observers.

6 As Chinn (1980: 747–8) shows, households in Peking were allowed to accumulate unused grain ration coupons in a savings account. He knew several households who had ten years' worth of accumulated coupons they

could draw on when necessary. This provided an alternative form of savings guaranteed in real terms. It was probably available for only a very limited number of households who had a large number of working members entitled to generous rations.

7 See *Zhongguo Maoyi Wujia Tongji Ziliao 1952–83* (mainly pp. 357–451) and *China Trade and Price Statistics* (1987: 89–115).

8 China is of course the country with the longest tradition of using paper money. In 1023 the government took over the right to issue notes and banned their private issue by merchants. The Yuan dynasty (1271–1368) is regarded as the golden age of Chinese paper money. In the early days of government paper-money issue, refusal to accept the currency could be met with death, an extreme way for the government to invest its currency with value. Note issue by the private banks (*qian zhuang*) occurred in the late Qing dynasty (1644–1911); a national bank was not established until 1905. See *A History of Chinese Currency 16th Century BC – 20th Century AD* (pp. 49–72).

9 See Byrd (1983: 154), *Economy* (1984: 378–9), Bortolani and Santorum (1984: 54–6), Tam (1987: 101) and *Lilü Wenjian Huibao* (1986: 415–16, 443–4, 487–9, 555–9).

10 Such private chequing accounts were introduced in about 1987 for a very limited number of distinguished citizens and private businesspeople. They sometimes have difficulty getting their cheques accepted. A Chinese credit card, the Great Wall Credit Card, was introduced in June 1986 for holders of foreign exchange and from 1 February 1987 for individuals and organisations in China, denominated in *Renminbi*. This was available for a very limited number of people. The Special Economic Zones feature such modern facilities as cash-dispensing machines operated by the Bank of China.

11 They are the *Renmin Shengli Zheshi Gongzhai* (People's Commodity Victory Bonds) of 1950, *Guojia Jingji Jianshe Gongzhai* (State Economic Construction Bonds) of 1954–58 and *Zhonghua Renmin Gongheguo Guokuquan* (People's Republic of China State Treasury Bonds) of the 1980s. See Ma (1982a: 462–3) who explains the rates of interest and redemption procedures.

12 Other centralised state systems have operated using these two spheres of circulation. The anthropologist Crump (1981: 203–4) quotes a case where state accounts were made in units of barley ('documentary barley') purely as an accounting device, and the people used silver. This was in Ur more than 4000 years ago. Crump is citing the work of fellow anthropologist Lambert.

13 See Borisov (1966). This distinction is found in the Soviet balance of money incomes and expenditures of the population, which is clearly divided into one section for transactions between the government sector and the individual, and another section for transactions between individuals. This latter section is also of importance to the planners for it is through this channel that purchasing power is redistributed across the country and that planners must, at least in theory, reallocate goods to meet the changing geographical distribution of consumer demand.

14 See *Zhongguo Maoyi Wujia Tongji Ziliao 1952–83* (pp. 8–9).

15 See *Statistical Yearbook of China 1986* (p. 444).

16 Komija (1989: 75) renders *huilong* even more literally as 'calling the birds (cash currency, *Renminbi* RMB) back to the cage (the central bank)'. *Long* means cage or basket.

17 It is interesting to note that, in its tables of members' 'reserve money' and

the 'ratio of reserve money to money plus quasi-money', issues of *International Financial Statistics Yearbook* omit China from these tables. The concept of 'reserve money' cannot be identified in China.

18 See Borisov (1966) and Kuschèpta (1978) for the concept, Peebles (1981) and Birman (1981) for attempts at reconstructing it for the Soviet Union, and Rudcenko (1979) for some Eastern European data.

19 The term is Bruce Reynolds's (1987: xvii). These young economists were responsible for the reports published by the China Economic System Reform Research Institute (CESRRI) eventuating in Reynolds (1987).

20 Confusingly, another source, *Lishide Xiongbian (A Sketch of Chinese Economy: 1949–1988)* (1989: 147) contains a graph of what it labels '*dangnian jieyu huobi*', which is translatable as 'that year's surplus money' but which the publication translates as 'remaining money (current year)' (p. 51). This 'surplus money' is in fact a flow, not a stock. It is shown in column 5 of Table I.3 and is the difference between *SPP* and *SME*.

21 Apart from some minor discrepancies between the two texts there is one important misleading statement in the English text where the authors are made to state that estimated surplus purchasing power in 1985 was 'approximately 60 per cent more than 1985 gross retail sales' (p. 96). In fact their original words state more or less correctly that this amount would constitute 'more than sixty per cent of 1985's total retail sales, corresponding to 7–8 month's of retail sales value' (Li and Xia, 1986: 97). This last clarification is omitted from the English translation. It is interesting to see the young economists continuing to use the ratio of outstanding money to annual retail sales as a rough criterion for judging monetary circulation. Table I.5, column 5, shows the ratio to have been 58.6 per cent.

22 I wrote to the editors in Peking in 1987 asking why this is the case and have received no reply. The figures remained the same in the *Statistical Yearbook of China 1987* (pp. 480–2).

23 See *Zhongguo Tongji Nianjian 1981* (p. 399) for the former and *1983* (p. 450) for the latter shorter version.

24 The data in later Chinese sources are somewhat different. See *Zhongguo Tongji Nianjian 1987* (p. 369) and *1988* (p. 769). The difference seems mainly to be an adjustment in the 'other' categories and in enterprise deposits.

25 See *Statistical Yearbook of China 1986* (p. 530).

26 Other versions of these balances call this item 'money advanced to the Ministry of Finance'. See, for example, *1882/3 China Official Annual Report*, English edition, Hong Kong: Kingsway International Publishers, 1982 (p. 452).

27 It was this consideration that probably induced Friedman (1980) to describe Chinese monetary planners as monetarists. See *Huobi Liutong Guanli Xue* (1985: 25–6) for a brief summary of Chinese monetary-policy objectives.

28 See also *Jianming Jinrong Cidian* (1984: 152–3).

29 See *Beijing Review*, no. 35, 29 August–4 September 1988 (pp. 8–9).

30 This shows one way in which socialist governments react to emerging market processes, here a black market competing with the official one; the government either accepts them and tries to benefit from them itself, or forbids them. Here the black market was virtually recognised and legitimised and the government took it over. Certain other market processes were stopped.

31 Aimed at encouraging exports this de facto recognition of a further devalued *Renminbi* had discouraging effects on foreign joint ventures that

were earning *Renminbi* and wished to repatriate some of their profits. They were forced to the swap centres to buy foreign exchange at this unfavourable rate. I know of some joint ventures that were established around 1985 at a time when they thought that they would be able to buy foreign exchange at the official rate. They suffered as they were forced, unexpectedly and illegally in the minds of some partners, to deal at the swap centres at a disadvantageous exchange rate. As Kwon (1989: 266–7) shows, inflation and devaluation also increase the effective tax rate paid by overseas direct investors in China.

Chapter 5

1 It is almost certain that they are the same person. Zheng (1986a: 56) describes the author as a researcher in the Finance and Banking department of Zhongnan Finance and Economics University and Zheng (1986b: 53) simply as working at Zhongnan Finance and Economics University.
2 Peebles (1983) points out this large increase but refers to it as the 'money accumulation ratio', that is, the proportion of household income not being returned to the state sector in any period and hence accumulating as household holdings of currency and savings deposits.
3 Naughton (1986) reports *t*-statistics and Naughton (1987) standard errors.
4 Recently published Chinese data show sustained excess demand for the entire period 1983–88 (Li Ping, 1990: 24; Peebles, 1990).
5 It is interesting to note this way of putting a point that has no doubt occurred to many people studying planned economies. Many of the relationships observed in capitalist economies do appear to be reversed there. This would make a good basis for an empirical comparative study of basic economic phenomena in the two systems. It recalls Joseph Stalin's prose, especially in Russian, in which he would list features of capitalist economies (supply exceeds demand, for example) and then, for each observation, say that 'with us, it's the other way around' (*u nas naoborot*).
6 Chen's source for the currency series for 1952–83, including the 1952 figure, is Chow (1987: 324). His data for 1984 and 1985 are from the *Statistical Yearbook of China 1986* (p. 530). His figure for 1985 is given as 987.38 (100 million *yuan*) whereas the correct figure is 987.83. Correcting both figures would probably not change the results much.

Chapter 6

1 These statements are based on Peebles (1985: 42–4) on the basis of various Chinese sources of the early 1980s. More recently, Ash (1988: 541) states that in 1979 the grain above-quota price rose by a further 50 per cent. This is ambiguous and cannot be correct. In fact Sicular (1988: 684) gives the same over-quota bonus figures as Peebles (1985) using different Chinese sources; that is, the 30 per cent bonuses for grain and oil crops that were offered in the 1970s were both increased to 50 per cent in 1979, and a bonus of 30 per cent was introduced for cotton.
2 Average price would also rise as extra output is sold at higher market prices. The statistics on sales do not allow us to separate the different markets precisely.
3 See the analysis of the Macroeconomic Research Office, Economic Structure Reform Research Institute of China, in its 'An analysis of the economic situation in 1986', *Chinese Economic Studies*, spring 1988 (pp. 9–11 in particular).
4 The data are probably not an accurate reflection of savings deposit holdings. Farmers who visit towns to sell their produce often have accounts at

an urban branch. Urban residents are less likely to have deposits in rural branches. The change in the definition of a town makes comparisons with the years after 1983 impossible.

5 The figure given for 1984 of 49 413 must be a misprint (for 4 941 perhaps). It is repeated in other editions and in the Mainland Chinese editions such as *Zhongguo Tongji Nianjian 1986* (p. 615) and *1988* (p. 768).

6 See *Huobi Liutong Guanli Xue* (1985: 15).

7 See *Huobi Liutong Guanli Xue* (1985: 15–16).

8 This graph follows the method of presentation of Naughton (1986: 34).

9 See *Huobi Liutong Guanli Xue* (1985: 16–17).

10 For example, in Hong Kong, the currency ratio increased from 0.66 in December 1984 to 0.74 in February 1985 and the money multiplier (of *M1*) fell from 2.13 to 2.00 (Peebles, 1988: 152).

11 The correct currency figure for 1952, the first observation, is considerably lower than the one used by Chow (1987): 2.75 against his 3.855. In a simple two-variable regression for the period 1952–83 this would tend to reduce the slope coefficient, but it would not do so in the regression for the longer period 1952–85.

12 A regression using the currency data of Table I.1 and real national income (index form) yields the result

$$\underset{}{\ln P} = \underset{(0.0469)}{1.0902} + \underset{(0.0158)}{0.2686} \ln (CRC/RNI) \qquad \begin{aligned} R^2 &= 0.9006 \\ s &= 0.0318 \\ DW &= 1.2577 \\ n &= 34 \end{aligned}$$

The slope coefficient remains the same.

13 This view was formulated before I had any data to construct any measure of *PPI*, so it can be regarded as an hypothesis, not just as an ex post reconstruction obtained by examining the data and their relationship.

14 See Wang (1988) and Peebles (1989) for different interpretations of these events.

15 This issue of the possible lag of price changes behind *PPI* can be settled by the following result for 1954–85:

$$\text{pd}P = \underset{(0.4981)}{0.6538} + \underset{(0.0598)}{0.2286}\, PPI + \underset{(0.0614)}{0.1545}\, PPI_{-1} \qquad \begin{aligned} R^2 &= 0.5076 \\ s &= 2.7286 \\ F[2, 29] &= 14.94 \\ DW &= 1.8299 \\ n &= 33 \end{aligned}$$

There *is* such a lagged effect, and it shows up in the regression of list prices on the same variables. The Chinese economists identified in note 2 believe that in China the lag of price increases behind demand expansion is six months to one year. Hence, imbalances detected in the middle of a year could produce price increases in the following year.

16 These regressions and statements are based on a value of pd*LP* for 1984 of 6.4. This figure could be only 2.7 (see the discussion in the notes to Table III.2). If this figure is used, the regressions become for the 33 observations

$$\text{pd}LP = \underset{(0.3069)}{0.7140} + \underset{(0.0353)}{0.1593}\, PPI \qquad \begin{aligned} R^2 &= 0.3966 \\ s &= 1.7108 \\ DW &= 1.5303 \\ n &= 33 \end{aligned}$$

and for the seventeen observations

$$\text{pd}LP = 1.2217 + 0.2076\ PPI \qquad R^2 = 0.5599$$
$$(0.4853)\quad (0.0475) \qquad s = 1.8902$$
$$DW = 2.0447$$
$$n = 17$$

The conclusions remain the same.

17 For empirical purposes it is not really necessary to perform the regressions of pd*LP* on *PPI* in order to show that pd*P* is a function of *PPI*. Scientific method just requires the assumption that *list* prices are the dominant element of the retail price index (*pace* Chow, 1987), an hypothesis explaining when list prices will be changed and then evidence that the general retail price index does actually change in these circumstances. The regression of pd*LP* on *PPI* is just a link in establishing the dependence of pd*P* on *PPI*; it could be omitted but is included in the text as extra evidence of *why* the general retail price index changes.

18 It can be seen that 1970 was a year of large negative *PPI* in Table III.2, and this explains why national monetary holdings fell in this year.

19 Not all these differences can be attributed to the unit price increases as revenue from the same volume of commodities will increase as the composition of consumption shifts to relatively more expensive items, in which case the average price paid will rise.

20 These are the verdicts of the economists of the Macroeconomic Research Office, Structural Reform Research Institute of China. See *Chinese Economic Studies*, spring 1988 (p. 16), cited in note 2.

21 There were no observations of other possible combinations.

22 This figure is similar to the time series graphs of the price index and an index of money per unit output used to illustrate the Quantity Theory. See, for example, M. Friedman and R. Friedman (1980: 300–6). Such graphs have to be supported by strong and acceptable arguments about the direction of causation.

23 Nearly all of *RNI* is produced by the state sector, and as long as state production grows at a roughly similar rate as *RNI* then the *SPP*/*RNI* ratio will remain a good indicator of changes in the state sector's unit costs.

24 Western economists would tend to explain the causation as follows. In the bottom sections of Figure 6.8 the budget deficit and the growth of currency exert expansionary effects on aggregate demand by shifting the *IS* and *LM* curves to the right. In the face of less than perfectly elastic aggregate supply the shift in demand increases the price level and real output. The increase in the price level leads to a revision of inflationary expectations, and these shift the supply curve upwards, producing higher inflation and so on. However, the budget deficit is not an exogenous policy instrument used for expanding demand in China, nor is the amount of currency in circulation.

25 This may explain why Chinese economists in the 1980s said that the Cultural Revolution period saw excessive currency growth. This is not really true, but it shows that there was unexpectedly high currency growth given the state of the budget.

26 For example, on 7 February there was a demand that the purchasing power of social groups be strictly controlled, on 13 February there was a circular calling for the strengthening of price management and inspection, and on 10 August there was a promise that economic punishments would be meted out to those who violated price regulations. See *Lishide Xiongbian: A Sketch of Chinese Economy: 1949–1988* (pp. 415–16).

27 Other changes, such as the switch to taxes on enterprises instead of profit

remissions after 1983, also would have contributed to the budget deficit by reducing revenue from enterprises, and this revenue did fall steadily after 1979. After 1979 the revenue from industrial and commercial taxes became a more important source of revenue, rising from 40.3 per cent of total revenue in 1978 to 53.8 per cent in 1985.

28 See *Zhongguo Maoyi Wujia Tongji Ziliao 1952–83* (p. 402). The periods 1962–65 and 1967–1970 saw falling grain procurement costs and also a falling *SPP* ratio.

29 See *Lishide Xiongbian: a Sketch of Chinese Economy: 1949–1988* (p. 273), which plots four time series of price increases including the general retail price index, the grain procurement price index and agricultural byproducts. These computer-generated graphs are very interesting but must be interpreted with care. The price data are plotted as percentages of the previous year's figure. They naturally fluctuate around a horizontal line drawn roughly through the average of the observations. The height of this line is not specified, but by measuring its position on the marked axes it appears to be at about 106 per cent. In other words the line chosen for reference is a line of *constant inflation*, not constant price level, and the fluctuations around it are fluctuations in the annual inflation rate.

30 The simple correlation coefficient of *acc* on *ppi* for the first four periods is minus 0.973 and for the last three it is 0.950, but visual inspection is enough to confirm this interpretation.

31 This is an obvious point, but just to establish it we can quote a private trader in China in the mid 1980s: 'I need to be very careful and not to let the Government know how much I have' (Chung, 1989: 142). Note the use of 'have', not 'earn', and that this quotation is put in the context of fears of confiscation of savings deposits, not the imposition of taxes on income.

32 See *Lishide Xiongbian: A Sketch of Chinese Economy: 1949–1988* (p. 389).

33 See *Lishide Xiongbian: A Sketch of Chinese Economy: 1949–1988* (p. 404).

34 *People's Republic of China Yearbook 1985* (p. 307) states this in article 6 of the regulations applying to the 1985 bond issue.

35 Slightly different figures for Treasury Bond issue for 1984 and 1985 are given in *People's Republic of China Official Report 1986*, Beijing: Xinhua Publishers and Hong Kong: NCN Ltd (p. 321).

36 These are the rates given in the *People's Republic of China Yearbook 1986* (p. 324). The rates given by Tam for 1985 (1987: 101) are not for one-year fixed deposits as labelled but for six-month deposits.

37 Alternatives to a monetary explanation would be real explanations of the 'pressure on resources' type. In this view high rates of growth of real output put pressure on resources, driving up costs and hence prices. No detailed attempt to test such alternative views has been made here, but the evidence offered above goes against it. So does the following also. It might be expected that, if output grows more rapidly than planned, disproportions may arise and monetary planning may be upset, leading to price increases. I examined this view by looking at the divergence of actual industrial growth from planned industrial growth and at the resulting changes in retail prices. A pressure-on-resources view would expect to see a positive correlation; greater than planned industrial growth causes inflation. Using an interesting series of data of planned annual industrial growth rates in Chen Yue (1988: 84) I regressed pd*P* on the difference between the actual industrial growth rate and the planned rate for the

period 1953–85, omitting 1968 and 1969 as no data are reported and using the average of the planned figures given for 1975 and 1976. The results are a *negative* association; greater than planned industrial growth is associated with low inflation rates and vice versa. This is consistent with the view offered above that output growth is an indicator of supply availability. It must be admitted that this negative correlation largely depends on two outliers: 1961, of very low growth compared with plan and high open inflation, and 1958, of very high growth compared with plan and very moderate inflation. The remaining observations are just a cluster with no discernible pattern.

Chapter 7

1 A Keynesian economist, concentrating as is his or her wont on the short run in an actual economy, would add that it probably also depends on the existing rate of utilisation of capacity. Full utilisation and low unemployment years would produce high inflation and a low real output response, whereas years of underutilised capacity and high unemployment would probably see large real output increases and possibly moderate inflation.

2 The policies produced falling real retail sales for the first time in over ten years, large stockpiles of high-quality consumer goods, new marketing strategies by shops to turn inventories into cash, consumer expectations of falling prices, enterprises unable to meet their wage bill and paying workers 30 per cent in government bonds (there had been forced bond allocations to the population on a quota basis towards the end of 1988 also), many township enterprises being forced to close down because of the credit squeeze, unpaid bills and so on. See Lian (1989) for a brief account, and *Jiushi Niandai*, no. 11, 1989 (p. 6) for an interesting report on how Shanghai shops were tempting customers to buy by guaranteeing to take back any item sold and to refund the whole price or by guaranteeing to refund the difference between price paid and any future lower price. Interestingly, at about the same time the American motor car industry was doing the same thing to deal with its unsold stocks of recently produced cars.

3 *China News Analysis*, no. 1398, 1 December 1989 (p. 6).

4 This is shown by the facts that the ratio of highest to lowest value for the years 1980–87 is 11.4 for the monetary ratio and 5.7 for the *PPI* ratio, and that the coefficient of variation is 0.71 for the former and 0.46 for the latter. This shows that there is less variance in the pd*P*/*PPI* ratio. Similar relations hold for the period 1980–88.

5 If pd*P* equals pd*SPP* minus the percentage increase in retail sales in constant prices, *m* will stay constant. In the definition of *PPI*, pd*RNI* is used as a proxy for the increase in the supply of real retail sales. This is tantamount to assuming that the proportion of *RNI* that consists of consumer goods remains constant and that sales from stocks are ignored.

6 Most of the figures in this section were calculated from data in the statistical section of *Fenjinde Sishi Nian 1949–1989* (1989).

7 *Lishide Xiongbian* (p. 433). Another source (Lian, 1990: 49) is surprisingly conservative and puts the amount at 80 billion *yuan*, as does Liu Guoguang (1990: 15).

8 *Lishide Xiongbian* (1989: 436–7).

9 I owe this information to Dr On-kit Tam.

10 For comparison, typical figures of government revenue as a percentage of national income or a related concept for the mid 1980s for some economies are as follows: Hungary 59 per cent, the United Kingdom 43 per

cent, the United States 22 per cent, Singapore 44 per cent and Hong Kong 15 per cent. China's figure, then, is much closer to that of Hong Kong and the United States, which are relatively less interventionalist economies than Singapore or the United Kingdom. These ratios were calculated from data in *International Financial Statistics Yearbook 1987* (passim.).

11 See *China News Analysis*, no. 1398 (p. 1), which seems to cite the proportions from *Renmin Ribao*, 23 July 1987 and 2 September 1989 and *Caizheng* (Public Finance), no. 3, 1989 and no. 5, 1989. The figures cited in the text were calculated from the appropriate figures in *Fenjinde Sishi Nian 1949–1989* (1989: 340, 423). The author seems not to trust statistical yearbooks and uses data reluctantly ('numbers . . . may also hide some sophistry', p. 2) although they are essential to the argument advanced. He or she prefers the old-fashioned China-studies approach of relying on many diverse newspaper reports and articles as all his or her data are cited from such sources, not from convenient statistical yearbooks.

12 See *Zhongguo: Jinrong yu Touzi* (1989: 23).

13 Another possible example of price decontrol and inflation control in a 'planned economy' is sometimes thought to be provided by the experience of West Germany after the Second World War when a command war economy was liberalised. Japan's similar experiences are sometimes offered as a model also. However, in the German case there is controversy over what actually happened in this policy area.

14 The United States in the late 1980s was an economy that had a large government deficit with very limited monetary growth.

15 For example, they state that, in the case of the Construction Bank, out of 597 loan applications during some period, fewer than 1 per cent of the total were rejected. No source is given, and they obviously interpret less than 1 per cent as a small number.

16 I have had to estimate the data of *SPP* for 1987 and 1988 for the following reason. The *Statistical Yearbook of China 1987* (p. 480) contains a consistent series for the entire period 1952–86. Unfortunately, the later Chinese-language sources report a series that breaks in 1985, making the data for 1986 and after non-comparable. Interestingly, the *Statistical Yearbook of China 1988* (p. 611) reports the Chinese-language data source, even for the year 1986. I have taken the complete comparable series for the years 1952–86 and extended it to 1987 and 1988 by increasing the 1986 figure in the *Statistical Yearbook of China 1987* (as this is comparable with the 1985 figure) by the successive annual percentage increases in the series in the Chinese sources. These figures are comparable for 1986 and after. See *Zhongguo Tongji Nianjian 1989* (p. 599) for the required annual percentage increases.

The effect of the revision of the *Zhongguo Tongji Nianjian* series was to make the *SPP* for 1986 less than the previously published figure, meaning that anyone using the revised series to compute indicators of excess demand using absolute figures would get a lower number and a lower rate of increase in *SPP* for 1986.

Before the publication of *Zhongguo Tongji Nianjian 1989* there was confusion over the *SPP* figure for 1988, which requires clearing up. Wan (1989: 52) clearly states that for 1988 'social commodity purchasing power reached 870.0 billion *yuan* and was 5.4 times the 1978 level growing at an average annual growth rate of 18.4 per cent [*shehui shangpin goumaili da 8700 yi yuan, bi 1978 nian zengzhang 4.4 bei, pingjun meinian zengzhang 18.4%*]'. However, the relevant 1978 figure that I take for *SPP* (as it is labelled '*shehui shangpin goumaili, huobi shouru zong e*', *Zhongguo*

Tongji Nianjian 1988, p. 683) is 176.52 billion. Wan's 1988 figure is only 4.9 times this figure, not 5.4 times (increasing by 4.4 *bei* in Chinese means increasing to 5.4 times the original level). *Lishide Xiongbian* (1989: 436) states that in 1988 *shangpin goumaili* (commodity purchasing power) reached 870 billion *yuan* (*ba qian qi bai yi yuan*) and was 27 per cent higher than in the previous year. However, the *Zhongguo Tongji Nianjian 1988* figure for 1987 is 757.3, so 870 was only 14.9 per cent more than this. *Lishide Xiongbian* gives no comparable figure for 1987 to help establish exactly which concept is being referred to. The 870 billion *yuan* figure seems much too low. This is indicated by the fact that *VRS* in 1988 was 744 billion *yuan* and total unspent purchasing power was 127.11 billion *yuan*, which items in themselves total about 871 billion *yuan*. In addition to retail sales and monetary accumulation there are other items of expenditure that are met out of *SPP*. In 1987, for example, these totalled 72.8 billion *yuan*, and there is no reason to believe that they were any lower in 1988. This puts the 1988 *SPP* at a minimum of 944 billion *yuan*. Taking Wan's statement that the 1988 figure was 5.4 times that of 1978 gives 953 billion *yuan*; using *Lishide Xiongbian*'s that it was 27 per cent higher in 1987 gives 962 billion. I had the feeling that the statement that the 1988 figure grew 27 per cent over the 1987 figure was likely to be accurate. In fact the figure of 960.3 billion *yuan* eventually published in *Zhongguo Tongji Nianjian 1989* (p. 599) is 26.8 per cent more than the 1987 figure and 5.44 times the 1978 figure. This is obviously the correct figure. The increase in this 1988 figure over that of 1987, that is, 26.8 per cent, has been used to compute the 1988 figure in absolute terms, so it is comparable with the data before 1987. See above.

References

I have used *Hanyu pinyin* to transliterate all Chinese proper names and titles. If a name has been transliterated using a different system in a cited translation, I have retained the original, supplementing it wherever possible with the *pinyin* version; for example, Po Yi-po is Bo Yibo. Two-character Chinese names have caused problems for some citers in the past and have often been listed according to the given name, not surname. For example, Chao Kang, Chi Ti and Lin Wei (surnames first) have sometimes been listed under Kang, Ti and Wei—this last case probably due to the publisher's own mistake on the book's cover. As far as I have been able to ascertain these people are surnamed Chao, Chi and Lin respectively, although Wei is also a surname. Against my own inclination I have listed K.H.Y. Huang Hsiao under Hsiao, not Huang Hsiao, because she herself does so. Chinese proper names in *pinyin* are given without a comma between surname and given name(s), following the Chinese practice. However, when only the surname and initials are known and used in the cited source, a comma is used to separate the surname and the initials as would be the case with an English name. If a Chinese language source also carries an English title, this has been given as part of the complete title even if it is not a direct translation of the Chinese title.

'A mystery: where is the money going?' (1988) *China News Analysis* no. 1366a, 15 August

Abbott, Graham J. (1984) 'National saving and financial development in Asian developing countries' *Asian Development Review* vol. 2, no. 2, pp. 1–22

—— (1985) 'A survey on savings and financial development in Asian developing countries' *Saving and Development* no. 4, pp. 395–419

Adam, Jan (1979) *Wage Control and Inflation in Soviet Bloc Countries* London: Macmillan

—— (ed.) (1982) *Employment Policies in the Soviet Union and Eastern Europe* New York: St Martin's Press

Agliardi, E. (1988) 'Microeconomic foundations of macroeconomics in the post-Keynesian approach' *Metroeconomica* vol. 39, no. 3, pp. 275–97

Amelung, Gerold (1982) *Die Rolle der Preise in der Industriallen Entwicklung der Volksrepublick China 1961–1976* (The Role of Prices in the Industrial Development of the People's Republic of China) Hamburg: Mitteilungen des Instituts für Asienkunk Hamburg

Arndt, H.W. (1983) 'Financial development in Asia' *Asian Development Review* vol. 1, no. 1, pp. 86–100

Artis, M.J. and Lewis, M.K. (1981) *Monetary Control in the United Kingdom* London: Philip Allan

Ash, Robert F. (1988) 'The evolution of agricultural policy' *The China Quarterly* no. 116, December, pp. 529–55

Ashbrook Jnr, Arthur G. (1967) 'Main lines in Chinese economic policy' in US Congress (1967) pp. 15–44

—— (1972) 'China: economic policy and economic result, 1934–71' in US Congress (1972) pp. 3–51

Asian Development Outlook 1990 (1990) Manila: Asian Development Bank

Asselain, Jean-Charles (1981) 'Mythe ou réalité de l'epargne forcée dans les pays socialistes (Fiction or fact of forced saving in socialist countries)' in Lavigne (1981) pp. 115–50

Auyeung Pak-kuen (1989) 'Operational problems of mainland China's tax system: 1949–85' *Issues and Studies* vol. 25, no. 6, June, pp. 72–94

Bachman, David (1987) 'Implementing Chinese tax policy' in Lampton (1987) pp. 119–53

—— (1989) 'The Ministry of Finance and Chinese politics' *Pacific Affairs* vol. 62, no. 2, Summer, pp. 167–87

Balasa, B. (1982) 'Economic reform in China' *Banca Nazionale del Lavoro Quarterly Review* (National Labour Bank Quarterly Review) no. 142, September, pp. 307–33

'Banking reform favours centralization' (1984) (interview with Lu Peijian) *Beijing Review* no. 15, 9 April, pp. 16–18

Barber, Noel (1979) *The Fall of Shanghai: the Communist Takeover of 1949* London: Macmillan

Barnham, Oliver (1988) 'Banking and financial reform in China' *China News Analysis* no. 1356, 15 March

Barro, Robert J. (1987) *Macroeconomics* 2nd edn, New York: Wiley

Barro, Robert J. and Grossman, H.I. (1974) 'Suppressed inflation and the supply multiplier' *Review of Economic Studies* vol. 41, January, pp. 87–104

Baumol, William (1952) 'The transactions demand for cash: an inventory theoretic approach' *Quarterly Journal of Economics* vol. 66, November, pp. 545–56

Baumol, William and Tobin, James (1989) 'The optimum cash balance proposition: Maurice Allais' priority' *Journal of Economic Literature* vol. 27, no. 3, September, pp. 1160–2

Bennett, Gordon (ed.) (1978) *China's Finance and Trade: a Policy Reader* White Plains, NY: M.E. Sharpe

Berger, Roland (1974), 'Financial aspects of Chinese planning' *Bulletin of Concerned Asian Scholars* vol. 6, no. 2, April–August, pp. 15–19

Bertinelli, Roberto (1981) 'Alcune considerazioni sulla moneta nella PRC (Some thoughts on money in the People's Republic of China)' *Revista Internazionale di Scienze Economiche e Commerciali* (International Review of Economics and Commerce) vol. 28, September, pp. 852–63

Bettelheim, Charles (1988) 'Economic reform in China' *Journal of Development Studies* vol. 24, no. 4, July, pp. 15–49

Birman, Igor (1980a) 'The financial crisis in the USSR' *Soviet Studies* vol. 32, no. 1, January, pp. 84–105

—— (1980b) 'A reply to Professor Pickersgill' *Soviet Studies* vol. 32, no. 4, October, pp. 586–91

—— (1981) *Secret Incomes of the Soviet State Budget* The Hague: Martinus Nijhoff

Birman, Igor and Clarke, Roger (1985) 'Inflation and the money supply in the Soviet economy' *Soviet Studies* vol. 37, no. 4, October, pp. 494–504

Bonavia, David (1980) *The Chinese* New York: Lippincott and Crowell

Bordo, Michael D. (ed.) (1989) *Money, History, and International Finance: Essays in Honor of Anna J. Schwartz* Chicago and London: University of Chicago Press

Bordo, Michael D. and Jonung, Lars (1981) 'The long-run behaviour of the income velocity of money in five advanced countries, 1870–1975: an institutional approach' *Economic Enquiry* vol. 19, no. 1, January, pp. 96–116

—— (1987) *The Long-run Behaviour of the Velocity of Circulation* Cambridge: Cambridge University Press

—— (1988) 'Some questions about the test of the institutional hypotheses of the long-run behaviour of velocity: a reply' *Economic Enquiry* vol. 26, no. 3, pp. 547–9

Borisov, V. (1966) *Balans Denezhnikh Dokhodov i Raskhodov Naseleniya* (The Balance of Money Incomes and Expenditures of the Population) Moscow

Bornstein, Morris (ed.) (1979) *Comparative Economic Systems: Models and Cases* 4th edn, Homewood, Ill.: Irwin

Bortolani, Sergio and Santorum, Anita (1984) *Moneta e Banca in Cina* (Money and Banking in China) Milan: Finafrica

Bos, P.C. (1969) *Money in Development* Rotterdam: Rotterdam University Press

Bowles, Paul and White, Gordon (1989) 'Contradictions in China's financial reforms: the relationship between banks and enterprises' *Cambridge Journal of Economics* vol. 13, no. 4, December, pp. 481–95

Brada, J.C. and King, A.E. (1986) 'Taut plans, repressed inflation and the supply of effort in centrally planned economies' *Economics of Planning* vol. 20, pp. 162–78

Brotman, David (1985) 'Reforming the domestic banking system' *The China Business Review* no. 2, March–April, pp. 17–23

Brunner, Karl (1987), 'Money supply' in Eatwell, Milgate and Newman (1987) vol. 3, pp. 527–9

Buck, Trevor and Cole, John (1987) *Modern Soviet Economic Performance* Oxford: Basil Blackwell

Bucknall, Kevin (1979) 'Capitalism and Chinese agriculture, 1960–1966' *The Australian Journal of Chinese Affairs* no. 1, January, pp. 69–90

Butterfield, Fox (1983) *China—Alive in the Bitter Sea* London: Coronet

Byrd, William (1983) *China's Financial System: the Changing Role of Banks* Boulder, Col.: Westview Press

—— (1987a) The Market Mechanism and Economic Reforms in Chinese Industry, unpublished PhD thesis, Harvard University, March

—— (1987b) 'The impact of the two-tier plan/market system in Chinese industry' *Journal of Comparative Economics* vol. 11, no. 3, September, pp. 295–308; also in Reynolds (1988) pp. 5–18

Cagan, Phillip (1989) 'Money-income causality—a critical review of the literature since *A Monetary History*' in Bordo (1989) ch. 3

The Cambridge Encyclopedia of China (1982) Cambridge: Cambridge University Press

The Cambridge Encyclopedia of Russia and the Soviet Union (1982) Cambridge: Cambridge University Press

'Can China's prices be stabilized?' (1981) (interview with Liu Zhuofu) *Beijing Review* no. 20, 18 May, pp. 21–2

Capie, Forrest and Weber, Alan (1985) *A Monetary History of the United Kingdom 1870–1982* vol. 1, London: George Allen and Unwin

Cassel, Dieter (1984) *Inflation in Socialist Planning Economies: Causes, Effects and Policy Options of Inflation in Soviet-type Command Economies* Discussion Paper no. 64, Duisburg: Fachbereich Wirtschaftswissenschaft Universitat Duisburg Gesanthochshule, July

—— (1990) 'Phenomenon and effects of inflation in centrally planned socialist economies' *Comparative Economic Studies* vol. 32, no. 1, Spring, pp. 1–41

Cassou, Pierre-Henri (1974) 'The Chinese monetary system' *The China Quarterly* no. 59, July/September, pp. 559–66; also in *Chinese Economic Studies* vol. 9, no. 4, Summer 1976; and in Bennett (1978), pp. 171–85

CIA (Central Intelligence Agency) (1989) *The Chinese Economy in 1988 and 1989: Reforms on Hold, Economic Problems Mount* Report to the Subcommittee on Technology and National Security, 7 July, Washington, DC

Chai, C.H. (1981) 'Money and banking reforms in China' *Hong Kong Economic Papers* no. 14, pp. 37–52

Chai, Joseph C.H. (1987a) 'Introduction: China's economic reforms: an interim assessment' in Chai and Leung (1987) pp. viii–xviii

—— (1987b) 'Reform of China's industrial prices 1979–1985' in Chai and Leung (1987) pp. 584–608

Chai, Joseph C.H. and Leung, C.K. (eds) (1987) *China's Economic Reforms* Occasional Papers and Monographs no. 73, Hong Kong: Centre of Asian Studies, University of Hong Kong

Chan, Thomas M.H. (1987) 'China's price reform in the period of economic reform' *The Australian Journal of Chinese Affairs* no. 18, July, pp. 85–108

—— (1989) 'China's price reform in the 1980s' in Cheng (1989) ch. 9

Chandavarkar, Anand G. (1977) 'Monetization of developing economies' *International Monetary Fund Staff Papers* vol. 24, no. 3, pp. 665–721

Chandler, Lester Vernon (1962) *Central Banking and Economic Development* Bombay: University of Bombay Press

Chang Chun-qiao (Zhang Chunqiao) (1975) *On Exercising All-round Dictatorship over the Bourgeoisie* Peking: Foreign Languages Press

Chang Kia-ngau (1958) *The Inflationary Spiral: the Experience in China, 1939–50* Cambridge, Mass.: Wiley and the Technology Press of the Massachusetts Institute of Technology

Chang, Valerie (1989) 'The new look of China's banks' *The China Business Review* May–June, pp. 20–2

Chao Kang (1970) *Agricultural Production in Communist China 1949–1965* Madison: University of Wisconsin Press

Charemza, W. and Gronicki, M. (1988) *Plans and Disequilibrium in Centrally-Planned Economies: Empirical Investigations for Poland* Amsterdam: North-Holland

Charlesworth, Harold Karl (1956) *The Economics of Repressed Inflation* London: George Allen and Unwin

Chen Chien-Hsun (1989) 'Monetary aggregates and macroeconomic performance in mainland China' *Journal of Comparative Economics* vol. 13, no. 2, June, pp. 314–24

Chen Hsi-yüan (1989) 'Mainland China's economic difficulties' *Issues and Studies* vol. 25, no. 9, September, pp. 71–84

Chen Nai-ruenn (1967) *Chinese Economic Statistics* Chicago: Aldine

Chen Nai-ruenn and Chi-ming Hou (1986) 'China's inflation, 1979–1983: measurement and analysis' *Economic Development and Cultural Change* vol. 34, no. 4, July, pp. 811–35

Chen Nai-ruenn and Galenson, Walter (1969) *The Chinese Economy under Communism* Chicago: Aldine

Chen Te-sheng (1990) 'The interaction between economic and political reform in mainland China, 1978–89' *Issues and Studies* vol. 26, no. 2, February, pp. 13–34

Chen Wenlin (1984) 'Controversies over the value basis of the Renminbi' *Social Sciences in China* vol. 5, no. 4, December, pp. 23–44

—— (1989) *Zhongguo Huobi Zhengce Gaige Jianlun* (A Brief Essay on the Reform of China's Monetary Policy) Peking: China Finance and Economics Publishing House

Chen Yige (1990) 'Renminbi bianzhi: yuanyin yu yingxiang (The *Renminbi* devaluation: reasons and effects)' *Jiushi Niandai* (The Nineties), no. 1, pp. 52–3

Chen Youping (1989) 'Dui woguo tonghuo pengzhangde shenceng fansi (A deep reassessment of inflation in China)' *Caizheng Yanjiu* (Financial Research), no. 7, pp. 27–31

Chen Yue (1988) 'Zhongguo jingji zhouqi wenti yanjiu (Research on economic cycles in China)' in Zhang Fengbo (1988b) ch. 3

Chen Yun (1949) 'The problem of commodity prices and the issuance of government bond' in China Committee for the Promotion of International Trade (1952 year of publication) pp. 33–58

—— (1950a) 'The economic situation and problems concerning readjustment of industry, commerce and taxation' in China Committee for the Promotion of International Trade (1952) pp. 61–78

—— (1950b) 'Financial and economic situation in the People's Republic of China during the past year' in China Committee for the Promotion of International Trade (1952)

Cheng Cho-yuan (1954) *Monetary Affairs of Communist China* Hong Kong: The Union Research Institute

Cheng Chu-yuan (1957) *Income and Standard of Living in Mainland China* 2 vols, Hong Kong: The Union Research Institute

—— (1963) *Communist China's Economy 1969–1962: Structural Changes and Crisis* South Orange, NJ: Seton Hall University Press

—— (1971) *The Economy of Communist China 1949–1969* Michigan Papers for Chinese Studies no. 9, Ann Arbor: University of Michigan Press

—— (1982) *China's Economic Development: Growth and Structural Change* Boulder, Col.: Westview Press

Cheng, Elizabeth (1989) 'China on the cheap' *Far Eastern Economic Review* 28 December, p. 39

Cheng Hang-Sheng (1981) 'Money and credit in China' *Federal Reserve Bank of San Francisco Economic Review* Fall, pp. 19–36

—— (ed.) (1986) *Financial Policy and Reform in Pacific Basin Countries* Lexington, Mass.: D.C. Heath

—— (1987) 'Monetary policy and inflation in China' paper presented at the Challenges to Monetary Policy in Pacific Basin Countries Conference at the Federal Reserve Bank of San Francisco, 23–5 September; revised version in Cheng (1988) pp. 401–29

—— (ed.) (1988) *Monetary Policy in Pacific Basin Countries* Boston: Kulwer Academic Publishers

Cheng, Joseph Y.S. (ed.) (1989) *China: Modernization in the 1980s* Hong Kong: Chinese University Press

Cheng Zhiping (1986) 'Dangqian jiage gaigede jige wenti' (Some issues of current price reform)' *Hong Qi* (Red Flag) no. 1, pp. 14–17

Chi Ti (1975) 'Stable prices and the reasons' *Peking Review* no. 19, 9 May, pp. 17–20

Chi Ts'ai ch'eng (Ji Caicheng) (1961) *A Brief Review of Comprehensive Financial Planning* Peking, October; trans. and published by CCM Information Corporation, New York, 1970

China—a General Survey (1981) new rev. edn, Peking: Foreign Languages Press

China: ASEAN Bankers Examine China's Rural Banking System (1984) United Nations: Economic and Social Commission for Asia and the Pacific

China Committee for the Promotion of International Trade (1952) *New China's Economic Achievements* Peking

China Monthly Statistics (monthly) Chicago

China Trade and Price Statistics (1987) Hong Kong: New World Press and China Statistical Information and Consultancy Service Centre

Chinn, Dennis L. (1980) 'Basic commodity distribution in the People's Republic of China' *The China Quarterly* no. 84, December, pp. 744–54

'China's banks face challenge of new financing policies' (1981) (interview with Li Baohua) *Economic Reporter* (Hong Kong) August, pp. 8–10

China's Economy and Development Principles (A Report by Premier Zhao Ziyang) (1982) Peking: Foreign Languages Press

'China's stock and bond market' (1989) *Beijing Review* no. 44, 30 October–5 November, pp. 20–3

Chou Chao-yang (1961) 'Discussion of the problem of currency under the socialist system' *Guangming Ribao* (Enlightenment Daily) 21 January; trans. in *Translations of Communist China's Trade, Finance, Transportation and Communications* no. 38, New York: CCM Information Corporation, 1970

Chou Shun-hsin (1963) *The Chinese Inflation 1937–1949* New York: Columbia University Press

Chow, Gregory C. (1985a) *The Chinese Economy* New York: Harper and Row

—— (1985b) 'A model of Chinese national income determination' *Journal of Political Economy* vol. 93, no. 4, August, pp. 782–92

—— (1986) 'Chinese statistics' *The American Statistician* vol. 40, no. 3, August, pp. 191–6

—— (1987) 'Money and price level determination in China' *Journal of Comparative Economics* vol. 11, no. 3, September, pp. 319–33; also in Reynolds (1988) pp. 29–43

—— (1988) 'Economic analysis of the People's Republic of China' *Journal of Economic Education* vol. 19, no. 1, Winter, pp. 53–64

Chrystal, K. Alec (1989) 'In defence of monetarism' in Llewellyn (1989) pp. 37–57

Chung, Helene (1989) *Shouting from China* Ringwood, Vic.: Penguin Australia

Coats, Warren L. and Khatkhate, Denna R. (eds) (1980) *Money and Monetary Policy in Less Developed Countries: A Survey of Issues and Evidence* Oxford: Pergamon Press

Cody, John, Hughes, Helen and Wall, David (eds) (1980) *Policies for Industrial Progress in Developing Countries* New York: Oxford University Press for the World Bank

Cole, David C. (1988) 'Financial development in Asia' *Asian–Pacific Economic Literature* vol. 2, no. 2, September, pp. 26–47

Committee on the Working of the Monetary System: Report (1959) (Radcliffe Report) Command 827, London: Her Majesty's Stationery Office; reprinted 1970

Congdon, Tim (1989) 'Credit, broad money and the economy' in Llewellyn (1989) pp. 59–82

Constitution of the People's Republic of China (December 4 1982) (1983) Peking: Foreign Languages Press

'Contradictions between socialist principles and "capitalist" development' (1986) *Asian Monetary Monitor* May–June, pp. 11–22

Cowitt, Philip P. (ed.) *World Currency Yearbook 1984* Brooklyn: New York International Currency Analysis

Crump, Thomas (1981) *The Phenomenon of Money* London: Routledge and Kegan Paul

Darby, Michael R., Mascaro, Angelo R. and Marlow, Michael L. (1989) 'The empirical reliability of monetary aggregates as indicators: 1983–1987' *Economic Inquiry* vol. 27, no. 4, October, pp. 555–85

Davis, Christopher and Charemza, Wojciech (eds) (1989) *Models of Disequilibrium and Shortage in Centrally Planned Economies* London: Chapman and Hall

Davis, James A. (1985) *The Logic of Causal Order* Sage University Paper Series on Quantitative Applications in the Social Sciences, series no. 55, Beverly Hills: Sage Publications

Day, Richard B. (1975) 'Preobrazhensky and the theory of the transition period' *Soviet Studies* vol. 27, no. 2, April, pp. 196–219

De Wulf, L. (1985a) 'Economic reform in China' *Finance and Development* March, pp. 8–12

—— (1985b) 'Financial reform in China' *Finance and Development* December, pp. 19–22

De Wulf, L. and Goldsbrough, D. (1986) 'The evolving role of monetary policy in China' *International Monetary Fund Staff Papers* vol. 33, no. 2, June, pp. 209–42

'Decision of the Central Committee of the Communist Party of China on reform of the economic structure (20th October 1984)' (1984) *Beijing Review* no. 44, 29 October

Decision of the Central Committee of the Communist Party of China on Reform of the Economic Structure (20th October 1984) (1984) Hong Kong: Joint Publishing Co.

Deleyne, Jan (1973) *The Chinese Economy* London: Andre Deutsch

Delfs, Robert (1982) 'The high cost of stable prices' *Far Eastern Economic Review* 12 March, pp. 84–6

—— (1986) 'Peking cuts its losses' *Far Eastern Economic Review* 17 July, pp. 50–1

—— (1989) 'Carry on Mr Li' *Far Eastern Economic Review* 2 November, pp. 49–50

Dembinski, Pawel, H. (1988) 'Quantity versus allocation of money: monetary problems of the centrally planned economies reconsidered' *Kyklos* vol. 41, fasc. 2, pp. 281–300

Deng Ziji (principal ed.) (1981) *Caizheng yu Xindai* (Finance and Credit) Peking: China Finance and Economics Publishing House

Dernberger, Robert F. (1985) 'Mainland China's economic system: a new model or variations on an old theme?' *Issues and Studies* vol. 21, no. 4, April, pp. 44–72

Desai, M. (1981) *Testing Monetarism* London: Frances Pinter

Desai, P. (ed.) (1983) *Marxism, Central Planning, and the Soviet Economy* Cambridge, Mass.: MIT Press

Dirksen, Erik (1981) 'The control of inflation? Errors in the interpretation of CPE data' *Economica* vol. 48, August, pp. 305–8

Dobb, Maurice H. (1948) *Soviet Economic Development since 1917* London: Routledge and Kegan Paul

Documents of the First Session of the Fourth National People's Congress of the People's Republic of China (1975) Peking: Foreign Languages Press

Documents of the First Session of the Fifth National People's Congress of the People's Republic of China (1978) Peking: Foreign Languages Press

Dong Fureng (1980) *Shehuizhuyi Zaishengchan he Guomin Shouru Wenti* (Issues of Reproduction and National Income under Socialism) Peking: Sanlian Bookstore

—— (1982) 'Relationship between accumulation and consumption' in Xu (1982) pp. 79–101

—— (1986) 'China's price reform' *Cambridge Journal of Economics* vol. 10, pp. 291–300

Donnithorne, Audrey (1967) *China's Economic System* London: George Allen and Unwin

—— (1974) 'China's anti-inflationary policy' *The Three Banks Review* no. 103, September, pp. 3–25

—— (1978) 'The control of inflation in China' *Current Scene* vol. 16, nos 4–5, April–May, pp. 1–11

—— (1983a) 'The Chinese economy today' *Journal of Northeast Asian Studies* vol. 2, no. 3, September, pp. 3–21

—— (1983b) 'Fiscal relations' *The China Business Review* November–December, pp. 25–7

—— (1989) 'Reform of the fiscal and banking systems in China' in Cheng (1989) pp. 355–87

Drake, P.J. (1980) *Money, Finance and Development* Oxford: Martin Robertson

Durand, Francois J. (1965) *Le Financement du Budget en Chine Populaire: un Example de Développement Fiscal dans une Économie de Croissance* (Financing the Budget in the People's Republic of China: an Example of Fiscal Development in a Growing Economy) Hong Kong: Editions Sirey

E-Han Jingji Cihui (1982) (A Russian–Chinese Economic Lexicon) Peking: China Social Sciences Publishing House

Eatwell, J., Milgate, M. and Newman, P. (eds) (1987) *The New Palgrave: A Dictionary of Economics* London: Macmillan Press

Eckland, George N. (1973) 'Banking and finance' in Wu (1973) pp. 579–93

Eckstein, Alexander (1976) *China's Economic Development: the Interplay of Scarcity and Ideology* Ann Arbor: University of Michigan Press

—— (1977) *China's Economic Revolution* Cambridge: Cambridge University Press

—— (ed.) (1980) *Quantitative Measures of China's Economic Output* Ann Arbor: University of Michigan Press

Eckstein, Alexander, Galenson, W. and Lin Ta-ching (1968) *Economic Trends in Communist China* Chicago: Aldine

'Economic structural imbalance: its causes and corrections' (1989) *Beijing Review* no. 36, 4–10 September, pp. 18–24

Egawa, Hiyoshi (1981) 'Chinese statistics: how reliable?' *China Newsletter* no. 33, July–August, pp. 12–15

Ellman, Michael (1989) *Socialist Planning* 2nd edn, Cambridge: Cambridge University Press

Engels, Frederick (1978) 'Preface' to the first German edition of Marx (1978)

Engle, Tom (1985) 'Reforming the labour system' *The China Business Review* vol. 12, no. 2, March/April, pp. 40–4

—— (1986) 'Stocks: new domestic financial tool' *The China Business Review* vol. 13, no. 1, January/February, pp. 35–8

Erdös, T. (1989) 'Monetary regulation and its perplexities in Hungary' *Acta—conomica* vol. 40, nos 1–2, pp. 1–15

Erlich, Alexander (1967) *The Soviet Industrialization Debate 1924–1928* Cambridge, Mass.: Harvard University Press

Etienne, Gilbert (1974) *La Voie Chinoise: la Longue Marche de l'Économie 1949–74* (The Chinese Way: the Long March of the Economy 1949–74) Paris: Presses Universitaires de France

Ezekiel, H. and Adekunle, J.O. (1969) 'The secular behaviour of income and velocity' *International Monetary Fund Staff Papers* vol. 16, no. 2, pp. 224–37

Farrell, John P. (1989) 'Financial "crisis" in the CPEs or "vsyo normalno"?' *Comparative Economic Studies* vol. 31, no. 4, Winter, pp. 1–9

Feltenstein, Andrew and Farhadian, Ziba (1987) 'Fiscal policy, monetary targets, and the price level in a centrally planned economy: an application to the case of China' *Journal of Money, Credit, and Banking* vol. 19, no. 2, May, pp. 137–56

Feltenstein, Andrew, Lebow, David and van Wijnbergen, Sweder (1990) 'Savings, commodity market rationing, and the real rate of interest in

China' *Journal of Money, Credit, and Banking* vol. 22, no. 2, May, pp. 235–52

Feng Gongqi (1989) 'Tigao xiaoyi yin tonghuo pengzhang er shi qi kuguo (Increase efficiency and reap the bitter fruits due to inflation)' *Caijing Wenti Yanjiu* (Research on Financial and Economic Issues) no. 6, pp. 1–8

Fenjinde Sishi Nian 1949–1989 (1989) (Forty Years of Struggle and Progress) Peking: China Statistical Publishing House

Feuchtwang, Stephan and Hussain, Athar (eds) (1983) *The Chinese Economic Reforms* London: Croom Helm

Field, Robert Michael, McGlynn, Kathleen M. and Abnett, William B. (1978) 'Political conflict and industrial growth in China: 1965–77' in US Congress (1978) vol. 1, pp. 239–83

'Financial reforms fare well in China' (1987) *Beijing Review* no. 1, 5 January, pp. 16–19

Fisher, Douglas (1971) *Money and Banking* Homewood, Ill.: Irwin

Fleming, Miles (1972) *Monetary Theory* London: Macmillan

Friedman, Milton (1959) 'The demand for money: some theoretical and empirical results' *Journal of Political Economy* vol. 67, no. 4, August, pp. 327–51

—— (1968a) 'Money: quantity theory' *International Encyclopedia of the Social Sciences* vol. 10, New York: Macmillan and the Free Press, pp. 432–47

—— (1968b) 'The role of monetary policy' *American Economic Review* vol. 58, no. 1, March, pp. 1–17

—— (1969) *The Optimum Quantity of Money and Other Essays* Chicago: Aldine

—— (1973) *Money and Development* New York: Praeger

—— (1980) 'Marx and money' *Newsweek* 27 October, p. 49

—— (1987a) 'The quantity theory of money' in Eatwell, Milgate and Newman (1987) vol. 4, pp. 3–20

—— (1987b) 'Review of Thomas J. Sargent *Rational Expectations and Inflation*' *Journal of Political Economy* vol. 95, no. 1, February, pp. 218–21

Friedman, Milton and Friedman, Rose (1980) *Free to Choose* Harmondsworth: Penguin

Friedman, Milton and Schwartz, Anna J. (1963) *A Monetary History of the United States, 1867–1960* Princeton: Princeton University Press

—— (1982) *Monetary Trends in the United States and the United Kingdom* Chicago and London: University of Chicago Press

Frisch, Helmut (1983) *Theories of Inflation* Cambridge: Cambridge University Press

Fry, Maxwell J. (1978) 'Money, capital or financial deepening in economic development' *Journal of Money, Credit, and Banking* vol. 10, no. 4, November; reprinted in Coats and Khatakhate (1980) pp. 107–13

—— (1980) 'Saving, investment, growth and the cost of financial repression' *World Development* vol. 8, pp. 317–27

—— (1984) 'Saving, financial intermediation and economic growth in Asia' *Asian Development Review* vol. 2, no. 1, pp. 82–91

—— (1988) *Money, Interest and Banking in Economic Development* Baltimore and London: Johns Hopkins University Press

Fujimoto, Akira (1980) 'The reform of China's financial administrative system' *China Newsletter* no. 25, March, pp. 2–9

—— (1983a) 'China's fiscal and financial reforms' *China Newsletter* no. 44, May–June, pp. 2–7, 17

—— (1983b) 'China's state finance in the course of readjustment' *China Newsletter* no. 45, July–August, pp. 2–9

Furusawa, Kenji (1984) 'Pricing China's industrial products: difficulties in the reform of China's pricing system' *China Newsletter* no. 52, September–October, pp. 2–6

Gablis, Vicente (1977) 'Financial intermediation and economic growth in less-developed countries: a theoretical appraisal' *Journal of Development Studies* vol. 13, no. 2, January, pp. 58–72; reprinted in Coats and Khatakhate (1980)

Gailliot, Henry John (1973) Long Run Determinants of the Distribution of International Reserves, unpublished PhD dissertation, Carnegie-Mellon University

Galbraith, John Kenneth (1975) *Money: Whence it Came, Where it Went* Harmondsworth: Penguin

Gao Shangquan (principal ed.) (1987) *Zhongguo: Fazhang yu Gaige* (China: Development and Reform) Chengdu: Sichuan People's Publishing House

Gardner, H. Stephen (1988) *Comparative Economic Systems* New York: Dryden Press

Garvy, George (1964) 'The role of the state bank in soviet planning' in Nove and Degras (1964) pp. 46–76

—— (1972) 'The monetary system and the payments flow' in Nove and Nuti (1972) pp. 275–306

—— (1977) *Money, Financial Flows, and Credit in the Soviet Union* Cambridge, Mass.: National Bureau of Economic Research

Gedeon, Shirley Jean (1982) Yugoslav Monetary Theory and its Implications for Self-Management, unpublished PhD dissertation, University of Massachusetts, September

—— (1985–86) 'The post Keynesian theory of money: a summary and an Eastern European example' *Journal of Post Keynesian Economics* vol. 8, no. 2, pp. 208–21

Ghatak, Subrata (1981) *Monetary Economics in Developing Countries* London: Macmillan

Goldsmith, Raymond W. (1969) *Financial Structure and Development* New Haven and London: Yale University Press

Goodhart, Charles (1987) 'Monetary base' in Eatwell, Milgate and Newman (1987) vol. 3, pp. 500–2

—— (1989) 'The conduct of monetary policy' *Economic Journal* vol. 99, June, pp. 293–346

Goodstadt, Leo (1975) 'Peking's firm hold on the money supply' *Far Eastern Economic Review* 13 June, pp. 39–40

—— (1976) 'China: debating the role of money' *Far Eastern Economic Review* 2 January, pp. 31–5

Gordon, Robert J. (1987) *Macroeconomics* 4th edn, Boston: Little Brown

Gowland, David (1984) *Controlling the Money Supply* 2nd edn, London: Croom Helm

Griffiths, Brian and Wood, Geoffrey E. (eds) (1984) *Monetarism in the United Kingdom* London: Macmillan in association with the Centre for Banking and International Finance, the City University

Griliches, Zvi (1985) 'Data and econometricians—the uneasy alliance' *American Economic Review—Papers and Proceedings* vol. 75, no. 2, May, pp. 196–205

Guanghuide Sanshiwu Nian, 1949–84 (1984) (Glorious Thirty-Five Years, 1949–84) Peking: China Statistics Publishing House

Gupta, K.L. (1984) *Finance and Economic Growth in Developing Countries* London: Croom Helm

Gurley, John G. (1976) *China's Economy and the Maoist Strategy* New York and London: Monthly Review Press

Gutowski, A., Arnaudo, A.A. and Scherrer, H-E. (eds) (1985) *Financing Problems of Developing Countries* London: Macmillan

Grassman, Sven and Lundberg, Erik (1981) *The World Economic Order: Past and Prospects* London: Macmillan

Haddad, L. (1977) 'Inflation under socialism' *Australian Economic Papers* June, pp. 44–52

Han Guojian (1989) 'Moonlighting craze hits China' *Beijing Review* no. 45, 6–12 November, pp. 21–3

Hansen, Bent (1951) *A Study in the Theory of Inflation* London: George Allen and Unwin

Harris, J.W. (1979) 'Financial deepening as a prerequisite to investment growth' *The Developing Economies* vol. 17, no. 3, September, pp. 245–308

Harris, Laurence (1981) *Monetary Theory* New York: McGraw-Hill

Hartwig, Karl-Hans (1983) 'Involuntary liquid assets in Eastern Europe: some critical remarks' *Soviet Studies* vol. 35, no. 1, January, pp. 103–5

Haulaman, Clyde A. (1987) 'Financial innovation and the Chinese enterprise' *Journal of Northeast Asian Studies* vol. 6, no. 2, Summer, pp. 67–74

He Daofeng, Duan Yingbi and Yuan Chongfa (1987) 'Lun woguo jinnian tonghuo pengzhangde fasheng jizhi yu jiegou biaoxian (On the causative mechanism and structural manifestation of our inflation in recent years)' *Jingji Yanjiu* (Economic Research) no. 11, pp. 21–8

Heinsohn, Gunnar and Steiger, Otto (1989) 'The veil of barter: the solution to "the task of obtaining representations of an economy in which money is essential"' in Kregel (1989) pp. 175–201

Hendry, D.H. and Ericsson, N.R. (1983) 'Assertion without empirical basis: an econometric appraisal of Friedman and Schwartz *Monetary Trends in . . . the United Kingdom*' in Bank of England, Panel of Academic Consultants *Monetary Trends in the United Kingdom* Panel Paper no. 22, Bank of England, October, pp. 45–101

Hewett, Ed A. (1989) 'Economic reforms in the USSR, Eastern Europe, and China: the politics of economics' *American Economic Review—Papers and Proceedings* vol. 79, no. 2, May, pp. 16–20

Hicks, John (1977) *Economic Perspectives: Further Essays on Money and Growth* Oxford: Clarendon Press

—— (1986) 'Abdication of money' *Hong Kong Economic Papers* no. 17, pp. 1–10

Hidasi, G. (1975) 'China's economy in the mid-1970s and its development perspectives' *Acta—conomica* vol. 14, pp. 355–81

—— (1979) 'China's economy in the late 1970s and its development prospects up to the mid-1980s' *Acta—conomica*, vol. 23, pp. 157–91

—— (1981) 'China's economy in the nineteen-eighties' *Acta—conomica* vol. 27, pp. 141–62

Hirsch, Fred and Goldthorpe, John H. (eds) (1978) *The Political Economy of Inflation* Oxford: Martin Robertson

Hishida, Masaharu (1984) 'China's customs clearance statistics and general administration of customs' *China Newsletter* no. 48, January–February, pp. 16–18

Ho, Henry C.Y. (1987) 'Distribution of profits and the change from profit remittance to taxation for state enterprises in China' in Chai and Leung (1987) pp. 562–83

Hooke, A.W. (ed.) (1983) *The Fund and China in the International Monetary System* n.p., probably Washington, DC: International Monetary Fund

Hosjoi, Yasushi (1985) 'China's present financial system' *China Newsletter* no. 58, September–October, pp. 7–10

Howard, David H. (1976a) 'A note on hidden inflation in the Soviet Union' *Soviet Studies* vol. 28, no. 4, October, pp. 599–608

—— (1976b) 'The disequilibrium model in a controlled economy: an empirical test of the Barro–Grossman model' *American Economic Review* vol. 66, no. 5, December, pp. 871–9

—— (1979a) *The disequilibrium Model in a Controlled Economy* Lexington: D.C. Heath

—— (1979b) 'The disequilibrium model in a controlled economy: reply and further results' *American Economic Review* vol. 69, no. 4, September, pp. 733–8

—— (1982) 'Hidden inflation in the Soviet Union: a final reply' *Soviet Studies* vol. 34, no. 2, April, pp. 300–3

Howe, Christopher (1973) *Wage Patterns and Wage Policy in Modern China, 1919–1972* Cambridge: Cambridge University Press

—— (1978) *China's Economy: A Basic Guide* London: Paul Elek/Granada

Hsia, Ronald (1955) *Economic Planning in Communist China* New York: International Secretariat, Institute of Pacific Relations

Hsia Wei (1975) 'Long-term balance in revenue and expenditure' *Peking Review* no. 20, 16 May, pp. 15–17

Hsiao, Gene T. (1977) *The Foreign Trade of China: Policy, Law and Practice* Berkeley: University of California Press

Hsiao, Katharine H.Y. Huang (1971) *Money and Monetary Policy in Communist China* New York and London: Columbia University Press

—— (1982) 'Money and banking in the People's Republic of China: recent developments' *The China Quarterly* no. 91, September, pp. 462–75

—— (1984) *Money and Banking in the Chinese Mainland* Taipei: Chung-hua Institution for Economic Research

—— (1987) *The Government Budget and Fiscal Policy in Mainland China* Taipei: Chung-hua Institution for Economic Research

Hsu, John C. (1982) 'Economic reforms in China: an assessment' *Asian Affairs* vol. 4, no. 3, September, pp. 253–62

—— (1989) *China's Foreign Trade Reforms: Impact on Growth and Stability* Cambridge: Cambridge University Press

Hsu, Robert C. (1982) *Food for One Billion: China's Agriculture since 1949* Boulder, Col.: Westview Press

Hu Xiaofen and Han Shuying (principal eds) (1983) *Zhongguo Shehuizhuyi Jingji Wenti Taolun Gangyao* (An Outline of Discussions of the Economic Problems of Chinese Socialism) Jilin: Jilin People's Publishing House

Huang Da (1981) 'Some problems concerning pricing' *Social Sciences in China* vol. 2, no. 1, March, pp. 136–56

—— (1985) 'Guanyu kongzhi huobi gongjiliang wentide tantao (On inquiries into the problem of controlling the money supply)' *Caimao Jingji* (Finance and Trade Economics) no. 7, pp. 1–8

Huang Da, Chen Gong, Hou Mengchan, Zhou Shengye and Han Yingjie (1981) *Shehuizhuyi Caizheng Jinrong Wenti* (Issues of Socialist Public Finance and Banking) 2 vols, Peking: People's University Publishing House

Huang Xu (1988a) 'Woguo huobi gongqiu yu jiage shuiping jueding (The demand and supply of money and the determination of the price level in China)' *Jingji Yanjiu* (Economic Research) February, pp. 35–45

—— (1988b) 'Huobi gongqiu fenxi (An analysis of the supply and demand for money)' in Zhang Fengbo (1988b) ch. 6

Hughes, T.J. and Luard, D.E.T. (1961) *The Economic Development of Communist China 1949–1961* 2nd edn, London: Oxford University Press

Huobi Liutong Guanli Xue (1985) (The Study of the Management of Monetary

Circulation) Xi'an: Economic Science Training Centre of the Chinese Federation of Economics Organizations

Igarashi, Masaki (1985) 'Bonds in China' *China Newsletter* no. 59, November–December, pp. 7–11, 22

Information China (1989) 3 vols, Oxford: Pergamon Press

Ishihara, Kyoichi (1983) 'The price problem and economic reform' *China Newsletter* no. 46, September–October, pp. 2–7

Jackman, Richard, Mulvey, Charles and Trevithick, James (1981) *The Economics of Inflation* 2nd edn, Oxford: Martin Robertson

Jackson, Sukhan (1984) 'Profit sharing, state revenue and enterprise performance in the PRC' *The Australian Journal of Chinese Affairs* no. 12, July, pp. 98–112

Jao, Y.C. (1967–68) 'Some notes on repressed inflation: a suggested interpretation of money and prices in Communist China, 1950–57' *Union College Journal* vol. 6, pp. 99–114

—— (1976) 'Financial deepening and economic growth: a cross section analysis' *Malayan Economic Review* April, pp. 47–58

—— (1985) 'Financial deepening and economic growth: theory, evidence and policy' *Greek Economic Review* vol. 7, no. 3, December, pp. 187–225

—— (1986) 'Banking and currency in the Special Economic Zones' in Jao and Leung (1986) pp. 160–83

Jao, Y.C. and Leung, C.K. (eds) (1986) *China's Special Economic Zones: Policies, Problems and Perspectives* Hong Kong: Oxford University Press

Jiang Jiajun, You Xianxun and Zhou Zhenhan (1989) *Zhonghua Renmin Gongheguo Jingji Shi* (An Economic History of the People's Republic of China) Xi'an: Shanxi People's Publishing House

Jianming Jiage Cidian (1982) (A Concise Dictionary of Prices) Tianjin: Tianjin People's Publishing House

Jianming Jinrong Cidian (1984) (A Concise Dictionary of Finance) Tianjin: Tianjin People's Publishing House

Jin Li (1987) 'Dui lilü gaigede huigu yu sikao (A look back on and reflections on interest rate reform)' *Zhongguo Jinrong* (Chinese Finance) no. 8, pp. 38–40

Jingji Da Cidian—Caizheng Juan (1987) (The Great Economics Dictionary—Public Finance Volume) Shanghai: Shanghai Dictionary Publishing House

Jingji Da Cidian—Jinrong Juan (1987) (The Great Economics Dictionary—Money and Banking Volume) Shanghai: Shanghai Dictionary Publishing House

Johnson, D. Gale (1983) 'Discussion of Chen and Hou' in *Conference on Inflation in East Asian Countries* Taipei: Chung-hua Institution for Economic Research, pp. 443–6

Kaldor, Nicholas (1970) 'The new monetarism' *Lloyds Bank Review* no. 97, July, pp. 1–17; reprinted in Kaldor (1978)

—— (1978) *Further Essays on Applied Economics* London: Duckworth

—— (1983) *The Economic Consequences of Mrs Thatcher* London: Duckworth

—— (1985) *The Scourge of Monetarism* 2nd edn, Oxford: Oxford University Press

Kane, Penny (1988) *Famine in China, 1959–61: Demographic and Social Implications* London: Macmillan

Katz, Barbara (1979) 'The disequilibrium model in a controlled economy: comment' *American Economic Review* vol. 69, no. 4, September, pp. 721–5

Kemme, David M. (1989) 'The chronic excess demand hypothesis' in Davis and Charemza (1989) pp. 83–99

Kincade, William H. and Thomson, T. Keith (1990) 'Economic conversion in the USSR: its role in *perestroyka*' *Problems of Communism* January–February, pp. 83–92

King, Frank H.H. (1968) *A Concise Economic History of Modern China* Bombay: Vora and Co.

Klatt, W. (1979) 'China's new economic policy: a statistical appraisal' *The China Quarterly*, no. 80, December, pp. 716–33

Klenner, Wolfgang and Wiesgart, Kurt (1983) *The Chinese Economy: Structure and Reform in the Domestic Economy and in Foreign Trade* New Brunswick and Oxford: Transaction Books

Knaack, Rudd (1980) 'Economic reform in China' *ACES Bulletin* vol. 23, no. 2, Summer, pp. 1–30

Ko, C.T. (Ge Zhida) (1957) *China's Budget During the Transition Period* Peking; trans. and published by CCM Information Corporation, New York, 1970

—— (1962) 'The role of the state bank in socialist construction' *Da Gongbao* (Impartial Daily) (Peking) 15 October; reprinted in *Translations of Communist China's Trade, Finance, Transportation and Communications* New York: CCM Information Corporation, 1970

Kobayashi, Hironao (1987) 'Reform in the Chinese wage system' *China Newsletter* no. 67, March–April, pp. 10–18

Kojima, Reitsu (1985) 'Characteristics of China's present agricultural policy' *China Newsletter* no. 58, September–October, pp. 2–6

Komiya, Ryutaro (1989) 'Macroeconomic development of China: "overheating" in 1984–1987 and problems for reform' *Journal of the Japanese and International Economies* vol. 3, March, pp. 64–121

Kornai, János (1976) 'Pressure and suction on the market' in Thornton (1976)

—— (1980a) *Economics of Shortage* vols A and B, Amsterdam: North-Holland

—— (1980b) 'The dilemmas of a socialist economy: the Hungarian experience' *Cambridge Journal of Economics* no. 4, pp. 147–57

—— (1982) *Growth, Shortage and Efficiency* Oxford: Blackwell

—— (1986a) *Contradictions and Dilemmas: Studies on the Socialist Economy and Society* Cambridge, Mass.: MIT Press

—— (1986b) 'The soft budget constraint' *Kyklos* vol. 39, fasc. 1, pp. 3–30

Korzec, Michel and Whyte, Martin King (1981) 'The Chinese wage system' *The China Quarterly* no. 86, June, pp. 248–73

Kosta, Jiri and Meyer, Jan (1976) *Volksrepublik China* (The People's Republic of China) Frankfurt-am-Main: Europaische Verlagsanstalt

Kraus, Wily (1987) 'Private enterprise in the People's Republic of China: official statement, implementations and future prospects' in Chai and Leung (1987) pp. 64–97

Kregel, J.A. (ed.) (1989) *Inflation and Income Distribution in Capitalist Crisis* London: Macmillan

Kueh, Y.Y. (1989) 'The Maoist legacy and China's new industrialization strategy' *The China Quarterly* no. 119, September, pp. 420–47

—— (1990) 'Growth imperatives, economic recentralization and China's open door policy' *The Australian Journal of Chinese Affairs* no. 24, July, pp. 93–119

Kuschpèta, O. (1978) *The Banking and Credit System of the USSR* Boston: Martinus Nijhoff

Kwang Ching-wen (1966) 'The economic accounting system of state enterprises in mainland China' *International Journal of Accounting, Education, Research* vol. 1, no. 2, Spring, pp. 61–99

Kwon, O. Yul (1989) 'An analysis of China's taxation of foreign direct investment' *The Developing Economies* vol. 27, no. 3, September, pp. 251–68

Laidler, David E.W. (1985) *The Demand for Money: Theories, Evidence, and Problems* 3rd edn, New York: Harper & Row

Lampton, David M. (ed.) (1987) *Policy Implementation in Post-Mao China* Berkeley: University of California Press

Lardy, Nicholas R. (ed.) (1977) *Chinese Economic Planning* White Plains, NY: M.E. Sharpe

—— (1983a) *Agriculture in China's Modern Economic Development* Cambridge: Cambridge University Press

—— (1983b) *Agricultural Prices in China* World Bank Staff Working Papers, no. 606, Washington, DC: World Bank

—— (1983c) 'Subsidies' *The China Business Review* November–December, pp. 21–4

Lardy, Nicholas R. and Lieberthal, K. (eds) (1983) *Chen Yun's Strategy for China's Development: a non-Maoist Alternative* Armonk, NY: M.E. Sharpe

Laski, Kazimierz (1979) 'The problem of inflation in socialist countries' *East European Economics* Summer, pp. 3–84

Lavigne, Marie (1974) *The Socialist Economies of the Soviet Union and Europe* White Plains, NY: International Arts and Sciences Press

—— (ed.) (1981) *Travail et Monnaie en Système Socialiste* (Work and Money in the Socialist System) Paris: Economica

—— (1986) 'The creation of money by the state bank of the USSR' in Smith (1986) ch. 6

Lee, Tim (1985) 'People's Republic of China: problems of monetary control' *Asian Monetary Monitor* vol. 9, no. 4, pp. 13–21

Li Chengrui (1984) 'Are the 1967–76 statistics on China's economy reliable?' *Beijing Review* no. 12, 19 March, pp. 21–6

—— (1986) 'Money supply and macroeconomic controls' *Social Sciences in China* vol. 7, no. 3, September, pp. 51–62

—— (1986–87) 'An important question in macroeconomic management' *Chinese Economic Studies* vol. 20, no. 2, Winter, pp. 3–12

Li Chengrui and Zhang Zhongji (1982) 'Remarkable improvement in living standards' *Beijing Review* no. 17, 26 April, pp. 15–18, 28

Li Choh-ming (1959) *Economic Development of Communist China* Berkeley: University of California Press

—— (1962) *The Statistical System of Communist China* Berkeley: University of California Press

Li Chonghuai (1982) 'On the new stage in the development of monetary forms' *Social Sciences in China* vol. 3, no. 4, December, pp. 14–45

Li Fang (1985) 'Woguo huobi liutong liang daihou wenti tantao (An enquiry into the monetary lag question in our country)' *Shuliang Jingji Jishu Jingji Yanjiu* (Quantitative and Technical Economic Research) no. 6, pp. 41–7

Li Fuchen (1981) 'Youguan shehuizhuyi guojia tonghuo pengzhangde jige wenti (On several questions of inflation under socialism)' *Zhongguo Jinrong* (Chinese Finance) June, pp. 24–5, 4

Li Jun and Xia Xiaoxun (1986) 'Xiaofei pengzhang: gaige yu fazhan mianlinde yanjun tiaozhan (Consumption expansion: a serious challenge to reform and development)' in *Gaige: Women Mianlinde Tiaozhan yu Xuanze* compiled by the China Economic System Reform Research Institute Comprehensive Survey Group, Peking: China Economics Publishing House, pp. 90–111

Li Maosheng (1985) 'Yijiubasi nian huobi liutongde xingshi he womende duice (The monetary circulation situation in 1984 and our policy reaction)' *Caimao Jingji* (Finance and Trade Economics) no. 3, pp. 51–5

Li Ping (1989) 'Initial success for economic rectification and improvement' *Beijing Review* no. 48, 27 November – 3 December, pp. 16–18

—— (1990) 'China's inflation—its causes and plans for control' *Beijing Review* no. 8, 19–25 February, pp. 24–8

Li Rongchun (1982) 'Tantan chuxu he shangpin xiaoshoude guanxi (A discussion of the relationship between savings and commodity sales)' *Zhongguo Jinrong* (Chinese Finance) no. 22, pp. 34–5

Li Shuhe (1987) 'Huobi liutong sude biandong guize (Regularities in the change in money velocity)' *Caimao Jingji* (Finance and Trade Economics) no. 7, pp. 40–6, 6

Li Shurong (1985) 'Huobi liutong liang yao tong shangpin liutong keguan xuyao liang xiang shiying (The quantity of money in circulation must correspond to the objective demands from the amount of commodity circulation)' *Caimao Jingji* (Finance and Trade Economics), no. 8, pp. 40–1

Li Xiannian (1959) 'Zenyang renshi nongcun caimao guanali tizhi gaige (How to understand the improvement of the rural financial and commercial management system)' *Hongqi* (Red Flag) no. 2, pp. 1–8

Li Yining (1986) 'A preliminary study of the adjustment effects of monetary measures on China's present macroeconomy' *Social Sciences in China* vol. 7, no. 4, December, pp. 55–64

Lian Huawen (1989) 'Zhongguo jingji da huapo (The crash of China's economy)' *Jiushi Niandai* (The Nineties) no. 11, pp. 18–19

—— (1990) 'Da huapoxiade zhongguo jingji (China's economy during the crash)' *Jiushi Niandai* (The Nineties) no. 1, pp. 49–50

Liang Youcai and Klein, Lawrence R. (1989) 'The two-gap paradigm in the Chinese case: a pedagogical exercise' *China Economic Review* vol. 1, no. 1, Spring, pp. 1–8

Lilü Wenjian Huibao (1986) (Collected Documents on Interest Rates) compiled by the People's Bank of China Planning Department, n.p.: China Finance Publishing House

Lin Jiken (1981) 'Kongzhi huobi faxing, wending jinrong wujia (Control money issue, stabilize finance and prices)' *Zhongguo Jinrong* (Chinese Finance) no. 3, pp. 20–1

Lin Wei and Chao, Arnold (eds) (1982) *China's Economic Reforms* Philadelphia: University of Pennsylvania Press

Lin Ye (1989) 'Lun xiaofei jiegou biandong dui jingji zengzhang jiegou bianhuade yingxiang (On the influence of changes in the structure of consumer demand on the composition of economic growth)' *Xiaofei Jingji* (Consumer Economics) no. 2, pp. 17–22

Ling Bin (1982) 'Zhongguode wujia he wujia guanli (Prices and price management in China)' in *Zhongguo Jingji Nianjian 1982* (Economic Yearbook of China, 1982) pp. V-349–53

—— (1988) 'Food subsidies to float with price index' *Beijing Review* no. 14, 4–10 April, p. 4

Lippit, Victor D. (1974) *Land Reform and Economic Development in China: a Study of Institutional Change and Development Finance* White Plains, NY: International Arts and Sciences Press

Lishide Xiongbian: Zhongguo Jingji 1949–1988 Nian Sumiao: A Sketch of Chinese Economy: 1949–1988 (1989) Peking: China Economics Publishing House

Liu Guangdi (1981) 'Lun zhibi he huangjinde lianxi (On the relationship between paper money and gold)' *Zhongguo Shehui Kexue* (Social Sciences in China) no. 3, pp. 67–82

Liu Guoguang (1990) 'Retrenchment: a boon to reform' *Beijing Review* no. 3, 15–21 January, pp. 15–16

Liu Guoguang et al. (1986) 'Economic restructuring and macroeconomic management' *Social Sciences in China* vol. 7, March, pp. 9–35

Liu Hongru (1980) *Shehuizhuyi Huobi yu Yinhang Wenti* (Issues of Socialist Money and Banking) Peking: China Financial Economics Publishing House

—— (1986) 'Zhongguo yinhangde hongguan tiaojie he kongzhi (Macroeconomic adjustment and control by the central bank)' *Caijing Kexue* (Finance and Economics Science), no. 5, pp. 1–9

Liu, J.Y.W. (1962) 'Monetary system of Communist China' in Szczepanik (1962) pp. 72–81

Liu Suinian and Wu Qungan (1986) *China's Socialist Economy: An Outline History (1949–1984)* Peking: Beijing Review

Liu Ta-chung and Yeh Kung-chia (1965) *The Economy of the Chinese Mainland: National Income and Economic Development, 1933–1959* Princeton, NJ: Princeton University Press

Liu, William H. (1985) 'Foreign trade factor in a centrally planned economy' *Issues and Studies* vol. 21, no. 4, April, pp. 73–107

Liu Yusheng, Chu Xiangyan, Han Feng and Zheng Baoxin (1984) *Shehui Goumailide Diaocha yu Yuce* (The Investigation and Forecasting of Social Purchasing Power) Harbin: Heilongjiang People's Publishing House

Liu Zhuofu (1982) 'Zenyang kan dangqian shichang wujia wenti (How to view the present market price question)' *Hongqi* (Red Flag), no. 2, pp. 33–6

Llewellyn, David T. (ed.) (1989) *Reflections on Money* London: Macmillan

Lomax, Rachel (1984) 'Bade and Parkin: Is £M3 the right aggregate?' in Griffiths and Wood (1984) pp. 294–330

Lothian, James R. (1985) 'Equilibrium relations between money and other variables' *American Economic Review* vol. 74, no. 4, September, pp. 828–36

Lu Baifu, Wang Dashu and Wang Guangqian (eds) (1989) *Tonghuo Pengzhang Wenti Yanjiu* (Research on the Issue of Inflation) Peking: China Finance and Economics Publishing House

Lu Kequn (1982) 'Kongzhi bushi xiao shangpin shengchan wending huobi liutong (Control does not suit commodity production stabilising money circulation)' *Caimao Jingji* (Finance and Trade Economics) no. 12, pp. 17–20

Lu Yun (1984a) 'Rural responsibility system (I) Peasants' initiative unleashed by contracts' *Beijing Review* no. 44, 29 October, pp. 18–21, 29

—— (1984b) 'Rural responsibility system (II) Is it a retreat to capitalism?' *Beijing Review* no. 45, 5 November, pp. 23–5

—— (1984c) 'Rural responsibility system (III) Gap between rich and poor is bridged' *Beijing Review* no. 46, 12 November, pp. 24–7

—— (1984d) 'Rural responsibility system (IV) Will farm mechanization be slowed?' *Beijing Review* no. 47, 19 November, pp. 20–2

—— (1984e) 'Rural responsibility system (V) Specialized households emerge' *Beijing Review* no. 49, 3 December, pp. 23–7

Lucas, Robert E. (1980) 'Two illustrations of the quantity theory of money' *American Economic Review* vol. 70, no. 5, December, pp. 1005–14

Luo Gengmo (1982a) 'Wo guode tonghuo pengzhang yu xifang guojiade qubie (The difference between inflation in our country and that in Western countries)' *Caimao Jingji* (Finance and Trade Economics) no. 9, pp. 1–3

—— (1982b) 'Socialism and inflation' *Beijing Review* no. 44, 1 November, pp. 20–3

Luo Hanxian (1985) *Economic Change in Rural China* Peking: New World Press

Lutz, Robert E. (1983) 'The general administration for the control of industry and commerce' *The China Business Review* March–April, pp. 25–9

Lyons, Thomas P. and Wang Yan (1988) *Planning and Finance in China's*

Economic Reforms Cornell University East Asia Papers no. 46 Ithica, NY: East Asia Program, Cornell University

Ma Hong (principal ed.) (1982a) *Xiandai Zhongguo Jingji Shidian* (The Contemporary Chinese Economy: a Compendium) Peking: China Social Sciences Publishing House

—— (1982b) *Zhongguo Jingji Tiaozheng Gaige yu Fazhan* (The Adjustment and Reform of the Chinese Economy) Shanxi People's Publishing House

—— (1983) *New Strategy for China's Economy* Peking: New World Press

Ma Kai (1984) 'Factors affecting planned prices and the objective basis of two-track prices' *Social Sciences in China* vol. 5, no. 2, June, pp. 55–82

—— (1987) 'Gongzi gaige yu jingji xiaoyi (Wage reform and economic efficiency)' in Chai and Leung (1987) pp. 204–13

Ma Shu-yun (1986) 'Convertibility of China's *Renminbi*' *China Newsletter* no. 60, January–February, pp. 12–15

Ma Yingchun (1984) 'The booming China market (Zhongguo chengxiang shichang kongqian huoyue)' *China Market* (*Zhongguo Shichang*) no. 9, pp. 23–5

Macesich, George and Hui-Liang Tsai (1982) *Money in Economic Systems* New York: Praeger

Macroeconomic Research Office, Economic Structural Reform Research Institute of China (1988) 'An analysis of the economic situation in 1986' *China Economic Studies* vol. 21, no. 3, Spring, pp. 3–23

Makinen, Gail E. and Woodward, G. Thomas (1989) 'The Taiwanese hyperinflation and stabilization of 1945–1952' *Journal of Money, Credit, and Banking* vol. 21, no. 1, February, pp. 90–105

Mankiw, N. Gregory and Summers, Lawrence H. (1986) 'Money demand and the effects of fiscal policies' *Journal of Money, Credit, and Banking* vol. 11, no. 4, November, pp. 415–29

Mao Shang (1984) 'Changes in China's rural market (Bianhuazhongde zhongguo nongcun shichang)' *China Market* (*Zhongguo Shichang*) no. 12, pp. 34–8

Mao Yushi and Hare, Paul (1989) 'Chinese experience in the introduction of a market mechanism into a planned economy: the role of pricing' *Journal of Economic Surveys* vol. 3, no. 2, pp. 137–58

Marx, Karl (1978) *The Poverty of Philosophy* Peking: Foreign Languages Press

McKinnon, Ronald I. (1973) *Money and Capital in Economic Development* Washington, DC: The Brookings Institute

—— (ed.) (1976) *Money and Finance in Economic Growth and Development* New York: Decker

—— (1980) 'Financial policies' in Cody, Hughes and Wall (1980) pp. 93–120

—— (1981) 'Financial repression and the liberalization problem within less-developed countries' in Grassman and Lundberg (1981) pp. 365–86

—— (1985) 'How to manage a repressed economy' in Gutowski, Arnaudo and Scherrer (1985) pp. 182–209

McLure Jnr, Charles E. and Thirsk, Wayne R. (1978) 'The inequity of taxing iniquity: a plea for reducing sumptuary taxes in developing countries' *Economic Development and Cultural Change* vol. 26, no. 3, April, pp. 487–503

Miyashita, Tadao (1966) *The Currency and Financial System of Mainland China* Tokyo: Institute of Asian Economic Affairs

Moazzami, B. and Wong, E. (1988) 'Income and price elasticities of China's trade' *The Asian Economic Review* vol. 30, August, pp. 218–29

Moise, Edwin Evariste (1977) Land Reform in China and North Vietnam: Revolution at the Village Level, unpublished PhD dissertation, University of Michigan, 2 vols

Molho, Lazaros E. (1986) 'Interest rates, saving, and investment in developing countries' *International Monetary Fund Staff Papers* vol. 33, March, pp. 90–106

Molodtsova, L. (1988) 'Modernization of Statistics' *Far Eastern Affairs* (Moscow) no. 6, pp. 45–52, 189

Moore, Basil J. (1988) *Horizontalists and Verticalists: the Macroeconomics of Credit Money* Cambridge: Cambridge University Press

—— (1989) 'On the endogeneity of money once more' *Journal of Post Keynesian Economics* vol. 11, no. 3, Spring, pp. 479–87

'Muqian huobi liutong zhuangkuang he yijiubaer nian renwu' (1982) (The present conditions of monetary circulation and the tasks for 1982) *Zhongguo Jinrong* (Chinese Finance) no. 9, pp. 1–3

Muscatteli, Vito Antonio (1988) 'Review of Bordo and Jonung (1987)' *Economic Journal* vol. 98, December, pp. 1234–6

Myers, Ramon H. (1985) 'Price reforms and property rights in China since 1978' *Issues and Studies* vol. 21, no. 10, October, pp. 13–33

Nambu, Minoru (1985) 'Inflation in China' *China Newsletter* no. 59, November–December, pp. 2–6, 22

Naughton, Barry John (1986) Saving and Investment in China: a Macroeconomic Analysis, unpublished PhD dissertation, Yale University, May

—— (1987) 'Macroeconomic policy and response in the Chinese economy: the impact of the reform process' *Journal of Comparative Economics* vol. 1, no. 3, September, pp. 334–53; also in Reynolds (1988) pp. 44–63

—— (1989) 'Inflation and economic reform in China' *Current History* vol. 88, September, pp. 269–70, 289–91

Nissanke, Machiko K. (1979) 'The disequilibrium model in a controlled economy: comment' *American Economic Review* vol. 69, no. 4, September, pp. 726–32

Nolan, Peter (1988) *The Political Economy of Collective Farms: an Analysis of China's Post-Mao Reforms* Cambridge: Polity Press

Nove, Alec (1980) *The Soviet Economic System* 2nd edn, London: George Allen and Unwin

—— (1982) *An Economic History of the USSR* Harmondsworth: Penguin

Nove, Alec and Degras, Jane (eds) (1964) *Soviet Planning* Oxford: Basil Blackwell

Nove, Alec and Nuti, D.M. (eds) (1972) *Socialist Economics* Harmondsworth: Penguin

Nuti, D.M. (1986) 'Inflation in soviet-type economies' *Contributions to Political Economy* vol. 5, March, pp. 37–81

'Of birds and cages: the Chinese financial system' (1989) *China News Analysis* no. 1398, 1 December

Oi, Jean C. (1989) *State and Peasant in Contemporary China: the Political Economy of Village Government* Berkeley: University of California Press

Okazaki, Funiusa (ed.) (1961) *Analysis of Prices in Communist China* Tokyo; published by CCM Information Corporation, New York, 1970

Oxnam, R.B. and Bush, R.C. (eds) (1980) *China Briefing* Boulder, Col.: Westview Press

Pan Ling (1984) *Old Shanghai: Gangsters in Paradise* Hong Kong: Heinemann Asia

Patinkin, Don (1981a) 'The Chicago tradition, the quantity theory, and Friedman' in Patinkin (1981b) pp. 241–74

—— (1981b) *Essays on and in the Chicago Tradition* Durham, NC: Duke University Press

Peebles, Gavin (1981) 'Money incomes and expenditures of the population of the Soviet Union: an East European comparison' *Hong Kong Economic Papers* no. 14, pp. 53–78

—— (1983) 'Inflation, money and banking in China: in support of the purchasing power approach' *ACES Bulletin* vol. 25, no. 2, Summer, pp. 81–103

—— (1984a) 'Inflation in the People's Republic of China, 1950–82' *The Three Banks Review* no. 142, June, pp. 37–57

—— (1984b) 'Review of Jan Adam (1982)' *ACES Bulletin* vol. 26, no. 4, Winter, pp. 73–6

—— (1984c) Chinese Monetary Planning, 1950–1982: a Comparative Socialist View, unpublished PhD thesis, University of Hong Kong, December

—— (1985) 'Soviet-style agricultural bonuses and their effect on prices in China: a search for perversity and its consequences' *Hong Kong Economic Papers* no. 16, pp. 40–53

—— (1986a) 'On the importance of establishing the inverse relationship between open inflation and household liquidity growth under socialism: a critique of Jan Winiecki's savings deposit data' *Comparative Economic Studies* vol. 28, no. 4, Winter, pp. 85–91

—— (1986b) 'Aggregate retail price changes in socialist countries: identification, theory and evidence for China and the Soviet Union' *Soviet Studies* vol. 38, no. 4, October, pp. 477–507

—— (1986c) 'Review of Perry and Wong (1985)' *Journal of Economic Literature* vol. 24, December, pp. 1838–9

—— (1987a) 'Review of *Zhongguo Tongji Nianjian/Statistical Yearbook of China 1986*' *Comparative Economic Studies* vol. 29, no. 2, Summer, pp. 106–9

—— (1987b) 'Chinese monetary management, 1953–82' in Chai and Leung (1987) pp. 503–50

—— (1988) *Hong Kong's Economy: an Introductory Macroeconomic Analysis* Hong Kong and New York: Oxford University Press

—— (1989a) 'Aggregate retail price changes in China: a reply to Wang Tongeng' *Soviet Studies* vol. 41, no. 1, January, pp. 149–53

—— (1989b) '*China Trade and Price Statistics/Statistical Yearbook of China 1987*—book review' *Comparative Economic Studies* vol. 31, no. 2, Summer, pp. 143–5

—— (1990a) *China's Macroeconomy in the 1980s: the Impact of Reform on Structure and Performance* China Working Paper 90/5, Canberra: National Centre for Development Studies, Australian National University

—— (1990b) 'Explaining macroeconomic imbalances in Mainland China under reform' *Issues and Studies* vol. 26, no. 10, pp. 65–83

—— (1991) *A Short History of Socialist Money*, Sydney: Allen and Unwin, 1991

Peng Kuang-hsi (Peng Guangxi) (1976) *Why China has no Inflation* Peking: Foreign Languages Press

Peng Ziqin (1981) 'Shilun wending huobi dui wending jiagede zhongyao yiyi (On the importance of stabilising money for the stability of prices)' *Zhongguo Jinrong* (Chinese Finance) no. 3, pp. 22–3

Perkins, Dwight H. (1964) 'Price stability and development in mainland China (1951–1963)' *Journal of Political Economy* vol. 72, pp. 360–75

—— (1966) *Market Control and Planning in Communist China* Cambridge, Mass.: Harvard University Press

—— (1973a) 'Plans and their implementation in the People's Republic of China' *American Economic Review—Papers and Proceedings* vol. 63, no. 2, May, pp. 224–231

—— (1973b) 'An economic reappraisal' *Problems of Communism* vol. 22, no. 3, May–June, pp. 1–13

—— (1988) 'Reforming China's economic system' *Journal of Economic Literature* vol. 26, June, pp. 601–45

Perry, Elizabeth J. and Wong, Christine (eds) (1985) *The Political Economy of Reform in Post-Mao China* Cambridge, Mass.: The Council for East Asian Studies/Harvard University

Pesek, Boris (1958) 'Monetary reforms and monetary equilibrium' *Journal of Political Economy* vol. 66, no. 5, October, pp. 375–88

—— (1988) *Microeconomics of Money and Banking and Other Essays* Hemel Hempstead: Harvester Wheatsheaf

Pickersgill, Joyce (1976) 'Soviet household saving behaviour' *Review of Economics and Statistics* vol. 58, May, pp. 139–47

—— (1980a) 'The financial crisis in the USSR—a comment' *Soviet Studies* vol. 32, no. 4, October, pp. 583–5

—— (1980b) 'Recent evidence on soviet household saving behaviour' *Review of Economics and Statistics* November, pp. 628–33

Pick's Currency Yearbook (various years) New York: Pick Publishing Corporation

Pien Yu-yuan (1985) 'The price reform in mainland China' *Issues and Studies* vol. 21, no. 6, June, pp. 1–5

Po Yi-po (Bo Yibo) (1949) 'The draft budget for 1950' in China Council for the Promotion of International Trade (1952) pp. 39–45

Podkaminer, Leon (1989) 'Macroeconomic disequilibria in centrally planned economies: identifiability of econometric models based on the theory of household behaviour under quantity constraints' *Journal of Comparative Economics* vol. 13, no. 1, March, pp. 47–60

Polak, Jacques J. (1989) *Financial Policies and Development* Paris: Development Centre of the Organization for Economic Cooperation and Development

Portes, Richard (1977) 'The control of inflation: lessons from East European experience' *Economica* vol. 44, no. 174, May, pp. 109–29; slightly revised version in Bornstein (1979) pp. 448–68

—— (1978) 'Inflation under central planning' in Hirsch and Goldthorpe (1978) ch. 3

—— (1981) 'Reply to E. Dirksen "The control of inflation? Errors in the interpretation of CPE data"' *Economica* vol. 48, August, pp. 309–11

—— (1982) 'Prices' in *The Cambridge Encyclopedia of Russia and the Soviet Union* (1982) pp. 362–4

—— (1983) 'Central planning and monetarism: fellow travellers?' in Desai (1983) ch. 9

—— (1989) 'The theory and measurement of macroeconomic disequilibrium in centrally planned economies' in Davis and Charemza (1989) pp. 27–48

Portes, Richard and Santorum, Anita (1987) 'Money and consumption goods market in China' *Journal of Comparative Economics* vol. 11, no. 3, September, pp. 354–71; also in Reynolds (1988) pp. 64–81

Portes, Richard and Winter, David (1977) 'The supply of consumption goods in centrally planned economies' *Journal of Comparative Economics* vol. 1, no. 1, pp. 351–65

—— (1978) 'The demand for money and for consumption goods in centrally planned economies' *Review of Economics and Statistics* vol. 60, no. 1, February, pp. 8–18

—— (1980) 'Disequilibrium estimates for consumption goods markets in centrally planned economies' *Review of Economics and Statistics* vol. 47, pp. 137–59

Prachnowny, Martin F. (1985) *Money in the Economy* Cambridge: Cambridge University Press

Prybyla, Jan S. (1975) 'A note on incomes and prices in China' *Asian Survey* vol. 15, no. 3, March, pp. 262–78

—— (1976) 'Work incentives in the People's Republic of China' *Weltwirtschaftliches Archiv* (Review of World Economics) vol. 112, no. 4, pp. 767–91

—— (1979) 'Changes in the Chinese economy: an interpretation' *Asian Survey* vol. 19, no. 5, May, pp. 409–35

—— (1980a) *Issues in Socialist Economic Modernization* New York: Praeger

—— (1980b) *The Chinese Economy: Problems and Policies* 2nd edn, Columbia, SC: University of South Carolina Press

—— (1981) 'Key issues in the Chinese economy' *Asian Survey* vol. 21, no. 9, September, pp. 925–46

—— (1982a) 'China's economic development: demise of a model (review essay)' *Problems of Communism* vol. 33, no. 3, May–June, pp. 38–42

—— (1982b) 'Where is China's economy headed? A systems analysis' *Journal of Northeast Asian Studies* vol. 1, no. 4, December, pp. 3–24

—— (1989) 'China's economic experiment: back from the market?' *Problems of Communism* vol. 38, January–February, pp. 1–18

Qian Jiaju and Guo Yan'gang (1985) *Zhongguo Huobi Shi Gangyao* (An Outline History of Money in China) Shanghai: Shanghai People's Publishing House

Qian Yingyi (1988) 'Urban and rural household saving in China' *International Monetary Fund Staff Papers* vol. 35, no. 4, December, pp. 592–627

Qiu Tairu (1987) 'Lun pengzhang (On inflation)' *Caimao Jingji* (Finance and Trade Economics) no. 8, pp. 34–6

Raj, Balder and Siklos, Pierre L. (1988) 'Some qualms about the test of the institutionalist hypothesis of the long-run behaviour of velocity' *Economic Inquiry* vol. 26, no. 3, July, pp. 537–45

Reading, Brian (1989) 'Monetarism and stagflation' in Llewellyn (1989) pp. 91–107

Redl, Harry and Hughes, Richard (1962) *Exodus from China* Hong Kong: Dragonfly Books

'Report on the final state accounts for 1980 and implementation of the final estimates for 1981' (1982) by Wang Bingqian *Beijing Review* no. 2, 11 January, pp. 14–25

'Retrenchment and economic growth' (1989) (interview with Li Guixian) *Beijing Review* no. 44, 30 October – 5 November, pp. 17–20

Reynolds, Bruce L. (1983) 'Economic reform and external imbalance in China, 1978–81' *American Economic Review—Papers and Proceedings* vol. 73, no. 2, May, pp. 325–8

—— (ed.) (1987) *Reform in China: Challenges and Choices* Armonk, NY and London: M.E. Sharpe

—— (ed.) (1988) *Chinese Economic Reform: How Far, How Fast?* San Diego, Ca.: Academic Press

Reynolds, Paul D. (1982) *China's International Banking and Financial System* New York: Praeger

Riskin, Carl (1987) *China's Political Economy: the Quest for Development since 1949* New York: Oxford University Press

Rivlin, Alice M. (1987) 'Economics and the political process' *American Economic Review* vol. 77, no. 1, March, pp. 1–10

Robinson, Joan (1975) *Economic Management in China* 2nd edn, London: Anglo-Chinese Educational Institute

—— (1979) *Aspects of Development and Underdevelopment* Cambridge: Cambridge University Press

Roland, Gérard (1990) 'On the meaning of aggregate excess supply and demand for consumer goods in Soviet-type economies' *Cambridge Journal of Economics* vol. 14, no. 1, March, pp. 49–62

Rosefielde, Steven (1980) 'A comment on David Howard's estimate of hidden inflation in the Soviet retail sales sector' *Soviet Studies* vol. 32, no. 3, July, pp. 423–7

—— (1981) 'Hidden inflation in the Soviet Union: a rejoinder to David Howard' *Soviet Studies* vol. 33, no. 4, October, pp. 610–15

Rousseas, Stephen (1986) *Post Keynesian Monetary Economics* London: Macmillan

Rudcenko, S. (1979) 'Household money income, expenditure and monetary assets in Czechoslovakia, GDR, Hungary, and Poland, 1956–1975' *Jahrbuch der Wirtschaft Osteuropas* (Yearbook of East European Economies) vol. 8, pp. 431–59

Samansky, Arthur W. (1981) *China's Banking System: Its Modern History and Development* Research Paper no. 8108, New York: Federal Reserve Bank of New York, December

Schran, Peter (1969) *The Development of Chinese Agriculture 1950–1959* Urbana, Ill.: University of Illinois Press

—— (1977) 'China's price stability: its meaning and distributional consequences' *Journal of Comparative Economics* vol. 1, pp. 367–88

Schroeder, Gertrude E. (1982) 'Managing labour shortage in the Soviet Union' in Adam (1982) pp. 3–25

Schulze, D.L. (1986) 'Monetization in ASEAN: 1970–1984' *The Singapore Economic Review* vol. 31, no. 2, October, pp. 57–66

Schwartz, Anna J. (1984) 'Comment' in Griffiths and Wood (1984) pp. 129–36

Shaw, Edward Stone (1973) *Financial Deepening in Economic Development* New York: Oxford University Press

Shehuizhuyi Huobi Xinyong Xue (1981) (The Study of Socialist Money and Credit) Peking: China Finance and Economics Publishing House

Sheng Hong and Huang Tieying (1989–90) 'Arguing for rapid economic growth' *Chinese Economic Studies* vol. 23, no. 2, Winter, pp. 34–54

Sheng Hong and Zou Gang (1990) 'On money supply in the course of economic development: the so-called loss of control over money in 1984' *Chinese Economic Studies* vol. 23, no. 3, Spring pp. 75–90

Sherer, John L. (1978–85) *China Facts and Figures Annual* vols 1–8, Gulf Breeze, Fl.: Academic Institutions Press

Shi Lei (1982) 'Jiangdingde zhixing wending huobi fangzhen (Resolutely implement a policy of monetary stability)' *Zhongguo Jinrong* (Chinese Finance) no. 2, pp. 2–4

Short, B.K. (1980) 'The velocity of money and per capita income in developing countries' in Coats and Khatakhe (1980)

Shubik, Martin (1987) 'Fiat money' in Eatwell, Milgate and Newman (1987) vol. 2, pp. 316–17

Sicular, Terry (1988) 'Agricultural planning and pricing in the post-Mao period' *The China Quarterly* no. 116, December, pp. 671–707

Skinner, G. William (1978) 'Vegetable supply and marketing in Chinese cities' *The China Quarterly* no. 76, December, pp. 733–93

Skully, Michael T. (1982) *Financial Institutions and Markets in the Far East* London: Macmillan

Skully, Michael T. and Viksnins, George J. (1987) *Financing East Asia's Suc-*

cess: Comparative Financial Development in Eight Asian Countries London: Macmillan in association with the American Enterprise Institute for Public Policy Research

Smith, Alan H. (1983) *The Planned Economies of Eastern Europe* London and Canberra: Croom Helm

Smith, David (1987) *The Rise and Fall of Monetarism* London: Penguin

Smith, Keith (ed.) (1986) *Soviet Industrialization and Soviet Maturity* London and New York: Routledge and Kegan Paul

Solinger, Dorothy (1984) *Chinese Business under Socialism: the Politics of Domestic Commerce 1949–1980* Berkeley: University of California Press

—— (1987) 'The 1980 inflation and the politics of price control' in Lampton (1987) pp. 81–118

Solntseva, M. (1990) 'Can inflation be beaten?' *Far Eastern Affairs* no. 2, pp. 81–92

Song Guoqing and Zhang Weiying (1985) 'Guanyu hongguan pingheng yu hongguan kongzhide jige lilun wenti (Some theoretical issues of macroeconomic balance and control)' *Jingji Yanjiu* (Economic Research) no. 6, pp. 25–35; also in Gao (1987) pp. 85–96

Soviet Financial System (1966) Moscow: Progress Publishers

Statistical Abstract of the United States 1986 Washington, DC: US Government Printing Office

Statistical Yearbook of China 1981 (1982) Hong Kong: Economic Information and Agency

—— *1983, 1984, 1985* Hong Kong: Economic Information and Agency

Statistical Yearbook of China 1986 (1986) Hong Kong: Economic Information and Agency and China Statistical Information and Consultancy

Statistical Yearbook of China 1987 (1988) Hong Kong: Longman (Far East) and China Statistical Information and Consultancy

Statistical Yearbook of China 1988 (1988) Hong Kong: International Centre for the Advancement of Science and Technology

Stiefl, M. and Wertheim, W.F. (1983) *Production, Equality and Participation in Rural China* London: Zed Press

Su Wenming (1986) *Opening the Doors: 14 Coastal Cities and Hainan* Peking: Beijing Review

Sun Ping (1984) 'Individual economy under socialism' *Beijing Review* no. 33, 13 August, pp. 25–30

Surrey, M.J.C. (1989) 'Money, commodity prices and inflation: some simple tests' *Oxford Bulletin of Economics and Statistics* vol. 51, no. 3, August, pp. 219–38

Swamy, Subramanian (1969) 'Retail price index in the People's Republic of China' *Review of Economics and Statistics* vol. 51, pp. 309–19

Szczepanik, E. (ed.) (1962) *Symposium on Economic and Social Problems of the Far East* Hong Kong: Hong Kong University Press

Tam On-kit (1986) 'Reform of China's banking system' *World Economy* vol. 9, no. 4, December, pp. 427–40

—— (1987) 'Development of China's financial system' *The Australian Journal of Chinese Affairs* no. 17, January, pp. 95–113

Tan Shouding (1984) 'On the demonetization of gold: a reply to Professor Li Chonghuai' *Social Sciences in China* vol. 5, no. 2, June, pp. 83–96

Tang De-piao and Hu Teh-Wei (1983) 'Money, prices and causality: the Chinese hyperinflation, 1945–1949' *Journal of Macroeconomics* vol. 5, no. 4, pp. 503–10

Tardos, M. (1988) 'Can Hungary's monetary policy succeed?' *Acta—conomica* vol. 39, nos 1–2, pp. 61–79

Taubmann, Wolfgang and Widmer, Urs (1987) 'Supply and marketing in

Chinese cities: reform in the urban commercial system' in Chai and Leung (1987) pp. 331–66
Temin, Peter (1976) *Did Monetary Forces Cause the Great Depression?* New York: Norton
Ten Great Years (1960) Peking: Foreign Languages Press
Thirwall, A.P. (1974) *Inflation, Saving and Growth in Developing Countries* London: Macmillan
Thomas, R. Leighton (1985) *Introductory Econometrics: Theory and Applications* London: Longman
Thornton, Judith (ed.) (1976) *Economic Analysis of the Soviet-type System* Cambridge: Cambridge University Press
Tian Shanfu (1985) 'Bange shiji yilai woguo gongnongye chanpin jiage "jiandaocha" de bianhua (The "scissors" price changes between agriculture and industry in China during the last half-century)' *Caimao Jingji* (Finance and Trade Economics) no. 5, pp. 30–4, 21
Tian Yinong (1985) 'How to view China's budget deficit' *Beijing Review* no. 12, 25 March, pp. 16–17
Tidrick, Gene and Chen Jiyuan (eds) (1987) *China's Industrial Reform* New York: Oxford University Press for the World Bank
Tobin, James (1970) 'Money and income: post hoc ergo propter hoc?' *Quarterly Journal of Economics* vol. 84, pp. 301–17
Tobin, James and Houthakker, H.S. (1951) 'The effects of rationing on demand elasticities' *The Review of Economic Studies*, vol. 18, no. 3, November, pp. 140–53
Travers, S. Lee (1984) 'Post-1978 rural economic policy and peasant income in China' *The China Quarterly* no. 98, June, pp. 241–59
—— (1985) 'Getting rich through diligence: peasant income after the reform' in Perry and Wong (1985) pp. 111–30
Tsakok, Isabelle (1976) Inflation Control in the People's Republic of China, 1949–1974, unpublished PhD thesis, Harvard University, June
—— (1979) 'Inflation control in the People's Republic of China, 1949–1974' *World Development* vol. 7, pp. 865–75
Tsang Shu-ki (1990) 'Controlling money during socialist economic reform: the Chinese experience' *Economy and Society* vol. 19, no. 2, May, pp. 219–41
Tseng Ling and Han Lei (1959) *The Circulation of Money in the People's Republic of China* Moscow; published by CCM Information Corporation, New York, 1970
Tsiang, S.C. (1967) 'Money and banking in Communist China' in US Congress (1967) pp. 323–39
Tsien Tche-hao (1979) *L'Empire du Milieu Retrouve: la Chine Populaire a Trente Ans* (The Middle Kingdom Rediscovered: the People's Republic of China at Thirty Years) Paris: Flammarion
US Congress (1967) Joint Economic Committee *An Economic Profile of Mainland China* vol. 1 Washington, DC: US Government Printing Office
—— (1972) Joint Economic Committee *People's Republic of China: an Economic Assessment* Washington, DC: US Government Printing Office
—— (1978) Joint Economic Committee *Chinese Economy Post-Mao* Washington, DC: US Government Printing Office
Usack, A.H. and Batsavage, R.E. (1972) 'The international trade of the People's Republic of China' in US Congress (1972) pp. 335–70
Van Brabant, Jozef M. (1990) 'Socialist economies: the disequilibrium school and the shortage economy' *Journal of Economic Perspectives* vol. 4, no. 2, Spring, pp. 157–75
Van der Lijn, N.J. (Nick) (1990) 'Repressed inflation on the consumption

goods market: disequilibrium estimates for the German Democratic Republic, 1957–1985' *Journal of Comparative Economics* vol. 14, no. 1, March, pp. 120–9

Vermeer, E.B. (1982) 'Rural economic change and the role of the state in China, 1962–1978' *Asian Survey* vol. 22, no. 9, September, pp. 823–42

Viksnins, George J. (1980) *Financial Deepening in Asian Countries* Hawaii: Pacific Forum

Viksnins, George J. and Skully, Michael T. (1987) 'Asian financial development: a comparative perspective of eight countries' *Asian Survey* vol. 27, no. 5, May, pp. 535–51

Walder, Andrew G. (1986) *Communist Neo-traditionalism: Work and Authority in Chinese Industry* Berkeley: University of California Press

Walters, A.A. (1970) *Money in Boom and Slump* 2nd edn, London: Institute of Economic Affairs

Wan Dianwu (1984) 'Commerce' in Yu (1984) pp. 351–401

Wan Zhigui (1989) 'Shichang fanrong huoye (The market is flourishing and brisk)' in *Fenjinde Sihi Nian 1949–1989* pp. 50–3

Wang Guangqian (1985) 'Wending huobi gongying zhengzhange lü wenti (The question of stabilising the growth rate of the money supply)' *Jingji Yanjiu* (Economic Research) no. 10, pp. 68–73

Wang Guichen, Zhou Qiren et al. (1985) *Smashing the Communal Pot* Peking: New World Press

Wang Jiye (1989) 'The state, the market and the enterprise' *Beijing Review* no. 15, 10–16 April, pp. 16–21

Wang Ping (1975) 'Long-term stability of "Renminbi"' *Peking Review* no. 21, 23 May, pp. 18–21

Wang Shaofei (1985) 'Huobi faxingde shuliang jiexian yu kongzhi cuoshi (Quantitative limits on the amount of money issue and steps to control it)' *Caimao Jingji* (Finance and Trade Economics) no. 8, pp. 35–8

Wang Tong-eng (1980) *Economic Policies and Price Stability in China* Berkeley: Institute of East Asian Studies, University of California, Berkeley, Centre for Chinese Studies

—— (1988) 'Aggregate price changes in China: a comment' *Soviet Studies* vol. 40, no. 1, January, pp. 142–5

Wang Weicai (1986) 'China's economic and financial reform' in Cheng (1986) ch. 16

Wang Xiyi (1981) 'Yao jixu jianchi huilong huobide fangzhen (We must continue to adhere to the policy of withdrawing money from circulation)' *Zhongguo Jinrong* (Chinese Finance) no. 7, pp. 22–3

Wang Yan (1988) 'Financial reform: decentralization and liberalization' in Lyons and Wang (1988) pp. 27–46

Wang Yuanhong and Yang Yong (1989) '1988 nian wujia xingshide huigu yu fenxi (A look back at 1988s price situation and an analysis)' *Caijing Wenti Yanjiu* (Research on Financial and Economic Issues) no. 6, pp. 9–15

Wang Zhenzhi and Wang Yongzhi (1982) 'Epilogue: prices in China' in Lin and Chao (1982) pp. 220–34

Wanless, P.T. (1985) 'Inflation in the consumer goods market in Poland, 1971–82' *Soviet Studies* vol. 37, no. 3, July, pp. 403–16

Watson, Andrew (ed.) (1980) *Mao Zedong and the Political Economy of the Border Region: a Translation of Mao's 'Economic and Financial Problems'* Cambridge: Cambridge University Press

Wei Ai (1985) 'The Special Economic Zones in Mainland China: an analytical study' *Issues and Studies* vol. 21, no. 6, June, pp. 117–35

Wei Hsia (1975) 'No inflation in China: long-term balance in revenue and expenditure' *Peking Review* no. 10, 16 May, pp. 16–17

Weintraub, Robert E. (1970) *Introduction to Monetary Economics* New York: The Ronald Press

Weintraub, Sidney (1959) *A General Theory of the Price Level, Output, Income Distribution and Economic Growth* Philadelphia and New York: Chilton

—— (1961) *Classical Keynesianism, Monetary Theory and the Price Level* Philadelphia and New York: Chilton

—— (1978a) *Keynes, Keynesians and Monetarists* Philadelphia: University of Pennsylvania Press

—— (1978b) *Capitalism's Inflation and Unemployment Crisis* Reading, Mass.: Addison-Wesley

—— (1978–79) 'The missing theory of money wages' *Journal of Post Keynesian Economics* vol. 1, no. 2, Winter, pp. 59–78

'Wending huobi yu fazhan jingji' (1983) '(Stabilise money and develop the economy)' by a special commentator *Zhongguo Jinrong* (Chinese Finance) no. 1, pp. 6–10

White, Gordon (1988) 'State and market in China's labour reforms' *Journal of Development Studies* vol. 24, no. 4, July, pp. 180–220

White, Gordon and Bowles, Paul (1988) 'China's banking reforms: aims, methods and problems' *National Westminster Bank Quarterly Review* November, pp. 28–37

Whyte, Martin King and Parish, William L. (1984) *Urban Life in Contemporary China* Chicago and London: University of Chicago Press

Wiens, T.B. (1983) 'Price adjustment, the responsibility system, and agricultural productivity' *American Economic Review—Papers and Proceedings* vol. 73, no. 2, May, pp. 319–24

Wilczynski, J. (1978) *Comparative Monetary Economics* London: Macmillan

Wilson, Dick (1986) 'China's bankers learn a new game' *The Banker* vol. 136, no. 726, pp. 14–25

Wimberley, James (1981) 'The Soviet financial crisis? A comment' *Soviet Studies* vol. 33, no. 3, July, pp. 444–5

Winiecki, Jan (1985) 'Portes ante portas: a critique of the revisionist interpretation of inflation under central planning' *Comparative Economic Studies* vol. 27, no. 2, Summer, pp. 25–51

—— (1988) *The Distorted World of Soviet-type Economies* London and New York: Routledge

Wong, John (1973a) *Land Reform in the People's Republic of China: Institutional Transformation in Agriculture* New York: Praeger

—— (1973b) *Chinese Land Reform in Retrospect* Hong Kong: Centre of Asian Studies, University of Hong Kong

Wood, Adrian (1989) 'Deceleration of inflation with acceleration of price reform: Vietnam's remarkable recent experience' *Cambridge Journal of Economics* vol. 13, no. 4, December, pp. 563–71

World Bank (1983) *China: Socialist Economic Development* 3 vols, Washington, DC: World Bank

—— (1989) *World Development Report 1988* New York: Oxford University Press for the World Bank

—— (1990a) *China: Macroeconomic Stability and Industrial Growth under Decentralized Socialism* Washington, DC: World Bank

—— (1990b) *China: Revenue Mobilization and Tax Policy* Washington, DC: World Bank

Wu, C.T. (1987) 'Impact of rural reforms' in Chai and Leung (1987) pp. 265–92

Wu Jinglian (1990) 'On differences concerning macroeconomic problems: a reply to comrade Zhang Xuejun' *Chinese Economic Studies* vol. 23, no. 3, Spring, pp. 91–101

Wu Jinglian and Zhao Renwei (1987) 'The dual pricing system in China's industry' *Journal of Comparative Economics* vol. 11, no. 3, September, pp. 309–18; also in Reynolds (1988) pp. 19–28

Wu Yuanfu (1982) 'Country fairs and free markets' *China Reconstructs* vol. 31, no. 2, February, pp. 44–5, 48

Wu Yuan-li (1956) *An Economic Survey of Communist China* New York: Bookman Associates

—— (ed.) (1973) *China: a Handbook* Encyclopedia Britannica Inc., Australia

Wujia Wenjian Xuanbian 1984–1985 Nian (1986) (Selected Documents on Prices 1984–1985) compiled by the State Price Bureau Research Institute, Peking: China Goods and Materials Publishing House

Wyzan, Michael L. (1985) 'Soviet agricultural procurement pricing: a study in perversity' *Journal of Comparative Economics* vol. 9, no. 1, March, pp. 24–45

Xia Xiaoxun and Li Jun (1987) 'Consumption expansion: a grave challenge to reform and development' in Reynolds (1987) ch. 6

Xiandai Shiyong Jinrong Cidian (1987) (A Contemporary Practical Dictionary of Finance) Shenyang: Liaoning People's Publishing House

Xiao Zhuoji (1980) 'The law of price movements in China' *Social Sciences in China* vol. 1, no. 4, December, pp. 44–59

Xie Yuhuai (1983) 'Dui dangqian huobi liutong liang yanjiuzhong ruogan wentide renshi (The understanding of some problems in current research on the quantity of money in circulation)' *Caimao Jingji* (Finance and Trade Economics) no. 2, pp. 32–5

Xiong Zhijun (1989) 'Lüe lun woguo tonghuo pengzhang chanshengde keguan jichu ji qi jiegou tezheng (A brief discussion of the objective basis of inflation in our country and its structural characteristics)' in Lu, Wang and Wang (1989) pp. 209–19

Xu Dixin et al. (1982) *China's Search for Economic Growth* Peking: New World Press

Xu Xuehan and Huang Xu (1987) 'Dangqian jinrong xingshi he yinhang jin yibu gaigede fangxiang (The present financial situation and the direction of further bank reform)' *Caimao Jingji* (Finance and Trade Economics) no. 6, pp. 18–25

Xu Yi and Chen Baosen (1981) 'On the necessity and possibility of stabilizing prices' *Social Sciences in China* vol. 2, no. 3, pp. 121–38

—— (1984) 'Finance' in Yu (1984) pp. 437–526

Xue Muqiao (1980) *Dangqian Woguo Jingji Ruogan Wenti* (Some Current Economic Problems in Our Country) Peking: People's Publishing House

—— (1981) *China's Socialist Economy* Peking: Foreign Languages Press

—— (1982a) *Current Economic Problems in China* Boulder, Col.: Westview Press

—— (1982b) *Zhongguo Shehuizhuyi Jingji Wenti Yanjiu* (Research on the Problems of China's Socialist Economy) Peking: People's Publishing House

—— (1985) 'Tiaozheng jiage he gaige jiage guanli tizhi (Readjust prices and reform the price administration system)' *Jingji Yanjiu* (Economic Research) no. 1, pp. 3–7

Xue Muqiao, Wu Kaitai and Li Kemu (1985) 'Liushi niandai qianqi wujiade wending yu tiaozheng (The stabilisation and adjustment of prices in the early 1960s)' *Jingji Yanjiu* (Economic Research) no. 3, pp. 41–50

Yamanouchi, Kazuo (1986) 'The Chinese price system and the thrust of reform' *China Newsletter* no. 60, January–February, pp. 2–11, 15

Yang Junchang (1985) 'Jingji faxing yu tonghu pengzhang (Money issue and inflation)' *Caimao Jingji* (Finance and Trade Economics) no. 6, pp. 32–4

Yang Pei-hsin (Yang Peixin) (1975) 'Why China has no inflation' *China Reconstructs* no. 4, April, pp. 4–9

Yang Peixin (1984) 'Banking' in Yu (1984) pp. 404–36

Yang Po (1964) 'New China's price policy' *Peking Review* no. 47, 20 November, pp. 6–11

Yang Zhongwei and Li Bo (1986) 'Pricing and price reforms' *Social Sciences in China* vol. 7, no. 1, March, pp. 69–80

Yao Kuan (1964) 'Socialist commerce in China' *Peking Review* no. 8, 21 February, pp. 8–11

Yao Yilin (1952) 'The readjustment and development of China's commerce since 1949' in China Committee for the Promotion of International Trade (1952) pp. 219–35

Yeh Chang-mei (1985) 'Mainland China's financial reforms: money and banking' *Issues and Studies* vol. 21, no. 6, June, pp. 80–99

Yeh, K.C. (1973) 'Agricultural policies and performance' in Wu (1973)

—— (1975) 'Assessing the Chinese economy (review article)' *Problems of Communism* May–June, pp. 55–62

Yi Xing (1981) 'Readjustment brings more consumer goods' *China Reconstructs* no. 9, September, pp. 32–3

Ying–Han Jingji Cihui (1983) (An English–Chinese Economic Lexicon) Chongqing: China Social Sciences Publishing House

Yong Xiaojun and Zheng Fengbo (1988) 'Jumin xiaofeide jingji fenxi' (An economic analysis of household consumption) in Zhang Fengbo (1988b) ch. 10

Yu Guangyuan (ed.) (1984) *China's Socialist Modernization* Peking: Foreign Languages Press

Zeng Qixian (1983) 'Comments on consumption and savings' *Social Sciences in China* vol. 4, no. 4, pp. 137–63

'Zenyang renshi dangqiande wujia wenti' (1981) '(How to understand the current price question)' by the editor *Hong Qi* (Red Flag) no. 1, pp. 26–7

'Zenyang kan dangqian jingji xingshi' (1981) '(How to view the current economic situation)' by a special commentator *Hong Qi* (Red Flag) no. 6, pp. 2–7

Zhan Wu and Liu Wenpu (1984) 'Agriculture' in Yu (1984) pp. 207–70

Zhang Chaohuang (1989) 'Wujia biange xi yu you (Price reform has its good side and its worries)' in *Fenjinde Sishi Nian 1949–1989* (1989) pp. 54–7

Zhang Fengbo (1987a) 'Woguo wujia biandongde jiben yuanyin fenxi (An analysis of the basic reasons for price changes in our country)' *Caimao Jingji* (Finance and Trade Economics) no. 11, pp. 37–45

—— (1987b) 'Woguo hongguan jingjizhong ruogan wentide sikao yu fenxi (Some thoughts on and analysis of certain macroeconomic problems in China)' in Gao (1987) pp. 76–85

—— (1988a) 'A theoretical study of several current macroeconomic problems' *Chinese Economic Studies* vol. 21, no. 3, Spring, pp. 40–58

—— (principal ed.) (1988b) *Zhongguo Hongguan Jingji Jiegou yu Zhengce* (China's Macroeconomy: Structure and Policy) Peking: China Finance and Economics Publishing House

Zhang Junkuo (1988a) 'Huobi, wujia yu jingji zengzhangde shizheng fenxi (An empirical analysis of money, inflation and economic growth)' *Caimao Jingji* (Finance and Trade Economics) no. 8, pp. 30–5; also in Lu, Wang and Wang (1989) pp. 220–34

—— (1988b) 'Jingji zengzhang ji qi yinsu fenxi (An analysis of economic growth and its elements)' in Zhang Fengbo (1988b) ch. 2

Zhang Kuifeng and Li Xiaofeng (1985) 'Shehuizhuyi shangyede shangpin xiaoshou (Commodity sales under socialist commerce) *Caimao Jingji* (Finance and Trade Economics) no. 7, pp. 68–80

Zhang Weiying (1985) 'On the role of prices' *Social Sciences in China* vol. 6, no. 4, December, pp. 177–94

Zhang Yigeng (1983) 'Structural changes of consumer goods supply on China's markets' *China Market* (*Zhongguo Shichang*) no. 1, pp. 23–7

—— (1984a) 'Multiple economic elements in the Chinese market (Duozhong jingji chengfen zai zhongguo ge xian shentong)' *China Market* (*Zhongguo Shichang*) no. 10, pp. 18–20

—— (1984b) 'Marked improvement in people's life since 1949 (Jianguo yilai renmin shenghuo xianzhu tigao)' *China Market* (*Zhongguo Shichang*) no. 11, pp. 18–20

—— (1985) 'Woguo lingshou jaige zhishude jingji yiyi he bianzhi fangfa (Our country's retail price index: its economic significance and method of compilation)' *Jingji Yanjiu* (Economic Research) no. 5, pp. 30–6

Zhang Yutang (1986a) 'Huobi gongji chaoqian zengzhang shi guilü ma? (Is the excessive increase of money supply a law?)' *Jingji Yanjiu* (Economic Research) no. 7, pp. 75–7, 25

—— (1986b) 'Huobi xuqiu zongliang jingji moxing tantao (A study of economic models of aggregate monetary demand)' *Caimao Jingji* (Finance and Trade Economics) no. 10, pp. 26–30, 25

Zhao Chunping (1989) 'Jinrong shiye xian shengji (Financial undertakings show vitality)' in *Fenjinde Sishi Nian 1949–1989* (1989) pp. 67–70

Zhao Dexin (principal ed.) (1988) *Zhonghua Renmin Gongheguo Jingji shi 1949–1966* (The Economic History of the People's Republic of China 1949–1966) Zhengzhou: Henan People's Publishing House

—— (1989) *Zhonghua Renmin Gongheguo Jingji shi 1967–1984* (The Economic History of the People's Republic of China 1967–1984) Zhengzhou: Henan People's Publishing House

Zhao Mingyang (1982) 'Shichang huobi liangde xingcheng yu fenxi (The formation and analysis of money on the market)' *Caizheng Jinrong* (Public Finance) no. 2, pp. 75–83

Zheng Jingsheng (1988) 'Shehui gongxu guanxi ji hongguan tiaokong (The social demand and supply relationship and macroeconomic control)' in Zhang Fengbo (1988b) ch. 4

Zheng Xianbing (1986a) 'Huobi gongji choqian zengzhang guilü tansuo (An inquiry into the law of more rapid increase of the money supply)' *Jingji Yanjiu* (Economic Research) no. 2, pp. 62–5, 56

—— (1986b) 'Lun huobi liutong sudu dizeng guilü (A discussion of the law of progressively increasing monetary velocity)' *Caimo Jingji* (Finance and Trade Economics) no. 9, pp. 31–7

Zhong Xuan (1981) 'Ekonomiaj atingoij de Cinio en la pasintaj 30 jaroj (The economic achievements of China during the last 30 years)' *El Popola Cinio* (From People's China) no. 8, pp. 7–12

Zhongguo Jingji Nianjian 1982 (1982) (Almanac of the Chinese Economy 1982) Peking: Economic Management Publishing House

—— *1983, 1984, 1985, 1986, 1987, 1988* Peking: Economic Management Publishing House

Zhongguo: Jinrong yu Touzi (1989) (China: Finance and Investment) Peking: China Finance and Economics Publishing House

Zhongguo Maoyi Wujia Tongji Ziliao 1952–1983 (1984) (Statistical Materials on Trade and Prices in China 1952–1983) Peking: China Statistical Publishing House

Zhongguo Nongye Nianjian 1980 (1981) (Chinese Agricultural Yearbook) Peking: Agricultural Publishing House

'Zhongguo Renmin Yinhang zhaokai quanguo huobi liutong xingshi fenxi hui (The People's Bank of China calls a meeting to analyse the nation's monetary situation)' (1981) *Zhongguo Jinrong* (Chinese Finance) no. 6, pp. 1–4

Zhongguo Tongji Nianjian 1981 (1982) (China Statistics Yearbook 1981) overseas Chinese-language edn, Hong Kong: Economic Information and Agency

—— *1983, 1984, 1985* Hong Kong: Economic Information and Agency

—— *1987, 1988, 1989* Peking: China Statistical Publishing House

Zhongguo Wujia Nianjian 1989 (China Prices Yearbook 1989) Peking: China Prices Publishing House

Zhongguo Wujia Tongji Nianjian 1988 (China Price Statistics Yearbook 1988) Peking: China Statistical Publishing House

Zhou Cequan (1986) 'Shilun huobi gongjide "chaoqian" quxiang ji qi shuliang jiexian (The "excessive" trend of the money supply and its quantitative limits)' *Caimao Jingji* (Finance and Trade Economics) no. 2, pp. 30–5, 25

Zhou Jun (1986) 'Huobi junheng (Monetary equilibrium)' *Caimao Jingji* (Finance and Trade Economics) no. 4, pp. 8–14, 68

Zhou Xiaochuan and Zhu Li (1987) 'China's banking system: current status, perspective on reform' *Journal of Comparative Economics* vol. 11, no. 3, September, pp. 399–409

Zhou Zhenhua (1987) 'Tonghuo pengzhangde bijiao fenxi (A comparative analysis of inflation)' *Caimao Jingji* (Finance and Trade Economics) no. 11, pp. 56–60

Zuo Wosheng (1988) 'Jiage jiegou yu jiage tiaozheng (The structure of prices and their adjustment)' in Zhang Fengbo (1988b) ch. 7

Zwass, Adam (1979) *Money, Banking, and Credit in the Soviet Union and Eastern Europe* London: Macmillan

Index